EYEWITNESS
*The Negro in American History*

# EYEWITNESS

## *The Negro in American History*

WILLIAM LOREN KATZ

Pitman Publishing Corporation
New York · Toronto · London

*The author gratefully acknowledges the cooperation of the following institutions, which provided many of the illustrations used in this book:* the Department of the Army; the Department of State; the United States Signal Corps; the Library of Congress; the National Archives; the New York Public Library Picture Collection; the Schomburg Collection of the New York Public Library; the United Nations; United Press International; the United States Air Force; the Student Nonviolent Coordinating Committee; the Association for the Study of Negro Life and History; and the Explorers Club.

1st printing, October 1967
2nd printing, December 1967
**3rd printing, May 1968**
*4th Printing, July 1968*

Copyright © 1967 by Pitman Publishing Corporation
*All rights reserved.*

*Typography and binding by Anita Duncan*
*Library of Congress Catalog Card Number: 67-10838*
*Manufactured in the United States of America*

1.987654

*For Naomi and Michael*

We do not believe that things will always continue the same. The time must come when the Declaration of Independence will be felt in the heart, as well as uttered from the mouth, and when the rights of all shall be properly acknowledged and appreciated. God hasten that time. This is our home, and this is our country. Beneath its sod lie the bones of our fathers; for it, some of them fought, bled, and died. Here we were born, and here we will die.

*Meeting of New York Negroes, 1831*

# *Preface*

THIS book began to take shape many years before the Negro revolution of the 1960's. Although it began in my high school days during World War II, this growing interest took on a deeper meaning in 1952 when I began teaching secondary school American history. School texts distorted the Negro's part in our history, picturing him as contented under slavery and bewildered by freedom. Since I felt it a grim cruelty to assign such readings to students of any race, I began to introduce materials, often eyewitness accounts, that highlighted the Negro's gift to America. Students of both races and their parents responded enthusiastically to the new material.

In the 1960's I was able to broaden my research through the aid of the New World Foundation and the New York State Department of Education. Summers were spent at the National Archives, the Library of Congress, Howard University's Moorland-Spingarn Collection, and the Schomburg Collection of the New York Public Library. It was fascinating work.

My first acknowledgment must go to my students at Woodlands High School, for they helped select the contents of this volume. Many thanks to my colleagues on the Woodlands staff for their aid and comfort, especially Thelma Macon, Bernard Gaughran, Ronnie Vann, Jane Mahoney, Julian Asher, Ray LaVigne, and Mr. and Mrs. Dan Smith. Very special thanks must go to Kenneth Haskins for his severe criticism and complete support—a true friend.

Frank Jennings of the New World Foundation has been a source of aid and inspiration since the time this project was only an armful of dittoed sheets. New World Foundation Executive Director Vernon Eagle has also been very helpful. Leonard Stern, Demonstration Chief of President Kennedy's Committee on Juvenile Delinquency and Youth Development, has been of enormous assistance, as has Nida Thomas of the New York State Department of Education.

Special aid in gathering pictures of the current scene came from James C. Evans, Office of the Secretary of Defense, Eddie N. Williams of the State Department, and Elizabeth Sutherland of SNCC. Dr. Jerome S. Ozer of the Pitman Publishing Corporation has been a constant source of encouragement as well as a superb editor. Cathy Baldino generously volunteered to type large sections of the final manuscript.

Among the many others who contributed to the completion of this project were: Dr. Martin Luther King, Jr., former Congressman Charles Weltner of Georgia, Mrs. George E. Haynes, Cecily Brownstone, Floyd W. Crawford, Henry Moon, Phyllis Murrel, Julia Schiff, Dr. James McPherson, Dorothy Sterling, Vernon Alleyne, Herbert Frisby, and Dr. George Blair.

Among the many librarians whose aid was essential, several went far beyond any call of duty to aid this project: Dorothy Porter of the Moorland-Spingarn Collection, Mother E. O'Connor of Manhattanville College of the Sacred Heart, and Ernest Kaiser of the Schomburg Collection, the outstanding bibliographer of this field. To Sara Jackson of the War Records Office of the National Archives, this writer and this book are so deeply indebted that appreciation cannot be adequately expressed. May all researchers find Sara Jacksons.

This book would not have been completed without the unstinting efforts and total commitment of my parents; Bernard Katz, who has done research for *American Heritage*, and Phyllis B. Katz, associate editor of *Parents' Magazine*.

For the most part this story is told in the words and pictures of those who made history. Each quotation used in the narrative, as well as the eyewitness sections, is by a person contemporaneous with the events or people described. Documents have been edited without distorting meaning and all omissions have been indicated by ellipses. Original spelling (or misspelling) has been preserved, except for the word Negro which has been capitalized throughout in accordance with modern usage. Because the history of the Negro in America is an integral part of American history, I have organized this book along the lines of the typical course in American history. The author assumes responsibility for any errors of fact or judgment.

I have attempted to tell this fascinating American story in unadorned prose, avoiding moral preaching or special pleading. To the extent I have succeeded in this, mind has conquered heart, for this has been a labor of love.

William Loren Katz

# Contents

# EYEWITNESS
*The Negro in American History*

# 11

# The Opening
# of New Worlds

FOR all who came to these shores, America was a land of freedom, hope, and opportunity. For all—except the Negro. He came in chains and for hundreds of years had to fight just to be free. With few friends, and against almost hopeless odds, black men and women struggled to stay alive, to obtain their freedom, and to share in the American dream of human dignity and justice for all.

The Negro came to America as a slave who had been captured —captured, as Frederick Douglass wrote, by "a band of successful robbers who had left their homes, and gone to Africa, and stolen us from our homes, and in a strange land reduced us to slavery." For more than four centuries this trade drained Africa of its healthiest sons and daughters.

Slavery had been a part of civilization since the day when man first learned to plant, harvest crops, and develop a surplus. The ancient Egyptians, Greeks, Romans, and Africans had both held and been slaves during the course of history and slavery was described in and sanctioned by the Bible. Even white Christians had been enslaved by their fellow Europeans as well as other peoples. Before the African slave trade, the slave was usually a prisoner of war or a criminal paying his debt to society. He was often protected in certain rights by both laws and customs, although he was an outcast and not an accepted member of society. Many bondsmen were allowed their liberty after years of faithful service. Only the slavery of North America denied the humanity of the slave and called him inferior because of his color.

The trade that began in 1442 when ten Africans were brought to Prince Henry of Portugal and the discovery of the New World a half century later were both part of a single historical movement. They were two aspects of the bold European explorers' conquests during the 15th and 16th centuries. And they grew out of a strange combination of religious zeal and greed for new land and cheap labor.

The Europeans needed a labor force to develop the mines, forests, and fertile fields of the New World. In Africa they found a hearty people, familiar with agriculture and used to hard work, which could turn the abundant natural resources of the Americas into staggering profits. Using the most advanced weapons of the time and a diplomacy based on deceit, the conquerors exploited the resources of both regions.

This new source of wealth from Africa attracted nobles as well as pirates. The Duke of York, who captured New Amsterdam from the Dutch in 1664, had, two years earlier, formed a "Company of Royal Adventurers" that captured people in the African kingdom of Guinea and sold them for gold. So much money poured into the British treasury from this trade that the King issued a new coin called the *guinea*.

The enormous profits of the slave trade became the most convincing argument for its continuation despite its known horrors. The European and American merchants who profited from this trade justified themselves by pointing out that Africans were not

An African chief sells prisoners of war to European slave merchants. Slavery was common in Africa; it was used as a punishment for crimes or making war. However, African slavery protected the basic rights of the prisoner and allowed him to own property, marry (even a member of the owner's family), and eventually gain his freedom. Slavery in the New World would be very different.

Christians. Since the idea of enslaving non-Christians was generally acceptable, the slave traders became wealthy and respected members of their communities. They built universities and churches and even gave their ships such names as *Jesus* and *Grace of God*. The New World, they claimed, offered the Africans contact with both Christianity and civilization in place of "African savagery."

The real Africa was very different from the Africa described by the slave trader. For one thing, it could no more be spoken of as one unified continent than Europe could. Africa was a land of many languages, religions, colors, and stages of development. In the years before the arrival of the Europeans, Africans achieved a cultural progress equal to and often superior to that of Europe. During the African metal age that began 500 years before the birth of Christ, the African people began to cultivate the soil, build great cities, develop their arts, smelt and work iron ore, and build complex social systems. African craftsmen were skilled in leather, wood, glass, gold, ivory, copper, tin, silver, and bronze. In the kingdom of the Congo, every clan had its special crafts such as weaving, winemaking, pottery, and smithery. Each craft sent representatives to the national council that advised the monarch. For centuries, African kings combined religion and business by making pilgrimages to Mecca in huge caravans that displayed their enormous riches.

*Ancient bronze statue of an African hunter carrying home an antelope. Considered a masterpiece, this statue was found in Benin City in 1897 and is now on display at the British Museum.*

*Congo knives. While Africans were a diverse population of many tribes, all shared a great skill in handicrafts and created some of the world's greatest art. However, beautiful weapons were no match for European rifles and cannons.*

*Gezo, King of Dahomey. Wealth and education were not uncommon in the urban centers of Africa before and during the slave trade era.*

The kingdom of Songhay in West Africa had developed a banking system, a school system, and a complete code of laws by the fifteenth century, and instituted economic reforms that made it prosperous. It traded with European and African nations, and its University of Sankoré at Timbuktu offered courses in surgery, law, and literature to African, Asiatic, and European scholars. Leo Africanus, a highly educated Spanish Moor who visited Timbuktu, noticed a "great store of doctors, judges, priests, and other learned men, [and] . . . manuscripts or written books . . . which are sold for more money than any other merchandise." In the year that Columbus discovered the New World, Songhay ruled an empire that was larger than all of Europe. The slave traders of Portugal, Spain, Holland, Denmark, France, and England wrecked much of this civilization as they plundered Africa for slaves and battled each other for control of the slave trade.

While the African came to the New World as a prisoner, he did not leave his homeland without a struggle or submit easily to bondage. Captain Philip Drake, a slave trader for 50 years, reported: "The Negroes fought like wild beasts. . . . Slavery is a dangerous business at sea as well as ashore." A seaman aboard a slave ship wrote in his diary: "If care not be taken they [the slaves] will mutiny and destroy the ship's crew in hopes to get away. To prevent such misfortunes we visit them daily, narrowly searching every corner between decks, to see whether they have . . . any pieces of iron, or wood or knives." Clearly, the seething human cargo packed below the decks of the slavers made the trip dangerous.

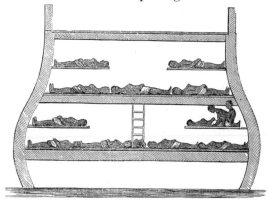

*Crossection of a slave ship showing the crowded conditions. Insufficient food and water, crowding, and disease often left the slaves too weak to revolt. But more than one hundred slave mutinies took place on board the ships bringing Africans to the New World.*

Insufficient food and water and the outbreak of epidemics took many lives among both slaves and crew. The seamen kept away from their human cargo and its special misery. Slaver Thomas Branagan described how the Negroes "struggle, they resist; but all in vain. No eye pities; no hand helps." But through their own efforts Negro slaves successfully revolted more than a hundred times on the high seas. Resistance to tyranny began at the birth of tyranny.

## Spanish and Portuguese Explorations

Africans served the European conquerors in many ways. Some traveled as seamen and officers to the Americas. Negroes traveled with Columbus and, in 1513, thirty Negroes marched with Balboa to the Pacific and built the first ships on that coast. Six years later, 300 Negroes dragged the heavy Spanish artillery that Cortez used to defeat the Aztecs of Mexico. The first wheat crop in the New World was planted and harvested by one of Cortez's black men. Negroes accompanied Pizarro in his conquest of Peru, and in 1565 they built St. Augustine, America's first city.

The best-known African explorer with the Spanish expeditions was Estevanico. A man of rare courage and ability, Estevanico served as an adviser to Cortez, and as a guide to Cabeza de Vaca and Father Marcos de Niza. He explored Florida, Mexico, and parts of Arizona and New Mexico. During a Florida expedition in 1528, Estevanico, Cabeza de Vaca, and two companions were captured by Indians. They escaped, only to spend eight years wandering through swamps and forests trying to find their way to the Spanish headquarters in Mexico. It was during this time that the four explorers first heard of Cibola from the Indians. Cibola, or the "Seven Cities of Gold," was said to lie somewhere north of Mexico. The attempt to reach this legendary land was to lead to Estevanico's last journey.

In 1539, the Spanish explorer Father Marcos de Niza led an expedition to search for the Seven Cities of Gold and his scout was Estevanico. A member of the group told how important Estevanico was to the expedition: "It was the Negro who talked to them [the Indians] all the time; he inquired about the roads we should follow, the villages; in short, about everything we wished to know." Estevanico was sent ahead with two large greyhounds and a group of Indian guides. In his earlier trip Estevanico had posed as a medicine

*A Spanish missionary. Negroes accompanied the early missionaries and explorers of the New World. These priests were credited with softening Latin American slavery because they considered Africans to be persons with immortal souls. Negroes were baptized and married by the Church in Catholic countries.*

man in order to survive among the Indians. This time he again assumed this disguise and carried a large gourd decorated with strings of bells and a red and a white feather. The gourd was supposed to be either a source of magic or a symbol of peace.

Father Marcos had instructed Estevanico to send back wooden crosses to show his progress. The closer he got to Cibola the larger the crosses were to be. Excitement rose in Father Marcos' camp when one by one large white crosses began to arrive almost immediately and, with them, news of Estevanico's fast progress. News came of gifts of leather and turquoise that were being showered on the explorer. As many as 300 Indian men and women joined Estevanico's group on its march to Cibola. Every few days another large cross arrived for Father Marcos.

Then no word. Weeks later an Indian staggered in with the frightening news of Estevanico's murder and the massacre of his party by the hostile Indians surrounding the Seven Cities of Gold. Father Marcos' party fled back to Mexico, but the story of Estevanico's discovery spurred De Soto, Coronado, and other Spanish explorers to search for Cibola in the southwestern territory of the United States. Hundreds of years after Estevanico's death, the Zuñi Indians, whose villages he was approaching when he met his death, still told stories about a strange black man who had once entered their land.

The vast majority of Negroes brought by the Spanish adventurers came, not as explorers like Estevanico, but as laborers. Less than fifty years after Columbus first landed in the New World, the Spanish Governor of Mexico wrote that Negroes were "indispensible for the cultivation of the land and the royal revenue." The letters of King Ferdinand of Spain show a lively interest in the economic value of the black slaves.

But keeping Africans in slavery was a difficult and dangerous business. They "fled among the Indians and taught them bad customs and never would be recaptured," wrote the Governor of Mexico in 1502. The first settlement within the present borders of the United States, near the Pedee River, was the scene of a successful slave uprising. In the winter of 1526, in this South Carolina colony of 500 Spaniards and 100 Negroes, slaves rebelled and fled to the Indians.

The pattern of Negro resistance to slavery continued for centuries. In the early 19th century, slave trader Philip Drake wrote of the Spanish colonies: "In Barbadoes, Trinidad, and St. Thomas, the whites lived in constant fear of massacre." Three hundred years after the first slave revolt in a Spanish colony, Rio de Janeiro slaves set fire to crops, smashed machinery, and were only defeated (although not captured) by the use of troops. They were led by a giant Ashanti warrior named Quobah who was never found.

The Portuguese colonies also had trouble controlling their Negro slaves. In 1607 the Governor of Bahia in Brazil complained to the King of Portugal of a large slave revolt. The King issued a long series of instructions and orders concerning the suppression of rebellions.

Some runaway slaves began their own colonies, the largest of which was the Republic of Palmares in northeastern Brazil. This colony sheltered 20,000 people within its three great walls. The runaways grew beans, cane, and bananas which they traded with other villages. Courts of justice carried out the many laws of the Negro government and many of the customs of Africa were kept alive during the 67 years of the city's existence. One of its leaders, Zambi, was described as "a Negro of singular courage, great presence of mind, and unusual devotion." Twenty-five Portuguese attempts to crush Palmares ended in failure. One of the defeated officers described the city as "so well fortified as to be lacking only in artillery." An overwhelming army of Portuguese was finally able to capture and destroy the city in 1697. According to legend, the defeated soldiers, led by their ruler, hurled themselves from a cliff rather than surrender.

The slavery that developed in the Spanish and Portuguese colonies was different, in a number of important respects, from the system of bondage developed in North America. In Latin America, a powerful Catholic Church, interested in the soul of the Negro, protected him from many abuses. In America, no church or any other power dared tell a slaveholder how to treat his slaves. The Church in Latin America encouraged owners to liberate slaves who became Christians. Marriages between blacks and whites were not opposed by the Church and Latin American slavery was not infected with racial prejudice. The South American slave was thought of as a member of the human race and not as part of an "inferior race." Slaves who were severely beaten could protest to the court and some even won their liberty from cruel owners. In Brazil, a slave could purchase his freedom by raising the amount of money which had originally been paid for him. In Cuba, slaves were allowed to buy their freedom on the installment plan, paying their masters a down payment and a set amount each month.

Early in the history of Latin America, free Negroes owned property and took part in the religious life of the colonies. In 1540, a Negro was admitted into the priesthood in the Spanish colonies.

An example of how high a Negro might rise in New Spain was provided by Brother Martin de Porres. Born in Lima, Peru in 1579, this tall, soft-voiced young man became a surgeon's apprentice and later a doctor in his own right. He tended patients who could pay as well as those who could not. He raised funds for the poor, for orphans, and even took care of sick dogs and cats. Brother de Porres is noted for starting Peru's first orphanage, and today it still carries on the work he began. Made a member of the Dominican Order before his death in 1639, de Porres often said, "I could do nothing without Christ." Two centuries later Pope Gregory XVI bestowed the title of "Blessed" on Brother de Porres. In 1962 Brother Martin de Porres became the world's first Negro saint.

## The Dutch Colonies

The Dutch colony of New Amsterdam, founded in 1626, included 11 male slaves. Women slaves were brought to the colony a few years later. Slaves were considered so necessary to the settlement that the Dutch would not execute six Negroes who had taken part in a murder. Instead, the six were told to draw lots so that one could be chosen for hanging. When the man chosen, a giant in size, broke the hangman's ropes, he was freed to the general delight of the community.

In 1644, the Dutch liberated a dozen slaves and gave them "their freedom on the same footing as other free peoples." Obviously the Dutch placed Africans on the same level with other indentured servants who were set free after a specified amount of service. In 1661, the first American slave petition for freedom came from a slave couple in New Amsterdam and was sent to Peter Stuyvesant. Its plea was for the liberty of a son—and it was granted. But when the British captured the colony a few years later, Negro servants were declared to be held in *perpetual* slavery.

However, all was not peaceful in Dutch colonies in South America. Negroes in the Dutch colony of Surinam fought for their liberty in a thirty-six-year war. In 1761 a newspaper reported that "the Dutch Governor, finding himself unable to subdue the rebel Negroes of that country by force, hath wisely . . . concluded an amicable treaty with them; in consequence of which, all the Negroes of the woods are acknowledged to be free. . . ." In 1772, fighting again broke out between the Dutch and the Negroes. The Negroes were led by a man named Baron and called themselves the "Black Rangers." They almost succeeded in capturing the colony.

As in the Spanish and Portuguese colonies, slaves worked in a variety of trades. They built forts and public projects and even served as armed deputies to rent-collectors. While the colony's Jews were not allowed to serve in the militia or to own land, Negroes were. The legislature three times passed laws to keep settlers from aiding slaves fleeing their masters. Slaves' petitions for freedom were often accompanied by petitions of whites supporting their rights to be free.

## The French Colonies

The earliest French explorers of the New World brought Negroes along on their expeditions. They journeyed down the Mississippi River to the Indian settlements with Marquette and Joliet. The French Jesuit colony in Kaskaskia, Illinois included 70 Negroes. They served as farmers, blacksmiths, carpenters, brewers, and masons. In 1720, Philippe Renault, a Paris banker, brought white and colored laborers to work in the lead, copper, and silver mines of New France.

The best-known Negro explorer of the French expeditions was Jean Baptiste Pointe du Sable, a tall, handsome Negro who had been educated in Paris. He came to New France in 1765 and later built a trading post at the mouth of the Chicago River. Like many other French traders and trappers, du Sable married an Indian woman. His trading post spread out to include a forty-foot house, bakehouse, dairy, smokehouse, workshop, stable, and barn. Eventually it became the site of the city of Chicago. The Indians joked that the first white man to come to Chicago was a black man.

The French colony of Haiti in the Caribbean was the scene of the only successful slave revolt in human history. The revolution began in August, 1791, when a half million Negro slaves rose against their French masters. They were joined by thousands of free Negroes who lived on the island. For ten years, French, Spanish, and

*Toussaint L'Ouverture, liberator of Haiti. His successful rebellion against French rule was the only completely victorious land-based slave revolt in history. The French finally tricked L'Ouverture, captured him, and took him to France where he died of starvation in prison.*

English armies tried in vain to crush the rebellion. The invaders, including Napoleon's powerful armies, were driven into the sea. The Haitian forces were led by Toussaint L'Ouverture, a short, slight ex-slave coachman of 50, with a remarkable knowledge of military tactics. In 1803, the revolutionists declared their freedom and announced: "Restored to our primitive dignity, we have asserted our rights; we swear never to yield them to any power on earth."

Emperor Napoleon had learned an important lesson from his defeat in Haiti—how impossible it was to hold colonies so far from France. When a delegation from Thomas Jefferson, President of the United States, arrived to discuss the purchase of New Orleans, Napoleon surprised them by offering to sell the entire Louisiana territory, from the Gulf of Mexico to the Canadian border. The Americans gladly agreed and this $15,000,000 bargain (four cents an acre) doubled the size of the United States.

# Africa During the Slave Trade

[*What was Africa like during the slave trade? What were the Africans like? A slave trader, Captain Theodore Canot, tells about the town of Timbo in West Africa, and of a visit he made to a tribe called the Bagers.*]

. . . It was the height of the dry season, when everything was parched by the sun, yet I could trace the outlines of fine plantations, gardens, and rice-fields. Every where I found abundance of peppers, onions, garlic, tomatoes, sweet potatoes, and cassava, while tasteful fences were garlanded with immense vines and flowers. Fowles, goats, sheep, and oxen stalked about. . . .

. . . I strolled repeatedly through the town. I became excessively familiar with its narrow streets, low houses, mud walls, cul-de-sacs [dead-end streets], and mosques. I saw no fine bazaars, market-places, or shops. The chief wants of life were supplied by peddlers. Platters, jars, and baskets of fruit, vegetables, and meat, were borne around twice or thrice daily. Horsemen dashed about on beautiful steeds towards the fields in the morning, or came home at nightfall at a slower pace. *I never saw man or woman bask lazily in the sun.* Females were constantly busy over their cotton and spinning wheels when not engaged in household occupations; and often have I seen an elderly dame quietly crouched in her hovel at sunset reading the Koran. Nor are the men of Timbo less thrifty. Their city wall is said to hem in about ten thousand individuals, representing all the social industries. They weave cotton, work in leather, fabricate iron from the bar, engage diligently in agriculture, and, whenever not laboriously employed, devote themselves to reading and writing, of which they are excessively fond.

[*Captain Canot visited the Bager people to check on a chest of his goods that had been left among them.*]

I opened the chest, which, to my surprise, was unlocked, and found it nearly full of the merchandise I had placed in it. I shook the cask, and its weight seemed hardly diminished. I turned the spiggot, and lo! the rum trickled on my feet. . . .

"Good!" said the chief, "it is all there,—is it not? We Bagers are neither Soosoos, Mandingoes, Foulahs, nor *Whitemen*, that the goods of a stranger are not safe in our towns! We work for a living; we want little; big ships never come to us, and we neither steal from our guests nor go to war to sell one another!" . . .

. . . [The chief] then sent a crier through the town, informing the women that a white stranger would be their guest during the night; and, in less than half an hour, my hut was visited by most of the village dames and damsels. One brought a pint of rice; another some roots of *cassava;* another, a few spoonfuls of palm oil; another a bunch of peppers; while the oldest lady of the party made herself particularly remarkable by the gift of a splendid fowl. . . .

There was nothing peculiar in this exhibition of hospitality, on account of my nationality. It was the mere fulfillment of a Bager law; and the poorest *black stranger* would have shared the rite as well as myself. I could not help thinking that I might have travelled from one end of England or America to the other, without meeting a Bager *welcome*. Indeed, it seemed somewhat questionable, whether it were better for the English to civilize Africa, or for the Bagers to send missionaries to their brethren in Britain!

---

Brantz Meyer, ed., *Captain Canot, or Twenty Years of an African Slaver* (New York, 1854), pp. 120-122, 177-180.

# A Slaver Describes the African Trade

[*Long after the slave trade had been outlawed by the nations of the world, it continued openly. It was a dangerous but highly profitable business. Captain James Smith was one of the few traders captured and punished, and his sentence was only two years in prison and a $1,000 fine. Captain Smith freely and honestly answered the questions of a newspaper editor.*]

"New York," said Captain Smith, "is the chief port in the world for the Slave Trade." He repeated two or three times, "*It is the greatest place in the universe for it.* Neither in Cuba nor in the Brazils is it carried on so extensively. Ships that convey Slaves to the West Indies and South America are fitted out from New York. Now and then one sails from Boston and Philadelphia; but New York is our headquarters. My vessel was the brig 'Julia Moulton.' I got her in Boston, and brought her here, and sailed from this port direct for the coast of Africa."

"But do you mean to say that this business is going on now?"

"*Yes, all the while. Not so many vessels have been sent out this year—perhaps not over twenty-five. But last year there were thirty-five.*"

"Are there large shipping-houses engaged in it?"

"Yes; I can go down to South Street, and go into a number of houses that help to fit out ships for the business. I don't know how far they own the vessels, or receive the profits of the cargoes. But these houses know all about it. . . ."

"But when you reach the African coast, are you not in great danger from British Ships-of-War?"

"Oh, no, we don't care a button for an English squadron. *We run up the American flag, and if they come aboard, all we have to do is to show our American papers, and they have no right to search us.*" . . .

"How many Slaves could you carry on your vessel?"

"We took on board 664. We might have stowed away 800. If she had been going to the Brazils, we should have taken that number. She would carry 750 with ease. The boys and women we kept on the upper deck. But all the strong men—those giant Africans that might make us trouble—we put below on the Slave deck."

"Did you chain them or put on handcuffs?"

"No, never; they would die. We let them move about."

"Are you very severe with them?"

"We have to be very strict at first—for a week or so—to make them feel that we are masters. Then we lighten up for the rest of the voyage."

"How do you pack them at night?"

"They lie down upon the deck, on their sides, body to body. There would not be room enough for all to lie on their backs."

"Did many die on the passage?"

"Yes. I lost a good many the last cruise—more than ever before. *Sometimes we find them dead when we go below in the morning.* Then we throw them overboard."

"Are the profits of the trade large?"

"Yes, sir, very large. My Brig cost $13,000 to fit her out completely. My last cargo to Cuba was worth $220,000."

"Did you ever get chased by the English ships?"

"Yes; once a Man-of-War chased two of us. The mate betrayed me. I never liked the man. He was scared. He had no heart. You see, it takes a man of a particular constitution to engage in our business. . . . We belong to no country. We are under the protection of no law. We must defend ourselves. A man must have a great deal of nerve in such a situation when he is liable to be chased by ships-of-war, or perhaps, finds himself suddenly in the midst of a whole fleet." . . .

"But are you not tired of this business?"

"Why, I didn't want to go out the last voyage. I tried to get another Captain to take charge of my ship. I wanted to stay at home and get married. But *good men* in our business are scarce. And I had to go."

---

Geo. W. Carleton, *The Suppressed Book About Slavery!* (New York, 1864), pp. 408-411.

# Stephan Dorantez (Estevanico) Finds the Seven Cities of Gold—and Death!

[*Estevanico or "Little Stephan," as he was called, had been chief scout in the 1528 Cabeza de Vaca expedition into Florida. In 1539, at the orders of the viceroy of Mexico and Nueva Espanna, he went with Friar Marcos de Niza into the American Southwest in search of the Seven Cities of Gold (Ceuola or Cibola) supposed to be hidden there. Here Father de Niza, leader of the expedition, tells of Estevanico's last great adventure.*]

. . . I sent Stephan Dorantez the Negro another way, whom I commaunded to goe directly northward fiftie or threescore leagues, to see if by that way hee might learne any newes of any notable thing which wee sought to discover, and I agreed with him, that if hee found any knowledge of any peopled and riche Countrey which were of great importance, that hee should goe no further, but should returne in person, or shoulde sende mee certaine Indians with that token which wee were agreed upon, to wit, that if it were but a meane thing, hee shoulde sende mee a White Crosse of one handfull long; and if it were any great matter, one of two handfuls long; and if it were a Countrey greater and better than Nueva Espanna, hee should send mee a great crosse. So the sayde Stephan departed from mee on Passion-sunday after dinner: and within foure dayes after the messengers of Stephan returned unto me with a great Crosse as high as a man, and they brought me word from Stephan, that I should forthwith come away after him, for hee had found people which gave him information of a very mighty Province, and that he had sent me one of the said Indians. This Indian told me, that it was thirtie dayes journey from the Towne where Stephan was, unto the first Citie of the sayde Province, which is called Ceuola. Hee affirmed also that there are seven great Cities in this Province, all under one Lord, the houses whereof are made of Lyme and Stone, and are very great . . . and that in the gates of the principall houses there are many Turques-stones cunningly wrought. . . .

[*After days of additional travel and more messages from Estevanico, Father Marcos saw another of his Negro's Indian guides.*]

[The guide] came in a great fright, having his face and ·body all covered with sweat . . . and he told mee that a dayes journey before Stephan came to Ceuola [and sent his gourd] and two feathers one white and another red, in token that he demanded safe conduct, and that he came peaceably. . . .

[*The magistrate refused the peace offer and forbade Stephan's entrance. Two other Indians stumbled into Father Marcos' camp with the final details.*]

These wounded Indians I asked for Stephan, and they agreeing in all poynts with [what] the first Indian sayd, that after they had put him into the . . . house without giving him meat or drinke all that day and all that night, they took from Stephan all the things which hee carried with him. The next day when the Sunne was a lance high, Stephan went out of the house [and suddenly saw a crowd of people coming at him from the city,] whom as soone as hee sawe he began to run away and we likewise, and foorthwith they shot at us and wounded us, and certain men fell dead upon us . . . and after this we could not see Stephan any more, and we thinke they have shot him to death, as they have done all the rest which went with him, so that none are escaped but we onely.

---

Richard Hakluyt, *Hakluyt's Collection of the Early Voyages, Travels, and Discoveries of the English Nation* (London, 1810), pp. 438-445.

# St. Malo Leads a Slave Revolt in New Spain

*[Although slave revolts in the New World were frequent, few records were kept of them. A description of a slave revolt leader in Spanish New Orleans is preserved in this song, "The Dirge of St. Malo," still sung many years later (in 1880) by "old Madeline," a Negro woman from New Orleans. The "Cabildo men" mentioned were the Spanish judges, police, and jailers.]*

Alas! young men, come, make lament
For poor St. Malo in distress!
They chased, they hunted him with dogs,
They fired at him with a gun,

. . . . . . . . . . . .

They hauled him from the cypress swamp—
His arms they tied behind his back,
They tied his hands in front of him;
They tied him to a horse's tail,
They dragged him up into the town.
Before those grand Cabildo men
They charged that he had made a plot
To cut the throats of all the whites.
They asked him who his comrades were;
Poor St. Malo said not a word!
The judge his sentence read to him,
And then they raised the gallows-tree.
They drew the horse—the cart moved off—
And left St. Malo hanging there.
The sun was up an hour high
When on the Levee he was hung;
They left his body swinging there,
For carrion crows to feed upon.

George W. Cable, "Creole Slave Songs," *Century Magazine*, Vol. 31 (April, 1886), pp. 814-815.

# 2

# *The English Colonies*

IN 1619 the new English colony of Jamestown was the scene of two events of great importance in the history of American democracy. Twenty African laborers were brought into the port and sold by the captain of a Dutch ship, and the House of Burgesses, America's first representative assembly, met for the first time. For close to 250 years, Africans would be used as forced labor in the world's first representative democracy.

## *Slave Life in Colonial America*

The cargo of Africans was purchased to help relieve Jamestown's labor shortage. In that same year, one hundred London boys were brought to the colony for the same purpose. Both Negroes and whites were freed following an agreed-upon number of years of labor —for they were indentured servants rather than slaves. Members of both groups became landowners and slaveholders. In fact, the first runaway slave case in Virginia involved a Negro master.

Two generations later, however, the House of Burgesses passed laws making newly arrived Africans, and the children born to them, slaves forever. The excuse for enslaving them was that they were neither Christian nor white. As soon as a few became Christians, Virginia adopted a law declaring "that baptisme of slaves doth not exempt them from bondage."

Indians had been used as slaves but they had proved unsuited to plantation labor. They died from the white man's diseases or from the rigors of the slave system. Many escaped to the woods which they knew better than their captors, or to their tribes. A few remained in slavery and were subjected to the same rules as Negroes. Unlike the Indian, the African was used to agricultural labor. Furthermore, he was thousands of miles from home and friends, so that even when he managed to escape, his skin color made him an easy target for recapture in a land of whites.

## The Southern Colonies

Slaves in the Southern colonies worked largely on the rice, tobacco, and sugar cane crops. A British officer described their working day as lasting from "day break" to "late in the evening." At night, "they sleep on a bench, or on the ground, with an old scanty blanket, which serves them at once for bed and covering."

Not all the Southern slaves worked in the fields. Some were skilled craftsmen, and others became servants in the "big house" of their masters. Slaves built the mansions of Mount Vernon and Monticello. Some worked as chimney sweepers in Charleston, where, in 1763, they combined to protest their working conditions. Others helped to protect the city from Indian attacks in 1708 by serving as cowboy patrols. George Washington saw slave "pioneers or hatchet men" employed on the Virginia frontier. Abel, a talented Virginia slave who escaped, was described by his owner in glowing terms: "He plays on the violin . . . a pilot for the York river and the Bay. He can write so as to be understood. He has gone off in a Boat with two Masts, schooner rigged. . . . A White lad went off with him." Abel may have been one of the many Negroes who worked alongside white indentured servants and free laborers.

While slave labor was important in all of the English colonies, it became vital to the development of the Southern colonies. Even Georgia, which began with a ban on slavery, gave up the restriction after a generation. "All unanimously agree," wrote one of its leaders in 1740, "that without Negroes Georgia can never be a colony of any consequence." By the time the American Revolution began, the slave population exceeded the free population in many areas of the South. Slaves comprised 65 per cent of South Carolina's total population.

The fear of rebellion led to strict "slave codes" in regions of dense slave populations.

The colonial period, however, even in the South, was marked by a more tolerant attitude toward Negroes than the pre-Civil War period. Negro and white apprentices were treated in much the same manner in South Carolina. As early as 1740, Alexander Garden of Charleston proposed a school for slaves. His unique idea included the suggestion that its instruction "must be by Negro Schoolmasters . . . equally Property as other Slaves, but educated for this Service. . . ." Garden's plan was accepted and he selected two slave boys of fifteen, Andrew and Harry, for training as schoolmasters. In 1743 the school opened under the direction of Harry, whom Garden called a "Genius." Within a year Harry was instructing sixty slave scholars, mainly in "the principles of our holy Religion." The school continued until Harry's death in 1764.

## The Middle and New England Colonies

The farther North one went the smaller was the slave population. New England's slaves never numbered more than two per cent of the total population. Slavery in the North often was more humane than in the South. New York City provided schools for Negroes in 1705 and Philadelphia did so in 1758. Puritan minister Cotton Mather insisted that masters treat their slaves "according to the rules of humanity" as persons with "immortal souls in them and . . . not mere beasts of burden."

Life for the New England slave was rarely as burdensome as it was for his Southern brother. Puritan masters thought it wrong to work their slaves on the Sabbath. They also made sure the Negroes were admitted to the white hospitals when ill. Cotton Mather formed a society to instruct Negroes in Christianity and performed slave marriages with Christian dignity. He told other ministers to preach "Thy Negro is thy neighbor" to their congregations. Furthermore, he practiced what he preached: "I would remember, that my servants are in some sense my children. . . . Nor will I leave them ignorant of anything, wherein I may instruct them to be useful to their generation." He added that "I will put Bibles and other good and proper books into their hands."

Slaves took part in every phase of the diverse economic life of the North. Twenty-four slave women worked in a Rhode Island creamery. The famous Touro Synagogue in Newport, an excellent example of colonial New England architecture, was built during the French and Indian War with the aid of hired Negro craftsmen. Prince Fowle was a slave who served as a pressman on New Hampshire's first newspaper. Many of New England's sailors were Negroes. Quaker Anthony Benezet, who began a school for Negro children in Philadelphia, reported: "I have found amongst the Negroes as great variety of talents as amongst a like number of whites." Benezet stated that the belief "that the blacks are inferior in their capacities, is a vulgar prejudice, founded on . . . pride or ignorance." The Quaker devoted the rest of his life to Negro education.

The Salem witch-hunts of the 1690's touched the lives of several Negroes. They were among the accused and accusers. A slave named Candy was accused of "wickedly, malliciously and felloniously [sic]" practicing witchcraft on a woman named Ann Putnam. Unlike many other victims of the hysteria, Candy was found not guilty and freed. In this case, as in many others, Negroes were tried before judges and juries and had the same legal rights that whites had.

It was easier for the New England slave to improve his condition or gain his freedom than it was for his Southern brother. Slave soldiers received the same pay and treatment as whites. More than a few slaves successfully sued their owners for their freedom. In 1769 a slave named James took his master to court in Concord, claiming he had "restrained him of his liberty and held him in servitude." When he lost the case, James took it to a higher court and finally won. Owners such as Cotton Mather freed their slaves out of kindness or Christian principle.

The free New England Negro was, at times, able to rise to a high position in the colonial society of the 18th century. Newport Gardner of Rhode Island opened a music school for Negroes and whites and his former master took lessons at his studio. Emmanuel Bernoon opened the first catering business in Providence, Rhode Island.

However, discrimination kept the Negro from rising as far as he might have. A French traveler to New England wrote:

*Tituba, a Salem house slave, delighted and frightened Puritan teenagers with strange stories and "sorcery." Accused of witchcraft, her testimony tore the community apart—leading to the Salem witch-hunt.*

> Those Negroes who keep shops live moderately and never augment their business beyond a certain point. The reason is obvious. The whites . . . like not to give them credit to enable them to undertake any extensive commerce nor even give them the means of [a] common education. . . .

Lucy Terry and her husband, Abijah Prince, were remarkable examples of slaves who became free and prosperous in colonial New England. Miss Terry was kidnapped from Africa when she was an infant and lived in Deerfield, Massachusetts from the age of five. It was here that she met Prince. In 1746 she witnessed a bloody Indian massacre in her village and wrote a rhymed description of it. It was the first poem written by a Negro on American soil.

Prince was freed and given land by the terms of his master's will. In 1756 the couple was married before a Justice of the Peace and Prince purchased Lucy's freedom. Another settler left him more land in Vermont in his will. When he became a charter member of the town of Sunderland in Vermont, he was granted still more land.

The Princes had six children and when Cesar, the oldest boy, was ready for college, Lucy Prince tried to enroll him in Williams College. For three hours she addressed the trustees, trying to persuade them to change their policy of not admitting Negroes. Despite the fact that she quoted "an abundance of law and Gospel, chapter and verse," she was unsuccessful. Cesar was one of the five thousand Negroes to serve their country in the Revolution. He probably marched with the Green Mountain Boys under Colonel Ethan Allen, who lived across the creek from the Prince family.

Lucy Prince went to court when a neighbor in Sunderland claimed part of the Prince farm as his land. One historian reported that she argued her case all the way from the court in her small town to the United States Supreme Court. According to this authority, Justice Samuel Chase told her she had made a better argument than any he had ever heard from a Vermont lawyer, and she won her case. For 18 years, until she died at the age of 91, Lucy Prince rode horseback over the Green Mountains each year to visit her husband's grave.

## The Fight Against Bondage

Slaveholders in all the colonies lived an uneasy life with their "property" often in revolt or flight. In 1657 Indians and Negroes attacked Hartford, Connecticut and burned homes. In 1690 Connecticut towns instituted a 9 o'clock curfew for Indians and Negroes. Some towns passed laws that forbade either group to come out of doors during fires. In 1727 Indians and Negroes attacked Virginia settlements. Obviously a number of black men had made common cause

*Hunting runaway slaves. George Washington thought slaves were "a very troublesome" kind of property because they ran away or planned revolts. Slaves owned by Washington, Patrick Henry, and George Mason, "father of the Bill of Rights," ran away to find freedom.*

with red men. To the Indian, slavery was unknown before the coming of the white man. Clearly the enemy of both the slave and the Indian was the same, the white man. When Natchez Indians massacred whites in 1730 they spared 106 Negroes. A Boston law forbade Negroes or Indians from carrying a stick or cane, day or night, which could "be fit for . . . fighting or anything of that nature."

From New England to Georgia, slaveholders had to be constantly alert to the escape of their slaves. Slaves ran away from all kinds of masters, both mean and kind. Even a strict but gentle master such as George Washington sold one of his slaves, Tom, because he had run away repeatedly. Washington advised Tom's new owner to keep him "handcuffed, lest he should attempt to escape."

Even the "Society of Negroes," which Cotton Mather began in 1693, aimed at curtailing slave resistance as well as fostering the Puritan gospel. Its members had to pledge themselves to provide runaways "*no Shelter*" and see they were "discovered and punished."

Slave resistance took many forms. In 1723 Boston slaves were accused of setting a dozen fires in one April week. In 1740 New York slaves were accused of trying to poison the water supply. The following year, the city crushed a slave revolt that included 25 whites and more than a hundred Negroes. Carolina slaves attacked a warehouse and seized guns and ammunition. A white eyewitness described the scene: "Being thus provided with arms, they elected one of their number captain, and agreed to follow him, marching towards the south-west, with colours flying and drums beating, like a disciplined company." Troops smashed this revolt.

When they could not flee or revolt, the bondsmen kept in touch with each other in many secret ways. John Adams wrote in 1775, "The Negroes have a wonderful art of communicating intelligence among themselves; it will run several hundred miles in a week or a fortnight."

Opposition to slavery did not come from Negroes alone. The persecuted Quakers of the middle colonies, who rejected war and violence, were the first group of white people to come to the aid of the slave. They saw slavery as a form of violence and freed their own slaves, before asking others to do the same. In 1688, the German-town, Pennsylvania Quakers issued the first group protest against slavery in America. They said: "What thing in the world can be done worse to us, than if men should rob or steal us away, and sell us for slaves to strange countries." After thus identifying themselves with the slaves, the Quakers asked if Negroes did not have "as much right to fight for their freedom, as you have to keep them slaves?"

Many important colonial figures were opposed to slavery. Samuel Sewall, Roger Williams, James Otis, and John Woolman were among the outstanding colonial leaders who denounced human bondage. The first of Thomas Paine's articles to be published in America (March, 1775), was a scathing attack on slavery and the

*Roger Williams opposed mistreatment of Indians and Negroes by whites.*

African trade. A month later Paine and Benjamin Franklin helped found the first antislavery society in America.

## Defending the Colonies

Negroes played an important role in the defending of frontier settlements from Indian attacks. One Virginia slave fired a gun full of nails to disperse an Indian raid on a fort. Another unknown hero barked orders and answered them himself to convince the Indians that his fort had many men. Although he was the only man present in the fort, his trick worked and the Indians retreated. One night in 1788 slave Dick Pointer "saved the lives of many citizens" at Fort Donnelly, Virginia by fighting off an Indian surprise attack single-handedly until the garrison awoke and came to his rescue.

The colonial militias often called Negroes into service and some slaves won their freedom by serving in the army. South Carolina promised freedom to any slave who slew or captured an enemy in battle. So many Negroes soon qualified that the offer was changed to ten pounds in cash. In 1747, South Carolina officially thanked its colored militiamen, who "in times of war, behaved themselves with great faithfulness and courage, in repelling the attacks of his Majesty's enemies." While paying them this compliment, the legislature limited the number of Negro militiamen to one-third of the total force. This made certain that there would always be more whites than Negroes with guns.*

The frontier dangers often made demands upon the women as well as the men. Major Arthur Campbell told how an unknown Negro woman saved a fort during Lord Dunmore's War in 1774.

> Last Thursday evening the Indians took a Negroe Wench Prisoner, belonging to Capt. Shelby. . . . After they took her some distance they . . . [asked

---

* Slaves and free Negroes served in Queen Anne's War (1702-1713), King George's War (1744-1748), and the French and Indian War (1754-1763). They fought and died alongside General Braddock and George Washington in 1755 and took part in the capture of Fort Ticonderoga and Crown Point in 1758. They also served aboard practically every ship in the colonial navy, receiving the same pay, food, and treatment as white sailors.

her] how many Guns was [sic] in the Fort, and other questions relative to the strength of the place. . . .

After they had carried her off about a Mile, they seen or heard a Boy coming from the Mill, they immediately tyed the Wench, and went off to catch the Boy, while they were gone, the Wench luckily got loose, and made her escape. She says they knocked her down twice, when she refused to tell in what situation the Fort was. . . .

The Spanish in St. Augustine tried to turn the slaves in the English colonies against their masters. They accepted those who managed to escape to Florida and invited others to leave the English. In 1687 eight men and two women fled their South Carolina plantation for St. Augustine. A dozen years later a Spanish decree promised protection "to all Negro deserters from the English who fled to St. Augustine and became Catholics." Many took up the offer of liberty and Catholicism. An English sea captain was astounded to find his runaway slaves walking the streets of St. Augustine. They made faces and laughed at him.

## Cultural Growth in Colonial America

*Gustavus Vasa was brought to America from Africa during Colonial times. After he gained his freedom, he wrote a book telling of his capture and mistreatment.*

Both slaves and free Negroes contributed to the scientific and cultural growth of the English colonies. Jupiter Hammon, a Long Island slave, published religious poems. Gustavus Vasa, captured in Nigeria, wrote a moving account of his life in Africa, his capture, and slave life in Virginia. His autobiography sold eight editions in America and England. As a free man, Vasa presented a petition against the slave trade to Parliament.

Several Negroes contributed to the medical and scientific knowledge of the colonies. A South Carolina slave named Cesar developed a series of cures for poisons that were successfully used. He was granted his freedom and an annuity of one hundred pounds for his discoveries.

James Derham, a slave in the post-Revolutionary period, was sold to a New Orleans physician who taught him to prepare drugs and gave him lessons in French and Spanish. When he was 21, Derham became a physician and practiced in New Orleans. Dr. Benjamin Rush, Surgeon-General of the Continental Army, and a signer of the Declaration of Independence, reported on his meeting with Dr. Derham:

> I have conversed with him upon most of the acute and epidemic diseases of the country where he lives, and was pleased to find him perfectly acquainted with the modern simple mode of practice in those diseases. I expected to have suggested some new medicines to him; but he suggested many more to me. He is very modest and engaging in his manners.

The colonial period was blessed with men like Thomas Jefferson and Benjamin Franklin whose capabilities ranged from political affairs to science. Benjamin Banneker, a Maryland free Negro, contributed to the fields of science, mathematics, and political affairs. A man of dignified dress and appearance (friends said he looked like

*Benjamin Banneker, a Maryland free Negro. A farmer and scientist, he was chosen by President George Washington to serve on the commission that planned the city of Washington, D. C.*

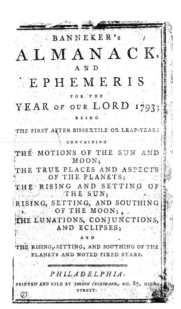

Banneker's Almanac *for 1793. For ten years Banneker published an almanac that provided information about the sun, moon, and tides. Thomas Jefferson was so impressed with it that he sent copies to French scientists and wrote to Banneker telling him of his high regard for the work. Banneker answered that if Negroes were free, many others could contribute to American life and culture.*

Benjamin Franklin), Banneker began his studies as a teenager. Using crude tools, he constructed a clock, the first one made entirely with American parts.

Banneker educated himself with books borrowed from a Quaker neighbor. His interest in scientific matters soon brought him to the attention of Thomas Jefferson, who sent samples of Banneker's Almanac to French scientists. Banneker then suggested that Jefferson lend his "aid and assistance" in helping to end slavery if Mr. Jefferson was impressed with his work. Jefferson promised that he would.

For a decade before his death, Banneker authored a popular almanac that included antislavery essays as well as carefully prepared tables giving information about the tides, moons, crops, and sun. But he is best remembered for the part he played in the commission of three that planned the city of Washington, D.C. Banneker was appointed to the commission upon Jefferson's suggestion to President Washington. With his Quaker friend, George Ellicott, Banneker chose the sites for the White House, the Capitol, and many other important government buildings.

When the French commission head quit and took the printed plans with him, Banneker and Ellicott were able to reconstruct them from memory. By the time Banneker died, in 1806, Thomas Jefferson was the occupant of the White House in the city that Banneker

*Phillis Wheatley, poet, from a portrait pub-
lished in her 1773 book of verse. Her work
was encouraged by her kind Boston mistress, who finally liberated her.*

had helped to plan. Three years before his death, however, the state
of Maryland passed a law forbidding free Negroes, such as Banneker, from voting in any election.

Phillis Wheatley, kidnapped from Africa at the age of 9, was
sold to a kind master in Boston. Her master's wife encouraged the
sensitive young lady to develop her poetic talents and she began writing poems when she was a teenager. Her first book of poems, published in London in 1773, was the second volume of poetry published
by a woman in America.

Miss Wheatley's poems drew favorable comments from Voltaire, John Hancock, Benjamin Franklin, and George Washington.
When she sent a poem to Washington praising him as Commander-
in-Chief of the Revolutionary army, he wrote to her and asked her to
visit him at his Cambridge headquarters. The slave poet and the
General met in 1776, but there is no record of what they said to each
other about either poetry or liberty.

## Life on Board a Colonial Slave Ship

[*Gustavus Vasa was only eleven when he was captured in Benin, Africa, and taken by slave ship to Virginia. This is his account of the trip.*]

The first object which saluted my eyes when I arrived on the coast was the sea, and a slaveship, which was then riding at anchor, and waiting for its cargo. These filled me with astonishment, which was soon converted into terror, which I am yet at a loss to describe, nor the then feelings of my mind. When I was carried on board I was immediately handled, and tossed up, to see if I were sound, by some of the crew; and I was now persuaded that I had got into a world of bad spirits, and that they were going to kill me. . . .

I was not long suffered to indulge my grief; I was soon put down under the decks, and there I received such a salutation in my nostrils as I had never experienced in my life; so that, with the loathsomeness of the stench, and crying together, I became so sick and low that I was not able to eat, nor had I the least desire to taste anything . . . but soon, to my grief, two of the white men offered me eatables; and, on my refusing to eat, one of them held me fast by the hands, and laid me across, I think, the windlass, and tied my feet, while the other flogged me severely. . . .

In a little time after, amongst the poor chained men, I found some of my own nation, which in a small degree gave ease to my mind. I inquired of them what was to be done with us? they gave me to understand we were to be carried to these white people's country to work for them. I then was a little revived, and thought, if it were no worse than working, my situation was not so desperate: but still I feared I should be put to death, the white people looked and acted, as I thought, in so savage a manner; for I had never seen among any people such instances of brutal cruelty; and this not only shewn towards us blacks, but also to some of the whites themselves. One white man in particular I saw, when we were permitted to be on deck, flogged so unmercifully with a large rope near the foremast, that he died in consequence of it; and they tossed him over the side as they would have done a brute. This made me fear these people the more; and I expected nothing less than to be treated in the same manner. . . .

The stench of the hold while we were on the coast was so intolerably loathsome, that it was dangerous to remain there for any time, and some of us had been permitted to stay on the deck for the fresh air; but now that the whole ship's cargo were confined together, it became absolutely pestilential. The closeness of the place, and the heat of the climate, added to the number in the ship, which was so crowded that each had scarcely room to turn himself, almost suffocated us. . . .

The shrieks of the women, and the groans of the dying, rendered the whole a scene of horror almost inconceivable. Happily perhaps for myself I was soon reduced so low here that it was thought necessary to keep me almost always on deck; and from my extreme youth I was not put in fetters. In this situation I expected every hour to share the fate of my companions, some of whom were almost daily brought upon deck at the point of death which I began to hope would soon put an end to my miseries. . . .

One day, when we had a smooth sea, and moderate wind, two of my wearied countrymen, who were chained together (I was near them at the time), preferring death to such a life of misery, somehow made through the nettings, and jumped into the sea; immediately another quite dejected fellow, who, on account of his illness, was suffered to be out of irons, also followed their example; and I believe many more would very soon have done the same, if they had not been prevented by the ship's crew, who were instantly alarmed. Those of us that were the most active were in a moment put down under the deck; and there was such a noise and confusion amongst the people of the ship as I never heard before, to stop her, and get the boat out to go after the slaves. However, two of the wretches were drowned, but they got the other, and afterwards flogged him unmercifully, for thus attempting to prefer death to slavery. In this manner we continued to undergo more hardships than I can now relate; hardships which are inseparable from this accursed trade. . . .

---

Gustavus Vasa, *The Interesting Narrative of the Life of Olandah Equiano or Gustavus Vasa, Written by Himself* (London, 1793) pp. 46-53.

## *The Colonial Slave Code*

[*A "slave code," designed to establish the rules of human bondage, was promulgated by each colonial legislature beginning in the 1660's. The following portions of these Southern laws indicate the conditions and problems faced by American slaves.*]

[*A Virginia law of 1669.*] . . . if any slave resist his master (or other by his master's order correcting him) and by the extremity of coercion could chance to die, that his death shall not be accounted felony, but the master (or that other person &c.) be acquitted from molestation, since it cannot be presumed that prepensed malice (which alone makes murder a felony) should induce any man to destroy his own estate.

John Codman Hurd, *The Law of Freedom and Bondage*, 1 (New York, 1858), p. 232.

[*A South Carolina law of 1740.*] Whereas many owners of slaves, and others who have the care, management, and overseeing of slaves, do confine them so closely to hard labor that they have not sufficient time for natural rest, Be it therefore enacted, That if any owner of slaves, or other persons, who shall have the care, management or overseeing of slaves, shall work or put such slave or slaves to labor more than fifteen hours in twenty-four hours . . . every such person shall forfeit a sum not exceeding twenty pounds nor under five pounds current money, for every time he, she, or they shall offend [the law] . . . .

William Goodell, *The American Slave Code* (New York, 1853), pp. 128-129.

# *The First Written Antislavery Protests*

[*The first known antislavery statement was made in February, 1688, by a group of Pennsylvania Quakers. Its basic antislavery arguments left little room for improvement.*]

. . . There is a saying, that we should do to all men like as we will be done ourselves. . . . Here [in America] is liberty of conscience, which is right and reasonable; here ought to be likewise liberty of the body. . . . But to bring men hither, or to rob and sell them against their will, we stand against. . . . Pray, what thing in the world can be done worse towards us, that if men should rob or steal us away, and sell us for slaves to strange countries; separating husbands from their wives and children. . . .

. . . have these poor Negroes not as much right to fight for their freedom, as you have to keep them slaves?

George H. Moore, *Notes on the History of Slavery in Massachusetts* (New York, 1866), pp. 75-77.

[*In 1788 there appeared the first known Negro protest against slavery to be published. Its author, "Othello," has left no history.*]

. . . In you [whites] the superiority of power produces nothing but a superiority of brutality and barbarism. Weakness, which calls for protection, appears to provoke your inhumanity. Your fine political systems are sullied by the outrages committed against human nature and the devine majesty.

When America opposed the pretensions of England, she declared that all men have the same rights. After having manifested her hatred against tyrants, ought she to have abandoned her principles? . . .

H. Gregoire, *An Enquiry Concerning the Intellectual and Moral Faculties, and Literature of Negroes*, translated by D. B. Warren (Brooklyn, 1810), pp. 185-186.

## Slave Revolt in Colonial South Carolina

[*The most defiant action a group of slaves could take was that of open re-bellion. Periodic revolts were a part of colonial life, particularly in the South where the slave population was most numerous. The following de-scription by a Southern white eyewitness is of a rebellion in Stono, South Carolina around 1740.*]

. . . A number of Negroes haveing assembled together at Stono, first surprised and killed two young men in a ware-house, and then plundered it of guns and ammunition. Being thus provided with arms, they elected one of their number captain, and agreed to follow him, marching towards the south-west, with colours flying and drums beating, like a disciplined company. . . . *they plun-dered and burnt every house, killing every white person they found in them, and compelling the Negroes to join them.*

Governor Bull returning to Charleston from the southward, met them, and observing them armed, spread the alarm, which soon reached the Presbyterian Church at Wiltown. . . . By a law of the province, all Planters were obliged to carry their arms to Church, which at this critical juncture proved a very useful and necessary regulation. The women were left in Church trembling with fear, while the militia, under the command of Captain Bee, marched in quest of the Negroes, who by this time had become formidable, from the number [of slaves] that joined them.

They had marched about twelve miles, and *spread desolation through all the plantations in their way.* They halted in an open field, and began to sing and dance, by way of triumph. During these re-joicings, the militia discovered them. . . . One party advanced into the open field and attacked them, and, having killed some Negroes, the remainder took to the woods and dispersed. Many ran back to their plantations, in hopes of escaping suspicion from the absence of their masters; *but the greater part were taken and tried.* Such as had been compelled to join them, contrary to their inclination, were pardoned, but all the chosen leaders and first insurgents suffered death.

---

Cited in Edwin C. Holland (ed.), *A Refutation of the Calumnies Circulated Against the Southern and Western States, Respecting the Institution and Existence of Slavery Among Them* (Charleston, 1822), pp. 70-71.

# A Slave Report in Rhyme on the Indian Attack on Old Deerfield, August 25, 1746

[*Slave Lucy Terry wrote this description of an Indian massacre in her Massachusetts village. It is considered to be one of the best accounts of the event, and is presented here in complete form, for the first time.*]

August 'twas the twenty-fifth
Seventeen hundred forty-six
The Indians did in ambush lay
Some very valient men to slay
Twas nigh unto Sam Dickinson's mill,
The Indians there five men did kill
The names of whom I'll not leave out
Samuel Allen like a hero fout
And though he was so brave and bold
His face no more shall we behold
Eleazer Hawks was killed outright
Before he had time to fight
Before he did the Indians see
Was shot and killed immediately
Oliver Amsden he was slain
Which caused his friends much grief and pain
Simeon Amsden they found dead
Not many rods off from his head.
Adonijah Gillet, we do hear
Did lose his life which was so dear
John Saddler fled across the water
And so escaped the dreadful slaughter
Eunice Allen see the Indians comeing
And hoped to save herself by running
And had not her petticoats stopt her
The awful creatures had not cotched her
And tommyhawked her on the head
And left her on the ground for dead.
Young Samuel Allen, Oh! lack-a-day
Was taken and carried to Canada.

George Sheldon, "Negro Slavery in Old Deerfield," *The New England Magazine*, Vol. 8 (March, 1893), p. 56.

## A Quaker Speaks of Slaves and Slavery

[*John Bartram was a Quaker farm boy during the 18th century who became botanist to the King of England. In the following passage he explains to a visitor why his Negroes look so well and happy.*]

Though our erroneous prejudices and opinions once induced us to look upon them as fit only for slavery, though ancient custom had very unfortunately taught us to keep them in bondage; yet of late, in consequence of the remonstrances of several Friends, and of the good books they have published on that subject, our society treats them very differently. With us they are now free. I give those, whom thee didst see at my table, eighteen pounds a year, with victuals and clothes, and all other privileges which the white men enjoy. Our society treats them now as the companions of our labours; and, by this management as well as by means of the education we have given them, they are in general become a new set of beings. Those, whom I admit to my table, I have found to be good, trusty, moral, men; when they do not what we think they should do, we dismiss them, which is all the punishment we inflict. Other societies of Christians keep them still as slaves, without teaching them any kind of religious principles. What motive beside fear can they have to behave well? . . . . We gave them freedom, and yet few have quitted their ancient masters. The women breed in our families; and we become attached to one another. I taught mine to read and write; they love God, and fear his judgements. The oldest person among them transacts my business in Philadelphia with a punctuality from which he has never deviated. They constantly attend our meetings, they participate in health and sickness, infancy and old age in the advantages our society affords. Such are the means we have made use of to relieve them from that bondage and ignorance in which they were kept before.

J. Hector St. John (Crèvecoeur), Letter 11 of *Letters from an American Farmer* (London, 1782), pp. 262-263.

# *Phillis Wheatley's Poem on Her Own Slavery*

[*Phillis Wheatley seldom mentioned herself in her poetry. But in the original edition of her* Poems on Various Subjects, *published in 1773, is a portion of her one poem that tells quite a bit about her own life. As a child she was kidnapped in Africa and brought to Boston. A little more than a year later her Quaker master and mistress taught her to read, write, and speak English.*]

To the Right Honourable WILLIAM, Earl of Dartmouth, His Majesty's Principal Secretary of State for North America, and company.

No more *America* in mournful strain
Of wrongs, and grievance unredress'd complain,
No longer shall thou dread the iron chain,
Which wanton *Tyranny* with lawless hand
Has made, and which it meant t' enslave the land.
Should you, my lord, while you pursue my song,
Wonder from whence my love of *Freedom* sprung,
Whence flow these wishes for the common good,
By feeling hearts alone best understood,
I, young in life, by seeming cruel fate
Was snatch'd from *Afric's* fancy'd happy seat:
What pangs excruciating must molest,
What sorrows labour in my parent's breast?
Steel'd was the soul and by no misery mov'd
That from a father seiz'd his babe belov'd
Such, such my case. And can I then but pray
Others may never feel tyrannic sway?

---

Phillis Wheatley, *Poems on Various Subjects* (London, 1773) p. 74.

## A Slave Is Invited to Visit General Washington

[*In the first year of American independence, General George Washington wrote this letter to the slave-poet, Phillis Wheatley, thanking her for the poem which she had written about him. The two met shortly thereafter, at Washington's Cambridge, Massachusetts headquarters.*]

Miss. Phillis: Your favour of the 26th of October did not reach my hands 'till the middle of December. Time enough, you will say, to have given an answer ere this. Granted. . . .

I thank you most sincerely for your polite notice of me, in the elegant lines you enclosed; and however undeserving I may be of such encomium and panegyrick, the style and manner exhibit a striking proof of your great poetical Talents. In honour of which, and in a tribute justly due you, I would have published the Poem, had I not been apprehensive, that, while I only meant to give the World this new instance of your genius, I might have incurred the imputation of Vanity. This and nothing else, determined me not to give it place in the public prints.

If you should ever come to Cambridge, or near Head Quarters, I shall be happy to see a person so favoured by the Muses, and to whom Nature has been so liberal and beneficent in her dispensations. I am, with great Respect, etc.

Letter of February 28, 1776, in John C. Fitzpatrick, ed., *The Writings of George Washington from the Original Manuscript Sources 1754-1799*, Vol. 4 (Washington, 1938), pp. 360-361.

# George Washington's Position on Slavery

[*This 1786 letter written by George Washington to Robert Morris reveals the difficulties faced by a slaveholder—even one with good will and humanitarian beliefs. It also contains history's first mention of the underground railroad.*]

Dear Sir: I give you the trouble of this letter at the instance of Mr. Dalby of Alexandria; who is called to Philadelphia to attend what he conceives to be a vexatious lawsuit respecting a slave of his, whom a Society of Quakers in the city (formed for such purposes) have attempted to liberate. . . . And if the practice of this Society of which Mr. Dalby speaks, is not discountenanced, none of those whose *misfortune* it is to have slaves as attendants, will visit the City if they can possibly avoid it; because by so doing they hazard their property; or they must be at the expence (and this will not always succeed) of providing servants of another description for the trip.

I hope it will not be conceived from these observations, that it is my wish to hold the unhappy people, who are the subject of this letter, in slavery. I can only say that there is not a man living who wishes more sincerely than I do, to see a plan adopted for the abolition of it; but there is only one proper and effectual mode by which it can be accomplished and that is by Legislative authority; and this, as far as my suffrage will go, shall never be wanting. But when slaves who are happy and contented with their present masters, are tampered with and seduced to leave; when a conduct of this sort begets discontent on one side and resentment on the other, and when it happens to fall on a man, whose purse will not measure with that of the Society, and he looses [sic] his property for want of means to defend it; it is oppression in the latter case, and not humanity in any, because it introduces more evils than it can cure.

John C. Fitzpatrick, ed., *The Writings of George Washington from the Original Manuscript Sources 1754-1799*, Vol. 28 (Washington, 1938), pp. 407-408.

## *The Epitaph of a Proud Man*

[*A Concord, Massachusetts Negro who died in colonial times had this epitaph carved on his gravestone.*]

GOD
Wills us free;
Man
Wills us slaves,

I will as God wills,
God's will be done.

Here lies the body of JOHN JACK,
A native of Africa, who died March, 1773,
Aged about *sixty years.*

Tho' *born* in a land of *slavery,*
He was born *free;*
Tho' he lived in a land of *liberty,*
He lived a *slave.* . . .

Tho' not long before
Death, the grand Tyrant,
Gave him his final emancipation,
And set him on a footing with kings. . . .

*Harper's New Monthly Magazine,* Vol. 41 (August, 1870), p. 475.

## *America's First Negro Mason Discusses Discrimination*

[*Prince Hall devoted his life to making America a better place in which to live. After his enlistment petition went to John Hancock and George Washington, he was accepted in the Revolutionary army. As a Boston landowner and voter, he demanded that his state free its slaves and his city educate its Negro children. He soon established a school in his own home. In 1797 he addressed the Negro Masons on the discrimination which Negroes faced and on how they should respond.*]

. . . Patience I say, for were we not possessed of a great measure of it you could not bear up under the daily insults you meet with in the streets of Boston; much more on public days of recreation, how are you shamefully abus'd, and that at such a degree, that you may be truly said to carry your lives in your hands . . . [since many have been attacked] by a mob of shameless, low-lived, envious, spiteful persons, some of them not long since, servants in gentlemen's kitchens. . . .

My brethren, let us not be cast down under these and many abuses we at present labour under: for the darkest is before the break of day. . . .

Although you are deprived of the means of education; yet you are not deprived of the means of meditation. . . .

Live and act as Masons, that you may die as Masons; let those despisers see, altho' many of us cannot read, yet by our searches and researches into men and things, we have supplied that defect . . . [and] give the right hand of affection and fellowship to whom it justly belongs [and] let their colour and complexion be what it will: their nation be what it may, for they are your brethren.

Prince Hall, *A Charge Delivered to the African Lodge*, June 24, 1797, pp. 10-13.

# 3

# *Building of a Nation*

AT the end of the French and Indian War, the British increased the taxes on the thirteen colonies and sent officials and soldiers to collect these taxes. Boston became a center of resistance to both the taxes and the British soldiers. Irritation grew on both sides.

## *The Revolution*

On the snowy winter night of March 5, 1770, the inevitable happened. A group of Boston patriots met a company of British soldiers, but this time the usual name-calling, scuffling, and throwing of snowballs ended in bloodshed.

The leader of the crowd of Boston men and boys was Crispus Attucks, a tall runaway slave who had become a seaman. When Attucks waved his cordwood club and urged the crowd forward, someone gave the order to fire and the British muskets cut down Attucks and four other Bostonians. Unlike Attucks, whose death made him the first martyr to American independence, another Negro named Andrew fled into a doorway as bullets flew that fateful evening. Andrew lived to tell a court exactly what happened.

This "Boston Massacre" was the first battle of the American Revolution. Before the War for Independence ended at Yorktown, 5,000 more American Negroes would fight to help build the new nation.

*The Boston Massacre. British troops fire on a Boston mob led by runaway slave Crispus Attucks. A monument to Attucks and the four other American martyrs now stands in Boston.*

As the British and colonial forces moved toward full-scale war, "Minutemen" drilled everywhere. When the British advanced on Lexington and Concord, Lemuel Haynes was among those who answered Paul Revere's and William Dawes' call to arms. Haynes was only one of the several Negro Minutemen who, at Concord Bridge, on April 19, 1775, fired some of those shots "heard 'round the world."

A few weeks later Haynes, Primas Black, and Epheram Blackman had joined Ethan Allen and his Green Mountain Boys in the capture of Fort Ticonderoga.

In the next battle of the war, Bunker Hill, Negroes and whites, whose ammunition included nails and scraps of iron, as well as musket balls, cut down advancing forces of the British Army twice and retreated only when all the ammunition was gone. When the British commander, Major Pitcairn, appeared suddenly in front of the colonial lines and called on the rebels to surrender, "his commanding air at first startled the men immediately before him. They neither answered nor fired." Except for one man. "At this critical moment, a Negro soldier [Peter Salem] stepped forward, and aiming his musket directly at the major's bosom, blew him through."

*Battle of Bunker Hill. It was actually fought on Breed's Hill.*

Another patriot, Salem Poor, was singled out for special commendation by Colonel William Prescott, the colonial field commander in the battle. Prescott (who early in the battle had shouted the immortal words "Don't fire until you see the whites of their eyes!") now, with thirteen other officers, commended: "A Negro man named Salem Poor," who "behaved like an experienced officer, as well as an excellent soldier."

Negroes were in every battle of importance. A Hessian soldier wrote: "No regiment is to be seen in which there are not Negroes in abundance and among them are able-bodied, strong, and brave fellows." Negroes served with Francis Marion, the Swamp Fox, in the Carolinas, and in the United States Navy with John Paul Jones. At fourteen, James Forten sailed with Stephen Decatur aboard the *Royal Louis* as a powderboy. When he was captured and offered a chance to go to England, the boy answered "I AM HERE A PRISONER FOR THE LIBERTIES OF MY COUNTRY. I *never*, NEVER, *shall prove a traitor to her interests.*"

*Swamp Fox Francis Marion welcomed Negroes in his guerrilla band. They struck at British forces in South Carolina, cutting communication lines and driving off Tories.*

Other Negroes served as spies and won praise and, sometimes, their liberty for repeatedly going behind enemy lines to obtain military information. James Armistead was a spy for General Lafayette and was granted his freedom at the Frenchman's request. Negro soldiers froze in Washington's army at Valley Forge. In the boats crossing the Delaware with their commander were Prince Whipple, an African slave, and Oliver Cromwell, a New Jersey Negro freeman. On that Christmas night of 1776, they took part in the surprise attack and capture of the British garrison of Hessians at Trenton, New Jersey.

One soldier, "Robert Shurtliff," turned out to be a woman, generally believed to be colored, who had served eighteen months in the patriot army. Her state of Massachusetts rewarded Deborah Gannett for an "extraordinary instance of female heroism."

Negroes served in the Revolutionary army and navy in spite of attempts by some Americans to keep them out. Slaveholders in the Continental Congress had George Washington halt enlistments of Negroes. But steps taken by the British soon led to a change in this policy. The British Governor of Virginia, Lord Dunmore, offered freedom to any slaves reaching his lines. Many made the attempt. The Continental Army decided to accept Negroes rather than see them used by the enemy. Northern colonies formed special Negro regiments and a white soldier named Harris witnessed a battle in which they took part:

*Slave James Armistead spied on British fortifications for Lafayette. In 1786 the Virginia legislature granted Armistead his freedom because he had helped the American cause "at the peril of his life."*

> Had they been unfaithful, or given way before the enemy all would have been lost. *Three times in succession* they were attacked, with most desperate valor and fury, by well disciplined and veteran [British] troops, and *three times* did they successfully repel the assault, and thus preserve our army from capture. They fought through the war. They were brave, hardy troops. They helped gain our liberty and independence.

In 1779, when the scene of warfare shifted from the North to the South, Virginians began to accept free Negroes and even slaves into the patriot army. These soldiers became part of regular combat units where they ate and fought alongside white soldiers. Many served on the sea, some as ship pilots. Caesar Tarrant served four years as pilot of the *Patriot* and the ship captured a British vessel while under his command. Others served aboard the *Liberty* during its twenty battles with the enemy.

Saul Matthews, a Virginia Negro, entered a British garrison in 1781 on a spy mission. He not only brought back valuable information for his fellow Americans, but led a raid on the British troops that same night. His amazing courage was highly praised by Baron Von Steuben, Lafayette, and General Nathaniel Greene.

*General Washington accepts surrender of Lord Cornwallis at Yorktown.*

Many of the slaves enlisted when they were promised their freedom. But the slaves who had fled to Lord Dunmore were often betrayed and were sent, still slaves, to the West Indies. Some American slaveholders also refused to keep their word. But others did, and many a former slave soldier enjoyed some of the freedoms he helped to establish.

The role which Negroes from other lands played in the American Revolution is comparatively unknown. Yet, like Lafayette, Von Steuben, Pulaski, and Kosciusko, the Fontages Legion from Haiti served gallantly with the Continental Army. At the battle of Savannah on October 9, 1779, more than five hundred of these Haitian freemen held back a fierce British attack that might well have wiped out the French and American armies. One of those wounded in the battle was Sergeant Henri Christophe. He returned to his country and later became second in command to Haiti's "George Washington," Toussaint L'Ouverture. After L'Ouverture's death, Henri Christophe became Emperor of Haiti.

Two months after the ringing words of the Declaration of Independence had sounded in the colonies, the Massachusetts legislature issued a proclamation calling slavery "utterly inconsistent with the . . . struggle for liberty." Before America's first year of independence drew to a close, several Massachusetts towns voted to end slavery. For the first time in the history of the human race, governments voted to end human bondage. It was an important beginning.

## The Critical Period Leads to the Constitution

In the years that followed the Revolution, the poor who had fought in the struggle for independence sought a greater measure of the liberty that they had helped to win. It was an era of turbulence, marked by the revolt of debtor farmers in western Massachusetts, led by a Revolutionary hero, Daniel Shays. Among Shays' men, indicted a year later, was Moses Sash, a five-foot-eight black soldier of the Revolution, the only man of the group to be indicted twice. Sash was charged as "a Captain" and a member of Shays' "Councill," and his indictment read:

> . . . that Moses Sash of Worthington . . . a Negro man and labourer being a disorderly, riotous & seditious person [did] . . . promote, incite, & maintain riots, mobs, tumults, [and] insurrections in this Commonwealth . . . to disturb, impede, & prevent the Government . . . and to prevent the Courts of justice from sitting as by Law [and] . . . did procure guns, bayonets, pistols, swords, gunpowder, bullets, blankets, & provisions & other warlike supplies.

When John Hancock was elected governor of Massachusetts he pardoned Shays, Sash, and the other revolt leaders.

While the Confederation Congress lacked the power to suppress Shays' rebellion, it did establish a democratic government for the states being formed out of the Northwest territory. It also forbade slavery there in its famous Northwest Ordinance issued in 1787. In that same year, American leaders in Philadelphia met to draw up a new Constitution. What would they do about slavery?

The Founding Fathers had opposed slavery and the slave trade. "Among my first wishes," Washington had written, "is to see some plan adopted by which slavery in this country may be abolished." Jefferson had predicted that "nothing is more certainly written in the Book of Fate, than that this people shall be free." Patrick Henry said about slavery: "I will not, I cannot justify it." Benjamin Franklin became a leader of Pennsylvania's Society for Promoting the Abolition of Slavery, and Alexander Hamilton became a leader of the New York Manumission Society.

The men who met at Philadelphia to write a new Constitution, however, came to build a strong and united country, not to solve the slavery question. To keep the loyalty of the slaveholders and slave traders in the North and South, they agreed to protect slave property in three separate sections of the Constitution:

> 1. They gave the African slave trade twenty more years in which to cease operations.
> 2. They provided that all runaway slaves had to be returned to their owners.
> 3. Because slaveholders were to be taxed for their slaves, as property, they were allowed three votes for every five slaves owned.

In spite of this bargain with those who traded in men, women, and children, most of the delegates left the Convention convinced that slavery was dying. They thought the Northwest Ordinance proved that Congress had the power to halt slavery's growth forever. They reasoned that the end of the slave trade in twenty years would dry up the source of the evil. And they knew that several states had already ended human bondage and that others had banned the slave trade. They felt sure that their compromises were a temporary arrangement, at worst.

Certainly they could not foresee the invention of the cotton gin which took place just 6 years later. The 55 men at Philadelphia could not realize that slaveholders, made wealthy and greedy by profits from cotton, would use these compromises to shield slavery

*The United States Constitution provided for an end of slave-trading after 1807. But the Southern planters always needed more laborers and the traders were unwilling to give up their profitable business. Although slave-trading was considered piracy after 1808, it continued until the Civil War. The death penalty was not carried out against any slave-trader until 1862, when Nathaniel Gordon was found guilty of the crime and hanged.*

and protect its growth. The practical result of these compromises was that slave merchants continued to import Africans, ignored the Constitution, and violated all legal attempts to halt the trade.

*Richard Allen, Negro civic and religious leader. He and Absalom Jones led a 1787 "kneel-in" in Philadelphia just as the delegates to the Constitutional Convention were leaving for home and George Mason was writing the Bill of Rights. During the War of 1812 Allen and Jones, at that time leaders of America's first Negro church, raised a force of 2,500 men to protect Philadelphia from the British. Shortly before his death in 1831 Allen wrote, "This land, which we have watered with our tears and our blood, is now our mother country."*

## The War of 1812

On a June morning in 1807, the British man-of-war *Leopard*, a few miles outside of Norfolk harbor, fired upon the United States Navy's *Chesapeake*, killing three and wounding eighteen men. British officers speedily boarded the *Chesapeake* and seized four men whom they charged with desertion from the Royal Navy. One *was* a deserter and he was promptly executed. But Daniel Martin, William Ware, and John Strachan, all Negro seamen, were able to prove they were Americans and were finally freed. The attack on the *Chesapeake* and the attempt to seize its sailors became the best-known instance of thousands of such foreign seizures of American seamen.

American anger rose to the boiling point over the *Chesapeake* incident. To halt these insults, irate citizens began a boycott of English goods, Congress passed an Embargo Act, and many called for armed action.

When war finally came in 1812, the young American Navy was well prepared. Both Negro and white seamen had shown their gallantry in our undeclared naval war with France, 1798-1800. One Negro seaman, William Brown, serving aboard the *Constellation*, was wounded in the battle and capture of the French warship *L'Insurgente*. A year later Brown fought again, this time against *La Vengeance* which escaped from the American fleet. He was granted 160 acres of land for his service and wound.

*Perry at the Battle of Lake Erie.*

By the War of 1812, at least one of every six members of the United States Navy was a Negro. In the war they fought on privateers as well as ships of the line. They won praise from both Captain Perry, who at first had doubted their ability, and Commodore Chauncey, who never had. When Perry objected to the Negro sailors that Chauncey sent him, the Commodore answered that they "are not surpassed by any seamen we have in the fleet and I have yet to learn that the color of the skin or the cut and trimming of the coat can affect a man's qualifications or usefulness. I have nearly fifty blacks on board of this ship, and many of them are among my best men." After his triumph at Lake Erie, Perry admitted that his black sailors were among the bravest men on his ship.

## The Battle of New Orleans

When Andrew Jackson heard that a large British force was moving toward New Orleans, he made a special appeal for help to the city's free Negroes. Four hundred volunteered to fight when Jackson promised them equality of treatment and pay. One battalion was made up of merchants, craftsmen, and laborers and the other of refugees from Santo Domingo. Even the slaves from nearby plantations volunteered to help build the American defenses.

At 7:00 A.M. on January 8, 1815, General Edward Pakenham led his British troops forward toward the American lines. Facing Pakenham's trained soldiers were the two Negro battalions, a group of New Orleans business and professional men called "Beale's Famous Rifles"—Mississippi riflemen who were unshaven, had long hair, and carried knives and tomahawks—Jean Lafitte's pirates rounded up from his hideout and from the New Orleans jail, regular army troops, Choctaw Indians in full war paint, and Kentucky draftees in ragged clothes and carrying old muskets. A sharp two-hour battle began in a heavy fog. Although outnumbered two to one, Jackson's "integrated" army killed and wounded more than 1,500 of Pakenham's men and lost only a handful of their own. Never again would a foreign army attempt to invade the United States.

Emperor Napoleon of France was so astounded by the American victory that he wrote for information about it. Andrew Jackson wrote an explanation of the battle which ended with this description of the death of Pakenham: "I have always believed he fell from the bullet of a free man of color, who was a famous rifle-shot. . . ."

*The death of General Pakenham at New Orleans. Andrew Jackson credited a Negro sharp-shooter with firing the fatal shot.*

When an Army paymaster held up pay for the Indians and Negroes, Jackson told him to pay all "without inquiring whether the troops are white, black, or tea." As usual Jackson's order was quickly obeyed.

All New Orleans turned out to honor Jackson and his troops after their glorious victory. Loud cheers greeted the free men of color and Jordan B. Noble, their young drummer boy. But for many years afterward the colored veterans were not permitted to march in the annual celebration. Slaveholders had become fearful of black heroes. In 1862, with New Orleans under the control of the Union Army, the drummer boy marched again—at the head of a victorious Union Army.

# *Crispus Attucks and the Boston Massacre of 1770*

[*When Crispus Attucks, leading a crowd of Boston patriots against British soldiers, was shot down, he became one of the first martyrs to American independence. This eyewitness description of the event, given at the trial of the British soldiers, is by a Negro slave named Andrew. It gives a believable picture of the witness himself and of the actions of Attucks, referred to as a "stout man" or "Mulatto."*]

### Andrew (Mr. Oliver Wendell's Negro)—sworn

On the evening of the 5th of March I was at home, I heard the bells ring, and went to the gate, and saw one of my acquaintances, and we run down to the end of the lane and saw another acquaintance coming up, holding his arm; I asked him what's the matter, he said the soldiers were fighting, had got cutlasses, and were killing everybody, and that one of them had struck him on the arm, and almost cut it off: He told me I had best not go down; I said a good club was better than a cutlass. . . . I went to the Town House, saw the Sentinels placed at the main guard standing by Mr. Bowe's corner; numbers of boys on the other side of the way were throwing snow balls at them; the Sentinels were enraged and swearing at the boys: the boys called them lobsters, bloody backs, and hallooed who buys lobsters. . . .

I turned about and saw the officer standing before the men, and one or two persons engaged in talk with him. A number were jumping on the backs of those that were talking with the officer, to get as near as they could. Upon this I went as close to the officer as I could; one of the persons who was talking with the officer turned about quick to the people, and said, Damn him, he is going to fire; upon that they gave a shout, and cried out, fire and be Damn'd, who cares for you, you dare not fire, and began to throw snow balls and other things which then flew very thick.

*Q.* Did they hit any of them?

*A.* Yes, I saw two or three of them hit, one struck a grenadier on the hat, and the people who were right before them had sticks; and as the soldiers were pushing with their guns back and forth, they struck their guns, and one hit a grenadier on the fingers. At this time, the people up at the Town House called again, come away, come away. . . . The people seemed to be leaving the soldiers, and to turn from them, when there came down a number from Jackson's Corner, huzzaing and crying, damn them, they dare not fire, we are not afraid of them; one of these people, a stout [heavy-set] man with a long cordwood stick, threw himself in, and made a blow at the officer; I saw the officer try to ward off the stroke, whether he struck him or not I do not know; the stout man then turned round, and struck the grenadier's gun at the captain's right hand, and immediately fell in with his club, and knocked his gun away, and struck him over the head, the blow came either on the soldier's cheek or hat. This stout man held the bayonet with his left hand, and twitched it and cried kill the dogs, knock them over; this was the general cry; the people then crowded in, and upon that the grenadier gave a twitch back and relieved his gun, and he up with it and began to pay away on the people. I was then betwixt the officer and this grenadier, I turned to go off, when I heard the word fire; at the word fire I thought I heard the report of a gun, and upon my hearing the report, I saw the same grenadier swing his gun, and immediately he discharged it.

Q. Do you know who this stout man was, that fell in and struck the grenadier?

A. I thought and still think, it was the Mulatto who was shot.

Q. Do you know the grenadier who was thus assaulted and fired?

A. I then thought it was Killroy, and I told Mr. Quincy so the next morning after the affair happened, I now think it was he from my best observation but I can't positively swear it.

Q. Did the soldiers of that party, or any of them, step or move out of the rank in which they stood to push the people?

A. No, and if they had they might have killed me and many others with their bayonets.

Q. Did you, as you passed through the people towards Royal-Exchange lane and the party, see a number of people take up any and every thing they could find in the street, and throw them at the soldiers?

A. Yes, I saw ten or fifteen round me do it.

Q. Did you yourself pick up everything you could find and throw at them?

*A.* Yes, I did.

*Q.* After the gun fired, where did you go?

*A.* I run as fast as I could into the first door I saw open, which I think was Mr. Dehon's, I was very much frightened.

---

*The Trial of the British Soldiers of the 29th Regiment of Foot for the Murder of Crispus Attucks, Samuel Gray, Samuel Maverick, James Caldwell, and Patrick Carr on Monday Evening, March 5, 1770* (Boston, 1824), pp. 71-73.

## Congressman Eustis Describes Negro Soldiers

[*Congressman William Eustis who served throughout the Revolution as an army surgeon tells of Northern Negro's role in the War for Independence. Eustis, who later became Governor of Massachusetts, indicates why many in the North favored ending slavery.*]

At the commencement of the Revolutionary War, there were found in the Middle and Northern States, many blacks, and other people of color, capable of bearing arms; a part of them free, the greater part slaves. The freemen entered our ranks with the whites. The time of those who were slaves was purchased by the States; and they were induced to enter the service in consequence of a law, by which, on condition of their serving in the ranks during the war, they were made freemen. In Rhode Island, where their numbers were more considerable, they were formed, under the same considerations, into a regiment commanded by white officers; and it is required, in justice to them, to add, that they discharged their duty with zeal and fidelity. The gallant defence of Red Bank, in which this black regiment bore a part, is among the proofs of their valor.

Among the traits which distinguished this regiment was their devotion to their officers: when their brave Col. Greene was afterwards cut down and mortally wounded, the sabres of the enemy reached his body only through the limbs of his faithful guard of blacks, who hovered over him and protected him, every one of whom was killed, and whom he was not ashamed to call his children. . . .

The war over, and peace restored, these men returned to their respective states; and who could have said to them, on their return to civil life, after having shed their blood in common with the whites in the defense of the liberties of the country: "You are not to participate in the rights secured by the struggle, or in the liberty for which you have been fighting"? Certainly no white man in Massachusetts.

George Livermore, *An Historical Research Respecting the Opinions of the Founders of the Republic on Negroes as Slaves, as Citizens and as Soldiers*, Annals of Congress, Sixteenth Congress, Second Session (Boston, 1862), p. 154.

## Salem Poor at Bunker Hill

[*This was the citation for Bunker Hill soldier Salem Poor, signed by Colonel William Prescott and thirteen other officers.*]

The subscribers beg leave to report to your Honorable House (which we do in justice to the character of so brave a man), that under our own observation, we declare that a Negro man named Salem Poor, of Col. Frye's regiment, Capt. Ame's company, in the late battle at Charleston, behaved like an experienced officer, as well as an excellent soldier. To set forth particulars of his conduct would be tedious. We only beg leave to say, in the person of this said Negro, centers a brave and gallant soldier. The reward due to so great and distinguished a character, we submit to Congress.

Joseph T. Wilson, *The Black Phalanx* (Hartford, 1890), p. 37.

## Negroes of Philadelphia Stage a "Kneel In," and Start Their Own Church

[*The Right Reverend Richard Allen tells of the incidents leading up to the establishment of the African Methodist Episcopal Church of Philadelphia. The date was a Sunday in November, 1787—only a month after the Constitutional Convention ended.*]

A number of us usually attended St. George's Church in Fourth street; and when the colored people began to get numerous in attending the church, they moved us from the seats we usually sat on, and placed us around the wall, and on Sabbath morning we went to church and the sexton stood at the door, and told us to go in the gallery. He told us to go, and we would see where to sit. We expected to take the seats over the ones we formerly occupied below, not knowing any better. We took those seats. Meeting had begun, and they were nearly done singing, and just as we got to the seats, the elder said, "Let us pray." We had not been long upon our knees before I heard considerable scuffling and low talking. I raised my head up and saw one of the trustees, H———M———, having hold of the Rev. Absalom Jones, pulling him up off of his knees, and saying, "You must get up—you must not kneel here." Mr. Jones replied, "Wait until prayer is over." Mr. H———M——— said. "No, you must get up now, or I will call for aid and force you away." Mr. Jones said, "Wait until prayer is over, and I will get up and trouble you no more." With that he [Mr. H———M———] beckoned to one of the other trustees, Mr. L———S———to come to his assistance. He came, and went to William White to pull him up. By this time prayer was over, and we all went out of the church in a body, and they were no more plagued with us in the church.

Richard Allen, *The Life, Experience and Gospel Labors of the Rt. Rev. Richard Allen, Written by Himself* (Philadelphia, 1887), pp. 14-15.

## Halting the Yellow Fever Epidemic in Philadelphia

[*In 1793 Philadelphia was swept by a yellow fever epidemic that drove President Washington and other government officials from the city. Negro leaders Absalom Jones and Richard Allen offered the aid of the city's Negro community. This is their account of the epidemic.*]

In order the better to regulate our conduct, we called on the mayor next day, to consult with him how to proceed, so as to be most useful. The first object he recommended was a strict attention to the sick, and the procuring of nurses. This was attended to by Absalom Jones and William Gray. . . . Soon after, the mortality increasing, the difficulty of getting a corpse taken away, was such, that few were willing to do it, [even] when offered great rewards. The black people were looked to. We then offered our services in the public papers, by advertising that we would remove the dead and procure nurses. Our services were the production of real sensibility;—we sought not fee nor reward. . . . It was very uncommon, at this time, to find any one that would go near, much more, handle, a sick or dead person.

. . . Here it ought to be remarked . . . that two thirds of the persons who rendered these essential services, were people of colour. . . . May the Lord reward them, both temporally and spiritually.

When the sickness became general, and several of the physicians died, and most of the survivors were exhausted by sickness or fatigue; that good man, Doctor Rush, called us more immediately to attend upon the sick . . . and accordingly directed us where to procure medicine duly prepared, with proper directions how to administer them, and at what stages of the disorder to bleed. . . . This has been no small satisfaction to us; for, we think, that when a physician was not attainable, we have been the instruments in the hand of God, for saving the lives of some hundreds of our suffering fellow mortals.

A.J. and R.A. [Absalom Jones and Richard Allen], *A Narrative of the Proceedings of the Black People During the Late Awful Calamity in Philadelphia, in the Year 1793* (Philadelphia: William W. Woodward, 1794), pp. 4-5.

[*Dr. Benjamin Rush, America's most noted medical man of the time, describes his work with the Negroes during the epidemic.*]

Dear Sir. . . . The only information which I am capable of giving you relates to the conduct of the Africans of our city. In procuring nurses for the sick, Wm. Grey and Absalom Jones were indefatigable, often sacrificing for that purpose whole nights of sleep without the least compensation. Richard Allen was extremely useful in performing the mournful duties, which were connected with burying the dead. Many of the black nurses, it is true, were ignorant, and some of them were negligent, but many of them did their duty to the sick with a degree of patience and tenderness that did them great credit.

During the indisposition and confinement of the greatest part of the Physicians of the City, Richard Allen and Absalom Jones procured copies of the printed directions for curing the fever—went among the poor who were sick—gave them the mercurial purges—bled them freely, and by these means, they this day informed me, they had recovered between two and three hundred people.

I am the more pleased with the above communication as it sheweth the safety and simplicity of the mode of treating the disease, which they politely said was generally successful. . . .

*Magazine of American History*, Vol. 27 (January, 1891), p. 68.

# *The Amazing Benjamin Banneker*

[*Benjamin Banneker, a Maryland free Negro, was a respected mathematician and scientist whose work came to the attention of Thomas Jefferson and, through Jefferson, to the Marquis de Condorcet of the French Academy of Science. In 1790, Banneker was chosen to serve on the commission of three that planned the federal city at Washington, D.C. Banneker and Major Ellicott decided where the Capitol, the White House, the United States Treasury, and the other public buildings ought to be located. Mrs. Martha Ellicott Tyson, a friend of Banneker's, gives further details of the commission's work.*]

After the adoption of the Constitution of the United States, the States of Maryland and Virginia ceded a portion of their territory to constitute a seat for the metropolis of the country. . . . The survey [of the area] subsequently, in the year 1790, devolved upon Major Andrew Ellicott, of Ellicott's Upper Mills.

Major Ellicott selected Benjamin Banneker as his assistant upon this occasion, and it was with his aid that the lines of the Federal Territory, as the District of Columbia was then called, were run.

It was the work, also, of Major Ellicott, under the orders of General Washington, then President of the United States, to locate the sites of the Capitol, [the] President's house, [the] Treasury, and other public buildings. In this, also, Banneker was his assistant.

---

"Banneker, the Afric-American Astronomer," in *The Posthumous Papers of Martha E. Tyson*, edited by her daughter (Philadelphia, 1884), pp. 36-37.

[*In 1791 Banneker sent a handwritten copy of an almanac he was about to publish to Thomas Jefferson, then Secretary of State. Here is Jefferson's letter in reply.*]

Philadelphia. Aug. 30, 1791

Sir,—I thank you sincerely for your letter of the 19th instant and for the Almanac it contained. No body wishes more than I do to see such proofs as you exhibit, that nature has given to our black brethren, talents equal to those of the other colors of men, and that the appearance of a want of them is owing merely to the degraded condition of their existence, both in Africa & America. I can add with truth, that no body wishes more ardently to see a good system commenced for raising the condition both of their body & mind to what it ought to be, as fast as the imbecility of their present existence, and other circumstances which cannot be neglected, will admit. I have taken the liberty of sending your Almanac to Monsieur de Condorcet, Secretary of the Academy of Sciences at Paris, and member of the Philanthropic society, because I considered it as a document to which your whole colour had a right for their justification against the doubts which have been entertained of them. I am with great esteem, Sir Your most obed$^t$ humble serv$^t$.

[*On that same day, Jefferson sent Banneker's almanac to the head of France's Academy of Science with the letter that follows.*]

Philadelphia. Aug. 30, 1791

To the Marquis de Condorcet

Dear Sir, . . . I am happy to be able to inform you that we have now in the United States a Negro, the son of a black man born in Africa, and of a black woman born in the United States, who is a very respectable mathematician. I procured him to be employed under one of our chief directors in laying out the new federal city on the Potowmac, & in the intervals of his leisure, while on that work, he made an Almanac for the next year, which he sent me in his own hand writing, & which I inclose to you. I have seen very elegant solutions of Geometrical problems by him. Add to this that he is a very worthy & respectable member of society. He is a free man. I shall be delighted to see these instances of moral eminence so multiplied as to prove that the want of talents observed in them is merely the effect of their degraded condition, and not proceeding from any difference in the structure of the parts on which intellect depends. . . .

Present my affectionate respects to Madame de Condorcet, and accept yourself assurances of the sentiments of esteem & attachment which I have the honour to be Dear Sir your most obed$^t$ & most humble serv$^t$.

---

Paul Leicester Ford, *The Writings of Thomas Jefferson*, Vol. 5 (New York and London, G. P. Putnam's Sons, 1895), pp. 377-378 and pp. 378-379.

# *Andrew Jackson Appeals to the Free Colored Population of New Orleans*

[*As British forces approached New Orleans in the last days of the War of 1812, Andrew Jackson issued this appeal for help on September 21, 1814.*]

## PROCLAMATION
### *To the free colored inhabitants of Louisiana.*

Through a mistaken policy you have heretofore been deprived of a participation in the glorious struggle for national rights in which our country is engaged. This no longer shall exist.

As sons of freedom, you are now called upon to defend our most inestimable blessing. As Americans, your country looks with confidence to her adopted children, for a valorous support, as a faithful return for the advantages enjoyed under her mild and equitable government. As fathers, husbands, and brothers, you are summoned to rally round the standard of the Eagle, to defend all which is dear in existence.

Your country, although calling for your exertions, does not wish you to engage in her cause, without amply remunerating you for the services rendered. Your intelligent minds are not to be led away by false representations.—Your love of honor would cause you to despise the man who should attempt to deceive you. In the sincerity of a soldier, and the language of truth I address you.

To every noble hearted, generous, freeman of color, volunteering to serve during the present contest with Great Britain, and no longer, there will be paid the same bounty in money and lands, now received by the white soldiers of the U. States, viz. one hundred and twenty-four dollars in money, and one hundred and sixty acres of land. The non-commissioned officers and privates will also be entitled to the same monthly pay and daily rations, and clothes furnished to any American soldier.

On enrolling yourselves in companies, the major-general commanding will select officers for your government, from your white fellow citizens. Your non-commissioned officers will be appointed from among yourselves.

Due regard will be paid to the feelings of freemen and soldiers. You will not, by being associated with white men in the same corps, be exposed to improper comparisons or unjust sarcasm. As a distinct, independent battalion or regiment, pursuing the path of glory, you will, undivided, receive the applause and gratitude of your countrymen.

To assure you of the sincerity of my intentions and my anxiety to engage your invaluable services to our country, I have communicated my wishes to the governor of Louisiana, who is fully informed as to the manner of enrolment, and will give you every necessary information on the subject of this address.

> *Head quarters*, 7th military district,
>
> Mobile, Sept. 21st 1814
>
> *Andrew Jackson*,
>
> Maj.gen, commanding

---

*Niles' Weekly Register*, Vol. 7, December 3, 1814, p. 205.

[*As the British prepared for their final attack on New Orleans, General Jackson reviewed the 6,000 troops under his command. Of this force, about 500 were Negroes in two battalions. After the review by Jackson these battalions and their commanders, Majors Lacoste and Savory, were read the address by Jackson that follows:*]

### TO THE MEN OF COLOR

Soldiers— . . . you surpass my hopes. I have found in you, united to those qualities, that noble enthusiasm which impels to great deeds.

Soldiers—The President of the United States shall be informed of your conduct on the present occasion, and the voice of the representatives of the American nation shall applaud your valor, as your general now praises your ardor. The enemy is near; his "sails cover the lakes;" but the brave are united; and if he finds us contending among ourselves, it will be for the prize of valor and fame its noblest reward.

> By command, *Thomas L. Butler*, Aid-de-camp.

---

*Niles' Weekly Register*, Vol. 7, January 28, 1815, p. 346.

# General Andrew Jackson Describes the Battle of New Orleans

[*In a letter written to Napoleon Bonaparte, Jackson gave this firsthand description of his famous victory at New Orleans.*]

The battle commenced at a very little before 7 A.M., January 8, 1815, and as far as the infantry was concerned it was over by 9 A.M. My force was very much mixed. I had portions of the Seventh and Forty-fourth regular infantry regiments, Kentucky and Tennessee riflemen, creoles, United States marines and sailors, Baratarian men [Lafitte's Pirates] . . . and two battalions of free Negroes. . . . The British strength was almost the same as mine, but vastly superior in drill and discipline. Of their force my riflemen killed and wounded 2117 in less than an hour, including two general officers (both died on the field, each a division commander), seven full colonels, with seventy-five line and staff officers. I lost 6 killed and 7 wounded. . . .

There was a very heavy fog on the river that morning, and the British had formed and were moving before I knew it. . . .

. . . "God help us!" I muttered, watching the rapidly advancing line. Seventy, sixty, fifty, finally forty yards, were they from the silent kneeling riflemen. All of my men I could see was their long rifles rested on the logs before them. . . . not a shot was fired until the redcoats were within forty yards. I heard Coffee's voice as he roared out: "Now, men, aim for the center of the crossbelts: Fire!" . . . in a few seconds after the first fire there came another sharp, ringing volley. . . . The British were falling back in a confused, disorderly mass, and the entire first ranks of their column were blown away. For two hundred yards in our front the ground was covered with a mass of writhing wounded, dead, and dying redcoats. By the time the rifles were wiped the British line was reformed, and on it came again. This time they were led by General Pakenham in person, gallantly mounted, and riding as though he was on parade. . . . I heard a single rifle-shot from a group of country carts we had been using, about one hundred and seventy-five yards distant, and a moment thereafter I saw Pakenham reel and pitch out of his saddle. I have always believed he fell from the bullet of a free man of color, who was a famous rifle-shot, and came from the Atakappas region of Louisiana [probably Major Savory of the Santo Domingo battalion]. . . .

They sent a flag to me, asking leave to gather up their wounded and bury their dead, which, of course, I granted. I was told by a wounded officer that the rank and file absolutely refused to make a third charge. "We have no chance with such shooting as these Americans do," they said.

William Hugh Robarts, "Napoleon's Interest in the Battle of New Orleans," *Century Magazine*, Vol. 53 (January, 1897), pp. 360-361.

## Serving at Sea in the War of 1812

[*Commander Nathaniel Shaler of the United States privateer* Gov. Tompkins *wrote this letter on January 1, 1813, describing a sea battle and the heroism of his mixed crew.*]

. . . At sunrise, three ships were discovered ahead. We made all sail in chase. The wind being light, we came slowly up with them. On a nearer approach, they proved to be two ships and a brig.—One of the ships had all the appearance of a large transport. . . . At 3 P.M. . . . before I could get our light sails in, and almost before I could turn round, I was under the guns, (not of a transport) but of a large *frigate!*—and not more than a quarter of a mile from her.

I immediately . . . commenced a brisk fire from our little battery; but this was returned with woful interest. Her first broadside killed two men and wounded six others. . . .

The name of one of my poor fellows who was killed ought to be registered in the book of fame, and remembered with reverence as long as bravery is considered a virtue; he was a black man by the name of *John Johnson;* a 24 lb. shot struck him in the hip and took away all the lower part of his body; in this state the poor brave fellow lay on the deck, and several times exclaimed to his shipmates, "*Fire away my boy, no haul a color down.*" The other was also a black man, by the name of *John Davis*, and was struck in much the same way: he fell near me, and several times requested to be thrown overboard, saying, he was only in the way of others.

While America has such tars, she has little to fear from the tyrants of the ocean.

*Niles' Weekly Register*, Vol. 5, February 26, 1814, p. 430.

# 4

# *Frontiersmen Conquer the Wilderness, 1800-1860*

PIONEER explorers, trappers, missionaries, and settlers opened the vast American continent from the Atlantic to the Pacific coasts in the years before the Civil War. Despite Indian attacks, hunger, epidemics, storms, droughts, stampedes, wild animals, freezing cold, and blazing heat, they established a civilization in the wilderness. This strong breed of men and women was made up of all sorts of Americans. Negroes, as slave laborers or free men and women, moved with each wave.

## *Slave Frontiersmen*

Most Negroes who went West followed the wagons of their masters, sometimes in chains. They prodded cattle onward, searched for water, or hunted for game. Later they cleared the land and built the cabins. Slaves raised crops in Mississippi, dug gold in California, roped and branded cattle in Texas. Some ran off at the first opportunity, sensing that man was meant to be free in this beautiful new country.

Others stood by their masters, even during Indian raids. Jim Bowie, inventor of the famous throwing knife, and his slave were in a party that fought off a Comanche attack near San Antonio in 1831. During the long battle, shielded by the fire of white men, the big slave darted to a spring and brought water back to the thirsty men. Another slave, Bob Anderson, and his master were surprised by Indians while working near their cabin. Both men were saved by the women of the family who came to their rescue with blazing shotguns. A teenage slave named Smith was attacked by three Indians as he worked in his master's corn field. With a butcher knife in one hand and a pistol in the other, he fought back, killing one, wounding another, and sending the third screaming to the woods.

Bold and decisive action brought liberty to some frontier slaves. For example, a slave named Tom won his freedom in Texas for his courageous defense of his master. The two men were ambushed by Apaches while prospecting. When the master was badly wounded, Tom had to drive off the Indians alone. Afterward, he carried his master thirty miles to a doctor.

The Lewis and Clark Expedition into the Louisiana territory benefited from the strong muscles and fine mind of York, Clark's Negro slave. Well over six feet in height and 200 pounds in weight, York was an excellent swimmer, fisherman, and hunter. Along with Sacajawea, the Indian guide, he proved to be of great help in making friends with the Indians. Lewis reported that tribesmen came from all over to see this black giant with short curly hair. An agile man despite his size, York delighted the Indians with the wild leaps and bounds which he called dancing. The tribes, wrote Lewis, "seemed as anxious to see this monster as they were the merchandize which we had to barter for their horses." Although York "spoke bad French and worse English," according to another member of the expedition, he and Sacajawea acted as interpreters for the party. Clark freed York at the end of the two-and-one-half-year trip.

## Red Men Meet Black Men

York's unusual success with the Indians was matched by many other Negro slaves. The Indians were quick to note that the black slaves and the red men had a common enemy—the white man. Negroes and Indians often realized they could be allies, and Negroes were admitted to many tribes.

The acceptance of slaves by Indian villages was obvious and annoying to many whites on the frontier. A United States Army survey of the Choctaw Indians in 1831 showed that the tribe included 512 Negroes. Edmonia Lewis, the first important Negro sculptress, was born into this tribe. The Pamunky Indians of Virginia included so many Negroes that whites petitioned the government to take their land away, claiming they were no longer Indians at all, but Negroes. The Shawnees and the Cherokees used their villages as stations for runaway slaves on the famous underground railroad that led to Canada.

In many instances Negroes rose to leadership in various tribes. James Beckwourth became chief of the Crow nation and an ex-slave named Garcia manned a British fort full of Indians and Negroes in Florida in 1816. During an Indian raid in Texas in 1839 the settlers were surprised to find that the leader was "a big French Negro, weighing about two hundred pounds." "This Negro," reported a settler, "claimed to have always been free, but would not acknowledge any allegiance to the Texas government." He was promptly shot.

In some instances Indian tribes kept captured Negroes (and whites) as slaves, but it seems to have been a very different form of slavery from that which Negroes faced in the South. A European visitor to Oklahoma in 1853 told how Indians had learned to keep slaves by observing whites. "But these slaves receive from their Indian masters more Christian treatment than among the Christian whites." He noted that Negroes were treated like other members of the tribe "and [that] the Negro is regarded as a companion and helper, to whom thanks and kindness are due when he exerts himself for the welfare of the household."

*James Beckwourth, frontiersman and Indian fighter. The picture is from his 1856 story of his life and adventures.*

## Free Negroes as Trappers and Missionaries

The men who blazed the earliest trails across this huge land were trappers seeking fur and pelts from the Indians. "The old fur traders," Colonel James Stevenson, an old trapper, recalled, "always got a Negro, if possible, to negotiate for them with the Indians, because of their 'pacifying effect.' They could manage [the Indians] better than the white men, and with less friction."

Many of these early black trappers married into Indian tribes. Pierre Bonza, one of this hearty breed, married a Chippewa and lived in her village. Their son George followed in his father's footsteps and became a wealthy man working for the American Fur Company and later serving as an interpreter for Governor Lewis Cass of the Michigan territory. George Bonza laughingly told his friends he was one of "the first two white men that came into this country."

*Photograph of James Beckwourth. The man who helped him write his life story said: "Probably no man ever lived who has met with more personal adventure involving danger to life." Made Chief of the Crow Indians, Beckwourth was called "Morning Star."*

The most important Negro frontiersman of this period was James Beckwourth, a handy man with a Bowie knife, gun, or hatchet. He headed west from St. Louis when he was 19, leaving a life of slavery. He quickly picked up the skills necessary for survival on the frontier. Beckwourth was a pugnacious, short-tempered fellow and a reporter who knew him in 1860 called him "the most famous Indian fighter of this generation."

Beckwourth lived a life full of daring adventures and unusual opportunities. When an old Indian woman claimed Beckwourth was her long lost son, he was taken into the Crow tribe and named "Morning Star." He soon became their Chief and led them into many battles shouting, "I will show you how to fight." Often, he reported, "my battle-axe was red with the blood of the enemy." His reputation prompted General Stephen Kearny to ask for Beckwourth's assistance in California's war for independence: "You like war, and I have good use for you now."

But Beckwourth's claim to a place in history does not rest upon his exploits as a patriot, an Indian fighter, or an Indian chief. In April, 1850, James Beckwourth discovered a pass through the Sierra Nevadas that became an important gateway to California during the Gold Rush. The pass still bears his name. By 1852 Beckwourth established a hotel and trading post in Beckwourth Valley, but he was not destined to live out his life as a peaceful innkeeper.

The Crows, according to one legend, invited Beckwourth to a tribal feast, intent on convincing him to lead them again. When Beckwourth turned them down, he was poisoned. According to this version of his death, if the Crows could not have him as a live chief, they intended to keep Beckwourth in the tribal burial ground.

At the same time Beckwourth started west, determined to master the ways of the frontier, two gentle Negro missionaries came west to preach the Christian gospel to the Indians. John Marrant of New York instructed Cherokees, Creeks, and other tribes in the word of God. John Stewart, a Virginia Baptist minister, brought his message of faith and salvation to the Wyandot tribe: "Pray to the Lord both day and night with a sincere heart and He will uphold you in all your trials and troubles." Marrant managed to convert the Cherokee chief and his daughter and Stewart was so successful that his church sent some additional ministers to assist in his important work.

Following the trappers and missionaries west were the settlers. In 1833 a party of 385 men, women, and children left a life of slavery in Virginia's Roanoke River Valley for a life of freedom on their own land in Ohio. They had been set free by the terms of Senator John Randolph's will and this kind master had also provided them with parcels of land to divide in Mercer County. After a long trip by wagon and boat, the slaves were stunned to find that they had been cheated out of their land by their master's relatives. In their search for jobs and homes some pushed on into Indiana and some migrated to other parts of Ohio. Some met white citizens who offered them the help needed to begin their new life.

## The United States Acquires Florida

Hundreds of Negroes crossed the American border into Spanish Florida to escape slavery. The swamps and forests became their home. The men built houses for their families and raised crops in this hidden and fertile land. For fifty miles along the banks of the Appalachicola River, their corn fields supplied them with food and their horses and cattle grazed in the clearings.

Many of these fugitives joined the Seminoles, a tribe that had left the Creek Indians (Seminole means *runaway*). America's first foreign treaty (1790) demanded that the Creeks "deliver" those Negroes who lived among them. But the Indians continued to protect their new black friends in defiance of all authority. Generation after generation of Negroes lived in this quiet valley.

*Runaway slave in Florida.*

*Creek Indians hired by the United States took part in the invasion of Florida in 1816. After the destruction of Fort Negro, they marched the survivors back to Georgia.*

By the time the War of 1812 ended, the furious slaveholders demanded that force be used to eliminate Florida as "a perpetual harbor for our slaves," as General Andrew Jackson called it. Jackson dispatched two gunboats, an army regiment, and 500 Creeks to subdue the Seminoles and their Negro allies. The immediate objective of this expedition was a powerful wooden fort abandoned by the British and left to the Negro leader, Garcia. As the gunboats approached it, the sailors noted that it still flew the British flag. After a few shots to determine the distance, one of the gunboats hit the fort's powder magazine with a heated cannonball. "The explosion was awful and the scene horrible beyond description," wrote an American officer. Most of the fort's 300 men, women, and children were killed and only three were uninjured. Those who survived the explosion were either put to death or sold into slavery.

This daring invasion of Spanish soil was a powerful argument in convincing Spain to sell Florida before Jackson merely took it. But the sale of Florida in 1819 did not end the problem of Negro runaways and their Indian friends. Three Seminole Wars were necessary to break the spirit of resistance and move the Seminoles to Oklahoma. Throughout the conflict the ex-slaves were the most determined fighters. John T. Sprague, an American soldier in the third Seminole War, noted: "The Negroes exercised a wonderful control [over the Seminoles]. . . . It was not until the Negroes capitulated that the Seminoles ever thought of emigrating."

This last Seminole War lasted eight years (1835–1842) and cost the United States 1,500 men and $20,000,000: it was the most expensive Indian war waged by this country. It began, according to one story, with a fight between Chief Osceola and an American officer at the United States port of Fort King. When slave catchers seized Osceola's Negro wife, Morning Dew, the Chief battled furiously, striking an officer who came to restrain him. In jail, Osceola vowed revenge. His black and red tribesmen took to the warpath, effectively using hit and run tactics. After the war had been under way for a year, General Thomas Jesup of the American forces stated: "This, you may be assured, is a Negro, not an Indian war."

It is interesting to note that Negroes served on both sides during the eight-year conflict. Gopher John was one of several Negroes used as scouts and interpreters by the American forces. Louis Pacheco, a slave hired by the Americans, took on the role of a counterspy. He notified the Seminoles of the path he would use for the United States troops and then led them into an ambush. After this famous "Dade massacre," Pacheco lived on with his Seminole and Negro friends. While some of the tribes moved to the West, others stayed on and never surrendered to American authority.

*Negro Abraham (center) served as an interpreter for the Seminole Indians in their 1825 negotiations with the United States in Washington, D. C. One Army officer described him as having "the crouch and spring of a panther." He admitted bitterly that Abraham had "ruled all the councils and actions of the Indians in this region." In 1838 Abraham tried to convince the tribes to accept the United States demand that they move to Oklahoma: "We do not live for ourselves only, but for our wives and children, who are as dear to us as those of any other men." But it was the overwhelming United States force that finally convinced most of the Seminoles and their Negro allies to accept the new location.*

## Defenders of the Lone Star Republic

*In Texas slave cowboys broke in horses.*

When the Mexican government offered Americans Texas land, slaveholders and their human property followed Stephen Austin into the Texas plains. Many of these slaves served as cowhands and drove cattle up the trails to Kansas.

One was Bose Ikard. Charles Goodnight, founder of the Goodnight-Loving trail from Texas to Montana, brought Ikard to Texas when he was five. Goodnight remembered him as one of his strongest cowboys, one who "surpassed any man I had in endurance and stamina. There was a dignity, a cleanliness, and a reliability about him that was wonderful." Ikard, wrote his boss, "was very good in a fight and he was probably the most devoted man that I ever had. I have trusted him farther than any living man. He was my detective, banker, and everything in Colorado, New Mexico, and the other wild country I was in."

Other Negroes rode into Texas as free men, summoned by Stephen Austin's promise of cheap land and a chance to begin a new life. Greenbury Logan, who answered Austin's call in 1831, was one of those to receive both land and Texas citizenship. Logan later wrote that he "loved the country" and stayed because he felt himself more a free man "then in the States." He was among the first to volunteer in the war for Texan independence. He fought in many battles and his severe wounds left him disabled.

From the Alamo to the final battle at San Jacinto, Negroes took part in the fight for the Lone Star Republic. Some were slaves whose bravery on the battlefield won them their freedom. Others were free men such as Hendrick Arnold, who served as a scout for three American armies.

As soon as the war ended with the surrender of Santa Ana to Sam Houston, however, the Negro patriots were forgotten. As Texas became an important slaveholding region, the legislature tried to eliminate the state's free Negroes. Greenbury Logan, too disabled to work his farm, was denied tax exemption. He and other Negroes found their rights restricted and their presence no longer wanted in the land they had helped to defend.

Some free Negroes stayed on through the efforts of their white friends in the Texas legislature. One staying was Aaron Ashworth, who went to Texas in 1833. Seventeen years later he owned 2,570 head of cattle and a large ranch and employed a white tutor for his children. The Ashworth family continued to contribute to the development of Texas for many years. Another free Negro, Isham Hicks, stayed on to supervise the construction of the First Methodist Church in Comanche county. He later died in an Indian raid.

## Oregon

Among the early American explorers of the Oregon territory was a free Negro, George William Bush, who fought at the battle of New Orleans under Andrew Jackson. Bush and a group of white companions found their way from the Mexican border to the Columbia River Valley. When the group heard that any Negro who entered the Oregon territory would be whipped, they decided that if anyone attempted to molest Bush, all of the members of the company would fight to protect him. The law was never carried out.

In 1844 Bush, his wife, and five children led several white couples in the trip to the Columbia River. One of Bush's companions remembers him giving the men of the wagon-train this advice: "Boys, you are going through a hard country. You have guns and ammunition. Take my advice: Anything you see as big as a blackbird, kill it and eat it." Bush's group became the first American settlers north of the Columbia River. Although Negroes were denied the right to homesteads, Bush's friend, Colonel Michael Simmons, a member of the Oregon legislature, had Congress pass a special act granting Bush a 640-acre plot.

The Bush family became wealthy, but often divided their crops with other less fortunate white settlers. One of Bush's sons raised a prize wheat crop (a sample of which was placed in the Smithsonian Institution) and another was twice elected to the state legislature. Bush is remembered today as one of the leading pioneers of Oregon and Washington, and Bush Prairie is named after him.

## On to California

Jacob Dodson, like Bush, was a free Negro who jumped at the chance to explore the West. United States Army Colonel John C. Frémont, "the Pathfinder," and scout Kit Carson took Dodson with them on three expeditions into California and Oregon. At the time of

their first trip, Frémont described his young expert with the lariat and the horse as "only eighteen, but strong and active and nearly six feet in height." Dodson fought alongside Frémont and Carson in California's war for independence.

Very few pioneers of any race became as wealthy as Alexander Leidesdorff who sailed his 106-ton schooner, *Julia Ann*, to California from New Orleans in 1841. Leidesdorff soon owned a 35,000-acre California estate he called *Rancho Americano*. He introduced the first steamboat to California as well as the first horse race. He served as an American government consul and built San Francisco's first hotel, but died before California joined the Union.

The discovery of gold brought many slaveholders to California and they brought their bondsmen to take care of the necessary labor. Some slaves such as Alvin Coffey and Daniel Rogers won their freedom by their work in the gold fields. Daniel Rogers was cheated out of his liberty by his master but whites from his native Arkansas responded by raising money to purchase his freedom and presented him with a certificate that praised his "honesty, industry and integrity."

Thousands of free Negroes were among the "forty-niners" who flocked to California seeking instant wealth. There were a thousand of them by 1850, and two years later the number had doubled. One became manager of the Frisbie Hotel in Sonoma. Two others became Pony Express riders, carrying the mail in California: George Munroe, whose route was from Merced to Mariposa, and William Robinson, who rode from Stockton to the mines. In one county 86 out of 123 free Negroes were listed as miners and in another it was 52 out of 62 people. More than a few became rich, for by 1855 California's Negro population had amassed $2,375,000, so that it was America's wealthiest Negro community. Along with the increased wealth came a large number of churches, many of which operated schools.

Many Californians of all races were helped through the efforts of two Negro reformers, Biddy Mason and J. B. Sanderson. Mrs. Mason trudged to California behind the three hundred wagons of her Mississippi master. Her job was to make sure the livestock stayed with the caravan. In California Mrs. Mason and her three daughters were freed. They settled in Los Angeles when it was a small town with eight white families and one other Negro family. Through hard work, saving, and shrewd business sense, Mrs. Mason soon became a rich landowner. "Grandma Mason" was soon well known to the poor, to the imprisoned, and to those left destitute by floods. Her gen-

*California's gold rush of 1849. It drew both masters and their slaves and by 1852 more than 2,000 Negroes lived in California. For Negroes California had more to offer than mere gold. Freedom must have been in the air, for many slaves fought their masters rather than return to the South. Slave Archy Lee fought his master in the California courts. A San Francisco court finally liberated him.*

erosity seemed unbounded. She purchased land for churches, built schools for nurses, and did welfare work among children of the poor.

Sanderson devoted his talents to starting schools for those children who were not admitted to the public schools. From San Francisco to Sacramento, he founded schools for Orientals, Negroes, and Indians. He taught in most of them until a replacement could be found.

In California, as elsewhere in the United States, Negro settlers took action to secure their civil rights. A "Franchise League" was formed in the state to campaign for repeal of the law forbidding Negroes the right to testify in trials involving whites. At an 1856 Negro convention, one delegate asked: "When will the people of this state learn that justice to the colored man is justice to themselves?" Five hundred white San Franciscans signed the petitions of the Franchise League and so did whites in five other counties. Under the leadership of Mary E. Pleasant, a former Georgia slave, the campaign achieved success by 1863. The following year Mrs. Pleasant put the law to practical use, successfully suing a streetcar company for rude treatment.

## Democracy and Slavery in the West

The westward movement can be credited with spreading the American ideals of democracy, brotherhood, and equality. On the frontier, man was judged by his skills rather than by his ancestors. Women played a key role in frontier homes and, therefore, demanded a larger

*The wagons that traveled westward. But democracy did not always follow the settlers. The new territories either tried to prevent Negroes from entering or denied them equality, citizenship, and the right to vote if they did accept them. Section I of Indiana's 1850 Constitution read: "No Negro or mulatto shall come into or settle in the State after the adoption of this Constitution."*

voice in many decisions. Cooperation was necessary to fight off Indian attacks, as well as to build homes and bring in the crops.

But the democracy that flowered on the frontier was lily white. Because the free Negro was associated with his slave brother, he faced greater hardships than other settlers. In no land of the Western plains could a Negro vote. To enter Iowa in 1839 he had to present a $500 bond and proof that he was free. Few had such proof and even fewer had $500. By 1844 Iowans announced that they would "never consent to open the doors of our beautiful state" to people of color for equality would lead to "discord and violence."

When Illinois passed restrictions on its free Negroes, one of the colored men who turned away in disgust was named George Washington. In 1855 he pushed westward into Washington, where he became the first settler in what became the city of Centralia.

While white Westerners opposed the free Negro, they battled slavery with equal vigor. Abraham Lincoln said that the new land must be kept "for homes of free white people. This cannot be, to any considerable extent, if slavery shall be planted within them." Lincoln pointed out that slave labor reduces the dignity of all labor and drives out "poor white people." Westerners resented both the slaveholder who did no work, and his slaves who were forced to work.

Congressman David Wilmot, whose famous proviso would have banned slavery in the Southwest, argued for a white man's West: "I plead the cause and the rights of white freemen. I would preserve to white labor a fair country, a rich inheritance, where the sons of toil of my own race and own color, can live without the disgrace which association with Negro slavery brings upon free labor."

But the Southern masters desperately needed new land to expand their slave economy. "Whenever slavery is confined . . . its future is doomed," said a Southern Congressman. Slavery used farming methods which tended to ruin the most fertile soil. Mississippi entered the Union in 1818, and by 1856 a soil expert reported "a large part of the state is already exhausted; the state is full of old deserted fields."

The most successful Southern attempt to take new land in the West involved the United States in a war with Mexico. The war was denounced by many in the North as caused by the greed of slaveholders. Ulysses S. Grant, who served in the war, said: "I do not think there was ever a more wicked war than that waged by the United States on Mexico." Henry David Thoreau went to jail rather than pay his taxes during the war. Congressman Abraham Lincoln thought that President Polk had sent American troops into Mexican land to provoke war. According to the terms of the peace treaty signed in 1848, Mexico lost one half of her national territory.

The Southern drive for new land continued during the 1850's. In 1853 William Walker of Tennessee tried to capture lower California from Mexico but failed miserably. He had greater success a few years later when he took over Nicaragua and had himself elected president. He restored slavery and looked forward to "a formal alliance with the seceding States." By the time that eleven Southern states had left the Union, Walker had been captured and shot by a South American firing squad.

From the bitter arguments over Missouri in 1819 to the savage warfare that engulfed Kansas in the 1850's, the West was the earliest battleground of the war over slavery. Slowly but surely the West became allied with the free North. It would be no accident of history that the President who ended slavery was born in a Kentucky log cabin, or that the first black troops to bear arms in defense of the Union were fugitive slaves living on the Kansas plains. They rode into Missouri to free their brothers held in bondage.

# *James Beckwourth, Frontiersman*

[*James Beckwourth was a runaway slave who became a tough frontier scout and chief of the Crow Indians. Like Kit Carson and other early Western heroes, Beckwourth was at home in the woods, living with the Indians, or shooting it out on many a firing line. Dacotah Indian Paul Dorion describes Beckwourth's battle with a large party of Blackfoot Indians.*]

"You are all fools and old women," he [Beckwourth] said to the Crows; "come with me, if any of you are brave enough, and I will show you how to fight."

He threw off his trapper's frock of buckskin and stripped himself naked, like the Indians themselves. He left his rifle on the ground, took in his hand a small light hatchet, and ran over the prairie to the right, concealed by a hollow from the eyes of the Blackfeet. Then climbing up the rocks, he gained the top of the precipice behind them. Forty or fifty young Crow warriors followed him. By the cries and whoops that rose from below he knew that the Blackfeet were just beneath him; and running forward he leaped down the rock into the midst of them. As he fell he caught one by the long loose hair, and dragging him down tomahawked him; then grasping another by the belt at his waist, he struck him also a stunning blow, and, gaining his feet, shouted the Crow war-cry. He swung his hatchet so fiercely around him, that the astonished Blackfeet bore back and gave him room. He might, had he chosen, have leaped over the breastwork and escaped; but this was not necessary, for with devilish yells the Crow warriors came dropping in quick succession over the rock among their enemies. The main body of the Crows, too, answered the cry from the front, and rushed up simultaneously. The convulsive struggle within the breastwork was frightful; for an instant the Blackfeet fought and yelled like pent-up tigers; but the butchery was soon complete, and the mangled bodies lay piled together under the precipice. Not a Blackfoot made his escape.

Francis Parkman, *The Oregon Trail* (Boston, 1872), p. 125.

[*The following passage is Beckwourth's own description of the discovery of the pass over the Sierra Nevada Mountains that still bears his name.*]

We proceeded in an easterly direction, and all busied themselves in searching for gold; but my errand was of a different character; I had come to discover what I suspected to be a pass.

It was the latter end of April when we entered upon an extensive valley at the northwest extremity of the Sierra range. . . . Swarms of wild geese and ducks were swimming on the surface of the cool crystal stream, which was the central fork of the Rio de las Plumas, or sailed the air in clouds over our heads. Deer and antelope filled the plains, and their boldness was conclusive that the hunter's rifle was to them unknown. Nowhere visible were any traces of the white man's approach, and it is probable that our steps were the first that ever marked the spot. We struck across this beautiful valley to the waters of the Yuba, from thence to the waters of the Truchy. . . . This, I at once saw, would afford the best waggon-road into the American Valley approaching from the eastward, and I imparted my views to three of my companions in whose judgment I placed the most confidence. They thought highly of the discovery, and even proposed to associate with me in opening the road. We also found gold, but not in sufficient quantity to warrant our working it. . . .

On my return to the American Valley, I made known my discovery to a Mr. Turner, proprietor of the American Ranch, who entered enthusiastically into my views; it was a thing, he said, he had never dreamed of before. If I could but carry out my plan, and divert travel into that road, he thought I should be a made man for life. Thereupon he drew up a subscription-list, setting forth the merits of the project, and showing how the road could be made practicable to Bidwell's Bar, and thence to Marysville. . . . He headed the subscription with two hundred dollars.

When I reached Bidwell's Bar and unfolded my project, the town was seized with a perfect mania for the opening of the route. The subscriptions toward the fund required for its accomplishment amounted to five hundred dollars. . . . While thus busily engaged I was seized with erysipelas, and abandoned all hopes of recovery; I was over one hundred miles away from medical assistance, and my only shelter was a brush tent. I made my will, and resigned myself to death. Life still lingered in me, however, and a train of waggons came up, and encamped near to where I lay. I was reduced to a very low condition, but I saw the drivers, and acquainted them with the object which had brought me out there. They offered to attempt the new road if I thought myself sufficiently strong to guide them through it. The women, God bless them! came to my assistance, and through their kind attentions and excellent nursing I rapidly recovered from my lingering sickness, until I was soon able to mount my horse, and lead the first train, consisting of seventeen waggons, through "Beckwourth's Pass." . . .

In the spring of 1852 I established myself in Beckwourth Valley, and finally found myself transformed into a hotel-keeper and chief of a trading-post. My house is considered the emigrant's landing-place, as it is the first ranch he arrives at in the golden state, and is the only house between this point and Salt Lake.

---

James Beckwourth, *The Life and Adventures of James Beckwourth, Mountaineer, Scout, Pioneer, and Chief of the Crow Nation of Indians*, written from his own dictation by T. D. Bonner (London, 1892), pp. 424-427.

## *The Destruction of Fort Negro, 1816*

[*Shortly after the end of the War of 1812 the United States government, prodded by angry slaveholders, began military operations against Spanish Florida. While the overall objective was the incorporation of this rich and fertile land into the United States, an immediate objective was the capture of hundreds of Negro slaves (and their families) who had taken refuge in Florida. Many had married into or joined the Seminoles and more than a few were leaders in the tribes. A fort manned by Negroes on the Appalachicola River was the first objective of the Federal forces.*]

[*Letter of General Andrew Jackson, of May 16th, 1816 to Gen. Gaines.*] I have little doubt of the fact, that this fort has been established by some villains for the purpose of rapine and plunder, and that it ought to be blown up, regardless of the ground on which it stands; and if your mind shall have formed the same conclusion, destroy it and return the stolen Negroes and property to their rightful owners.

---

Joshua R. Giddings, *The Exiles of Florida* (New York, 1863), p. 37.

[*Report of Colonel Clinch.*] At two o'clock on the morning of the 20th we landed within cannon shot of the Fort. . . . Finding it impossible to carry my plans into execution without . . . artillery, I ordered Major McIntosh to keep up an irregular fire.

. . . In the evening a deputation of chiefs went into the Fort and demanded its surrender, but they were abused and treated with the utmost contempt. The Black Chief [Garcia] heaped much abuse on the Americans, & said he had been left in command of the Fort by the British Government and that he would sink any American vessels that should attempt to pass it, and would blow up the Fort if he could not defend it. The chiefs also informed me that the Negroes had hoisted a red flag, and that the English Jack was flying over it. . . .

In the course of the evening after consulting with the commanding officer of the convoy I directed him to move up the two gun vessels at day light the next morning.

*Report of Col. Clinch of the destruction of Fort Negro, on the Appalachicola, July 29, 1816* (Washington: War Records Office, National Archives).

[*Report of Sailing-Master Loomis.*] At 4 A.M. on the morning of the 27th, we began warping the gun vessels to a proper position; at 5, getting within gun shot, the fort opened [fire] upon us which we returned; and after ascertaining our real distance with cold shot, we commenced with hot [heated cannon balls] . . . the *first* one of which entering their magazine, blew up, and completely destroyed the fort.

J. Loomis, *Letter of August 13, 1816*, in House Documents, Fifteenth Congress, Second Session, pp. 16-17.

[*Report of Colonel Clinch.*] The explosion was awful and the scene horrible beyond description. Our first care on arriving at the scene of destruction was to rescue and relieve the unfortunate beings that survived the explosion.

The war yells of the Indians, the cries and lamentations of the wounded, compel'd the soldier to pause in the midst of victory, and to drop a tear for the sufferings of his fellow beings, and to acknowledge that the great ruler of the Universe must have used us as an instrument in chastising the blood thirsty murderous wretches that defended the Fort. The Fort contained about one hundred effective men (including twenty five Choctaws) and about two hundred women and children not more than one sixth part of which number were saved. . . .

. . . The greater part of the Negroes belonged to the Spaniards and Indians. The American Negroes had principally settled in the river and a number of them had left their fields and gone over to the Seminoles on hearing of our approach. Their corn fields extended nearly fifty miles up the river and their numbers were daily increasing. The chief passed sentence of death on the outlawed Choctaw chief and the black commandant [Garcia] . . . and the sentence was immediately carried into execution.

Report of Col. Clinch, *op. cit.*

## Seminoles and Soldiers Argue the Negro Problem

[*Beginning in the early days of the Republic and continuing throughout the wars with the Seminole tribes, Indians and American army officers exchanged bitter notes and letters about the Indian's protection of runaway slaves or the attacks on Indian villages by slave catchers. Here is part of that war of words as revealed in American State Papers dating from 1818 to 1835.*]

[*General Gaines to the Seminole Chiefs.*] Your Seminoles are very bad people. . . . You have murdered many of my people, and stolen my cattle and many good horses, that cost me money; and many good houses that cost me money you have burnt for me; and now, that you see my writing, you'll think I have spoken right, I know it is so; you know it is so. . . . but just give me the murderers, and I will show them my law; and, when that is finished and past, if you will come about any of my people, you will see your friends; and if you see me, you will see your friend. . . .

I tell you this, that if you do not give me up the murderers who murdered my people, I say I have got good strong warriors, with scalping-knives and tomahawks. You harbor a great many of my black people among you at Sahwahnee. If you give me leave to go by you against them, I shall not hurt any thing belonging to you.*

[*King Hatchy Answers General Gaines.*] You charge me with killing your people, stealing your cattle and burning your houses; it is I that have cause to complain of the Americans. While one American has been justly killed, while in the act of stealing cattle, more than four Indians while hunting have been murdered by these lawless freebooters. I harbor no Negroes. When the Englishmen were at war with America, some [Negroes] took shelter among them; and it is for you white people to settle those things among yourselves, and not trouble us with what we know nothing about. I shall use force to stop any armed Americans from passing my towns or my lands.

*American State Papers*, Vol. I (Washington, 1832), p. 723.

[*Florida Governor William Duval to the Seminoles (1826).*] Chiefs and warriors: You hold Negroes in your nation that belong to the white people. By the treaty, you are bound to deliver all the Negroes that do not belong to the Indians to the [Indian] agent; this you have not done . . . you are now called upon to fulfill the treaty. You are not to mind what the Negroes say; they will lie, and lead you astray, in the hope to escape from their right owners, and that you will give them refuge and hide them; do your duty, and give them up. They care nothing for you, further than to make use of you to keep out of the hands of their masters.

Thus far the Negroes have made you their tools, and gained a protection, contrary to both justice and the treaty, and at the same time, laugh at you for being deceived by them. Your conduct in this matter is cause of loud, constant, and just complaint on the part of white people, who are thus deprived of their slaves. Deliver them up, rid your nation of a serious pest, and do what, as honest men, you should not hesitate to do; that your white brothers will say you have done them justice like honest, good men.

*American State Papers*, Indian Affairs, Vol. II (Washington, 1832), pp. 690-691.

[*Chief Emachutochustern, Seminole, to General Thompson, Indian Agent, 1835.*]

Dear Sir: I am induced to write you in consequence of the depredations making and attempting to be made on my farm by a company of men, Negro stealers, some of whom are from Columbus [Georgia]. . . . It is reported and believed by all the white people around here that a large number of them will very shortly come down here and attempt to take off Billy, Jim, Rose and her family, and others. These same men have been engaged in the same business up in the "Creek Nation." I should like to have your advice how I should act. I dislike to make any trouble, or to have any difficulty with any of the white people; but if they will trespass on my premises and on my rights, I must defend myself in the best way I can. . . . But is there no *civil law* that will protect me? Are the free Negroes and the Negroes belonging in this town to be stolen away publicly—in the face of all law and justice carried off and sold to fill the pockets of these worse than "land pirates?" Certainly not. I know you will not suffer it. Please direct me how to act in this matter. . . .

*John Walker*, his *X* mark, Chief Emachutochustern
*Jim Walker*, his *X* mark, Interpreter

*American State Papers*, Military Affairs, Vol. IV (Washington, 1861), p. 463.

## *Advice from a Negro Settler in Indiana*

[*During the 1820's and 1830's Negroes who had intermarried with Cherokees in North Carolina came to Indiana by covered wagon rather than face persecution. By 1832 enough had come to form the Roberts settlement in Hamilton County. This community later produced its share of lawyers, doctors, dentists, teachers, ministers, and Civil War soldiers. But in 1830, when settler Willis Roberts told his cousin "Long" James Roberts that he was thinking of returning to North Carolina, "Long" James wrote him this letter.*]

After leaving you on the 15th day of February, 1830, I feel it a duty for me to write a few lines to inform you of my mind on what you are going to do. . . .

It seems very plain to me that you are now going to make one of the worst mistakes that you ever made, in many ways. The first is that you are taking your children to an old country that is worn out and to slave on. . . .

. . . To think that you are going to take your small children to that place and can't tell how soon you may be taken away from them and they may come under the hands of some cruel slave holder, and you know that if they can get a colored child they will use them as bad again as they will one of their own slaves; it is right that parents should think of this, most especially if they are going to the very place and know it at the same time.

I would not this night, if I had children, take them to such a place and there to stay for the best five farms in three miles around where we came from, for I think I should be going to do something to bring them to see trouble and not enjoy themselves as free men but be in a place where they are not able to speak for their rights. . . .

I cannot do myself justice to think of living in such a country. When I think of it I can't tell how any man of color can think of going there with small children. It has been my intention ever since I had notice of such if I lived to be a man and God was willing I would leave such a place.

I wish you well and all your family and I hope that you all may do well, as much so as any people I ever saw or ever shall see, and I hope that you may see what you are going to do before it is too late. This is from the heart of one who wishes you well. . . .

[*Willis Roberts did visit North Carolina but returned to Indiana to live.*]

---

Letter from James Roberts to Willis Roberts, the Roberts Settlement Collection (Washington: Library of Congress, Manuscript Collection).

## *Greenbury Logan and the Lone Star Republic*

[*Greenbury Logan came to Texas at the invitation of Stephen Austin and fought in its war for independence. Because he was crippled from wounds received in the war, he wrote to a member of the Texas legislature asking for tax relief. His letter also mentions the burdens which a Texas Negro had to face in the state which he had helped to free from Mexico. The Texas legislature refused to pass a tax-relief bill for Logan.*]

I hope you will excuse me for taking the liberty of riting to you. I knew not of you being in the county until the night before you left for Austin. it was my wish to see you from the time you was elected but in consiquence of your absence I co[u]ld not. I presume it is unecessary to give you eny informasion abought my coming to Texas. I cam[e] here in 1831 invited by Col. Austin. it was not my intention to stay until I had saw Col. Austin who was then in Mexico. after se[e]ing him on his return and conversing with him relitive to my situation I got letters of sittizen ship. having no famoly with me I got one quarter League of land insted of a third. but I love the country and did stay because I felt myself mower a freeman then in the states. it is well known that Logan was the man that lifted his rifle in behalf of Texas as of fremans righted. it is also known that Logan was in everry fite with the Maxacans during the camppain of 35 until Bexhar was taken in which event I was the 3rd man that fell. my discharge will show the man[n]er in which I discharged my duty as a free man and a sol[d]ier but now look at my situation. every previleg dear to a freman is taken a way and logan liable to be imposed upon by eny that chose to doo it. no chance to collect a debt with out witness, no vote or say in eny way, yet liable for Taxes [as] eny other [person]. . . . I am on examination found perment injurd and can nom[o]re than support by myself now as everry thing that is deare to a freman is taken from me. the congress will not refuse to exempt my lands from tax or otherwise restoure what it has taken from me in the constitution. to leave I am two poor and imbarrased and cannot leav honerable as I came. I am tow old and cr[i]ppled to go on the world with my famaly recked. if my debts was payd I wo[u]ld be willing to leav the land though my blood has nearly all been shed for its rights—now my dear friend you are the first man I hav ever spoken to for eny assistance. I hombely hope you as a gentleman . . . will look into this errur and try if you cannot effect— something for my relief. I know I have friends in the house if a thing of the kind was brought up. . . . please euse your best exertions. . . . G. Logan

Harold Schoen, "The Free Negro in the Republic of Texas," Part IV, *Southwestern Historical Quarterly*, Vol. 41 (July, 1937), pp. 84-86. Reprinted with permission.

## George Bush Leads a Party to Oregon

[*Among the early settlers in the Oregon territory was a free Negro, George Bush, who had fought in Andrew Jackson's army at New Orleans. In Bush's party on the Oregon Trail were a group of white men, David Kindred, Gabriel Jones, and Colonel Michael T. Simmons. Later Simmons got a grant of six hundred and forty acres of farmland for his friend Bush. John Minton, a white pioneer who had met Bush in Missouri at the wagon train's starting point, met him again on the way west. The date was September 5, 1844.*]

I struck the road again in advance of my friends near Soda Springs. There was in sight, however, G. W. Bush, at whose camp table Rees and I had received the hospitalities of the Missouri rendezvous. Joining him, we went on to the Springs. Bush was a mulatto, but had means, and also a white woman for a wife, and a family of five children. Not many men of color left a slave state so well to do, and so generally respected; but it was not in the nature of things that he should be permitted to forget his color. As we went along together, he riding a mule and I on foot, he led the conversation to this subject. He told me he should watch, when we got to Oregon, what usuage was awarded to people of color, and if he could not have a free man's rights he would seek the protection of the Mexican Government in California or New Mexico. He said there were few in that train he would say as much to as he had just said to me. I told him I understood. This conversation enabled me afterwards to understand the chief reason for Col. M. T. Simmons and his kindred, and Bush and Jones determining to settle north of the Columbia [River]. It was understood that Bush was assisting at least two of these to get to Oregon, and while they were all Americans, they would take no part in ill treating G. W. Bush on account of his color.

[*As a matter of fact, when the party heard that any Negro trying to enter Oregon might be whipped, they decided that every one of them would fight to protect Bush.*]

No act of Colonel Simmons as a legislator in 1846 was more creditable to him than getting Mr. Bush exempt from the Oregon law, intended to deter mulattoes or Negroes from settling in Oregon—a law, however, happily never enforced.

---

John Minton, "Reminiscences of Experiences on the Oregon Trail in 1844," *The Quarterly of the Oregon Historical Society*, Vol. 2 (September, 1901), pp. 212-213.

## A Forty-Niner Makes a New Life in California

[*After Alvin Coffey and his master came to California during the Gold Rush, the master took away both the $5,000 which Coffey had earned for him in the mines and the $700 which the slave had earned for himself working nights. Then he sold the slave to a new master. Coffey convinced his new owner that he could earn enough in the mines to buy his freedom as well as the freedom of his wife and three children. The master agreed, and by 1860 Coffey's family were all with him, free and prosperous in Tehama County—and one of the noted pioneer families of California. Here is his own story of his first trip westward.*]

I started from St. Louis, Missouri, on the 2nd of April in 1849. There was quite a crowd of neighbors who drove through the mud and rain to St. Joe to see us off. About the first of May we organized the train. There were twenty wagons in number and from three to five men to each wagon.

We crossed the Missouri River at Savanna Landing on or about the 6th, no the 1st week in May. . . . At six in the morning, there were three more went to relieve those on guard. One of the three that came in had cholera so bad that he was in lots of misery. Dr. Bassett, the captain of the train, did all he could for him, but he died at 10 o'clock and we buried him. We got ready and started at 11 the same day and the moon was new just then.

We got news every day that people were dying by the hundreds in St. Joe and St. Louis. It was alarming. When we hitched up and got ready to move, [the] Dr. said, "Boys, we will have to drive day and night." . . . We drove night and day and got out of reach of the cholera. . . .

We got across the plains to Fort Larimie, the 16th of June and the ignorant driver broke down a good many oxen on the trains. There were a good many ahead of us, who had doubled up their trains and left tons upon tons of bacon and other provisions. . . .

Starting to cross the desert to Black Rock at 4 o'clock in the evening, we traveled all night. The next day it was hot and sandy. . . .

A great number of cattle perished before we got to Black Rock. . . . I drove our oxen all the time and I knew about how much an ox could stand. Between nine and ten o'clock a breeze came up and the oxen threw up their heads and seemed to have new life. At noon, we drove into Black Rock. . . .

We crossed the South Pass on the Fourth of July. The ice next morning was as thick as a dinner-plate.

[*The wagon train went on through Honey Lake to Deer Creek in Sacramento Valley and then to Redding Springs on Oct. 13, 1849.*]

On the morning of the 15th we went to dry-digging mining. We dug and dug to the first of November, at night it commenced raining, and rained and snowed pretty much all the winter. We had a tent but it barely kept us all dry. There were from eight to twelve in one camp. We cut down pine trees for stakes to make a cabin. It was a whole week before we had a cabin to keep us dry.

The first week in January, 1850, we bought a hundred pounds of bear meat at one dollar per pound.

---

Alvin Coffey, *Reminiscences*, taken from the bound unfolioed manuscript copy of *Reminiscences of Society Members* with the special permission of The Society of California Pioneers, San Francisco. [Coffey was the only nonwhite member of the Society.]

# 5

## The South When Cotton Was King

### Masters and Slaves

BY the time rebel guns opened fire on Fort Sumter in April, 1861, the South had become a backward agricultural region. It had few railroads, industries, schools, or libraries. While the writers of New England were blazing new paths in American literature, life among the slaveholders was pictured by one of their servants:

> Quarrels and brawls of the most violent description were frequent . . . and whenever they became especially dangerous, and glasses were thrown, dirks drawn, and pistols fired, it was the duty of the slaves to rush in, and each one drag his master from the fight, and carry him home.

Williams G. Simms, a noted South Carolina novelist and historian, described the effect of slavery on literature in these words: "No, sir, there never will be a literature worth the name in the Southern States so long as their aristocracy remains based on so many head of Negroes and so many bales of cotton."

Meanwhile, poor whites like Hinton Helper of North Carolina were complaining:

> We are compelled to go to the North for almost every article of utility or adornment, from matches, shoe-pegs, and paintings to cotton-mills, steamships, and

statuary . . . we are dependent on Northern capital-
ists for the means necessary to build our railroads,
canals and other public improvements.

Even the cotton gin, the invention that turned the South white with
cotton and dark with slaves, was devised by Eli Whitney, a Massachusetts schoolteacher.

Whitney's invention changed the course of Southern history. At
a time when slavery appeared to be dying, a machine was invented
which did the work previously done by 50 slaves. Cotton prices
dropped and world demand rose. The slave population leaped from
less than a million in 1793 to four million just before the Civil War.
More land was planted for cotton and still more was needed. The
price of slaves rose from $200 to $2,000 each. Cotton production
soared from a few million to two billion bales. The cotton frontier
moved west from the Carolinas into Alabama, Texas, southern Kansas, and California.

For the slave, the changes brought by the cotton gin were unfortunate. He became a cog in the vast, driving machine that piled up
cotton for the world market. Masters and overseers, a planter admitted, treated both slave and land as something to be "worn out, not
improved." The life span of the field slave fell as cotton production
rose.

*The cotton gin. As it drove down the price of cotton garments, it increased*
*the need for more slaves and more land for cotton planting.*

*A slave coachman. Skilled or house slaves were better treated than the field hands.*

Seven out of eight slaves worked on the Southern plantations, mainly in the Deep South. Their working day was from early sunrise to late sunset. Every plantation owner or overseer set the working conditions and served as judge and jury over his slaves. According to one Southerner, overseers, who were paid according to how much was produced, "care for nothing but to make a large crop." Slaves were not human—they were property. As property, they could be bought and sold at auctions, willed to relatives, rented out, lost at cards, or won in raffles.

Slaves did far more than labor in the fields. Some were house servants—butlers, cooks, maids, and nurses—and these were better treated than field slaves. Some were made overseers and given positions of trust. For example, Joe Anderson helped Cyrus McCormick invent his famous reaper. And Irish visitor Isaac Weld, touring the South at the end of the 18th century, noticed that slaveholders "have nearly everything they can want on their own estates. Amongst their slaves are found taylors, shoemakers, carpenters, smiths, turners, wheelwrights, weavers, tanners. . . ." A Georgia doctor admitted in 1837 that "without a population of blacks the whole country would become a desert."

## The Slaveholder Justifies Slavery

To the white Southerner, slavery was a social as well as a labor system. To justify it, masters developed elaborate theories. Alexander H. Stephens of Georgia said that "equality of the races is fundamentally wrong" and proclaimed "the great truth that the Negro is not equal to the white man; that slavery—subordination to the superior race—is his natural and normal condition." John C. Calhoun of South Carolina claimed that slaveholders took "low, degraded and savage" Africans and "civilized" and "improved" them. George Fitzhugh of Virginia said that slaves were "perhaps the happiest and the freest people in the world."

The slaveholders carefully taught the poor whites and their slaves this myth of superior and inferior races. Through this myth and their wealth, 3,000 leading slaveholders were able to control the South's eight million whites and four million blacks. In 1866, President Andrew Johnson, who had been a poor white, told Frederick Douglass: "There were twenty-seven non-slaveholders to one slaveholder [in Tennessee], and yet the slave power controlled the state." Ministers, editors, teachers, scientists, and sheriffs followed their

*A slave is auctioned off to the highest bidder. Whites and blacks alike were dehumanized by participating in and seeing such scenes.*

wishes. "There is no legislation except for the benefit of slavery and slaveholders," wrote Hinton Helper, a poor white from North Carolina who was also a famous writer. The South was organized to protect slave property and so the interests of the majority of its citizens were neglected. The economic progress and growth of democracy that took place on the free soil of the West and North left the South untouched. "We meet multitudes of poor whites on all our great roads, seeking new homes to the West or the South," wrote a South Carolina planter. "Slavery," bitterly concluded Hinton Helper, "destroys whatever it touches."

Although they suffered deeply from competition with slave labor, the poor whites supported this system that called them superior because of their white skins. They served in the nightly slave patrols for six cents an hour and hunted runaways for the rewards. Only a few of them helped slaves escape or took part in the many slave conspiracies and revolts.

## The Slave in Southern Cities

Half a million slaves worked in Southern cities and towns by 1860. They became ship pilots, lumberjacks, printers, or factory workers. They built bridges in Mississippi, hotels in Alabama, roads in Louisiana, and ships in Georgia and Maryland. One was a locomotive engineer. Another was a laboratory assistant in the United States Naval Academy in Maryland. When, in 1847, white workers of the Tredegar Iron Works of Virginia went on strike to protest the use of slaves, the manager replaced the strikers with more slaves. When the foreman who was making the Statue of Freedom for the Capitol at Washington went on strike, he was replaced by a slave. The *New York Tribune* reported: "The black master builder lifted the ponderous masses and bolted them together, joint by joint, piece by piece, 'till they blended into the majestic freedom." Many skilled whites migrated to the free lands of the West rather than face competition with slaves.

In the decades before the Civil War, masters increasingly trained their slaves in various trades so that they could rent them out at high rates. The slave preferred either skilled or city work to plantation work because of the freedom and dignity it gave him. When slave Emanuel Quivers was hired out to work at the Tredegar Iron Works, he persuaded the owner to buy him. Then Quivers worked extra hours for pay—and in four years was able to buy himself, his wife, and four children. As a free man he went to California during the Gold Rush and lived to see his children educated. His son became a foreman in a factory in Stockton.

The city slaves enjoyed greater liberty than the plantation hands. They learned self-reliance and often earned money for themselves by working extra hours. Slave Lunsford Lane had agents in three North Carolina cities selling his specially prepared pipe tobacco in fifteen cent packages. Lane soon made enough money to purchase his freedom and that of his large family. Citizens of Charleston bitterly resented the urban slaves because they were "in every way . . . conducting themselves as if they were not slaves." Another white warned that city slaves "get strange notions into their heads and grow discontented," which was true. In Richmond, Henry Brown, who worked in a tobacco factory, found a white man who was willing to seal him in a box and ship him to Philadelphia. In Baltimore, Frederick Douglass learned how to read and write from white playmates and later escaped to New York with a pass from a Negro seaman.

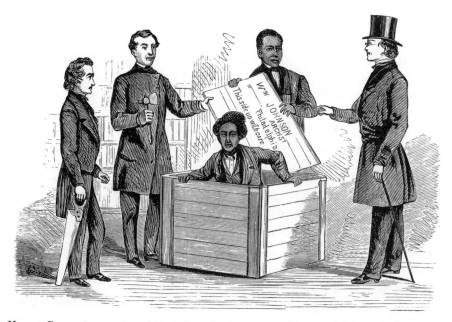

*Henry Brown emerging from the small box that carried him to freedom. Those Negroes who lived in towns or cities had a better chance to meet whites and Negroes who would help them. The white Southerner who helped Brown escape was sent to prison.*

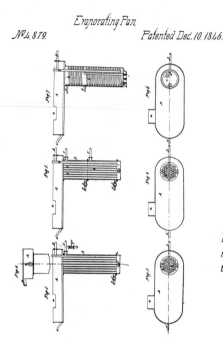

*Norbert Rillieux's evaporating pan for sugar refining. This invention revolutionized the sugar-refining industry.*

## The Free Negro Population

A quarter of a million free Negroes lived in the South by 1860. Despite severe restrictions, several achieved outstanding success. In 1846 Norbert Rillieux of New Orleans perfected a vacuum pan that revolutionized the sugar refining industry in Europe and America. Sent by his wealthy father to France to study, Rillieux taught applied mechanics in Paris and published many scientific papers by the time he was twenty-four. Dr. Charles Browne, sugar chemist of the United States Department of Agriculture, said: "Rillieux's invention is the greatest in the history of American chemical engineering, and I know of no other invention that has brought so great a saving to all branches of chemical engineering." Rillieux submitted a complicated proposal for a sewerage system for his city, but it was not accepted. He returned to Paris where he lived for the rest of his life.

There were other Negro inventors from the South but it is difficult to determine how many since, under the existing laws, they could be refused permission to patent their creations. However, Henry Blair of Maryland patented a seedplanter for corn in 1834, and in 1854 Henry Sigler of Galveston, Texas patented an improved fishhook and later sold his patent for only $625.

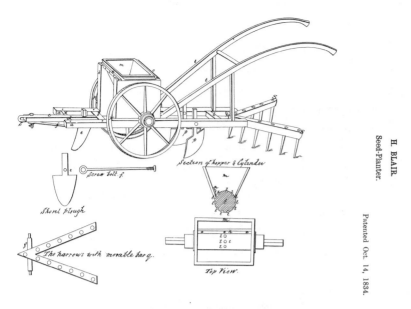

H. BLAIR.
Seed-Planter.

Patented Oct. 14, 1834.

*Patent drawing for Henry Blair's seedplanter, 1834. It is the first patent to be held by a Negro. Slaves could not hold patents. The master held patents for anything his slaves invented. There may have been a considerable number of inventions by slaves because the Southern Confederacy thought it necessary to include a section in its Constitution stating that the owner of a slave also controlled his invention.*

A large number of educated and talented New Orleans Negroes contributed to a book of French verse, *Les Cenelles*, edited in 1845 by Armand Lanusse. By 1816, the New Orleans Opera House established a segregated section in the upper tier for the many colored people who attended it.

Although the teaching of slaves—and sometimes of free Negroes—was forbidden by law, some schools operated illegally in much the same manner as prohibition distilleries, two of them with Negro principals. One of these principals, John Chavis of North Carolina, instructed whites during the day and Negroes at night (at lower fees). Daniel A. Payne, a South Carolina free Negro, established a school with a curriculum that included arithmetic, literature, science, chemistry, botany, zoology, astronomy, and geography, as well as reading and writing. Payne had taught himself these subjects as well as Greek, Latin, and French. Later, at Wilberforce, Payne would become the first Negro college president in America.

To most whites, the free Negroes were a dangerous third force in a society built for two—slave and master. "The superior condition of the free persons of color," complained a group of whites in Charleston in 1822, "excites discontent among our slaves, who continually have before their eyes, persons of the same color, many of whom they had known in slavery . . . freed from the control of masters, working where they please, going whither they please. . . ." Seeing these freemen, "the slave pants for liberty."

Despite the fact that the free Negroes were carefully watched, they helped many slaves escape. Their homes and stores were often the Southern stations of the underground railroad. Some forged passes for slaves, and others contributed money to help them escape. Samuel Martin of Mississippi, an ex-slave who became wealthy, bought six slaves and, in 1844, led them to the free soil of Pennsylvania. Four thousand other free Negroes owned slaves, usually family members or close friends, that the law would not allow them to liberate.

## Day-to-Day Resistance to Bondage

*Ellen Craft dressed as a young slaveholder. With her darker husband serving as her "coachman," the couple rode to freedom in high style, stopping at the best Southern hotels. They moved to England where they entered school so that they could learn to read and write.*

The South became a battleground in the slave's daily struggle to improve his lot, to live in dignity, or to escape to freedom. "My mother often hid us in the woods," wrote Moses Grandy, "to prevent master selling us." Alabama slave Cudjo Lewis reported that slave women "overpowered and soundly thrashed" an overseer who had insulted one of them. The slaves who labored in the fields destroyed tools and crops and sometimes tried to poison masters and overseers. They set so many fires that some companies refused to insure homes in the slave states. The slaves pretended to be lame, sick, blind, or insane and they often pretended stupidity or clumsiness to avoid work.

Dr. Samuel Cartwright of New Orleans, a respected Southern medical man, was convinced that Negroes suffered from special diseases. He called one *dysaethesia aethiopica* and claimed that it caused Negroes to "break, waste, and destroy everything they handle. . . . They slight their work—cut up corn, cane, cotton, or tobacco when hoeing it, as if for pure mischief. They raise disturbances with their overseers. . . ." His other discovery was "*drapetomania, or the disease causing negroes to run away.*" This "disease of the mind" was sometimes cured, he said, by "whipping the devil out of them." To those who claimed that slavery was such a happy life and so "natural" to the Negroes, their resistance could only be viewed as "*a disease peculiar to negroes.*"

Each year, thousands escaped to Southern cities, free states, Mexico, or Canada. Entire colonies lived in the woods or the swamps from Virginia to Florida. America's first treaty under the Constitution asked the Creek Indians to return slaves who were being hidden by their tribes in Georgia.

Slaves fled their masters long before the "Underground Railroad" was developed. They set out into an unknown land where every white face was a possible enemy. They hid in trees, tall grass, hollow logs, churches, schools, attics, and woods. They escaped aboard ships, sleds, horses, and wagons. Some got away in barrels, sacks, and coffins. Sometimes they had to battle slave catchers on the road. On Christmas Eve, 1855, a group of teenage boys and girls escaped by wagon from Virginia. They were well-armed and led by young, determined Ann Wood. When a posse surrounded them in Maryland, Ann Wood dared the whites to fire, holding "a double barrelled pistol in one hand and a long dirk knife in the other, utterly unterrified and fully ready for a death struggle." The posse retreated and the proud young people reached Philadelphia in safety.

*Despite every effort to control slaves, they fled to the swamps or planned revolts.*

*Ann Wood and the other teenagers drive off the slavecatchers.*

To prevent open rebellion and flight, planters took every precaution. They kept all knowledge of the outside world from their bondsmen. State laws provided severe punishments for anyone who taught a slave to read or write. "The increase of knowledge [among slaves] is the principal agent in evolving the spirit we have to fear," wrote a Carolina planter in 1800. Slaves who worked near water

*A slave gallops to freedom on his master's horse. "Don't be afraid to take the best horse, you're entitled to it," a group of runaways wrote to their friends in slavery.*

were "not allowed to learn the art of swimming" wrote slave Solomon Northup. Slave patrols guarded the countryside at night. Savage dogs, valued at $300 each, were kept in readiness to hunt runaways. White ministers preached to slaves that "they must always obey their masters." Rebellious slaves were publicly whipped or sold farther South so that the fearful price of resistance would be clear to all.

In many parts of the South, slaves waged a continuous battle to learn to read and write, to practice religion, or even to hear what was going on outside the plantation. "My father and other boys used to crawl under the house an' lie on the ground to hear massa read the newspaper to missus," recalled one slave. Another told how her mistress would spell out words she did not want the slave to know, but "I ran to uncle an' spelled them over to him, an' he told me what they meant."

Slave Booker T. Washington told how slaves "kept themselves informed of events by what was termed the 'grapevine' telegraph." Frederick Douglass conducted a Sunday school in the woods until he was warned that he would be killed if he did not stop teaching

Negroes. In 1870, an agent of the Freedmen's Bureau reported on the education of slaves by whites in St. Louis:

> There were not wanting those who at all risks under-
> took the task of teaching the slaves, and for a quarter
> of a century before the late rebellion schools were kept
> up in St. Louis with more or less regularity. Secretly,
> and sometimes with the connivance of the authorities,
> sometimes for a year or two without interruption, then
> broken up to be started again in some other quarter
> [these schools continued]. . . . Many of our leading
> colored men owe all the education they possess to op-
> portunities like these. [War Records Office, National
> Office, Washington, D.C.]

## The Slave Revolts

The greatest fear of the slaveholder was not the escape of his slaves but possible revolts. A Carolina planter warned a friend: "The love of freedom, sir, is an inborn sentiment . . . it springs forth and flourishes with a vigor that defies all check. There never have been slaves in any country, who have not seized the first favorable opportunity to revolt." It was not surprising, then, when a visitor to the South reported that "I have known times here when not a single planter had a calm night's rest. They never lie down to sleep without . . . loaded pistols at their sides."

Slave revolts were planned, or took place, in Southern cities, on plantations, or aboard ships. Except for those at sea, none could succeed, for the entire armed might of the local and state militia and the armed forces of the federal government stood ready to crush any rebellion. But plots and revolts marked the entire history of Negro slavery in the United States. They were a last, hopeless, and desperate battle against a system that held lives in contempt and destroyed human dignity.

In 1800, Gabriel Prosser, a Virginia slave, prepared thousands of his fellow bondsmen to attack Richmond. A violent storm saved the city. It washed out bridges and flooded roads and before Gabriel could regroup his men, the plot was betrayed by two house slaves. The leaders were arrested, tried, and sentenced to death. One told the court that he had only done for his people what George Washington had done for America: "I have ventured my life . . . to obtain the liberty of my countrymen."

In Charleston, South Carolina in 1822, a vast slave plot was uncovered. Its leader was a tall, muscular carpenter, Denmark Vesey, who spoke several languages. As a young man, Vesey had bought his own liberty when he won a $1,500 raffle. The conspiracy had been planned for four years, and the slaves involved had hidden away weapons and ammunition. The authorities, given information by two house slaves, arrested 131 suspects. An attempt to rescue the slaves was feared. Federal troops stood by to protect the city as the leaders were led to the gallows. Before the traps were sprung, the doomed men called on slaves everywhere to revolt until freedom was theirs.

It was the Nat Turner revolt of 1831 which so frightened the South that at least one state considered giving up slavery. Turner led his small band of Virginia slaves from plantation to plantation, murdering slaveholding families and recruiting their slaves. Before the rebellion was finally smashed, federal troops, artillery, and state forces had to be called in. For two months a panic-stricken Virginia legislature talked seriously of ending Negro slavery. But the lawmakers decided, instead, to crush all slave resistance with more severe laws and tighter controls over slaves. Since Nat Turner was a preacher and an educated man, Southern states increased their control of black preachers and the education of slaves. "To see you with a book in your hand, they would almost cut your throat," recalled one slave.

A member of the Virginia legislature admitted how far they would go to keep slaves from learning.

> We have, as far as possible, closed every avenue by which light might enter their minds. If you could extinguish the capacity to see the light, our work would be completed; they would then be on a level with the beasts of the field, and we should be safe! . . .

The spirit of defiance among slaves did not end with the death of Nat Turner. Two mutinies aboard the ships of the slave trade were successful. In 1839, Cinque, son of an African king, led 54 slaves in a revolt aboard the *Amistad*. "I would not see you serve the white men," he told them. "You had better be killed than live many moons in misery. . . . I could die happy if by dying I could save so many of my brothers from the bondage of the white men." Cinque and his men seized the ship and tried to sail it back to Africa. By the treachery of the slave dealers, whose lives they had spared, they were

*Joseph Cinque, leader of the* Amistad *slaves. He told his comrades: "Brothers . . . our hands are now clean for we have striven to regain the precious heritage we received from our fathers . . . I am resolved that it is better to die than be a white man's slave, and I will not complain if by dying I save you."*

landed on the Connecticut coast and captured. Cinque and the others were finally freed by the Supreme Court of the United States after a lengthy battle led by ex-President John Quincy Adams, who served as their lawyer.

In 1841, a slave named Madison Washington led a revolt aboard the *Creole* that also succeeded. Washington rescued his own lovely wife, who was held below decks with other slave women. The lives of the white members of the crew had been spared on promises of good behavior. However, the crew proved to be treacherous and the slaves wanted to execute them. At this point, Washington said: "We have got our liberty, and that is all that we have been fighting for. Let no more blood be shed." The free men and women of the *Creole* sailed to the West Indies where they lived out their lives in freedom.

Until Emancipation Day, slave men and women battled for their dignity and freedom in ways that appeared most practical. Many demonstrated the same raw bravery and stubborn courage as the Minutemen at Concord, or the ragged armies at Valley Forge.

## A Slave Picks Cotton

[*Solomon Northup was a free Negro who was kidnapped in Washington, D.C. and sold into slavery. He worked for 12 years as a plantation slave before he finally won his freedom. He describes cotton picking on a Louisiana plantation, in late August, the cotton-picking season.*]

When a new hand, one unaccustomed to the business, is sent for the first time into the field, he is whipped up smartly and made for that day to pick as fast as he can possibly. At night it is weighed, so that his capability in cotton picking is known. He must bring in the same weight each night following. If it falls short, it is considered evidence that he has been laggard, and a greater or less number of lashes is the penalty.

An ordinary day's work is two hundred pounds. A slave who is accustomed to picking, is punished, if he or she brings in a less quantity than that. There is a great difference among them as regards this kind of labor. Some of them seem to have a natural knack, or quickness, which enables them to pick with great celerity, and with both hands, while others, with whatever practice or industry, are utterly unable to come up to the ordinary standard. Such hands are taken from the cotton field and employed in other business. . . .

The hands are required to be in the cotton field as soon as it is light in the morning, and, with the exception of ten or fifteen minutes, which is given them at noon to swallow their allowance of cold bacon, they are not permitted to be a moment idle until it is too dark to see, and when the moon is full, they often times labor till the middle of the night. They do not dare to stop even at dinner time, nor return to the quarters, however late it be, until the order to halt is given by the driver.

The day's work over in the field, the baskets are "toted," or in other words, carried to the gin-house, where the cotton is weighed. . . . This done, the labor of the day is not yet ended, by any means. Each one must then attend to his respective chores. One feeds the mules, another the swine—another cuts the wood, and so forth; besides, the packing is all done by candlelight. Finally, at a late hour, they reach the quarters, sleepy and overcome with the long day's toil. Then a fire must be kindled in the cabin, the corn ground in the small hand-mill, and supper, and dinner for the next day in the field, pre-pared. All that is allowed them is corn and bacon, which is given out at the corncrib and smoke-house every Sunday morning. Each one receives, as his weekly allowance, three and a half pounds of bacon, and corn enough to make a peck of meal. That is all—no tea, coffee, sugar, and, with the exception of a very scanty sprinkling now and then, no salt. . . .

S. Northup, *Twelve Years a Slave* (Philadelphia, n.d.), pp. 165-169.

## Master and Slave Relationships

[*Along with the cruel and heartless masters, there were also some kind and trusting owners. In this last will of Judge Upshur one can see the kind of feeling that existed between this master and the slave who served him for twenty-four years.*]

I emancipate and set free my servant, David Rice, and direct my executors to give him *one hundred dollars.* I recommend him in the strongest manner to the respect, esteem, and confidence of any com-munity in which he may happen to live. He has been my slave for twenty-four years, during all which time he has been trusted to every extent, and in every respect; my confidence in him has been un-bounded; his relation to myself and family has always been such as to afford him daily opportunities to deceive and injure us; yet he has never been detected in any serious fault, nor even in an unintentional breach of decorum of his station. His intelligence is of a higher order, his integrity above all suspicion, and his sense of right and propriety correct, and even refined. I feel that he is justly entitled to carry this certificate from me in the new relations which he must now form; it is due to his long and most faithful services, and to the sin-cere and steady friendship which I bear to him. In . . . twenty-four years, I have never given him, nor had occasion to give him, one unpleasant word. I know of no man who has fewer faults or more excellences than he.

Harriet Beecher Stowe, *The Key to Uncle Tom's Cabin* (Boston, 1854), pp. 39-40.

[*Josiah Henson tells us of a completely different kind of relationship between a master and a slave. The kind of life which this master led made it necessary for him to place a good deal of faith in his slave.*]

. . . My master's habits were such as were common enough among the dissipated planters of the neighborhood; and one of their frequent practices was to assemble on Saturday or Sunday, which were their holidays, and gamble, run horses, or fight game-cocks, discuss politics, and drink whiskey and brandy and water all day long. Perfectly aware that they would not be able to find their own way home at night, each one ordered his body-servant to come after him and help him home. I was chosen for this confidential duty by my master; and many is the time I have held him on his horse, when he could not hold himself in the saddle, and walked by his side in darkness and mud from the tavern to his house. Of course, quarrels and brawls of the most violent description were frequent consequences of these meetings; and whenever they became especially dangerous, and glasses were thrown, dirks drawn, and pistols fired, it was the duty of the slaves to rush in, and each one drag his master from the fight, and carry him home. To tell the truth, this was a part of my business for which I felt no reluctance. I was young, remarkably athletic and self-relying, and in such affrays I carried it with a high hand, and would elbow my way among the whites,—whom it would have been almost death for me to strike—seize my master and drag him out, mount him on his horse, or crowd him into his buggy, with the ease with which I would handle a bag of corn. I knew that I was doing for him what he could not do for himself, and showing my superiority to others, and acquiring their respect in some degree, at the same time.

Josiah Henson, *Truth Stranger Than Fiction, Father Henson's Story of His Own Life* (Boston, 1858), pp. 31-33.

# For Frederick Douglass Life as a Slave Was One Continuous Battle

[*Edward Covey, a professional "slave breaker" for masters with hard-to-handle slaves, had already beaten Frederick Douglass several times, when Douglass decided to resist. This is the young slave's story of the fight.*]

The fighting madness had come upon me, and I found my strong fingers firmly attached to the throat of my cowardly tormentor; as heedless of consequences, at the moment, as though we stood as equals before the law. The very color of the man was forgotten. I felt as supple as a cat, and was ready for the snakish creature at every turn. Every blow of his was parried, though I dealt no blows in turn. I was strictly on the *defensive*, preventing him from injuring me, rather than trying to injure him. I flung him on the ground several times, when he meant to have hurled me there. I held him so firmly by the throat, that his blood followed my nails. He held me and I held him.

All was fair, thus far, and the contest was about equal. My resistance was entirely unexpected, and Covey was taken all aback by it, for he trembled in every limb. "*Are you going to resist*, you scoundrel?" said he. To which, I returned a polite "yes sir". . . . He called for his cousin Hughes, to come to his assistance. . . . I was still *defensive* toward Covey, but *aggressive* toward Hughes; and, at the first approach of the latter, I dealt a blow, in my desperation, which fairly sickened my youthful assailant. He went off, bending over with pain, and manifesting no disposition to come within my reach again. . . .

By this time, Bill, the hired man, came home. . . . "What shall I do, Mr. Covey?" said Bill. "Take hold of him—take hold of him!" said Covey. With a toss of his head, peculiar to Bill, he said . . . . "My master hired me here, to work, and *not* to help you whip Frederick." It was now my turn to speak. "Bill," said I, "don't put your hands on me." To which he replied "My God! Frederick, I aint goin' to tech ye," and Bill walked off, leaving Covey and myself to settle matters as best we might.

But, my present advantage was threatened when I saw Caroline (the slavewoman of Covey) coming to the cow yard for milk, for she was a powerful woman, and could have mastered me very easily, exhausted as I now was. As soon as she came into the yard, Covey attempted to rally her to his aid. Strangely—and, I may add, fortunately—Caroline was in no humor to take a hand in any such sport . . . . Caroline answered . . . precisely as Bill had answered, but in *her*, it was at greater peril so to answer; she was the slave of Covey. . . .

Covey at length [two hours had elapsed] gave up the contest. Letting me go, he said—puffing and blowing at a great rate—"now, you scoundrel, go to your work; I would not have whipped you half so much as I have had you not resisted." The fact was, *he had not whipped me at all.* . . .

During the whole six months that I lived with Covey, after this transaction, he never laid on me the weight of his finger in anger. . . .

[*In the Baltimore shipyard where Douglass worked as a caulker, white and free Negro carpenters were feuding. Though Douglass was a slave, the ill-feeling in the yard drew him into the fight.*]

The spirit . . . was one of malice and bitterness, toward colored people *generally*, and I suffered with the rest, and suffered severely. . . . Edward North, the biggest in everything . . . ventured to strike me, whereupon I picked him up, and threw him into the dock. Whenever any of them struck me, I struck back again, regardless of consequences. I could manage any of them *singly;* and, while I could keep them from combining, I succeeded very well. In the conflict which ended my stay at Mr. Gardiner's, I was beset by four of them at once. . . . Two of them were as large as myself, and they came near killing me, in broad day light. The attack was made suddenly, and simultaneously. One came in front, armed with a brick; there was one at each side and one behind, and they closed up around me. I was struck on all sides. . . . It was impossible to stand against so many. . . .

After making my escape from the ship yard, I went straight home, and related the story of the outrage to [my] Master Hugh Auld. . . .

. . . His indignation was really strong and healthy; but, unfortunately, it resulted from the thought that his rights of property, in my person, had not been respected, more than from any sense of the outrage committed on me *as a man*. . . . He related the outrage to the magistrate [Mr. Watson] . . . and seemed to expect that a warrant would, at once, be issued for the arrest of the lawless ruffians. . . .

"Mr. Auld, who saw this assault of which you speak?"

"It was done, sir, in the presence of a ship yard full of hands."

"Sir," said Watson, "I am sorry, but I cannot move in this matter except upon the oath of white witnesses."

"But here's the boy; look at his head and face . . . *they* show *what* has been done."

But Watson insisted that he was not authorized to do anything, unless *white* witnesses . . . would come forward, and testify to what had taken place. . . .

---

Frederick Douglass, *My Bondage and My Freedom* (New York and Auburn, 1855), pp. 242-246, 312-317.

## *The Break-Up of Slave Families*

[*Josiah Henson describes the auction at which his family was broken up for sale to different owners.*]

. . . the remembrance of the breaking up of McPherson's estate is photographed in its minutest features in my mind. The crowd collected round the stand, the huddling group of Negroes, the examination of muscle, teeth, the exhibition of agility, the look of the auctioneer, the agony of my mother—I can shut my eyes and see them all.

My brothers and sisters were bid off first, and one by one, while my mother, paralyzed by grief, held me by the hand. Her turn came, and she was bought by Isaac Riley of Montgomery county. Then I was offered to the assembled purchasers. My mother, half distracted with the thought of parting forever from all her children pushed through the crowd, while the bidding for me was going on, to the spot where Riley was standing. She fell at his feet, and clung to his knees, entreating him in tones that a mother could only command, to buy her *baby* as well as herself, and spare to her one, at least, of her little ones. Will it, can it be believed that this man, thus appealed to, was capable not merely of turning a deaf ear to her supplication, but of disengaging himself from her with such violent blows and kicks, as to reduce her to the necessity of creeping out of his reach, and mingling the groan of bodily suffering with the sob of a breaking heart? As she crawled away from the brutal man I heard her sob out, "Oh, Lord Jesus, how long, how long shall I suffer this way!" I must have been then between five and six years old. I seem to see and hear my poor weeping mother now. This was one of my earliest observations of men; an experience which I only shared with thousands of my race. . . .

Josiah Henson, *Truth Stranger Than Fiction, Father Henson's Story of His Own Life* (Boston, 1858), pp. 11-13.

## Efforts to Reunite the Slave Family

[*During the entire period of American slavery, slaves made efforts to rejoin loved ones sold away. These attempts to reunite families can be seen in the reward notices printed by owners in Southern newspapers.*]

Macon (Ga.) Messenger, November 23, 1837. $25 Reward.—Ran away, a Negro man, named Cain. He was brought from Florida, and has a wife near Mariana, and probably will attempt to make his way there.

Richmond (Va.) Compiler, September 8, 1837. Ran away from the subscriber, Ben. He ran off without any known cause, and I suppose he is aiming to go to his wife, who was carried from the neighborhood last winter.

Richmond (Va.) Enquirer, February 20, 1838. Stop the Runaway!!!—$25 Reward. Ran away from the Eagle Tavern, a Negro fellow named Nat. He is no doubt attempting to follow his wife, who was lately sold to a speculator named Redmond. The above reward will be paid by Mrs. Lucy M. Downman, of Sussex County, Va.

Savannah (Ga.) Republican, September 3, 1838. $20 Reward for my Negro man Jim.—Jim is about 50 or 55 years of age. It is probable he will aim for Savannah, as he said he had children in that vicinity.

Lexington (Ky.) Observer and Reporter, September 28, 1838. $50 Reward.—Ran away from the subscriber, a Negro girl, named Maria. She is of a copper color, between 13 and 14 years of age—bare headed and bare footed. She is small of her age—very sprightly and very likely. She stated she was going to see her mother at Maysville.

Theodore Dwight Weld, *American Slavery As It Is. Testimony of a Thousand Witnesses* (New York, 1839), pp. 164-166.

## Sold to Louisiana

[*Slaves feared being sold to the states of the Deep South. One slave describes the scene as a group is taken to the depot.*]

. . . the victims were to take the cars from a station called Clarkson turnout, which was about four miles from master's place. The excitement was so great that the overseer and driver could not control the relatives and friends of those that were going away, as a large crowd of both old and young went down to the depot to see them off. Louisiana was considered by the slaves as a place of slaughter, so those who were going did not expect to see their friends again. While passing along, many of the Negroes left their master's fields and joined us as we marched to the cars; some were yelling and wringing their hands, while others were singing little hymns that they were accustomed to for the consolation of those that were going away, such as,

> When we all meet in heaven,
> There is no parting there;
> When we all meet in heaven,
> There is parting no more.

We arrived at the depot and had to wait for the cars to bring the others from the Sumterville Jail, but they soon came in sight, and when the noise of the cars died away we heard wailing and shrieks from those in the cars. While some were weeping, others were fiddling, picking banjo, and dancing as they used to do in their cabins on the plantations. Those who were so merry had very bad masters, and even though they stood a chance of being sold to one as bad or even worse yet they were glad to be rid of the one they knew.

While the cars were at the depot, a large crowd of white people gathered, and were laughing and talking about the prospect of Negro traffic; but when the cars began to start and the conductor cried out, "all who are going on this train must get aboard without delay," the colored people cried out with one voice as though the heavens and earth were coming together, and it was so pitiful, that those hardhearted white men who had been accustomed to driving slaves all their lives, shed tears like children. As the cars moved away we heard the weeping and wailing from the slaves, as far as human voice could be heard; and from that time to the present I have neither seen nor heard from my two sisters, nor any of those who left Clarkson depot, on that memorable day.

Jacob Stroyer, *Sketches of My Life in the South*, Vol. 1 (Salem, 1879), pp. 29-31.

## Why the Slaves Sang

[*In 1855 Frederick Douglass wrote of some of the reasons the slaves were expected to sing and why their sad songs were so much a part of slavery.*]

. . . slaves are generally expected to sing as well as to work. A silent slave is not liked by masters or overseers. "*Make a noise*," "*make a noise*," and "*bear a hand*," are the words usually addressed to the slaves when there is silence amongst them. This may account for the almost constant singing heard in the Southern states. There was, generally, more or less singing among the teamsters, as it was one means of letting the overseer know where they were, and that they were moving on with the work. But, on allowance day, those who visited the great house farm were peculiarly excited and noisy. While on their way, they would make the dense old woods, for miles around, reverberate with their wild notes. These were not always merry because they were wild. On the contrary, they were mostly of a plaintive cast, and told a tale of grief and sorrow. In the most boisterous outbursts of rapturous sentiment, there was ever a tinge of deep melancholy. I have never heard any songs like those anywhere since I left slavery, except when in Ireland. There, I heard the same wailing notes, and was much affected by them. It was during the famine of 1845-6. . . .

I did not, when a slave, understand the deep meaning of those rude, and apparently incoherent songs. I was myself within a circle, so that I neither saw nor heard as those without might see and hear. They told a tale which was then altogether beyond my feeble comprehension; they were tones, loud, long, and deep, breathing the prayer and complaint of souls boiling over with the bitterest anguish. Every tone was a testimony against slavery, and a prayer to God for deliverance from chains. The hearing of those wild notes always depressed my spirits, and filled my heart with ineffable sadness. The mere recurrence, even now, afflicts my spirit, and while I am writing these lines, my tears are falling. To those songs I trace my first glimmering conceptions of the dehumanizing character of slavery. I can never get rid of that conception. Those songs still follow me, to deepen my hatred of slavery, and quicken my sympathies for my brethren in bonds.

---

Frederick Douglass, *My Bondage and My Freedom* (New York and Auburn, 1855), pp. 97-99.

# The Slave Inventor at the United States Naval Academy

[*In this letter, to one of those who had given money to help buy the freedom of slave Benjamin Bradley, we get some of the story of this remarkable young inventor. Bradley helped pay for his own freedom and later paid back all those who had helped him.*]

*Dear Sir:*—I am very happy to inform you that the freedom of the slave Benjamin Bradley has been accomplished by the payment of $1,000, to which you contributed the final $122 necessary to make it up. . . .

Bradley was owned by a master in Annapolis, Maryland. Eight years ago he was employed in a printing office there. He was then about sixteen, and showed great mechanical skill and ingenuity. With a piece of gun-barrel, some pewter, a couple of pieces of round steel, and some materials, he constructed a *working model of a steam engine*.

His master soon afterwards got him the place of a helper in the department of Natural and Experimental Philosophy in the Naval Academy at Annapolis. He sold his first steam engine to a Midship-man. With the proceeds, and what money he could lay up (his master allowing him five dollars a month out of his wages), he built an engine large enough to drive the first cutter of a sloop-of-war at the rate of sixteen knots an hour. . . .

Professor Hopkins, of the Academy, says that he gets up the experiments for the lecture-room very handsomely. Being shown once how to line up the parabolic mirrors for concentrating heat, he always succeeds afterwards. So with the chemical experiments. He makes all the gasses, and works with them, showing the Drummond light, &c. Prof. Hopkins remarks of him that "he looks for *the law* by which things act."

He has been taught to read and write, mainly by the Professor's children; has made very good progress in arithmetic, and will soon take hold of algebra and geometry.

---

*The Anglo-African Magazine*, Vol. 1 (November, 1859), p. 367. Reprinted from the *Journal of Commerce*.

## A Black Schoolmaster in the Deep South

[*Daniel A. Payne, a free Negro of Charleston, opened his first school in 1829. He taught three children during the day and three adult slaves at night. Each pupil paid 50 cents a month. As his expenses mounted he became discouraged and quit. Then a white man told him that the difference between a master and slave was "nothing but superior knowledge," and Payne decided to reopen his school.*]

On the first of the year 1830 I re-opened my school, which continued to increase in numbers until the room became too small, and I was constrained to procure [a larger] place. This in turn became too small, and one was built for me. . . .

During the three years of my attendance at the school of Mr. Thomas S. Bonneau I learned how to read, write, and spell; also arithmetic as far as the "Rule of Three." Spelling was a delightful exercise of my boyhood. In this I excelled. . . . History was my great delight. Of geography and map-drawing, English grammar and composition I knew nothing, because they were not taught in any of the schools for colored children. . . . [He then managed to find a geography and atlas for his classes.]

. . . at the same time with geography I studied and mastered English grammar. . . . I therefore added that to my curriculum.

Having now the groundwork, I began to build the superstructure. I commenced with "Playfair's Euclid," and proceeded as far as the first five books. The next thing that arrested my attention was botany. . . . Descriptive chemistry, natural philosophy, and descriptive astronomy followed in rapid succession. . . .

Then, on a Thursday morning, I bought a Greek grammar, a lexicon, and a Greek Testament. On the same day I mastered the Greek alphabet; on Friday I learned to write them; on Saturday morning I translated the first chapter of Mathew's Gospel from Greek into English. My very soul rejoiced and exulted in this glorious triumph. Next came the Latin and the French. Meanwhile I was pushing my studies in drawing and coloring till I was able to produce a respectable flower, fruit, or animal on paper and on velvet.

My researches in botany gave me a relish for zoology; but as I could never get hold of any work on this science, I had to *make books* for myself. This I did by killing such insects, toads, snakes, young alligators, fishes, and young sharks as I could catch. I then cleaned and stuffed those that I could, and hung them upon the walls of my school-room. . . .

My enthusiasm was the inspiration of my pupils. I used to take my first class into the woods every Saturday in search of insects, reptiles, and plants, and at the end of five years I had accumulated some fine specimens of each of these. . . .

. . . it was also one of my methods in order to interest my pupils to erect several gymnastic instruments, that they might develop their muscular systems and find amusement to break the monotony of the school-room; but in all their sports I led them in person. . . .

Bishop Daniel Alexander Payne, *Recollections of Seventy Years* (Nashville, 1888), pp. 19-25.

# The Christmas Season on the Plantation

[*Ex-slave Jacob Stroyer describes the Christmas holidays as one of the few times when slaves had days off, visited relatives, and were not required to work.*]

Both masters and slaves regarded Christmas as a great day. When the slaveholders made a large crop they were pleased, and gave the slaves from five to six days, which was much enjoyed by the Negroes, especially by those who could dance. Christmas morning was held sacred both by master and slave, but in the afternoon or in a part of the next day the slaves were required to devote themselves to the pleasure of their masters. Some of the masters would buy presents for the slaves, such as hats and tobacco for the men, handkerchiefs and little things for the women, these things were given after they had been pleased with them, after either dancing or something for their amusement.

When the slaves came up to their master and mistress the latter would welcome them, the men would take off their hats and bow and the women would make a low courtsy. There would be two or three large pails filled with sweetened water with a gallon or two of whisky in each, this was dealt out to them until they were partly drunk; while this was going on those who could talk very well would give tokens of well wishing to master and mistress, and some who were born in Africa would sing some of their songs, or tell different stories of the customs in Africa. After this they would spend half a day in dancing in some large cotton house or on a scaffold, the master providing fiddlers who came from other plantations if there were none in the place, and who received from fifteen to twenty dollars on these occasions.

A great many of the strict members of the church who did not dance would be forced to do it to please their masters, the favorite tunes were *The Fisher's Hornpipe*, *The Devil's Dream* and *Black-eyed Susan*. . . .

After the dancing was over we had our presents, master giving to the men, and mistress to the women, then the slaves would go to their quarters and continue to dance. . . .

Jacob Stroyer, *Sketches of My Life in the South*, Vol. 1 (Salem, 1879), pp. 34-35.

# The Denmark Vesey Plot of 1822

[*Denmark Vesey, a free Negro of Charleston, South Carolina, planned to capture the city. Before his slave followers struck, the plot was betrayed and the leaders arrested. First, Rolla, the slave of the governor, tells his story to the court.*]

I know Denmark Vesey, on one occasion he asked me, what news? I told him, none. He replied, we are free, but the white people here won't let us be so; and the only way is, to raise up and fight the whites. I went to his house one night, to learn where the meetings were held. . . . Vesey told me, he was the leader in this plot. . . . Vesey induced me to join. When I went to Vesey's house, there was a meeting there, the room was full of people, but none of them white. That night, at Vesey's, we determined to have arms made, and each man to put in twelve and a half cents towards that purpose. . . . At this meeting, Vesey said, we were to take the guardhouse and magazines, to get arms; that we ought to rise up against the whites to get our liberties. He was the first to rise up and speak, and he read to us from the bible, how the *children of Israel were delivered out of Egypt from bondage;* he said, that the rising would take place last Sunday night week (the 16th June), and that Peter Poyas was one [leader].

[*Jesse, a slave.*] I was invited to Denmark Vesey's house, and when I went, I found several men met together, among whom was Ned Bennett, Peter Poyas, and others, whom I did not know. Denmark opened the meeting by saying, he had an important secret to communicate to us, which we must not disclose to any one, and if we did, we should be put to instant death. He said, we were deprived of our rights and privileges by the white people, and that our church was shut up, so that we could not use it, and that it was high time for us to seek for our rights, and that we were fully able to conquer the whites, if we were only unanimous and courageous, as the St. Domingo people were. He then proceeded to explain his plan, by saying, that they intended to make the attack by setting the governour's mills on fire, and also some houses near the water, and as soon as the bells began to ring for fire, that they should kill every man, as he came out of his door. . . .

[*A Negro man reporting his talk with Peter Poyas.*] I asked what was the plan? . . . I am the captain, said he, to take the lower guardhouse and arsenal. But, I replied, when you are coming up, the sentinel will give the alarm. He said, he would advance a little distance ahead, and if he could only get a *grip at his throat he was a gone man*, for his sword was very sharp. . . . I then said, that this thing seems true. My man, said he, God has a hand in it, *we have been meeting for four years, and are not yet betrayed.* I told him, I was afraid, after all, of the white people from the back country, and Virginia, &c. He said that the blacks would collect so numerous from that country, we need not fear the whites from the other parts, for when we have once got the city we can keep them all out. . . .

James Hamilton, Jr., *Negro Plot—An account of the late intended insurrection among a portion of the Blacks of the City of Charleston, South Carolina published by the Authority of the Corporation of Charleston* (Boston, 1822), pp. 35, 36, 42.

## *The Nat Turner Rebellion, 1831*

[*The plantation rebellion that came closest to success was the one led by preacher Nat Turner in August, 1831. It is described here from the point of view of the slave master, and then from the point of view of the slaves.*]

[*A master.*] I have a horrible, a heart-rending tale to relate. . . .

. . . a band of insurgent slaves (some of them believed to be runaways from the neighboring swamps), had turned out on Sunday night last, and murdered several whole families, amounting to 40 or 50 individuals. . . .

The insurrection was represented as one of a most alarming character. . . . Unfortunately a large number of the effective male population was absent at camp meeting in Gates county, some miles off . . . and the panic which they [the slaves] struck at the moment prevented the assembling of a force sufficient to check their career.

As soon as this intelligence was received, our authorities met, and decided on making an immediate application to col. *House*, commanding at Fortress Monroe, who at 6 o'clock this morning embarked on board the steam boat *Hampton*, with three companies and a piece of artillery for Suffolk. These troops were re-inforced in the roads by detachments from the U.S. ships *Warren* and *Natchez*, the whole amounting to nearly 300 men.

. . . the few [slaves] who have thus rushed headlong into the arena, will be shot down like crows or captured and made examples of. The militia are collecting in all the neighboring counties, and the utmost vigilance prevails. . . .

*Niles' Weekly Register*, Vol. 40 (August 27, 1831), pp. 455-456.

Gen. Eppes, who is in command of the troops, reports under date of the 28th ult. [of August] that all the insurgents except Nat Turner, the leader, had either been taken or killed. On the 29th Gen. Broadnax reports to the governor that all was quiet and free from visible marauders; he thinks all have been killed or taken except four or five. He states that Nat, the ringleader, who calls himself general, and pretends to be a Baptist preacher, declares to his comrades that he is commissioned by Jesus Christ, and proceeds under his inspired directions . . . he is not taken, and the account of his being killed at the affair of the bridge is not correct. . . .

*Niles' Weekly Register*, Vol. 41 (September 3, 1831), p. 5.

[*Nat Turner tells how he hid himself and was captured.*] . . . I gave up all hope for the present, and on Thursday night, after having supplied myself with provisions . . . I scratched a hole under a pile of fence rails in a field, where I concealed myself for six weeks, never leaving my hiding place but for a few minutes in the dead of night to get water, which was very near. . . . I know not how long I might have led this life if accident had not betrayed me. A dog in the neighborhood passing by my hiding-place one night while I was out, was attracted by some meat I had in my cave, and crawled in and stole it, and was coming out just as I returned. A few nights after, two Negroes having started to go hunting with the same dog . . . discovered me. . . . On making myself known they fled from me. Knowing then they would betray me, I immediately left my hiding place, and was pursued almost incessantly until I was taken a fortnight afterwards by Mr. Benjamin Phipps, in a little hole I had dug out with my sword . . . under the top of a fallen tree.

T. R. Gray, *The Confession, Trial and Execution of Nat Turner* (Petersburg, Virginia, 1881), pp. 17-18.

[*Charity Bowery, an old slave woman.*] At the time of the old Prophet Nat, the colored folks was afraid to pray loud; for the whites threatened to punish 'em dreadfully, if the least noise was heard. The patrols was low drunken whites, and in Nat's time, if they heard any of the colored folks praying or singing a hymn, they would fall upon 'em and abuse 'em, and sometimes kill 'em afore master or missis could get to 'em. The brightest and best was killed in Nat's time. The whites always suspect such ones. They killed a great many at a place called Duplon. They killed Antonio, a slave of Mr. J. Stanley, whom they shot; then they pointed their guns at him, and told him to confess about the insurrection. He told 'em he didn't know anything about any insurrection. They shot several balls through him, quartered him, and put his head on a pole at the fork of the road leading to the court. It was there but a short time. He had no trial. They never do. In Nat's time, the patrols would tie up the free colored people, flog 'em, and try to make 'em lie against one another, and often killed them before anybody could interfere. Mr. James Cole, High Sheriff, said, if any of the patrols came on his plantation, he would lose his life in defense of his people. . . .

Thomas Wentworth Higginson, "Nat Turner's Insurrection," *Atlantic Monthly*, Vol. 8 (August, 1861), p. 180.

[*Moses Grandy, another slave.*] Formerly slaves were allowed to have religious meetings of their own; but after the insurrection which I spoke of before, they were forbidden to meet even for worship. Often they are flogged if they are found singing or praying at home. They may go to the places of worship used by the whites; but they like their own meetings better. My wife's brother Isaac was a colored preacher. A number of slaves went privately into a wood to hold meetings; when they were found out, they were flogged, and each was forced to tell who else was there. Three were shot, two of whom were killed, and the other was badly wounded. For preaching to them, Isaac was flogged. . . .

Moses Grandy, *Narrative of the Life of Moses Grandy* (Boston, 1844), pp. 35-36.

# "*Slavery Is Ruinous to the Whites . . . .*"

[*After the Nat Turner rebellion of 1831 had been crushed, the future of slavery was debated in the Virginia legislature. One of many delegates who attacked the system was T. Marshall, who pointed out its evil effect on whites.*]

Slavery is ruinous to the whites—retards improvement—roots out industrious population, banishes the yeomanry of the country—deprives the spinner, the weaver, the smith, the shoemaker, the carpenter of employment and support. The evil admits of no remedy—it is increasing, and will continue to increase, until the whole country[side] will be inundated with one black wave, covering its whole extent, with a few white faces here and there floating on the surface. The master has no capital but what is invested in human flesh—the father instead of being richer for his sons, is at a loss how to provide for them; there is no diversity of occupations, no incentive to enterprise. Labor of every species is disreputable because performed mostly by slaves. Our towns are stationary, our villages almost everywhere declining—and the general aspect of the country[side] marks the curse of a wasteful, idle, reckless population who have no interest in the soil, and care not how much it is impoverished. Public improvements are neglected, and the entire continent does not present a region, for which nature has done so much and art so little. . . .

*Niles' Weekly Register*, Vol. 43 (September 8, 1832), p. 23.

# *The Dream of Liberty and Peace*

[*What are the thoughts of a slave as he plans escape? Lewis Clarke, a Kentucky slave in the 1840's, tells the worries and fears that went through his mind when he was about to make a break for freedom. Clarke made good his escape.*]

I had long thought and dreamed of LIBERTY; I was now determined to make an effort to gain it. No tongue can tell the doubt, the perplexities, the anxiety, which a slave feels when making up his mind upon this subject. If he makes an effort and is not successful, he must be laughed at by his fellows, he will be beaten unmercifully by the master, and then watched and used the harder for it all his life.

And then, if he gets away, *who, what*, will he find? He is ignorant of the world. All the white part of mankind that he has ever seen are enemies to him and all his kindred. How can he venture where none but white faces shall greet him? The master tells him that abolitionists *decoy* slaves off into the free states to catch them and sell them to Louisiana or Mississippi; and, if he goes to Canada, the British will put him in a *mine under ground, with both eyes put out, for life*. How does he know what or whom to believe? A horror of great darkness comes upon him, as he thinks over what might befall him. Long, very long time did I think of escaping before I made the effort.

At length the report was started that I was to be sold for Louisiana. Then I thought it was time to act. My mind was made up.

Harriet Beecher Stowe, *The Key to Uncle Tom's Cabin* (Boston, 1854), pp. 21-22.

## *Troubles on the Road to Freedom*

[*After their escape two teen-age slaves, William and Charles Parker, ran into difficulties on the way from Maryland to Pennsylvania.*]

The first place at which we stopped to rest was a village on the old York road, called New Market. There nothing occurred to cause us alarm; so, after taking some refreshments, we proceeded towards York; but when near Logansville, we were interrupted by three white men, one of whom, a very large man, cried—

"Hallo!"

I answered,—"Hallo to you!"

"Which way are you travelling?" he asked.

We replied,—"To Little York."

"Why are you travelling so late?"

"We are not later than you are," I answered.

"Your business must be of consequence," he said.

"It is. We want to go to York to attend to it; and if you have any business, please attend to it, and don't be meddling with ours on the public highway. We have no business with you, and I am sure you have none with us."

"See here!" said he; "you are the fellows that this advertisement calls for," at the same time taking the paper out of his pocket, and reading it to us.

Sure enough, there we were, described exactly. He came closely to us, and said,—"You must go back."

I replied,—"If I must, I must, and you must take me."

"Oh, you need not make any big talk about it," he answered; "for I have taken back many a runaway, and I can take you. What's that you have in your hand?"

"A stick."

He put his hand into his pocket, as if to draw a pistol, and said,—"Come! give up your weapons."

I said again,—" 'Tis only a stick."

He then reached for it, when I stepped back and struck him a heavy blow on the arm. It fell as if broken; I think it was. Then he turned and ran, and I after him. As he ran, he would look back over his shoulder, see me coming, and then run faster, and haloo with all his might. I could not catch him, and it seemed, that, the longer he ran, the faster he went. The other two took to their heels at the first alarm,—thus illustrating the valor of the [Southern] chivalry!

At last I gave up the chase. The whole neighborhood by that time was aroused, and we thought best to retrace our steps to the place whence we started. Then we took a roundabout course until we reached the railroad, along which we travelled. For a long distance there was unusual stir and commotion. Every house was lighted up; and we heard people talking and horses galloping this way and that way, with other evidences of unusual excitement. This was between one and two o'clock in the morning.

William Parker, "The Freedman's Story," I, *Atlantic Monthly*, Vol. 17 (February, 1866), pp. 158-159.

# Henry "Box" Brown Has Himself Shipped *to Freedom*

[*This slave climbed into a box in Richmond, Virginia around the year 1848 and had a white friend nail it up and send him by express to Philadelphia. Here is his story of the trip, written by a white Abolitionist in 1849.*]

. . . I took my place in this narrow prison, with a mind full of uncertainty as to the result. It was a critical period of my life, I can assure you, reader; but if you have never been deprived of your liberty, as I was, you cannot realize the power of that hope of freedom. . . .

I laid me down in my darkened home of three feet by two, and . . . resigned myself to my fate. My friend was to accompany me but he failed to do so; and contented himself with sending a telegraph message to his correspondent in Philadelphia, that such a box was on its way to his care.

I took with me a bladder filled with water to bathe my neck with, in case of too great heat; and with no access to the fresh air, excepting three small . . . holes, I started on my perilous cruise. I was first carried to the express office, the box being placed on its end, so that I started with my head downwards, although the box was directed, "this side up with care." From the express office, I was carried to the depot, and from thence tumbled roughly into the baggage car, where I *happened* to fall "right side up," but no thanks to my transporters. But after a while the cars stopped, and I was put aboard a steamboat, *and placed on my head*. In this dreadful position, I remained the space of an hour and a half, it seemed to me, when I began to feel of my eyes and head, and found to my dismay, that my eyes were almost swollen out of their sockets, and the veins on my temple seemed ready to burst. I made no noise however, determining to obtain "*victory or death*," but endured the terrible pain, as well as I could, sustained under the whole by the thoughts of sweet liberty. About half an hour afterwards, I attempted again to lift my hands to my face, but I found I was not able to move them. A cold sweat now covered me from head to foot. . . . One half hour longer and my sufferings would have ended in that fate, which I preferred to slavery; but I lifted up my heart to God in prayer, believing that he would yet deliver me, when to my joy, I overheard two men say, "We have been here *two* hours and have travelled twenty miles, now let us sit down, and rest ourselves." They . . . turned the box over, containing my soul and body, thus delivering me from the power of the grim messenger of death, who a few moments previously had aimed his fatal shaft at my head, and had placed his icy hands on my throbbing heart. One of these men inquired of the other, what he supposed that box contained, to which his comrade replied, that he guessed it was the mail. "Yes," thought I, "it is a *male*, indeed, although not the *mail* of the United States."

Soon after this fortunate event, we arrived at Washington, where I was thrown from the wagon, and again as my luck would have it, fell on my head. . . . Pretty soon, I heard some one say, "there is no room for this box, it will have to remain behind." I then again applied to the Lord, my help in all my difficulties, and in a few minutes I heard a gentleman direct the hands to place it aboard, as "it came with the mail and must go on with it." I was then tumbled into the car, my head downwards again, as I seemed to be destined to escape on my head. . . . We had not proceeded far, however, before more baggage was placed in the car, at a stopping place, and I was again turned to my proper position. No farther difficulty occurred until my arrival in Philadelphia. I reached this place at three o'clock in the morning, and remained in the depot until six o'clock A.M., at which time, a waggon drove up. . . . I was soon placed on this waggon, and carried to the house of my friend's correspondent, where quite a number of persons were waiting to receive me. They appeared to be some afraid to open the box at first, but at length one of them rapped upon it, and with a trembling voice, asked, "Is all right within?" to which I replied, "All right." The joy of these friends was excessive . . . each one seized hold of some tool, and commenced opening my grave. At length the cover was removed, and I arose, and shook myself . . . and I swooned away.

George Stearns, *Narrative of Henry Box Brown by Himself* (Boston, 1849), pp. 60-62.

## The Contented Slave Who Ran Away

[*James Christian had all that a slave could want—except his freedom. He served the family of President Tyler in the White House, was always treated with kindness and generosity, could get as much spending money as he wanted, and lived well. Yet even this happy slave ran away and was interviewed at the Philadelphia station of the Underground Railroad.*]

"I have always been treated well; if I only have half as good times in the North as I have had in the South, I shall be perfectly satisfied. Any time I desired spending money, five or ten dollars were no object." . . . with regard to food also, he had fared as well as heart could wish, with abundance of leisure time at his command. His deportment was certainly very refined and gentlemanly. . . . He had been to William and Mary's College in his younger days, to wait on young master James B. C. where, through the kindness of some of the students, he had picked up a trifling amount of book learning. . . . On the death of the old Major [Christian, his owner] James fell into the hands of his son, Judge Christian. . . . Subsequently he fell into the hands of one of the Judge's sisters, Mrs. John Tyler (wife of ex-President Tyler), and then he became a member of the President's domestic household, was at the White House, under the President, from 1841 to 1845. . . .

"How did you like Mr. Tyler?" said an inquisitive member of the Vigilance Committee. "I didn't like Mr. Tyler much," was the reply. "Why?" again inquired the member of the Committee. "Because Mr. Tyler was a poor man. I never did like poor people. I didn't like his marrying into our family, who were considered very far Tyler's superiors." "On the plantation," he said, "Tyler was a very cross man, and treated the servants very cruelly; but the house servants were treated much better, owing to their having belonged to his wife, who protected them from persecution, as they had been favorite servants in her father's family." James estimated that "Tyler got about thirty-five thousand dollars and twenty-nine slaves, young and old, by his wife."

What prompted James to leave such pleasant quarters? It was this: He had become enamored of a young and respectable free girl in Richmond, with whom he could not be united in marriage solely because he was a slave. . . . So . . . the resolution came home to him very forcibly to make tracks for Canada.

---

William Still, *The Underground Rail Road* (Philadelphia, 1872) pp. 69-70.

## Varieties of Slave Resistance

[*A Virginia farmer describes some of the ways in which slaves fought against their masters.*]

The slave, if he is indisposed to work, and especially if he is not treated well, or does not like the master who has hired him, will sham sickness—even make himself sick or lame—that he need not work. But a more serious loss frequently arises, when the slave, thinking he is worked too hard, or being angered by punishment or unkind treatment, "getting the sulks," takes to "the swamp," and comes back when he has a mind to. . . .

"But, meanwhile, how does the Negro support life in the swamp?" I asked.

"Oh, he gets sheep and pigs and calves, and fowls and turkeys; sometimes they will kill a small cow. We have often seen the fires, where they were cooking them, through the woods, in the swamp yonder. If it is cold, he will crawl under a fodder-stack, or go into the cabins with some of the other Negroes, and in the same way, you see, he can get all the corn, or almost anything else he wants."

"He steals them from his master?"

"From anyone; frequently from me. I have had many a sheep taken by them."

"It is a common thing, then?"

"Certainly, it is, very common, and the loss is sometimes exceedingly provoking. One of my neighbors here was going to build, and hired two mechanics for a year. Just as he was ready to put his house up, the two men, taking offense at something, both ran away, and did not come back at all, till their year was out, and then their owner immediately hired them out again to another man."

These Negroes "in the swamp," he said, were often hunted after, but it was very difficult to find them, and, if caught, they would run again, and the other Negroes would hide and assist them. Dogs to track them he had never known to be used in Virginia.

Frederick Law Olmsted, *A Journey in the Seaboard Slave States* (New York, 1856), pp. 100-101.

# "I Do as I Am Bid"

[*John Capehart provided a special service for slaveholders. In his testimony before a court, he explains his job.*]

Q. Mr. Capehart, is it a part of your duty, as a policeman, to take up colored persons who are out after hours in the streets?

A. Yes, sir.

Q. What is done with them?

A. We put them in the lock-up, and in the morning they are brought into Court and ordered to be punished—those that are to be punished.

Q. What punishment do they get?

A. Not exceeding thirty-nine lashes.

Q. Who gives them these lashes?

A. Any of the Officers. I do, sometimes.

Q. Are you paid *extra* for this? How much?

A. Fifty cents a head. It used to be sixty-two cents. Now, it is only fifty. Fifty cents for each one we arrest, and fifty more for each one we flog.

Q. Are these persons you flog Men and Boys only, or are they Women and Girls also?

A. Men, Women, Boys, and Girls, just as it happens . . .

Q. Is your flogging confined to these cases? Do you not flog Slaves at the request of their Masters?

A. Sometimes I do. Certainly, when I am called upon.

Q. In these cases of private flogging, are the Negroes sent to you? Have you a place for flogging?

A. No; I go round, as I am sent for.

*Q.* Is this part of your duty as an Officer?

*A.* No, sir.

*Q.* In these cases of private flogging, do you inquire into the circumstances to see what the fault has been, or if there is any?

*A.* That's none of my business. I do as I am bid. The Master is responsible.

---

Geo. W. Carleton, *The Suppressed Book About Slavery* (New York, 1864), pp. 193-195.

# Dr. Cartwright Describes "Negro Diseases"

[*Dr. Samuel Cartwright of the University of Louisiana was a highly respected medical man whose articles were widely published by Southern journals.* De Bow's Review *printed this account of two diseases the doctor had discovered among the slaves.*]

### DRAPETOMANIA, OR THE DISEASE
### CAUSING NEGROES TO RUN AWAY

DRAPETOMANIA is from [a Greek word meaning] a runaway slave, and [another Greek word meaning] *mad or crazy.* It is unknown to our medical authorities, although its diagnostic symptom, the absconding from service, is well known to our planters and overseers. . . . The cause in most of the cases, that induces the Negro to run away from service, is as much a disease of the mind as any other species of mental alienation, and much more curable as a general rule. With the advantages of proper medical advice, strictly followed, this troublesome practice that many Negroes have of running away, can be almost entirely prevented, although the slaves be located on the borders of a free state, within a stone's throw of the abolitionists. . . .

Before Negroes run away, unless they are frightened or panic-struck, they become sulky and dissatisfied. The cause of this sulkiness and dissatisfaction should be inquired into and removed, or they are apt to run away or fall into Negro consumption. When sulky and dissatisfied with cause, the experience of those [overseers and owners] on the line and elsewhere, was decidedly in favor of whipping them out of it, as a preventive measure against absconding, or other bad conduct. It was called whipping the devil out of them.

DYSAETHESIA AETHIOPICA, OR HEBETUDE
OF THE MIND AND OBTUSE SENSIBILITY
OF BODY—A DISEASE PECULIAR TO NEGROES—
CALLED BY OVERSEERS, "RASCALITY"

From the careless movements of the individuals affected with the complaint, they are apt to do much mischief, which appears as if intentional, but is mostly owing to the stupidity of mind and insensibility of nerves induced by the disease. Thus, they break, waste, and destroy everything they handle,—abuse horses and cattle,—tear, burn, or rend their own clothing, and, paying no attention to the rights of property, steal others, to replace what they have destroyed. . . . They slight their work,—cut up corn, cane, cotton, or tobacco when hoeing it, as if for pure mischief. They raise disturbances with their overseers and fellow-servants, and seem insensible to pain when subjected to punishment. . . .

Dr. Cartwright of New Orleans, "1. Diseases and Peculiarities of the Negro Race," *De Bow's Review*, Vol. 11 (September, 1851), pp. 331-334.

## A Sermon for Slaves

[*When slaves were allowed or encouraged to attend religious services, these were conducted by white ministers who always included sermons on loyalty to owners and overseers. Bishop Meade of Virginia wrote this sermon for slaves.*]

. . . Having thus shown you the chief duties you owe to your great Master in heaven, I now come to lay before you the duties you owe to your masters and mistresses here upon earth. And for this you have one general rule, that you ought always to carry in your minds; and that is to do all service for them as if you did it for God himself.

Poor creatures! you little consider, when you are idle and neglectful of your masters' business, when you steal, and waste, and hurt any of their substance, when you are saucy and impudent, when you are telling them lies and deceiving them, or when you prove stubborn and sullen, and will not do the work you are set about without stripes and vexation—you do not consider, I say, that what faults you are guilty of towards your masters and mistresses are faults done against God himself, who hath set your masters and mistresses over you in his own stead, and expects that you would do for them just as you would do for him. And pray do not think that I want to deceive you when I tell you that your masters and mistresses are God's overseers, and that, if you are faulty towards them, God himself will punish you severely for it in the next world. . . .

Frederick Law Olmsted, *A Journey in the Seaboard Slave States* (New York, 1856), p. 119.

## Stealing an Education

[*In many parts of the South it was unlawful to teach a Negro to read or write. Violation of these laws sometimes was punishable by death. These are the ways in which Susie King Taylor and a boy named Frederick Douglass learned to read. Susie King Taylor, who later served as a nurse and teacher in the first Negro regiment in the Civil War, obtained her education in Savannah, Georgia; Frederick Douglass got his in Baltimore, Maryland. This is Mrs. Taylor's story.*]

I was born under the slave law in Georgia, in 1848, and was brought up by my grandmother in Savannah. There was three of us with her, my younger sister and brother. My brother and I being the two eldest, we were sent to a friend of my grandmother, Mrs. Woodhouse, a widow, to learn to read and write. She was a free woman and lived on Bay Lane, between Habersham and Price streets, about half a mile from my house. We went every day about nine o'clock, with our books wrapped in paper to prevent the police or white persons from seeing them. We went in, one at a time, through the gate, into the yard to the kitchen, which was the schoolroom. She had twenty five or thirty children whom she taught, assisted by her daughter, Mary Jane. The neighbors would see us going in sometimes, but they supposed we were there learning trades, as it was the custom to give children a trade of some kind. After school we left the same way we entered, one by one, when we would go to a square, about a block from the school and wait for each other.

Susie King Taylor, *Reminiscences of My Life in Camp* (Boston, 1902) p. 5.

[*Frederick Douglass had begun to learn his ABC's from his master's wife. Her husband, discovering what was going on, warned her that it was illegal and that, furthermore, the education of the small boy "would forever unfit him for the duties of a slave."*]

From this time I was most narrowly watched. If I was in a separate room any considerable length of time, I was sure to be suspected of having a book, and was at once called to give an account of myself. . . . The plan which I adopted, and the one by which I was most successful, was that of making friends of all the little white boys whom I met in the street. As many of these as I could, I converted into teachers. With their kindly aid, obtained at different times and in different places, I finally succeeded in learning to read. When I was sent on errands, I always took my book with me, and by going one part of my errand quickly, I found time to get a lesson before my return. I used also to carry bread with me, enough of which was always in the house, and to which I was always welcome; for I was much better off in this regard than many of the poor white children in our neighborhood. This bread I used to bestow upon the hungry little urchins, who, in return, would give me that more valuable bread of knowledge. I am strongly tempted to give the names of two or three of those little boys, as a testimonial of the gratitude and affection I bear them; but prudence forbids;—not that it would injure me, but it might embarrass them; for it is almost an unpardonable offense to teach slaves to read in this Christian country. It is enough to say of the dear little fellows, that they lived on Philpot Street, very near Durgin and Bailey's ship-yard. . . .

---

Frederick Douglass, *Narrative of the Life of Frederick Douglass* (Boston, 1845), p. 38.

# 6

# *Industrial and Cultural Growth in the Free North*

AS the South turned to cotton and slaves, the North entered into a period of industrial, commercial, and cultural growth. This growth, however, was fed by profits made by trading in cotton and slaves. Colonial New England's largest industry had been the distilling of the rum used to purchase slaves in Africa. New England merchants built factories and centers of learning with the fortunes they made in the slave trade. In Rhode Island the Brown brothers founded a university with their profits and Abraham Redwood endowed a library. But Northern factories also produced the whips and chains used by Southern slaveholders to control their restless slave population. Daniel Webster of Massachusetts said, "I hear the sound of the hammer, I see the smoke of the furnaces where manacles and fetters are forged for human hands." He was standing in Boston when he spoke.

## The North Chooses Free Labor

The North had liberated its slaves soon after the Revolution. Some men argued that slavery was wrong in a country that called itself "the land of the free" and others were impressed with the courageous role played by Negro soldiers and sailors both in the Revolution and in the War of 1812.

There was a strong economic reason for the North's abolition of slavery, however, that had nothing to do with sentiment: It did not pay. To use slaves on farms where there was little work for them during the long Northern winters was a waste of the money it cost to clothe and feed them. While a free laborer could be "laid off" when there was no work, a slave had to be cared for every day of the year. And white mechanics refused to compete with slaves. Vice-President John Adams wrote in 1795 that if Northern employers "had been permitted to hold slaves, the common white people would have put the slaves to death, and their masters too, perhaps."

Each Northern state liberated its slaves but refused them equality with whites. Gerritt Smith, a New York abolitionist, in the 1840's, said:

> Even the noblest black is denied that which is free to the vilest white. The omnibus, the car, the ballot-box, the jury box, the halls of legislation, the army, the public lands, the school, the church, the lecture room, the social circle, the table, are all either absolutely or virtually denied to him.

In 1819, in a New York Negro school, a teenager asked his graduating class these questions:

> What are my prospects? To what shall I turn my hand? Shall I be a mechanic? No one will employ me; white boys won't work with me. Shall I be a merchant? No one will have me in his office. Can you be surprised at my discouragement?

This student may have known that the TB rate was twice as high for Negroes as whites and that those families moving into white neighborhoods became targets of arsonists and mobs.

Even the wealthy Negro suffered because of Northern prejudice.\* Charlotte Forten's father could afford to send her to a private

*A passenger is asked to leave a Philadelphia railway car in 1856 and sit in the car set aside for Negroes. Through individual and group action segregated traveling facilities were eliminated from some Northern towns and states before the end of the Civil War.*

---

\* It is interesting to contrast the prejudice in the Northern states with the attitude of the Canadian government during the same period of time. In 1829, a delegation of Cincinnati Negroes, seeking refuge after being driven from the town by whites, interviewed Sir James Colebrook, Governor of Upper Canada. His answer to their plea included the following: "Tell the republicans on your side of the line, that we royalists do not know men by their color. Should you come to us you will be entitled to all the privileges of the rest of His Majesty's subjects." A sizable number of Negroes did migrate to Canada at this time, and formed the settlement of Wilburforce.

school near Boston. In school the teenager found the white girls friendly, but outside "they feared to recognize me." In 1854 she confided to her diary that:

> It is hard to go through life meeting contempt with contempt, hatred with hatred, fearing with too good reason, to love and trust hardly any one whose skin is white—however lovable, attractive, and congenial. . . . In the bitter, passionate feelings of my soul again and again there rise the questions "When, oh! when shall this cease?" "Is there no help?" . . . Let us take courage; never ceasing to work—hoping and believing that, if not for us, for another generation there is a better, brighter day in store. . . .

This sensitive young lady would later find her brighter day in the teaching of ex-slaves in South Carolina during the Civil War and in her long marriage to Francis J. Grimké, the noted Negro minister who was one of the founders of the NAACP.

Although all immigrant groups who came to America faced discrimination at first, they were eventually able to enjoy better jobs, finer homes, and the friendship of their neighbors. The Negro was forced to remain, permanently, on the bottom rung of the social ladder.

*New York mobs destroy a Negro Orphan Home in 1863. Anti-Negro rioting rocked many Northern cities before, during, and after the Civil War.*

Although most Negroes were poor, many had risen far from the point from which they had started. Of 2,600 Negroes in Cincinnati in 1835, 1,129 had been slaves and 476 of these had purchased their own freedom, paying a total of $215,522.04. More than a few of these had homes and businesses. One, Godfrey Brown of Greene County, paid $2,350 for himself and family, owned 550 acres and, in addition, was a shoemaker.

Even the great reform movements that swept the nation during Jackson's Presidency did nothing for the Negro. Presidents Jackson and Van Buren both opposed voting rights for free Negroes. And as states extended the right to vote to all white adult males without regard to property, several states took away the right to vote from property-owning Negroes who had voted before!

In 1841 Frederick Douglass and other abolitionists campaigned effectively in Rhode Island against a reform Constitution that would have barred Negroes from voting. In those states where Negroes could still vote, they supported Federalist or Whig candidates rather than Jacksonians. Between 1807 and 1837, as cotton fastened slavery on the South, five Northern states cut down Negro voting rights.

In spite of all these restrictions, the Liberty Party in 1855 elected John Mercer Langston to a town council post in Brownheim, Ohio. Langston, a brilliant and eloquent lawyer, became the first Negro elected to office in the United States. After the Civil War, he served as head of Howard University's Law School, as United States Minister to Haiti for eight years, and then as Virginia's only Negro Congressman.

*John M. Langston, first Negro elected to public office, served in the Brownheim, Ohio council in 1855. It was the beginning of a career in public service that later led to a diplomatic post in Haiti and a place in the United States Congress.*

## The North Becomes a Business Center

At the time when many of the rich merchants of the North were piling up wealth in the African slave trade, Paul Cuffe was a notable exception. Cuffe was born in 1759 and became a sailor aboard a whaling ship at 16. In a few years he was building his own ships. A tall, muscular, and serious young man, Cuffe and other Negro taxpayers of Massachusetts protested in 1780 to the Revolutionary government against "taxation without representation." Three years later a Massachusetts court ruled that Negroes did have the right to vote if they paid taxes.

By 1806 Cuffe's wealth included large parcels of New England land and many vessels. He often sailed as captain on his own

*In 1780 Paul Cuffe and eight other Massachusetts Negroes protested to their state government against taxation without representation. They noted Negroes "have cheerfully entered the field of Battle in Defence of the Common Cause," American independence from England.*

ships and hired Negro sailors. Cuffe established cultural relations with Africa, taught navigation in Sierra Leone, and brought African products to Europe and America. Twice Cuffe used his own funds and ships to carry Negro settlers to Africa. "I furnished them provisions . . . without fee or reward—my hope is in a coming day," he wrote in his diary. When Cuffe died in 1817, he was a respected member of his New Bedford community.

New England's ship building and fishing industries were able to make important strides because of the work of Negro inventors. Robert Lewis of Maine and Lewis Temple of Massachusetts invented devices that were used by the fishing fleets. In 1848 Temple, a New Bedford blacksmith, invented a toggle-harpoon that has been called the most important invention in the history of whaling. It resulted in the capture of a greater proportion of the whales harpooned than had been possible before and became the standard harpoon used in the industry.

James Forten of Philadelphia invented a device that aided in the control of sails. This veteran of the United States Navy, who had served in the Revolution, became wealthy and built a sail factory employing fifty Negro and white workers. Forten used the money his invention earned to further the abolitionist cause. He contributed a considerable sum to William Lloyd Garrison's *Liberator* during the first crucial years of its publication and was an important influence on the white editor. Forten became President of Philadelphia's Moral Reform Society, won a citation for saving a number of people from drowning, and helped recruit 2,500 Negroes to defend his city during the War of 1812.

*William Lloyd Garrison began his* Liberator *with funds supplied by Negroes. For years three-fourths of his readers were Negroes and they considered him one of them.*

A surprising number of Negroes—almost half of the total number of seamen aboard ships—played an important part in America's maritime industry. William Gross, who joined the United States Navy at 17, sailed with Commodore Perry to Japan to conclude America's first treaty with that nation. Three thousand others served in the whaling fleet, 6,000 in the Merchant Marine, and another 5,000 in river navigation within the nation's borders. At sea the Negro could proudly enjoy an equality he was denied on land. Several Southern ports saw the free Negro seamen as a great danger to their slave system and insisted on keeping them in jail until their ships were ready to set sail.

Long before the Civil War, several Negroes were owners of growing Northern businesses. Thomas L. Jennings, a New York tailor, invented a process for cleaning clothes, patented it, and made a fortune. One of his sons became a New Orleans dentist and another a successful Boston businessman. Jennings, like Forten, used his money to finance antislavery groups.

John Jones came to Chicago from North Carolina as a young man with only $3.50 in his pocket. He made a great deal of money in the tailoring business and used it to finance both the underground railroad and the fight against discrimination in his state. His efforts helped repeal Illinois' "Black Laws" that denied legal equality to his people in that state until 1865. Later he also secured the passage of a law that opened the Cook County (Chicago) schools to Negroes. After the Civil War he was twice elected Cook County Commissioner.

## Development of an Intellectual Class

William Whipper, who ran a successful lumber yard in Columbia, Pennsylvania, was a leading member of a Negro intellectual class that had begun to develop long before the Civil War. He used his own funds and money which he collected from local whites to help fugitive slaves on their way to Canada. For each of more than a dozen years, he spent one thousand dollars on this dangerous work, then contributed another five thousand dollars to the Union cause during the Civil War. In 1870 he wrote: "I would prefer to be penniless in the streets, rather than have withheld a single hour's labor or a dollar from the sacred cause of liberty, justice, and humanity."

Whipper was also vitally interested in the elevation of the North's free Negro population and spoke before several of the Negro "Reading Societies" which were springing up in Northern cities. In 1837 he delivered "An Address on Non-violent Resistance to Offensive Aggression," speaking in favor of the theory of nonviolent resistance to evil. This was a dozen years before Henry David Thoreau wrote his famous essay on civil disobedience and a hundred years before Mahatma Gandhi in India and Martin Luther King in America made this theory world-famous. Whipper claimed, much as Gandhi and King did, that nonviolence "is not only consistent with reason, but the surest method of obtaining a speedy triumph of the principles of universal peace."

*William Whipper, an early advocate of passive resistance to unjust laws.*

Whipper was only one of many Negro intellectuals who achieved fame in their own time, despite all odds. While few colleges admitted Negroes before 1860, 28 had graduated by that date and many others were on the way.

William Wells Brown was a runaway slave who taught himself to read and write. Brown helped rescue other runaways from slave catchers and saw them transported to safety in Canada aboard Great Lakes boats. Brown was one of the best-known abolitionist speakers in this country and Europe. "My religion," he said, "was to help do away with the curse of American slavery."

Despite his sufferings under slavery he never lost his sense of humor. Once, when telling what it meant to try to give a speech to a crowd that included 27 "babies in their mothers' arms," he wrote: "But they give us rice pudding out here for breakfast, and that gives me strength to meet the babies." Brown was America's first Negro novelist (1853) and playwright (1858) and later wrote three travel books and several short histories of his people.

*William Wells Brown, writer.*

Martin R. Delany was born free in Charles Town, Virginia in 1812. At 10 his parents brought him to the free soil of Pennsylvania so that he could go to school there. Delany studied medicine and law at Harvard. A tough little battler for Negro rights all his life, he was intensely proud of his color. Delany was recognized here and abroad as a geographer, anthropologist, and author. In his history of Amer-

*Martin R. Delany, a brilliant and fiery spokesman for Negro rights. A Harvard graduate, doctor, editor, world traveler, African explorer, and scientist, he became a major in the Union Army during the Civil War.*

ican Negroes, written in 1852, he concluded with this advice to his fellow colored men: "We must make an *Issue*, Create an *Event* and *Establish* a *National Position* for *Ourselves* . . . [do] some fearless, bold, and adventurous deeds of daring—contending against every [sic] odds—regardless of every consequence."

During the Civil War Delany visited President Lincoln at the White House to propose a special army unit staffed with Negro officers as well as soldiers. The President had "this most extraordinary and intelligent black man" (as he wrote to Secretary of War Stanton) appointed the first Negro field officer in the country's history. His rank was Major. After the Civil War Delany was a judge in Charleston, South Carolina and, in 1874, was nominated for lieutenant-governor of the state but was defeated.

Dr. John Rock of Boston had been a teacher, dentist, and doctor before he became a lawyer and Massachusetts judge. A dignified and eloquent orator, Rock could also read and write in three languages. He firmly believed that Negroes should be reformers. In a speech to Negroes, he said: "This being our country, we have made up our minds to remain in it, and to try to make it worth living in." In his speeches he tried to make other Americans aware of the plight of the educated Negro who "has no field for his talent" because of discrimination. In 1865 the Supreme Court of the United States accepted John Rock as the first Negro lawyer qualified to present cases before it.

Dr. James McCune Smith, a respected New York physician, used his vast knowledge of science and history in an attempt to destroy the myth that Negroes were physically or mentally suited to slavery. On two occasions he challenged the leading spokesman for slavery, John C. Calhoun. Calhoun had used the 1840 census statistics to prove that Negroes in the free states were more inclined to madness than Southern slaves. Dr. Smith was among those who found some important errors in the census figures. He found, for example, that the census listed 19 insane Negroes in six Maine towns where only one Negro lived and reported this in *The Liberator*. "To make 19 crazy men out of one man, is pretty fair calculation, . . ." he laughed. Then he became serious: "Freedom has not made us mad; it has strengthened our minds by throwing us upon our own resources, and has bound us to American institutions with a tenacity which nothing but death can overcome." Dr. Smith, on another occasion, demolished another Calhoun statement, that slaves lived longer than free Negroes, illustrating that the opposite was true.

Dr. Smith was also concerned that Negroes themselves play a leading part in the fight for justice. In 1855 he told a Negro convention in New York:

> The time is come when our people must assume the rank of a first-rate power in the battle against caste and Slavery; it is emphatically our battle; no one else can fight it for us, and with God's help we must fight it ourselves.

Smith practiced what he preached, leading the fight for civil rights in New York until his death in 1865.

One of the most outstanding contributions to world culture in the mid-nineteenth century was made by the actor Ira Aldridge, the son of a New York minister. To avoid riots by whites who resented serious theater performed by Negroes, Aldridge and the other New York actors of the "African Company" used comedy skits between the acts of their productions of Shakespeare. Aldridge went to Europe to study under the well-known English actor, Edmund Kean, and in 1833 both men opened at London's famous Covent Garden Theatre in *Othello*. Aldridge played the title role and his teacher played the role of the evil Iago.

*Surgeon A. T. Augusta of the Union Army challenged Washington, D. C. streetcar segregation during the Civil War.*

*Ira Aldridge, actor.*

*In 1833 Prudence Crandall, a Quaker school principal, opened her exclusive Connecticut girl's school to Negroes. The townspeople refused to sell her merchandise, jailed her, and finally set fire to the school and forced its closing.*

Aldridge not only achieved worldwide fame as Othello, the Moor, but played white parts as well, using white makeup. His acting was acclaimed from Ireland to Russia and he received medals from the kings of Prussia and Austria. A French drama critic who saw Aldridge perform in Russia wrote: "I have never seen an artist identify himself so perfectly with the character he represents. . . . Everybody, men and women, wept."

But Americans had no chance to see this famous actor. Because of public prejudice against a Negro actor appearing with a white cast, Aldridge had been forced to cancel an appearance in Baltimore. In 1867, with slavery abolished, the Negro actor planned to return to his native land and tour with his own Shakespearean company. Unfortunately for Americans, he died before he could complete the plans for his return.

James W. C. Pennington was an illiterate slave blacksmith who escaped to the North and educated himself. He mastered reading and writing in Greek, Latin, and German and wrote the first Negro history in 1841. Less than ten years after his escape from bondage, his ability as a preacher and lecturer won him a Doctor of Divinity degree from Heidelberg University. He returned to Brooklyn, New York to lead civil rights demonstrations there.

The Negro's long fight for equality in the North won public attention and some significant victories before the Civil War had ended. Court battles as well as "sit-ins" and "freedom rides" were part of the drive mounted by Negro leaders in the Northern states. From New England to California Negroes struggled for equality through petition campaigns, protest conventions, and legal actions. The earliest lawsuit to desegregate the public schools took place in Massachusetts in 1849 on behalf of six-year-old Sarah Roberts who had to walk past five white schools to reach her inferior colored school. Although the little girl's case was lost, victory came in 1855 with the desegregation of Boston's schools.

There were Negroes who used passive resistance and others who fought back with fury against those who tried to oppress them. But no matter which way they resisted unjust laws, many of the North's Negroes believed with their great leader, Frederick Douglass, that "if there is no struggle, there is no progress."

# Paul Cuffe, Merchant and Philanthropist

*[Paul Cuffe climbed high on America's ladder of success. He was one of ten children born to an ex-slave who died when Paul was fourteen. Though he never attended a day of school, Cuffe became a businessman by the time he was twenty-one. His great interest in Africa led to many interesting projects: He learned navigation in two weeks so that he could captain his* Traveller *to Africa with thirty-eight Negro settlers; he taught in Africa and brought its products to America, England, Russia, and the West Indies. Cuffe's letters and* Journal *have been preserved—providing a vivid look at this remarkable American. In an 1808 letter he explained his interest in Africa.]*

I have for some years had it impressed on my mind to make a voyage to Sierra Leon in order to inspect the situation of the country, and feeling a real desire that the inhabitants of Africa might become an enlightened people and be so favored as to give general satisfaction to all those who are endeavoring to establish them in the true light of Christianity. And as I am of the African race I feel myself interested for them and if I am favored with a talent I think I am willing that they should be benefited thereby.

---

Letter of June 6, 1808, in Paul Cuffe Papers (New Bedford Library).

*[After his 1811 trip to Africa Cuffe returned to America. Even this wealthy and respected American encountered prejudice when he traveled by public transportation from Washington to Baltimore. He recorded this 1812 incident in his* Journal.]*

Embarked this morning at 5 o'clock [from Washington]. . . . Arrived in Baltimore at 3 in the afternoon. When I took my seat, being the first in I took the after seat. When the passengers came,—in came a blustering powder headed man with stern countenance. [He said,] "Come away from that seat."

I . . . sat still. He then bustled along and said "I want to put my umbrella in the box." I arose. He then put his umbrella in. He then said "You must go out of this for there is a lady coming in." I entered into no discourse with him, but took my seat; he took his beside me but showed much evil contempt. At length the women and a girl made their appearance. I then arose and invited the women into the after seat saying "We always give way to accommodate the women." We set forward on our journey. On our way at the tavern I was overtaken by Wm Hunter member of Congress. He was very free and conversant, which this man above mentioned observed. Before we got to Baltimore, he became loving and openly accosted me "Captain take the after seat," but from the common custom I thanked him and wished him to keep his seat.

I believe if I am favored to keep my place, my enemies will become friendly. I note this for encouragement and memory.

When I arrived in Baltimore they utterly refused to take me in at the tavern or to get me a dinner unless I would go back among the servants. This I refused, not as I thought myself better than the servants, but from the nature of the case. I found my way to a tavern where I got my dinner.

---

Paul Cuffe, *Journal*, copy of entry for May 5, 1812, in Paul Cuffe Papers (New Bedford Library).

## *James Forten to Paul Cuffe: The Colonization Question*

[*In 1817 few Americans of any race were as wealthy as James Forten. After briefly attending a Quaker school, Forten became an apprentice to a sailmaker. At twenty Forten was promoted to foreman. His invention of a sailing device soon after that made him a "millionaire"—actually he made about $100,000. But his great goal was the salvation of his people and he soon became a leader in Philadelphia's Negro community. He came to the conclusion that Negroes would be better off in Africa—or any place but America—and corresponded with wealthy Paul Cuffe about his efforts to bring Negroes to Africa. But during a large meeting in January, Forten discovered that the city's poor Negroes rejected the very idea of going to Africa.*]

Esteemed friend . . .

The African Institution met at the Rev. R. Allens the very night your letter came to hand. I red that part to them that wished them a happy New Year, for which they desired me to return you many thanks. I must now mention to you that the whole continent seems to be agitated concerning Colonising the People of Colour. . . . Indeed the People of Colour, here was very much fritened at first. They were afrade that all the free people would be Compelled to go, particularly in the southern States. We had a large meeting of Males at the Rev. R. Allens Church the other evening Three thousand at least attended, and there was not one sole that was in favour of going to Africa. They think that the slave holders want to get rid of them so as to make their property more secure. However it appears to me that if the Father of all mercies, is in this interesting subject . . . the way will be made strate and clear. We however have agreed to remain silent, as the people here both the white & colour are decided against the measure. My opinion is that they will never become a people until they com out from amongst the white people, but as the majority is decidedly against me I am determined to remain silent, except as to my opinion which I freely give when asked. . . .

I remain very affectionately<br>
Yours unalterably,<br>
James Forten

[*In less than a year Forten altered his views, perhaps as a result of this unanimous opposition to colonization. He became a leading force in the abolitionist movement that demanded slaves be quickly freed and given their rights as Americans. Forten is credited with convincing William Lloyd Garrison that Negro colonization in Africa did nothing for the Negro but remove him from his homeland.*]

---

James Forten, Letter of January 25, 1817, in Paul Cuffe Papers (New Bedford Library).

# A Plea to Abolish Slavery in the North

[*Shortly after the Revolution, the Northern states began to put an end to slavery. At New York's Constitutional Convention of 1821, delegate Clarke argued that the bravery of Negro soldiers in the Revolution and in the War of 1812 entitled them to freedom.*]

In the War of the Revolution, these people helped to fight your battles by land and by sea. Some of your States were glad to turn out corps of colored men, and stand "shoulder to shoulder" with them.

In your late war [of 1812], they contributed largely towards some of your most splendid victories. On Lakes Erie and Champlain, where your fleets triumphed over a foe superior in numbers and engines of death, they were manned, in a large proportion, with men of color. And, in this very House, in the fall of 1814, a bill passed, receiving the approbation of all the branches of your government, authorizing the Governor to accept the services of a corps of two thousand free people of color. Sir, these were times which tried men's souls. In these times, it was no sporting matter to bear arms. . . . They were not compelled to go; they were not drafted. No; your pride had placed them beyond your compulsory power. But there was no necessity for its exercise; they were volunteers; yes, Sir, volunteers to defend that very country from the inroads and ravages of a ruthless foe, which had treated them with insult, degradation, and slavery.

Wm. C. Nell, *The Colored Patriots of the American Revolution* (Boston, 1855), pp. 148-149.

## American Voices from Africa, 1827

[*With the aid of the American Colonization Society and the federal government, a number of Negroes returned to Africa during the early years of the 19th century. The Liberian colony of Monrovia addressed this message to American Negroes on August 27, 1827.*]

The first consideration which caused our voluntary removal to this country, and the object, which we still regard with the deepest concern, is liberty—liberty, in the sober, simple, but complete sense of the word: not a licentious liberty, nor a liberty without government . . . —but that liberty of speech, action, and conscience, which distinguishes the free enfranchised citizens of a free State. We did not enjoy that freedom in our native country. . . . Our constitution secures to us, so far as our condition allows, "all the rights and privileges enjoyed by the citizens of the United States;" and these rights and privileges are ours. We are proprietors of the soil we live on, and possess the rights of freeholders. Our suffrages, and, what is of more importance, our sentiments and our opinions have their due weight in the government we live under. Our laws are altogether our own: they grow out of our circumstances; are framed for our exclusive benefit; and administered either by officers of our own appointment, or such as possess our confidence. We have a judiciary, chosen from among ourselves; we serve as jurors in the trial of others; and are liable to be tried only by juries of our fellow-citizens, ourselves. We have all that is meant by *Liberty of Conscience*. . . .

Forming a community of our own, in the land of our forefathers; having the commerce, and soil, and resources, of the country at our disposal; we know nothing of that debasing inferiority with which our very colour stamped us in America: there is nothing here to create the feeling on our part—nothing to cherish the feeling of superiority in the minds of foreigners who visit us. . . . The burden is gone from our shoulders: we now breathe and move freely; and know not . . . the empty name of liberty, which you endeavour to content yourselves with, in a country that is not yours. . . .

Archibald Alexander, *A History of Colonization of the Western Coast of Africa* (Philadelphia, 1846), pp. 288-289.

## *Ira Aldridge, World-Famous Actor*

[*Ira Aldridge learned to act while he was a student in New York City's African Free School. In Europe he achieved stardom for his roles in Shakespearean dramas. This is how his performances were received by European critics.*]

[London Weekly Times] Mr. Aldridge is an African of Mulatto tint, with wooly hair. His features are capable of much expression, his action is unrestrained and picturesque, and his voice clear, full, resonant. His powers of energetic declamation are very marked, and the whole of his acting appears impulsed by a current of feeling of no inconsiderable weight and vigor, yet controlled and guided in a manner that clearly shows the actor to be a person of much study and a great stage experience.

H. G. Adams, *God's Image in Ebony* (London, 1854), p. 158.

[*The St. Petersburg correspondent for* Le Nord] . . . The success of the Negro actor, Ira Aldridge has been wonderful. At his *debut*, people were curious to see an Othello who needed [nothing] . . . to blacken his face. . . . From his appearance on the stage the

African artist completely captivated his audience by his harmonious and resonant voice, and by a style full of simplicity, nature, and dignity.

[*Russian reporter for the* New York Herald] . . . An American Negro, named Ira Aldridge, has been performing at the Imperial Theater in several of Shakespear's pieces, and has met with great applause. His principal character, of course, is Othello, and he portrays the jealous African with . . . truth and energy. . . .

The Anglo-African Magazine, Vol. 1 (February, 1859), p. 63.

## Interview with a Young Sculptress

[*Edmonia Lewis was the first Negro to achieve fame in the field of sculpture. She attended Oberlin College and was trained in the studio of Edmund Brackett of Boston. Writer Lydia Maria Child interviewed her at an antislavery meeting during the Civil War and wrote this description of the talk.*]

One of the most interesting individuals I met at the reception was Edmonia Lewis, a colored girl about twenty years of age, who is devoting herself to sculpture. . . . I told her I judged by her complexion that there might be some of what was called white blood in her veins. She replied, "No; I have not a single drop of what is called white blood in my veins. My father was a full-blooded Negro, and my mother was a full-blooded Chippewa." . . .

"And have you lived with the Chippewas?"

"Yes. When my mother was dying, she wanted me to promise that I would live three years with her people, and I did."

"And what did you do while you were there?"

"I did as my mother's people did. I made baskets and embroidered moccasons and I went into the cities with my mother's people, to sell them." . . .

"But, surely," said I, "you have had some other education than that you received among your mother's people, for your language indicates it."

"I have a brother," she replied, "who went to California, and dug gold. When I had been three years with my mother's people, he came to me and said, 'Edmonia, I don't want you to stay here always. I want you to have some education.' He placed me at a school in Oberlin. I staid there two years, and then he brought me to Boston, as the best place for me to learn to be a sculptor. I went to Mr. Brackett for advice; for I thought the man who made a bust of John Brown must be a friend to my people. Mr. Brackett has been very kind to me."

She wanted me to go to her room to see . . . a head of Voltaire. "I don't want you to go to praise me," she said; "for I know praise is not good for me. Some praise me because I am a colored girl, and I don't want that kind of praise. I had rather you would point out my defects, for that will teach me something."

L. Maria Child, "Letter," *The Liberator* (February 19, 1864), p. 31.

## *Prejudice Destroys a School in Connecticut*

[*Principal Prudence Crandall decided to admit Sarah Harris, a Negro pupil, to her Connecticut school for girls in 1833. The white community of Canterbury reacted violently. Miss Crandall describes how it all began.*]

. . . The reason for changing my school of white pupils for a school for colored pupils is as follows: I had a nice colored girl, as help in my family, and her intended husband regularly received the "Liberator." The girl took the paper from the office and loaned it to me. Having been taught from early childhood the sin of slavery, my sympathies were greatly aroused. Sarah Harris, a respectable young woman and a member of the church, called often to see her friend Marcia, my family assistant. In some of her calls I ascertained that she wished to attend my school, and board at her own father's house at some little distance from the village. I allowed her to enter as one of my pupils. By this act I gave great offense. The wife of an Episcopalian clergyman who lived in the village told me that if I continued that colored girl in my school, it could not be sustained. I replied to her, *That it might sink, then, for I should not turn her out!*

I very soon found that some of my school would leave, not to return, if the colored girl was retained. Under these circumstances, I made up my mind that if it were possible I would teach colored girls exclusively.*

---

* Wendell Phillips Garrison, "Connecticut in the Middle Ages," *Century Magazine*, Vol. 9 (September, 1885), p. 780.

[*Reverend Samuel J. May, a white minister who tried to help Miss Crandall, describes what happened next.*]

Undismayed by the opposition of her neighbors and the violence of their threats, Miss Crandall received early in April fifteen or twenty colored young ladies and misses from Philadelphia, New York, Providence, and Boston. At once her persecutors commenced operations. All accommodations at the stores in Canterbury were denied her; so that she was obliged to send to neighboring villages for her needful supplies. She and her pupils were insulted whenever they appeared in the streets. The doors and door-steps of her house were besmeared, and her well was filled with filth. Had it not been for the assistance of her father and another Quaker friend who lived in the town, she might have been compelled to abandon "her castle" for the want of water and food. But she was enabled to "hold out," and Miss Crandall and her little band behaved somewhat like the besieged in the immortal Fort Sumter. The spirit that is in the children of men is usually roused by persecution. I visited them repeatedly, and always found teacher and pupils calm and resolute. . . .**

---

** Samuel J. May, *Some Recollections of Our Antislavery Conflict* (Boston, 1869), p. 50.

[*One of the Negro students wrote on May 24, 1833, of new events.*]

. . . There are thirteen scholars now in the school. The Canterburians are *savage*—they will not sell Miss Crandall an article from their shops. . . . But the happiness I enjoy here pays me for all. The place is delightful; all that is wanting to complete the scene is *civilized men*. Last evening the news reached us that the new Law [against the school] had been passed. The bell rang, and a cannon was fired for half an hour. Where is justice? In the midst of all this Miss Crandall is unmoved. When we walk out, horns are blown and pistols fired.†

---

*The Liberator*, June 22, 1833, p. 99.

[*Reverend May describes the sad end of the story.*]

. . . About twelve o'clock, on the night of the 9th of September, Miss Crandall's house was assaulted by a number of persons with heavy clubs and iron bars; five window sashes were demolished and ninety panes of glass dashed to pieces.

I was summoned next morning to the scene of destruction and the terror-stricken family. Never before had Miss Crandall seemed to quail, and her pupils had become afraid to remain another night under her roof. The front rooms of the house were hardly tenantable; and it seemed foolish to repair them only to be destroyed again. After due consideration, therefore, it was determined that the school should be abandoned. The pupils were called together, and I was requested to announce to them our decision. Never before had I felt so deeply sensible of the cruelty of the persecution which had been carried on for eighteen months, in that New England village against a family of defenceless females. Twenty harmless, well-behaved girls, whose only offence against the peace of the community was that they had come together there to obtain useful knowledge and moral culture, were to be told that they had better go away, because, forsooth, the house in which they dwelt would not be protected by the guardians of the town, the conservators of the peace, the officers of justice, the men of influence in the village where it was situated. The words almost blistered my lips. My bosom glowed with indignation. I felt ashamed of my country, ashamed of my color. . . .

Samuel J. May, *Some Recollections of Our Antislavery Conflict* (Boston, 1869), p. 71.

# Canaan, New Hampshire, and Negro Students

[*Negro students Alexander Crummell, Henry H. Garnet, and Thomas Sidney of New York were invited to attend school in Canaan, New Hampshire in 1835. Alexander Crummell tells the story.*]

It was a long and wearisome journey, of some four hundred and more miles; and rarely would an inn or a hotel give us food, and nowhere could we get shelter. . . . The sight of three black youths, in gentlemanly garb, traveling through New England was, *in those days, a most unusual sight;* started not only surprise, but brought out universal sneers and ridicule. We met a most cordial reception at Canaan from two score white students, and began, with the highest hopes, our studies. But our stay was the briefest. . . . On the 4th of July, with wonderful taste and felicity, the farmers, from a wide region around, assembled at Canaan and resolved to remove the academy as a public nuisance. On the 10th of August they gathered together from the neighboring towns, seized the building, and with ninety yoke of oxen carried it off into a swamp about a half mile from its site. They were two days in accomplishing this miserable work.

Meanwhile, under Garnet, as our leader, the boys in our boarding house were moulding bullets, expecting an attack upon our dwelling. About eleven o'clock at night the tramp of horses was heard approaching, and as one rapid rider passed the house and fired at it, Garnet quickly replied by a discharge from a double-barrelled shotgun which blazed away through the window. At once the hills, from many miles around, reverberated with the sound. Lights were seen in scores of houses on every side, and the towns and villages far and near were in a state of great excitement. But that musket shot by Garnet doubtless saved our lives. The cowardly ruffians dared not attack us. . . .

---

Alexander Crummell, *The Eulogy on Henry Highland Garnet* (Washington, 1882), pp. 12-13.

## William Wells Brown Foils a Kidnapping

[*The Northern Negro lived in constant fear of being captured by kidnappers and sold into Southern slavery. To combat this Negroes formed organizations patterned after the Minutemen. William Wells Brown, later famous as a novelist, lecturer, and world traveler, describes how his group managed to recover the Stanford family of New York from kidnappers.*]

. . . One man got on the track of the carriage, and followed it to the ferry at Black Rock, where he heard that it had crossed some three hours before. He went on to Buffalo, and gave the alarm to the colored people of that place. . . . The alarm was given just as the bells were ringing for church. . . . We started on a run for the livery-stable, where we found as many more of our own color trying to hire horses to go in search of the fugitives. . . .

We travelled on at a rapid rate, until . . . we met a man . . . who made signs for us to stop. . . . he informed us that the carriage we were in pursuit of was at the public house. . . .

We proceeded to the tavern, where we found the carriage standing in front of the door, with a pair of fresh horses ready to proceed on their journey. . . . We all dismounted, fastened our horses, and entered the house. We found four or five persons in the bar-room, who seemed to rejoice as we entered.

One of our company demanded the opening of the door, while others went out and surrounded the house. The kidnappers stationed one of their number at the door, and another at the window. They refused to let us enter the room, and the tavern-keeper, who was more favorable to us than we had anticipated, said to us: "Boys, get into the room in any way that you can; the house is mine, and I give you the liberty to break in through the door or window." This was all that we wanted, and we were soon making preparations to enter the room at all hazards. Those within had warned us that if we should attempt to enter they would "shoot the first one." One of our company, who had obtained a crowbar, went to the window, and succeeded in getting it under the sash, and soon we had the window up, and the kidnappers, together with their victims, in full view.

One of the kidnappers, while we were raising the window, kept crying at the top of his voice, "I'll shoot, I'll shoot!" but no one seemed to mind him. As soon as they saw that we were determined to rescue the slaves at all hazards, they gave up, one of their number telling us that we might "come in."

The door was thrown open, and we entered, and there found Stanford seated in one corner of the room, with his hands tied behind him, and his clothing, what little he had on, much stained with blood. Near him was his wife, with her child, but a few weeks old, in her arms. Neither of them had anything on except their night clothes. They had been gagged, to keep from alarming the people, and had been much beaten and bruised when first attacked by the kidnappers. Their countenances lighted up the moment we entered the room.

---

William Wells Brown, *Narrative of William W. Brown* (London, 1849), pp. 112-115.

## Prejudice and the Free Negro in Ohio in 1834

[*Students from Lane Seminary, near Cincinnati, investigated the conditions under which free Negroes of that city lived. Here is a part of their report.*]

A respectable master mechanic stated to us . . . that in 1830 the President of the Mechanical Association was publicly tried by the Society for the crime of assisting a colored young man to learn a trade. Such was the feeling among the mechanics that no colored boy could learn a trade, or colored journeyman find employment. A young man of exceptional character and an excellent workman purchased his freedom and learned the cabinet making business in Kentucky. On coming to this city, he was refused work by every man to whom he applied. At last he found a shop carried on by an Englishman, who agreed to employ him—but on entering the shop, the workmen threw down their tools and declared that he should leave or they would. . . . The unfortunate youth was accordingly dismissed.

In this extremity, having spent his last cent, he found a slaveholder who gave him employment in an iron store as a common laborer. Here he remained two years, when the gentleman finding he was a mechanic, exerted his influence and procured work for him as a rough carpenter. This man, by dint of perseverance and industry, has now become a master workman, employing at times six or eight journeymen. But, he tells us, he has not yet received a single job of work from a native born citizen of a free state.

This oppression of the mechanics still continues. One of the boys of our school last summer sought in vain for a place in this city to learn a trade. . . .

The combined oppression of public sentiment and law reduce the colored people to extreme misery.

*Proceedings of Ohio Anti-Slavery Convention* (Cincinnati, 1835), p. 19.

## Charles Langston Addresses an Ohio Court

*[Arrested with a score of other Ohioans for attempting to free a fugitive slave from United States marshals in Oberlin in 1859, Charles Langston tells the court that is about to sentence him what he thinks of prejudice in the North.]*

. . . "I was tried by a jury who were prejudiced; before a Court that was prejudiced; prosecuted by an officer who was prejudiced. . . .

"One more word, sir, and I have done. I went to Wellington, knowing that colored men have no rights in the United States, which white men are bound to respect; that the Courts had so decided; that Congress has so enacted; that the people had so decreed.

"There is not a spot in the wide country, not even by the altars of God . . . ; no, nor in the old Philadelphia Hall, where any colored man may dare to ask a mercy of a white man. Let me stand in that Hall and tell a United States Marshall that my father was a Revolutionary soldier; that he served under Lafayette, and fought through the whole war, and that he fought for *my* freedom as much as for his own; and he would sneer at me, and clutch me with his bloody fingers, and say he has a *right* to make me a slave! . . .

"Some say that there is no danger of free persons being seized and carried off as slaves. No one need labor under such a delusion. Sir, *four* of the eight persons who were first carried back under the act of 1850, were afterwards proved to be *free men*. . . ."

John M. Langston, *The Anglo-African Magazine*, Vol. 1 (July, 1859), p. 214.

*[Langston was sentenced to twenty days and one hundred dollars fine for his part in the rescue. He returned to his antislavery work as soon as he was released.]*

# Frederick Douglass' Freedom Ride

[*Northern railroads, for a great many years, restricted Negroes to "Jim Crow" railroad cars. Frederick Douglass tells how this practice was ended in Massachusetts.*]

. . . Attempting to start from Lynn, one day, for Newburyport, on the eastern railroad, I went, as my custom was, into one of the best railroad carriages on the road. The seats were very luxuriant and beautiful. I was soon waited upon by the conductor, and ordered out; whereupon I demanded the reason for my invidious removal. After a good deal of parleying, I was told that it was because I was black . . . I was soon waited on by half a dozen fellows of the baser sort, (just such as would volunteer to take a bull-dog out of a meeting-house in time of public worship,) and told that I must move out of that seat, and if I did not, they would drag me out. I refused to move, they clutched me, head, neck, and shoulders. But, in anticipation of the stretching to which I was about to be subjected, I had interwoven myself among the seats. In dragging me out, on this occasion, it must have cost the company twenty-five or thirty dollars, for I tore up seats and all. So great was the excitement in Lynn, on the subject, that the superintendent, Mr. Stephen A. Chase, ordered the trains to run through Lynn without stopping, while I remained in that town; and this ridiculous farce was enacted. For several days the trains went dashing through Lynn without stopping. At the same time that they excluded a free colored man from their cars, this same company allowed slaves, in company of their masters and mistresses to ride unmolested.

After many battles with the railroad conductors, and being roughly handled in not a few instances, this proscription was at last abandoned; and the "Jim Crow car"—set up for the degradation of colored people—is nowhere found in New England. This result was not brought about without the intervention of the people, and the threatened enactment of a law compelling railroad companies to respect the rights of travelers. . . .

---

Frederick Douglass, *My Bondage and My Freedom* (New York and Auburn, 1855), pp. 399-400.

## Dr. Pennington's Resistance to New York Streetcar Segregation

[*In the 1850's New York Negroes were compelled to ride on the front platform of Sixth Avenue horse-drawn streetcars. One of the many instances of Negro opposition to that policy was the direct action of Reverend James W. C. Pennington. A slave blacksmith who escaped to the North and achieved sufficient education to earn a Doctor of Divinity degree at Heidelberg University, Pennington was also the author of the first Negro history text in America. John P. Early, a white merchant, told the Superior Court of New York of Pennington's efforts.*]

. . . as the doctor took his seat on the right side of the car, the [white] passengers near him rose up and left a vacant space on both sides of him for three or four seats. A number of the passengers went to the conductor and requested him to turn Dr. P. out. [Pennington denied this.] He was approached and asked civilly to take a seat on the front platform, as that was the regulation on the road. He declined, but the conductor insisted on his leaving his seat to which he replied that he would maintain his rights. . . .

The conductor then asked the driver to stop the car, and remove the doctor. He stopped, took Dr. P. in his arms, embraced him, and carried him backward through the car, the doctor apparently making all the resistance in his power. He was, however, forced through the car, over the platform and into the street, near the sidewalk. . . .

*New York Daily Tribune,* December 19, 1856.

## Dr. James McCune Smith Calls on All Negroes to Join the Battle for Civil Rights

[*Dr. James McCune Smith, a brilliant scholar and physician who had first studied at New York City's African Free School and then earned his Bachelor of Arts and Master of Arts degrees at the University of Glasgow, where he also got his medical degree, urges all Negroes to fight their own battles. This speech was given at a Negro convention in New York City in 1855.*]

The influence of our land and its institutions reaches to the uttermost parts of the earth; and go where we may, we will find American prejudice, or at least the odor of it, to contend against. It is easiest, as well as manliest, to meet and contend with it here at the fountain head. . . . But the hour has come for us to take a direct and forward movement. We feel and know it. . . . We are awakened, as never before, to the fact that if Slavery and caste are to be removed from the land, we must remove them, and move them ourselves; others may aid and assist if they will, but the moving power rests with us. . . . We must act up to what we declare. . . . And from the mere act of riding in public conveyances, up to the liberation of every slave in the land do our duties extend—embracing a full and equal participation, politically and socially, in all the rights and immunities of American citizens. If our duties are weighty, we have the means to perform them. . . . [Some states have] made movements toward recognizing our rights as citizens thereof. But efforts on our own part have helped toward this good result: in Massachusetts mainly by the efforts of some colored citizens, led by a member of this Council, both houses of the Legislature, have done their share toward granting us equal suffrage, and the Governor has strongly recommended the same. In New-York, through the efforts of a member of this Council and the President of our State Council, aided by the moving eloquence of another member of our council, the Legislature passed a vote of equal suffrage. . . . In Pennsylvania strong and able effort has been made to obtain the franchise by our colored brethren, and not without some signs that the labors of her intelligent and energetic colored citizens have not been in vain. . . . The time is come when our people must assume the rank of a first-rate power in the battle against caste and Slavery; it is emphatically our battle; no one else can fight it for us, and with God's help we must fight it ourselves.

---

*New York Daily Tribune*, May 9, 1855, pp. 6-7.

# 7
# *The Age of Reform,*
# *1820-1860*

BOSTON'S Vigilance Committee—formed to battle slave catchers coming from the South to capture runaways—included, at one time, writer James Russell Lowell, lawyer and novelist Richard Henry Dana, educator and humanitarian Samuel G. Howe, and Reverend Theodore Parker, the city's outstanding minister. Ex-Presidents John Adams and John Quincy Adams served without fee as lawyers for fugitive slaves seized in Massachusetts. Northern writers such as Melville, Hawthorne, Emerson, Thoreau, Whittier, Longfellow, Bryant, and the Alcotts wrote, spoke, or took vigorous action against slavery. Women's rights leader Susan B. Anthony opened her Rochester, New York home to slaves fleeing to Canada and demanded that the North "prove to the South, by her acts, that she fully recognizes the humanity of the black man." In one of his poems Walt Whitman, poet of American democracy, spoke of his identification with the slave when he wrote: "I am the hounded slave, I wince at the bite of the dogs."

## The Great Reformers

This was the great age of reform in American history, and many white and Negro philosophers, writers, ministers, orators, and editors spoke out for justice for all people who were mistreated or denied the common rights of humanity. This movement in America was linked with a worldwide interest in reform that included such men as Richard Cobden in England, Daniel O'Connell in Ireland, and Victor Hugo in France. It sought to reshape the nation and the world along humanitarian lines—peace, concern for the unfortunate, an end to slavery, equality, education for all, and justice for men and women regardless of color.

In America this era included Horace Mann's campaign for public schools and Dorothea Dix's fight for understanding and help for those in jails and insane asylums. Samuel G. Howe sought to prove that the deaf, dumb, and blind could be educated, and Susan B. Anthony and Elizabeth Cady Stanton battled for equal rights for women. Negro leaders such as William Wells Brown, Frederick Douglass, and Sojourner Truth fought for increased education, women's rights, and universal peace—and several toured Europe to support these causes in England, Ireland, and France.

It was the time of Sojourner Truth, a tall, former New York slave, whose vibrant voice stirred antislavery meetings with moving stories of the wrongs heaped upon her long-suffering people. Although illiterate, she spoke for women's rights simply and clearly against men far more educated than herself. And she battled segregation on the streetcars of Washington by simply refusing to leave the white section, or creating a scene which convinced conductors that it was wiser to leave her alone.

*Sojourner Truth, a former New York slave, spoke for Negro freedom and women's rights.*
*Though unable to read or write, she became a masterful orator, clear and logical.*

## Frederick Douglass

No one better represented the age of reform than a tall, broad-shouldered, young runaway slave named Frederick Douglass. While a slave boy in Baltimore, Douglass learned to read and write despite his master's vigilance and the laws making it a crime for slaves to learn to read and write. When a slavebreaker named Covey tried to whip him into submission, Douglass—then a strapping teenager—fought him off for two hours and won. After his escape from Maryland, Douglass lectured for the antislavery cause and published the story of his life—daring his master to come and recapture him.

In the 1840's Douglass toured Europe to raise funds and make friends for the abolitionist cause. He also spoke out for Irish freedom, world peace, and political rights for all regardless of sex, wealth, or color. He told a London audience in 1846: "You may rely

*An English magazine's picture of Frederick Douglass addressing a British audience. Douglass spoke against slavery and for women's rights, Irish freedom, federal aid to education, and the right of the oppressed everywhere to equal protection of the laws. He told a London audience, "You may rely upon me as one who will never desert the cause of the poor, no matter whether black or white." He kept his word.*

upon me as one who will never desert the cause of the poor, no matter whether black or white."

Douglass spent five weeks lecturing in Ireland on home rule for the Irish and emancipation for the American Negro. He was introduced to Irish audiences by orator Daniel O'Connell as "the Black O'Connell of the United States." Seventy thousand citizens of Ireland had previously signed a petition calling on the American Irish to support the antislavery cause and treat Negroes as equals.

He returned to America to publish his own newspaper, the *North Star*. His editorials demanded the end of capital punishment, mistreatment of Chinese immigrants and American Indians, and neglect of education for the poor. For 50 years he wrote and spoke for justice and the rights of man. Douglass told of his opposition to slavery in these words:

> I have held all my life, and shall hold to the day of my death, that the fundamental and everlasting objection to slavery, is not that it sinks a Negro to the condition of a brute, but that it sinks a *man* to that condition.

He also pointed out a simple truth when he said: "Let us not forget that justice to the Negro is safety to the nation."

Douglass did more than speak for justice—he placed himself in the thick of the battle. He refused to leave Northern railroad cars set aside for whites and reported: "I was often dragged out of my seat, beaten, and severely bruised, by conductors and brakemen." In Indiana a mob broke his arm when he spoke out against slavery. His Rochester home was a station on the Underground Railroad, and his sons became conductors for fugitives traveling to Canada.

During the Civil War Douglass urged Lincoln to free the slaves and arm all Negro men. When Lincoln finally adopted these policies he asked Douglass to serve as his adviser. Douglass raised troops for the Union Army, and his two sons were among the first to enlist. After the war Douglass continued his battle for reform. He urged Congress to enact "a great national system of aid to education" and a series of laws that would protect the rights of the liberated Negroes. He was chosen to serve his government in several high posts in Washington, and as United States minister to Haiti. He died in 1895 shortly after delivering a speech on behalf of women's rights. He was a mental and physical giant who had helped pull his country and people from the depths of slavery.

## The Rise of Militant Abolitionism

The fight against slavery had been going on since the first slave ship left Africa. Flight was the most common form slaves used to end their bondage. Even when recaptured, they tried to break away. Josiah Quincy, a New England Federalist, was the lawyer for the first fugitive captured under the laws of the new Constitution. The case, however, was never ruled upon because his client knocked down two policemen and made his escape from the court.

Many of the early white organizations formed to help the slaves believed that the only solution to the problem was the deportation of Negroes to Africa. Even many slaveholders could support this idea. In 1821 the American Colonization Society, supported largely by slaveholders, with the aid of the United States Congress established a colony in Liberia. Some 12,000 Negroes were sent there, mostly slaves liberated on the condition that they accept this deportation.

But the most uncompromising fight against bondage began with the slaves themselves as well as the free Negroes. In 1829, David Walker, a Boston agent for the first Negro newspaper, issued an *Appeal* to those in bondage. His message was simple: If you are not given your liberty, rise in bloody rebellion. When copies of his *Appeal* were found in Southern cities from Virginia to Louisiana, slaveholders panicked. They offered a reward for Walker's capture, dead or alive. He disappeared mysteriously the following year, but the fight went on.

By 1830 there were 50 Negro antislavery groups in Northern cities and towns. They helped fugitives reach Canada and raised funds to purchase friends and family members who could not escape. During that same year Negro leaders from several states met in a first convention to discuss the problems of slavery and discrimination. In 1831 a declaration issued by a convention of Negroes in New York City spoke for most Negroes in rejecting the idea that they should migrate to Africa:

*The Reverend Henry Highland Garnet. In 1843 he called for massive slave rebellions as the best way to end human bondage. White abolitionists were not in agreement on the use of violence to free slaves.*

> The time must come when the Declaration of Independence will be felt in the heart, as well as uttered from the mouth, and when the rights of all shall be properly acknowledged and appreciated. God hasten that time. This is our home, and this is our country. Beneath its sod lie the bones of our fathers; for it, some of them fought, bled, and died. Here we were born, and here we will die.

## Growing White Support

When 26-year-old William Lloyd Garrison came to Boston and began to publish his famous *Liberator* on January 1, 1831, he found that his main support came from Negro abolitionists. Rich Negroes contributed money, black newsboys sold the paper on the streets, and three quarters of his readers were Negroes. This determined young man was the first of his race to look at the Negro's problems from the Negro's point of view. "In your sufferings I participate," he told Boston Negroes. He fiercely denounced slavery as a sin and violation of the rights of man, and forcefully proclaimed that there would be no compromise with it. Garrison said the government was protecting the evil and publicly burned a copy of the Constitution—"a blood-stained document"—because it regarded humans as property. "He will shake our nation to its center," said a minister who heard him for the first time, "but he will shake slavery out of it."

A number of whites had joined Garrison and the Negroes in the antislavery movement by the 1830's. Levi Coffin, Indiana Quaker

THE

# UNDERGROUND RAIL ROAD.

A RECORD

OF

FACTS, AUTHENTIC NARRATIVES, LETTERS, &C.,

Narrating the Hardships Hair-breadth Escapes and Death Struggles

OF THE

Slaves in their efforts for Freedom,

AS RELATED

BY THEMSELVES AND OTHERS, OR WITNESSED BY THE AUTHOR;

TOGETHER WITH

SKETCHES OF SOME OF THE LARGEST STOCKHOLDERS, AND

MOST LIBERAL AIDERS AND ADVISERS,

OF THE ROAD.

BY

WILLIAM STILL,

For many years connected with the Anti-Slavery Office in Philadelphia, and Chairman
of the Acting Vigilant Committee of the Philadelphia Branch of
the Underground Rail Road.

Illustrated with 70 fine Engravings by Bensell, Schell and others, and
Portraits from Photographs from Life.

Thou shalt not deliver unto his master the servant that has escaped from his master unto thee.—*Deut.* xxiii. 15.

SOLD ONLY BY SUBSCRIPTION.

PHILADELPHIA:

PORTER & COATES,

822, CHESTNUT STREET.

1872.

*William Still, secretary of the underground railway in Philadelphia. He decided to keep careful records when he discovered that a runaway he was interviewing was his brother.*

and banker, began using his Newport home to hide runaways even earlier when he found that the colored people of the town who had been hiding them lacked the money and resources to do it well. Coffin was soon called the "President of the Underground Railroad."

This "railroad" developed its own language. The "trains" were the large farm wagons that could conceal and carry a number of fugitives. The "tracks" were the back country roads which were used to escape the slave catchers. The "stations" were the homes where the slaves were fed and cared for as they moved from station to station. The "conductors" were the fearless men and women of both races who led the slaves toward freedom and the "passengers" or "parcels" were the slaves who dared to break for liberty. Passengers paid no fare and conductors received no pay.

This strange railroad had many ways of moving slaves. Twenty-eight slaves walked in a funeral procession from Kentucky to Ohio. Calvin Fairbank, a white minister who spent fourteen years in jail for his part in aiding runaways in the 1850's, described his work in these words:

> I piloted them through the forests, mostly at night;
> . . . boys dressed as girls, and girls as boys; on foot
> and on horseback, in buggies, carriages, common

wagons, in and under loads of hay, straw, old furniture, boxes, and bags . . . or in boats or skiffs; on rafts, and often on a pine log. And I never suffered one to be recaptured.

The most daring and successful conductor was Harriet Tubman, a former slave. She made 19 trips into the South to bring 300 relatives, friends, and strangers to freedom. Wanted dead or alive in the South, she was never captured and never lost a passenger. A thorough and determined worker, Harriet Tubman carried a gun for protection and drugs to quiet the crying babies in her rescue parties. During the Civil War, she went to South Carolina to guide Union raids deep into Confederate territory.

*Before she died at 93, Harriet Tubman had led 300 slaves to freedom, directed Union raiding parties during the Civil War, and built a home for ex-slaves who were too old or ill to work.*

The Underground Railroad united the efforts of Negroes and whites in its dangerous work. Thomas Garrett, a gentle, old white Quaker and Samuel Burris, a young, free Negro, ran the station in the slave state of Delaware during the 1840's. Garrett paid out a fortune in court fines for his crime of aiding fugitives, but said to a judge:

> Thee hasn't left me a dollar, but I wish to say to thee, and to all in the courtroom, that if anyone knows of a fugitive who wants shelter, and a friend, *send him to Thomas Garrett* and he will befriend him.

Burris was captured and was punished by being auctioned off as a

*Quaker Thomas Garrett (left) and free Negro Samuel Burris (right) ran a station of the underground railroad in slave Delaware.*

slave. No one knew that the highest bidder was sent by Thomas Garrett to buy him and return him to freedom.

The threat of losing millions of dollars invested in slave property brought a furious response from slaveholders, their Northern business associates, and their friends in the federal government. Abolitionists were driven from the South, their printing presses wrecked, and their literature burned. The federal government, from the early 1800's until the election of Lincoln in 1860, favored the minority of slaveholders who ruled the Southern states. In 1835, President Andrew Jackson forbade the Post Office to deliver abolitionist mail in the South. Congress, in clear violation of the Bill of Rights, decided not to accept any antislavery petitions. This "Gag Rule" was finally defeated after an eight-year Congressional battle led by the then Congressman (former President) John Quincy Adams.

In the North, abolitionists faced mobs of ruffians urged on by men whose business depended upon Southern slavery. In the 48 hours of October 21 and 22, 1835, abolitionist meetings in New York, Massachusetts, and Vermont were broken up by gangs of rowdies. William Lloyd Garrison was almost killed by a mob led by "respectable" Boston merchants. Reverend Elijah Lovejoy was killed by an Illinois mob two years later.

The antislavery crusaders were made of strong Yankee metal that did not bend and rarely broke. Though never a majority of the

American people, they aimed their appeal directly at the American conscience. They were ready, in the words of one, "to fight against slavery until Hell freezes and then continue the battle on the ice." Many white citizens felt that the abolitionists threatened the nation's peace, but Negroes saw them in quite a different light. A convention of fugitive slaves held in 1850 sent these words to their brothers in bondage: "The abolitionists act the part of friends and brothers to us and our only complaint against them is, that there are so few of them."

While the abolitionists were fearless and determined, they were rarely united. "Meetings were a disorderly convention, each [member] having his own plan or theory," wrote one minister. Ex-Presidents and ex-slaves, poets and politicians, men of God and atheists tried to set a common program. William Lloyd Garrison drove large numbers of Negro and white abolitionists out of the American Antislavery Society when he demanded that they follow his leadership and not vote in elections. James G. Birney, an Alabama slaveholder who had become an abolitionist, led a large number of Western Negroes and whites away from Garrison into the Liberty Party, which ran antislavery men for office. Frederick Douglass' newspaper supported Birney and urged Negroes to use political action to end slavery in America.

President Abraham Lincoln, a week before his death, said: "I have only been an instrument. The logic and moral power of Garrison, and the antislavery people of the country and the Army, have done all."

*Boston aristocrat Wendell Phillips joined the abolitionists after seeing a mob almost lynch William Lloyd Garrison. He became one of America's greatest orators and radical reformers. His speaking style was described as "easy and graceful, but powerful as the soft stretching of a tiger's paw." After the Civil War he continued his campaign for Negro rights, women's suffrage, and the rights of trade unions to strike.*

# The Philosophy of a Great American Reformer

[*The creed of Frederick Douglass, embodied in this speech delivered in 1857, is remarkably like that of civil rights reformers today.*]

Let me give you a word of the philosophy of reform. The whole history of the progress of human liberty shows that all concessions yet made to her august claims, have been born of earnest struggle. The conflict has been exciting, agitating, all-absorbing, and, for the time being, putting all other tumults to silence. It must do this or it does nothing. If there is no struggle there is no progress. Those who profess to favor freedom and yet deprecate agitation, are men who want crops without plowing up the ground, they want rain without thunder and lightning. They want the ocean without the awful roar of its many waters.

This struggle may be a moral one, or it may be a physical one, and it may be both moral and physical, but it must be a struggle. Power concedes nothing without a demand. It never did and it never will. Find out just what any people will quietly submit to and you have found out the exact measure of injustice and wrong which will be imposed upon them, and these will continue till they are resisted with either words or blows, or with both. The limits of tyrants are prescribed by the endurance of those whom they oppress. In the light of these ideas, Negroes will be hunted at the North, and held and flogged at the South so long as they submit to those devilish out-rages, and make no resistance, either moral or physical. Men may not get all they pay for in this world, but they must certainly pay for all they get. If we ever get free from the oppressions and wrongs heaped upon us, we must pay for their removal. We must do this by labor, by suffering, by sacrifice, and, if needs be, by our lives and the lives of others.

---

*Two Speeches by Frederick Douglass* (Rochester, 1857), pp. 21-22.

# David Walker's Call for Action

[*David Walker, born free in North Carolina, came to Boston where he learned to read and write. In his fiery pamphlet, written in 1829, he concluded that slave revolts were justified to end slavery and he advised Negroes to take action. He also had some words of advice for all Americans.*]

. . . Remember, Americans, that we must and shall be free and enlightened as you are, will you wait until we shall, under God, obtain our liberty by the crushing arm of power? Will it not be dreadful for you? I speak Americans for your good. We must and shall be free I say, in spite of you. You may do your best to keep us in wretchedness and misery, to enrich you and your children, but God will deliver us from under you. And wo, wo, will be to you if we have to obtain our freedom by fighting. Throw away your fears and prejudices then, and enlighten us and treat us like men, and we will like you more than we do now hate you, and tell us now no more about colonization [to Africa], for America is as much our country, as it is yours. —Treat us like men, and there is no danger but we will all live in peace and happiness together. For we are not like you, hard hearted, unmerciful, and unforgiving. What a happy country this will be, if the whites will listen. . . . But Americans, I declare to you, while you keep us and our children in bondage, and treat us like brutes, to make us support you and your families, we cannot be your friends. You do not look for it, do you? Treat us then like men, and we will be your friends. . . .

---

David Walker, *Walker's Appeal, in Four Articles* (Boston, 1830), pp. 79-80.

# A White Quaker Builds a "Station"

[*Levi Coffin, born and brought up in North Carolina, was a member of the Society of Friends and always opposed slavery. His work for the Underground Railroad began in earnest when he moved to Newport, Indiana.*]

. . . Soon after we located at Newport, I found that we were on a line of the U.G.R.R. [Underground Railroad]. Fugitives often passed through that place, and generally stopped among the colored people. . . . I learned that the fugitive slaves who took refuge with these people were often pursued and captured, the colored people not being very skillful in concealing them, or shrewd in making arrangements to forward them to Canada. . . . I was willing to receive and aid as many fugitives as were disposed to come to my house. I knew that my wife's feelings and sympathies regarding this matter were the same as mine, and that she was willing to do her part. . . .

In the winter of 1826-27, fugitives began to come to our house, and as it became more widely known on different routes that the slaves fleeing from bondage would find a welcome and shelter at our house, and be forwarded safely on their journey, the number increased. Friends in the neighborhood, who had formerly stood aloof from the work, fearful of the penalty of the law, were encouraged to engage in it when they saw the fearless manner in which I acted, and the success that attended my efforts. . . .

. . . the Underground Railroad business increased as time advanced, and it was attended with heavy expenses, which I could not have borne had not my affairs been prosperous. I found it necessary to keep a team and a wagon always at command, to convey the fugitive slaves on their journey. Sometimes, when we had large companies, one or two other teams and wagons were required. These journeys had to be made at night, often through deep mud and bad roads, and along by ways that were seldom traveled. Every precaution to evade pursuit had to be used, as the hunters were often on the track, and sometimes ahead of the slaves. . . .

I soon became extensively known to the friends of the slaves, at different points on the Ohio River, where fugitives generally crossed, and to those northward of us on the various routes leading to Canada. . . . Three principal lines from the South converged at my house: one from Cincinnati, one from Madison, and one from Jeffersonville, Indiana. The roads were always in running order, the connections were good, the conductors active and zealous, and there was no lack of passengers. Seldom a week passed without our receiving passengers by this mysterious road. . . .

---

Levi Coffin, *Reminiscences of Levi Coffin* (Cincinnati, 1876), pp. 107-112.

# New York Merchants vs. the Abolitionists

[*Many wealthy and important Northerners opposed the growing abolitionist groups. Reverend Samuel J. May found out why, one day in
1835.*]

At the annual meeting of the American Antislavery Society in
May, 1835, I was sitting upon the platform of the Houston Street
Presbyterian Church in New York, when I was surprised to see a
gentleman enter and take his seat who, I knew, was a partner in one
of the most prominent mercantile houses in the city. He had not been
seated long before he beckoned me to meet him at the door. I did
so. "Please walk out with me, sir," said he; "I have something of
great importance to communicate." When we had reached the sidewalk he said, with considerable emotion and emphasis: "Mr. May,
we are not such fools as not to know that slavery is a great evil, a
great wrong. But it was consented to by the founders of our Republic. It was provided for in the Constitution of our Union. A great
portion of the property of the Southerners is invested under its sanction; and the business of the North, as well as the South, has become
adjusted to it. There are millions upon millions of dollars due from
Southerners to the merchants and mechanics of this city alone, the
payment of which would be jeopardized by any rupture between the
North and South. We cannot afford, sir, to let you and your associates succeed in your endeavor to overthrow slavery. It is not a matter
of principle with us. It is a matter of business necessity. We cannot
afford to let you succeed. And I have called you out to let you know,
and to let your fellow-laborers know, that we do not mean to allow
you to succeed. We mean, sir," said he, with increased emphasis—
"we mean, sir, to put you Abolitionists down—by fair means if we
can, by foul means if we must."

---

Samuel J. May, *Some Recollections of Our Antislavery Conflict* (Boston, 1869), pp.
127-128.

## White Abolitionists Mobbed in New England in 1835

[*The antislavery fight often became a battle for the rights of free speech, press, and assembly. William Lloyd Garrison describes his capture by, and escape from, a Boston mob opposed to abolition.*]

. . . on seeing me, three or four of the rioters, uttering a yell, furiously dragged me to the window, with the intention of hurling me from that height to the ground, but one of them relented and said—"Don't let us kill him outright." So they drew me back, and coiled a rope about my body—probably to drag me through the streets. I bowed to the mob, and requesting them to wait patiently until I could descend, went down upon a ladder that was raised for that purpose. I fortunately extricated myself from the rope, and was seized by two or three powerful men [abolitionist friends]. . . . They led me along bareheaded, (for I had lost my hat), through a mighty crowd ever and anon shouting, "He shant be hurt! You shant hurt him! Don't hurt him! He's an American!" I was thus conducted through Wilson's Lane into State-street, in the rear of the City Hall, over the ground that was stained with the blood of the first martyr's in the cause of *Liberty* and *Independence*, by the memorable massacre of 1770. . . . My offense was in pleading for liberty—liberty for my enslaved countrymen, colored though they be. . . .

William Lloyd Garrison, *The Liberator*, November 7, 1835, p. 179.

[*Reverend Samuel J. May describes the breaking up of his New England speaking tour by repeated acts of mob violence.*]

. . . I had spoken about fifteen minutes, when the most hideous outcries, yells, from a crowd of men who had surrounded the house startled us, and then came heavy missiles against the doors and blinds of the windows. I persisted in speaking for a few minutes, hoping the blinds and doors were strong enough to stand the siege. But presently a heavy stone broke through one of the blinds, shattered a pane of glass and fell upon the head of a lady sitting near the centre of the hall. She uttered a shriek and fell bleeding into the arms of her sister. The panic-stricken audience rose *en masse*, and began a rush for the doors. Seeing the danger, I shouted in a voice louder than I ever uttered before or since,

> *Sit down, every one of you, sit down!* . . . If there is any one here whom the mob wish to injure, it is myself. I will stand here and wait until you are safely out of the house. But you must go in some order as I bid you.

To my great joy they obeyed. . . .

When the house was nearly empty I took on my arm a brave young lady, who would not leave me to go through the mob alone, and went out. Fortunately none of the ill-disposed knew me. So we passed through the lane of madmen unharmed, hearing their imprecations and threats of violence to the ———— Abolitionist when he should come out.

It was well we had delayed no longer to empty the hall, for at the corner of the street above we met a posse of men more savage than the rest, dragging a cannon, which they intended to explode against the building and at the same time tear away the stairs; so furious and bloodthirsty had "the baser sort" been made by the instigation of "the gentlemen of property and standing."

In October it was thought advisable for me to go and lecture in several of the principal towns of Vermont. I did so, and everywhere I met with contumely and insult. I was mobbed five times. In Rutland and Montpelier my meetings were dispersed with violence. . . .

---

Samuel J. May, *Some Recollections of Our Antislavery Conflict* (Boston, 1869), pp. 152-153.

## *Elijah Lovejoy and the Fight for Democracy*

[*Driven from Missouri, his presses thrown in the river, Reverend Elijah Lovejoy, a white antislavery fighter, went before a public meeting and announced that he intended to continue printing antislavery items in his Alton, Illinois newspaper.*]

. . . I plant myself, sir, down on my unquestionable *rights*, and the question to be decided is, whether I shall be protected in the exercise, and enjoyment of those rights—*that is the question, sir;*—whether my property shall be protected, whether I shall be suffered to go home to my family at night without being assailed, and threatened with tar and feathers, and assassination; whether my afflicted wife, whose life has been in jeopardy, from continued alarm and excitement, shall night after night be driven from a sick bed into the garret to save her life from the brickbats and violence of the mobs; *that sir, is the question. . . .* I have no personal fears. Not that I feel able to contest the matter with the whole community, I know perfectly well I am not. I know, sir, that you can tar and feather me, hang me up, or put me into the Mississippi, without the least difficulty. But what then? Where shall I go? I have been made to feel that if I am not safe at Alton, I shall not be safe any where. I recently visited St. Charles to bring home my family, and was torn from their frantic embrace by a mob. I have been beset night and day at Alton. And now if I leave here and go elsewhere, violence may overtake me in my retreat, and I have no more claim upon the protection of any other community than I have upon this; and I have concluded, after consultation, with my friends, and earnestly seeking counsel of God, *to remain at Alton,* and here to insist on protection in the exercise of my rights. If the civil authorities refuse to protect me, I must look to God; and if I die, I have determined to make my grave in Alton.

[*Shortly after this speech, on November 7, 1837, Lovejoy was killed by an Alton mob while protecting his press.*]

Joseph C. Lovejoy and Owen Lovejoy, *Memoir of the Rev. Elijah P. Lovejoy Who Was Murdered in Defense of the Liberty of the Press* (New York, 1838), pp. 280-281.

## A Call to Slaves

[*Reverend Henry H. Garnet of New York had been a slave until he was eleven. He escaped to the North, attended school, and graduated from Oneida Institute in 1840. Three years later, at twenty-seven, he spoke at a Negro Convention in Buffalo, New York, where he issued this call for slaves to revolt.*]

Brethren, it is as wrong for your lordly oppressors to keep you in slavery as it was for the man thief to steal our ancestors from the coast of Africa. You should therefore now use the same manner of

resistance as would have been just in our ancestors when the bloody
foot prints of the first remorseless soul-thief was placed upon the
shores of our fatherland. . . .

Brethren, the time has come when you must act for yourselves.
It is an old and true saying that, "if hereditary bondsmen would be
free, they must themselves strike the blow." You can plead your own
cause, and do the work of emancipation better than any others. . . .
Think of the undying glory that hangs around the ancient name of
Africa—and forget not that you are native-born American citizens,
and as such, you are justly entitled to all the rights that are granted
to the freest. Think how many tears you have poured out upon the
soil which you have cultivated with unrequited toil and enriched
with your blood; and then go to your lordly enslavers and tell them
plainly, that you *are determined to be free.* Appeal to their sense of
justice, and tell them that they have no more right to oppress you
than you have to enslave them. . . . Inform them that all you desire
is FREEDOM and that nothing else will suffice. Do this, and forever
after cease to toil for the heartless tyrants, who give you no other
reward but stripes and abuse. If they then commence work of death,
they, and not you, will be responsible for the consequences. You had
far better all die—*die immediately,* than live slaves, and entail your
wretchedness upon your posterity. If you would be free in this generation, here is your only hope. However much you and all of us may
desire it, there is not much hope of redemption without the shedding
of blood. If you must bleed, let it all come at once—rather *die freemen than to live to be slaves.* . . .

Brethren, arise, arise! Strike for your lives and liberties. Now is
the day and the hour. Let every slave throughout the land do this,
and the days of slavery are numbered. You cannot be more oppressed
than you have been—you cannot suffer greater cruelties than you
have already. *Rather die freemen than live to be slaves.* Remember
that you are FOUR MILLIONS!

[*The convention turned down Garnet's appeal for slave revolts by a
single vote. After the Civil War Garnet became President of Avery College in Pennsylvania and served as United States Minister to Liberia,
where he died.*]

---

*A Memorial Discourse by Rev. Henry Highland Garnet,* James McCune Smith, ed.
(Philadelphia, 1865), pp. 48-59.

## Frederick Douglass:
## Early Days as an Abolitionist

[*Three years after his escape from slavery, Frederick Douglass joined the abolitionists as a speaker. He describes these early days.*

Among the first duties assigned to me, on entering the ranks, was to travel, in company with Mr. George Foster, to secure subscribers to the *Anti-slavery Standard* and the *Liberator*. With him I traveled and lectured through the eastern counties of Massachusetts. Much interest was awakened—large meetings assembled. Many came, no doubt, from curiosity to hear what a Negro could say in his own cause. I was generally introduced as a "*chattel*"—a "*thing*"—a piece of southern "*property*"—the chairman assuring the audience that *it* could speak. Fugitive slaves, at that time, were not so plentiful as now [1855]; and as a fugitive slave lecturer, I had the advantage of being a "*brand new fact*"—the first one out. Up to that time a colored man was deemed a fool who confessed himself a runaway slave, not only because of the danger to which he exposed himself of being retaken, but because it was a confession of a very *low* origin. . . . The only precaution I took, at the beginning, to prevent Master Thomas from knowing where I was, and what I was about, was the withholding of my former name, my master's name, and the name of the state and county from which I came. During the first three or four months, my speeches were almost exclusively made up of narrations of my own personal experience as a slave. "Let us have the facts," said the people. . . . "Tell your story, Frederick," would whisper my then revered friend, William Lloyd Garrison, as I stepped upon the platform. I could not always obey, for I was now reading and thinking. New views of the subject were presented to my mind. It did not entirely satisfy me to *narrate* wrongs; I felt like *denouncing* them. . . .

---

Frederick Douglass, *My Bondage and My Freedom* (New York and Auburn, 1855), pp. 360-362.

# A Study in Courage: A Negro Station
# of the Underground Railroad in the South

[*This letter, dated June 13, 1858, from Camden, Maryland, indicates some of the problems faced by Negroes who were helping others to escape.*]

Mr. Still:—I writ to inform you that we stand in need of help if ever we wonted help it is in theas day, we have Bin trying to rais money to By a hors but there is so few here that we can trust our selves with for fear that they may serve us as tom otwell [a traitor] served them when he got them in dover Jail. But he is dun for ever, i wont to no if your friends can help us, we have a Road that more than 100 past over in 1857. it is one we made for them, seven in march after the lions had them [the seven runaways that Tom Otwell had turned over to the Dover police] there is no better [Road] in the State, we are 7 miles from Delaware Bay. you may understand what i mean. I wrote last december to the anti Slavery Society for James Mot and others concerning of purchasing a horse for this Bisnes if your friends can help us the work must stil go on for ther is much frait pases over this Road, But ther has Ben but 3 conductors for sum time. you may no that there is but few men, sum talks all dos nothing, there is horses owned by Collard peopel but not for this purpose. We wont one for to go when called for, one of our best men was nigh Cut [caught] By keeping of them too long, By not having means to convay them tha must Be convad if they pass over this Road safe tha go through in 2 nights to Wilmington, for i went there with 28 in one gang last November, tha had to ride for when thea com to us we go 15 miles, it is hard Road to travel i had sum conversation with mr. Evens and wos down here on a visit. pleas try what you can do for us this is the place we need help, 12 mile i live from mason and Dixson Line. I wod have come but cant have time, as yet there has been some fuss about a boy ho lived near Camden, he has gone away, he ses me and my brother nose about it but he dont. . . .

. . . Ancer this letter.

Pleas to writ let me no if you can do anything for us. I still remain your friend.

William Still, *The Underground Rail Road* (Philadelphia, 1872), pp. 448-449.

# John Fairfield, Southern White Conductor of the Underground Railroad

[*Levi Coffin, who came to be known as the President of the Underground Railroad, tells of a young man from a slaveholding family who became a daring conductor on the Underground Railroad.*]

. . . When quite a young man, he decided to make a visit to the State of Ohio, and seek his fortune in a free State. Thinking that it would be a good opportunity to put his anti-slavery principles into practice, he planned to take with him one of his uncle's slaves, a bright, intelligent young man, about his own age, to whom he was much attached. John and this young colored man had played together when boys, and had been brought up together. They had often discussed plans by which Bill, the slave, could make his escape to Canada, but no attempt had been made to carry them out, until young Fairfield determined to visit Ohio. The arrangement was then made for Bill to take one of his master's horses, and make his escape the night before Fairfield started, and wait for him at a rendezvous appointed. This plan was carried out, and Bill traveled as Fairfield's servant until they reached Ohio. Not feeling safe in that State, he went on to Canada. . . .

When Fairfield told me the story, some years afterward, I asked him if he did not feel guilty of encouraging horse-stealing, as well as Negro-stealing. I knew that death was the penalty for each of these crimes, according to the laws of Virginia and North Carolina.

The reply was: "No! I knew that Bill had earned several horses for his master, and he took only one. Bill had been a faithful fellow, and worked hard for many years, and that horse was all the pay he got. As to Negro-stealing, I would steal all the slaves in Virginia if I could." . . .

He was an inveterate hater of slavery, and this feeling supplied a motive for the actions of his whole life. He believed that every slave was justly entitled to freedom, and that if any person came between him and liberty, the slave had a perfect right to shoot him down. He always went heavily armed himself, and did not scruple to use his weapons whenever he thought the occasion required their use. He resorted to many stratagems to effect his object in the South, and brought away numbers of slaves from nearly every slave State in the Union. . . .

I reproved him for trying to kill any one. I told him it was better to suffer wrong than to do wrong, and that we should love our enemies.

"Love the devil!" he exclaimed. "Slaveholders are all devils, and it is no harm to kill the devil. I do not intend to hurt people if they keep out of the way, but if they step in between me and liberty, they must take the consequences. When I undertake to conduct slaves out of bondage I feel that it is my duty to defend them, even to the last drop of my blood."

I saw that it was useless to preach peace principles to John Fairfield. He would fight for the fugitives as long as his life lasted. . . .

[*In the following selection, Levi Coffin tells what a slave, one of a party of ten that Fairfield had led to freedom, told him about the young Southerner and their escape.*]

. . . "I never saw such a man as Fairfield. He told us he would take us out of slavery or die in the attempt, if we would do our part, which we promised to do. We all agreed to fight till we died, rather than be captured. Fairfield said he wanted no cowards in the company; if we were attacked and one of us showed cowardice or started to run, he would shoot him down."

They were attacked several times by patrolers, and fired upon, but always succeeded in driving the enemy and making their escape, keeping near their leader and obeying his commands. Fairfield said that they had a desperate battle one moonlight night with a company of armed men. They had been discovered by the patrolers, who had gathered a party of men and waylaid them at a bridge.

Fairfield said: "They were lying in ambush at each end of the bridge, and when we got fairly on the bridge they fired at us from each end. They thought, no doubt, that this sudden attack would intimidate us and that we would surrender, but in this they were mistaken. I ordered my men to charge to the front, and they did charge. We fired as we went, and the men in ambush scattered and ran like scared sheep."

"Was anybody hurt?" I asked.

In reply Fairfield showed me several bullet holes in his clothes, a slight flesh wound in one arm, and a slight flesh wound on the leg of one of the fugitives.

"You see," he said, "we were in close quarters, but my men were plucky. We shot to kill, and we made the devils run."

[*In another exploit, Fairfield gathered together a party of light-skinned slaves from Maryland, the District of Columbia, and Virginia and brought them out of slavery to relatives in Canada.*]

. . . After gaining their confidence and making them acquainted with his plans, Fairfield went to Philadelphia and bought wigs and powder. These cost him eighty dollars. . . . His first experiment with these articles of disguise was made at Baltimore. Having secretly collected the mulatto slaves of that city and vicinity, whom he had arranged to conduct to the North, he applied the powder and put on the wigs. The effect was satisfactory; the slaves looked like white people.

Fairfield bought tickets for them and they took the evening train to Harrisburg, where he had made arrangements for another person to meet them, who would accompany them to Cleveland and put them aboard the boat for Detroit.

Fairfield, having seen this party safely on the way, returned immediately to Washington City for another company, who, by the aid of wigs and powder, passed for white people. He put these fugitives on the train, and accompanied them to Pittsburg. I received a letter from a friend in Cleveland informing me of the arrival of both these parties. . . .

[*Just before the Civil War, after years as a conductor on the Underground Railroad, after many pitched battles with slaveholders, and numerous terms in Southern jails, John Fairfield disappeared. Coffin believed that he lost his life leading a slave revolt in Tennessee.*]

Levi Coffin, *Reminiscences of Levi Coffin* (Cincinnati, 1876), pp. 429-445.

## The Struggle for Women's Rights

[*The Seneca Falls Convention of 1848 launched the women's rights movement in America. One of its pioneer leaders was Elizabeth Cady Stanton. It was a tense moment when she decided to submit her motion proposing women be given the right to vote. Before the convention opened, she told her husband what she intended to do.*]

. . . "You will turn the proceedings," replied her husband, "into a farce; I wash my hands of the whole business. . . ." Lucretia Mott [another leader] also . . . said, "Lizzie, thou wilt make the convention ridiculous." But Lizzie was of a different opinion; and she withstood Mrs. Mott with modest courage and independence. . . . Mrs. Stanton . . . found only one person among the delegates who was willing from the first to champion her novel demand. This was the brave and high-souled Frederick Douglass, to whom she successfully appealed, saying,

> You, like myself, belong to a disfranchised class, and must see that the root of all our social and legal disabilities lies in our deprivation of the right to make laws for ourselves. Will you urge the convention to adopt this protest against injustice? I have never spoken in public, and cannot defend my own resolutions. I want your help.

"You shall have it," was the reply. Mr. Douglass, with his ready genius as an orator, proved more than equal to the occasion. Mrs. Stanton, too, greatly to her surprise, found that her tongue was loosed, and that she could rise and reply to objections with happy success. . . .

[*This historic resolution was passed and Douglass continued to fight for women's rights. His last speech, on the day of his death, concerned women's rights and was delivered in the presence of his good friend, Susan B. Anthony, another pioneer for women's rights.*]

---

Laura Curtis Bullard, "Elizabeth Cady Stanton," in *Our Famous Women* (Hartford, 1884), pp. 613-614.

## An American Negro Delegate to the Paris Peace Congress of 1849

[*The unity of European and American reform movements during the pre-Civil War period is shown in this report by William Wells Brown, a former slave who became a conductor for the Underground Railroad, an abolitionist lecturer, a world traveler, and a speaker for women's rights, peace, temperance, and antislavery causes.*]

. . . Victor Hugo took the chair as President of the Congress, supported by vice-presidents from the several nations represented [England, France, Germany, Switzerland, Greece, Spain, and the United States]. Mr. Richard, the secretary, read a dry report of the names of societies, committees, etc. which was deemed the opening of the Convention.

The president then arose, and delivered one of the most impressive and eloquent appeals in favor of peace that could possibly be imagined. . . . Victor Hugo concluded his speech amid the greatest enthusiasm on the part of the French, which was followed by hurras in the old English style. . . .

Well, at the close of the first sitting of the convention, and just as I was leaving Victor Hugo, to whom I had been introduced by an M.P., I observed near me a gentleman with his hat in hand, whom I recognized as one of the passengers who had crossed the Atlantic with me in the *Canada*, and who appeared to be the most horrified at having a Negro for a fellow-passenger. This gentleman, as I left M. Hugo, stepped up to me and said, "How do you do, Mr. Brown?"

"You have the advantage of me," said I.

"O, don't you know me? I was a fellow-passenger with you from America; I wish you would give me an introduction to Victor Hugo and Mr. Cobden."

I need not inform you that I declined introducing this pro-slavery American to these distinguished men. I only allude to this, to show what a change came over the dreams of my white American brother by crossing the ocean. . . .

William Wells Brown, *Sketches of Places and People Abroad* (Boston, 1855), pp. 59-61.

# Harriet Tubman's Last Trip

[*Harriet Tubman escaped from bondage and returned to the South 19 times to free 300 other slaves. This letter by Quaker conductor Thomas Garrett is about her last trip.*]

Respected Friend:—William Still:—I write to let thee know that Harriet Tubman is again in these parts. She arrived last evening from one of her trips of mercy to God's poor, bringing two men with her as far as New Castle. I agreed to pay a man last evening, to pilot them on their way to Chester county; the wife of one of the men, with two or three children, was left some thirty miles below, and I gave Harriet ten dollars, to hire a man with carriage, to take them to Chester county. She said a man had offered for that sum, to bring them on. I shall be very uneasy about them, till I hear they are safe. There is now much more risk on the road, till they arrive here, than there has been for several months past, as we find that some poor, worthless wretches are constantly on the look out on two roads, that they cannot well avoid more especially with carriage, yet, as it is Harriet who seems to have had a special angel to guard her on her journey of mercy, I have hope.

Thy Friend
*Thomas Garrett*

---

William Still, *The Underground Rail Road* (Philadelphia, 1872), p. 530.

[*After the Civil War, Frederick Douglass wrote to Harriet Tubman, telling of his appreciation of her efforts.*]

. . . I have had the applause of the crowd and the satisfaction that comes of being approved by the multitude, while the most that you have done has been witnessed by a few trembling, scarred, and foot-sore bondmen and women, whom you have led out of the house of bondage, and whose heartfelt "*God bless you*" has been your only reward. The midnight sky and the silent stars have been the witnesses of your devotion to freedom and of your heroism. Excepting John Brown—of sacred memory—I know of no one who has willingly encountered more perils and hardships to serve our enslaved people than you have. Much that you have done would seem improbable to those who do not know you as I know you. . . .

Sarah Bradford, *Harriet, The Moses of Her People* (New York, 1886), p. 135.

## *Sojourner Truth Speaks for Women's Rights*

[*When the leaders of a women's rights convention in May, 1851, saw a tall, gaunt black woman march toward the speaker's platform they did not know what to expect. Sojourner Truth, mother and former New York slave, had listened to male speakers state that women need not be given rights since they were mentally inferior to men.*]

. . . At her first word there was a profound hush. She spoke in deep tones, which, though not loud, reached every ear in the house, and away through the throng at the doors and windows.

"Wall, chilern, whar dar is so much racket dar must be somethin' out o' kilter. . . . What's all dis here talkin' 'bout?

"Dat man ober dar say dat womin needs to be helped into carriages, and lifted ober ditches, and to hab de best place everywhar. Nobody eber helps me into carriages, or ober mud-puddles, or gibs me any best place!" And raising herself to her full height, and her voice to a pitch like rolling thunder, she asked: "And a'n't I a woman? Look at me! Look at my arm! (and she bared her right arm to the shoulder, showing her tremendous muscular power). I have ploughed, and planted, and gathered into barns, and no man could head me! And a'n't I a woman? I could work as much and eat as much as a man—when I could get it—and bear de lash as well! And a'n't I a woman? I have borne thirteen chilern, and seen 'em mos' all sold off to slavery, and when I cried out with my mother's grief, none but Jesus heard me! And a'n't I a woman?

"Den day talks 'bout dis ting in de head; what dis dey call it?" ("Intellect," whispered someone near.) "Dat's it, honey. What's dat got to do wid womin's rights . . . ? If my cup won't hold but a pint, and yourn holds a quart, wouldn't ye be mean not to let me have my little half measure full?" And she pointed her significant finger, and sent a keen glance at the minister who had made the argument. The cheering was long and loud.

"Den dat little man in black dar, he say women can't have as much rights as men, 'cause Christ wan't a woman! Whar did your Christ come from?" Rolling thunder couldn't have stilled that crowd, as did those deep, wonderful tones, as she stood there with outstretched arms and eyes of fire. Raising her voice still louder, she repeated, "Whar did your Christ come from? From God and a woman! Man had nothin' to do wid Him." . . . .

. . . She ended by asserting: "If de fust woman God ever made was strong enough to turn de world upside down all alone, dese women togedder (and she glanced her eye over the platform) ought to be able to turn it back, and get it right side up again! And now dey is asking to do it, de men better let 'em." Long-continued cheering greeted this. . . .

Amid roars of applause, she returned to her corner, leaving more than one of us with streaming eyes, and hearts beating with gratitude. She had taken us up in her strong arms and carried us safely over the slough of difficulty turning the whole tide in our favor. . . .

Frances D. Gage, "Reminiscences by Frances D. Gage," in Elizabeth Cady Stanton, Susan B. Anthony, and Matilde Joselyn Gage, eds., *History of Woman Suffrage*, Vol. 1 (Rochester, 1887), pp. 115-117.

# 8

# *Steps to Civil War*

*Dred Scott. Two weeks after the Supreme Court denied his petition for freedom, his master liberated him. The two men had arranged the suit together, hoping that it would aid the cause of abolition.*

ON May 14, 1857, Frederick Douglass told a New York meeting: "My hopes were never brighter than now." Supreme Court Chief Justice Roger Taney, a Maryland slaveholder, had just handed down the Dred Scott decision, which opened new land to slavery. But Douglass, a former Maryland slave, pointed out that:

> Judge Taney can do many things, but he cannot perform impossibilities. He cannot bale out the ocean, annihilate this firm old earth, or pluck the silvery star of liberty from our Northern sky.

To prove that the Dred Scott decision could not fasten bondage on the country permanently, Douglass traced the history of past compromises. He said the slavery issue had not been settled by the Missouri Compromise, the annexation of Texas, the war with Mexico, the Compromise of 1850, or the opening of Kansas to slavery. "The fact is, the more the question has been settled, the more it has needed settling." Douglass clearly had that great ability to see beyond the defeats of the moment to the eventual victories that history must shape at last.

### The Fugitive Slave Law

Douglass was right. Ever since the birth of the United States, Americans had tried in every way possible to settle the slavery issue once and for all. But each agreement had only led to additional demands by the slaveholders. The Compromise of 1850 was called by some "a final settlement." It included a strong fugitive slave law, a penalty of six months' imprisonment, and a $1,000 fine for anyone caught helping a slave to escape. Southerners thought that this tough measure would be sufficient to halt the escape of their slaves. The Northern reaction to this law shocked them.

Both Negro and white members of the Underground Railroad went into action. Lewis Hayden of Boston, who had escaped slavery and hid many fugitives in his house, placed two kegs of dynamite in his cellar and announced he would blow up the house rather than let slave catchers enter. The fiery editor Martin R. Delany said:

> Sir, my house is my castle. . . . If any man approaches that house in search of a slave—I care not who he may be, whether constable or sheriff, magistrate or even judge of the Supreme Court . . . —if he crosses the threshold of my door, and I do not lay him a lifeless corpse at my feet, I hope the grave may refuse my body a resting place. . . .

A group of Ohio Quakers said they would continue to aid runaways "in defiance of all the enactments of all the governments on earth." White abolitionist Wendell Phillips told a cheering Boston audience that: "Law or no law, Constitution or no Constitution, humanity shall be paramount."

A group of Canadian Negroes who had escaped from American slavery held a convention in New York and wrote "our enslaved brethren" to "be prayerful, be brave—be hopeful." Many of these Canadians then joined the underground railroad to bring others out of bondage.

Abolitionists posted notices describing slave-catchers who entered Northern cities. Some followed these Southerners into stores and streetcars and pointed them out to all. Prominent lawyers volunteered, or were hired, to defend fugitives caught in the web of the new law. In some cases Negro defendants, with the help of abolitionists, escaped from courtrooms in broad daylight.

A Congressional committee reported that the effort to recapture fugitives in the North "often leads to most unpleasant, if not perilous collisions." President Millard Fillmore decried this resistance "by lawless and violent mobs." But opposition mounted.

In 1851, a Negro Vigilance Committee in Pennsylvania killed two members of a posse who had come to claim two runaways. To-

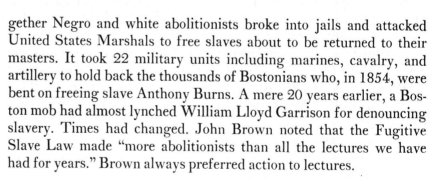

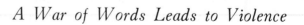

*Slave-catchers driven off by a Negro Vigilance Committee in Christiana, Pennsylvania. William Parker and his band then escaped to Canada with the help of Frederick Douglass.*

*Anthony Burns, captured in Boston, was returned to slavery in Virginia in 1854.*

*Harriet Beecher Stowe. Her* Uncle Tom's Cabin *dramatically exposed the evils of slavery and became a worldwide best seller.*

gether Negro and white abolitionists broke into jails and attacked United States Marshals to free slaves about to be returned to their masters. It took 22 military units including marines, cavalry, and artillery to hold back the thousands of Bostonians who, in 1854, were bent on freeing slave Anthony Burns. A mere 20 years earlier, a Boston mob had almost lynched William Lloyd Garrison for denouncing slavery. Times had changed. John Brown noted that the Fugitive Slave Law made "more abolitionists than all the lectures we have had for years." Brown always preferred action to lectures.

## A War of Words Leads to Violence

Moved by the plight of slave runaways under the new law, Harriet Beecher Stowe in 1852 wrote a novel to dramatize the evils of slave life. *Uncle Tom's Cabin* became a worldwide best seller and brought the evils of slavery home to any American who could read. Samuel Green, a free Negro, was sentenced to ten years in prison by a Maryland court for having a copy of the book in his possession.

In 1854, Congress, under the leadership of Senator Stephen A. Douglas, passed the Kansas-Nebraska Act, opening that territory to slavery. Armed settlers from the North and South entered Kansas to fight out the slavery issue. When one slaveholder tried to auction a slave boy at Iowa Point, a bloody clash occurred. "It was a bunch of 'free soilers' who were determined to break up the auction," recalled the boy.

> A man leading a riderless horse rushed up to me and shouted: "The moment your feet touched Kansas soil, you were a free man," and, then, he ordered me to mount the horse and we rode at a fast gallop, leaving the groups to fight it out.

"Some one planned to assassinate me," reported Governor John W. Geary of Kansas, but added, "I am perfectly cool . . . but I am more vigilant than ever."

Southerners who rode into Kansas from Missouri around election time shouted "every white-livered abolitionist who dares to set foot in Kansas should be hung." They added "every man north of Mason and Dixon's line is an abolitionist." But still the Northerners poured in.

Violence flared over the Kansas issue in the United States Senate. Abolitionist Senator Charles Sumner, seated behind his Senate desk, was beaten bloody and unconscious by the slashing cane of Congressman Preston Brooks of South Carolina. Brooks explained that Sumner had insulted slaveholders in a speech he made on "Bleeding Kansas." While Sumner became a martyr to the North, Brooks was applauded in the South. Other abolitionists "should catch it next," wrote a Richmond, Virginia paper, and Southerners sent Brooks more canes.

*Charles Sumner, long a defender of Negro rights.*

Out of the fighting in bloody Kansas rose a new party pledged to halt the growth of slavery—the Republican Party. One of the new party's leaders, Abraham Lincoln, asked in 1855: "Can we as a nation continue *permanently—forever*—half slave and half free?"

An iron-willed white man named John Brown stood watching Lawrence, Kansas set ablaze by proslavery night riders and gave his answer: "I have only a short time to live—only one death to die, and I will die fighting for this [antislavery] cause." Much earlier he had pledged his family to a crusade against slavery in a ceremony that took place in his family kitchen. John Brown, Jr., then about 18, recalled:

*John Brown. Because he was willing to defy any authority in his war on slavery, he has been called mad. A few years after his death Union soldiers sang "The John Brown Song" as they marched into battle.*

After prayer he [John Brown] asked us to raise our right hands, and then he administered to us an oath [that] bound us to secrecy and devotion to the purpose of fighting slavery by force and arms to the extent of our ability.

In 1859, John Brown completed his plans for a raid on the government arsenal at Harpers Ferry. It was to be his first step in the creation of a headquarters and Negro republic in the Virginia mountains. Frederick Douglass had spent long hours trying to convince Brown that he was entering "a perfect steel trap." But the old man had made up his mind. Only illness kept Harriet Tubman from joining the invaders.

Leading a group of nineteen men that included five Negroes and his own sons, Brown launched his attack. The assault bogged down and, within hours, it was overwhelmed by Marines led by Robert E. Lee. Tried and convicted, Brown and his men, knowing their cause to be just, calmly faced death. "I have thirteen children, and only four are left," said Mrs. Brown, "but if I am to see the ruin of my house, I cannot but hope that Providence may bring out of it some benefit for the poor slave."

The slaves continued to flee North during the 1850's. Despite the greater vigilance of Southerners, more escaped than ever before.

Abolitionist minister Thomas Wentworth Higginson, no stranger to the topic, wrote an article on "Physical Courage" in the *Atlantic Monthly*. He found the bravery of the slave runaways

> . . . beyond all Greek, all Roman fame. These men and women, who have tested their courage in the lonely swamp against the alligator and the bloodhound, who have starved on prairies, hidden in holds [of ships], clung to locomotives, ridden hundreds of miles cramped in boxes . . . —and who have then, after enduring all this, gone voluntarily back to risk it over again, for the sake of wife or child,—what are we pale faces, that we should claim a rival capacity with theirs for heroic deeds?

More white hands than ever reached out to aid the fleeing slaves and hinder their pursuers. Representative Joshua Giddings proudly told Congress how he defied the law by helping runaways: "I fed them, I clothed them, gave them money for their journey and sent them on their way rejoicing."

This decade that began with a compromise with slaveholders concluded with an election that spelled the end of compromise. Abraham Lincoln, dedicated to halting the growth of slavery, defeated a Democratic Party that was split down the middle over the slavery issue. Americans had finally elected a President opposed to the extension of slavery.

Abolitionist Wendell Phillips rejoiced: "For the first time in our history, the *slave* has chosen a President of the United States. . . . Lincoln is in *place*, Garrison is in *power*." (By 1863 the logic of events made this exaggeration come true!) But one thing was certain in 1860. The masters of the slaves were no longer the masters of the United States.

As slave states began to leave the Union, a tense nation prayed that Mr. Lincoln would measure up to the great challenge.

## *Negro Leaders Challenge the 1850 Fugitive Slave Law*

[*Dr. Martin R. Delany, lecturer, world traveler, medical man, and abolitionist editor and orator, gave his opinion of the Fugitive Slave Law of 1850 to a Pittsburgh meeting which included the Mayor.*]

Honorable mayor, whatever ideas of liberty I may have, have been received from reading the lives of your revolutionary fathers. I have therein learned that a man has a right to defend his castle with his life, even unto the taking of life. Sir, my house is my castle; in that castle are none but my wife and my children, as free as the angels of heaven, and whose liberty is as sacred as the pillars of God. If any man approaches that house in search of a slave—I care not who he may be, whether constable or sheriff, magistrate or even judge of the Supreme Court—nay, let it be he who sanctioned this act to become a law [President Millard Fillmore], surrounded by his cabinet as his body-guard, with the Declaration of Independence waving above his head as his banner, and the constitution of his country upon his breast as his shield,—if he crosses the threshold of my door, and I do not lay him a lifeless corpse at my feet, I hope the grave may refuse my body a resting-place, and righteous Heaven my spirit a home. O, no! he cannot enter that house and we both live.

Frank A. Rollin, *The Life and Public Services of Martin R. Delany* (Boston, 1883), p. 76.

[*Reverend Jarmain Loguen of Syracuse, New York, an escaped slave who used his home and church to hide runaways, made clear his determination to resist the new law in a speech before a public meeting in his city, on October 4, 1850.*]

. . . The time has come to change the tones of submission into tones of defiance,—and to tell Mr. Fillmore and Mr. Webster, if they propose to execute this measure upon us, to send their bloodhounds. . . .

. . . I don't respect this law—I don't fear it—I won't obey it! It outlaws me, and I outlaw it, and the men who attempt to enforce it on me. I place the government officials on the ground that they place me. I will not live a slave, and if force is employed to re-enslave me, I shall make preparations to meet the crisis as becomes a man.

---

J. W. Loguen, *The Rev. J. W. Loguen, As a Slave and As a Freeman* (Syracuse, 1859), pp. 392-393.

## *The Reception and Treatment of Kidnappers*

[*The following suggestions were published in the abolitionist* Liberator *by a member of a vigilance committee.*]

As soon as the arrival of one or more slave-hunters is known, let the Vigilance Committee appoint a sub-committee of the most active and devoted friends of liberty, sufficiently numerous for the thorough accomplishment of the following purposes, namely:

To keep themselves informed, by active, open, personal supervision, of every step the kidnappers take, every act they do, and every person they visit, as long as they remain in the place:

By personal interference, and calling aloud upon the citizens for rescue, to prevent them from seizing any man or woman as a slave:

To point them out to the people, wherever they go, as Slave-hunters: and, finally,

When they leave the town, to go with them and point them out to members of the Vigilance Committee or other friends of freedom in the first place in which they stop, that similar attention may be paid them there. . . .

As soon as the kidnappers arrive in any town, large handbills should be posted in all the public places, containing their names, with a description of their persons and the business on which they come.

An attempt should be made to induce the landlord of any hotel or boarding-house to which they may go, to refuse them entertainment, on the ground of their being persons infamous by profession, like pick-pockets, gamblers, or horse-stealers.

If this proves unsuccessful, some of the committee . . . should take lodgings in the same house with the kidnappers, and take, if possible, sleeping rooms and seats at a table directly opposite to them.

The doors of the house should be watched carefully, day and

night, and whenever they go out, two resolute, unarmed men should follow each of them wherever he goes, pointing him out from time to time with the word SLAVE-HUNTER. . . . He should not have a moment's relief from the feeling that his object is understood, that he cannot act in secret, that he is surrounded by those who loathe his person and detest his purpose, and who have means always at hand to prevent the possibility of success. . . .

C. K. W., "Reception and Treatment of Kidnappers," *The Liberator*, January 31, 1851, p. 20.

## Boston Defies the Fugitive Slave Law

[*Despite the penalties Boston's Negro community freed the first man arrested under the new law. Reverend Thomas Wentworth Higginson tells the story of the rescue of Shadrach.*]

. . . on the day of the arraignment of the alleged fugitive, the fact was noted in a newspaper by a colored man of great energy and character, employed by a firm in Boston and utterly unconnected with the Abolitionists. He asked leave of absence, and strolled into the Court-House. Many colored men were at the door and had been excluded; but, he, being known and trusted, was admitted, and the others, making a rush, followed in behind him with a hubbub of joking and laughter. There were but a few constables on duty, and it suddenly struck this leader, as he and his followers passed near the man under arrest, that they might as well keep on and pass out at the opposite door, taking among them the man under arrest, who was not handcuffed. After a moment's beckoning the prisoner saw his opportunity, fell in with the jubilant procession, and amid continued uproar was got outside the Court-House, when the crowd scattered in all directions.

It was an exploit which . . . was treated at Washington as if it had shaken the nation. Daniel Webster called it "a case of treason"; President Fillmore issued a special proclamation; and Henry Clay gave notice of a bill to lend added strength to the Fugitive Slave Law. . . .

Thomas Wentworth Higginson, *Cheerful Yesterdays* (Boston and New York, 1898), pp. 135-136.

# The Disappearing Defendant

[*Levi Coffin, called the "President of the Underground Railroad," describes the first important Ohio case under the new Fugitive Slave Law. A runaway named Louis had been captured and tried in Cincinnati in 1851. One of his two volunteer defense lawyers was Rutherford B. Hayes, who became President of the United States after the Civil War.*]

When the time set for the decision arrived, the court-room was crowded with interested listeners, white and black. . . . The judge was slow and tedious in reviewing the evidence, and as he spoke in a low tone, and the auditors were anxious to hear they leaned forward much absorbed, trying to catch every word, as they expected every moment to hear the Negro consigned to slavery.

Louis was crowded, and to gain more room, slipped his chair back a little way. Neither his master nor the marshal noticed the movement, as they were intently listening to the judge, and he slipped in his chair again, until he was back of them. I was standing close behind him and saw every movement. Next he rose quietly to his feet and took a step backward. Some abolitionists, friendly to his cause, gave him an encouraging touch on the foot, and he stepped farther back. Then a good hat was placed on his head by some one behind, and he quietly and cautiously made his way around the south end of the room, into the crowd of colored people on the west side, and, through it, toward the door. I and several other abolitionists had our eyes on him, and our hearts throbbed with suppressed excitement and anxiety lest he should be discovered. The door and passage were crowded with Germans, through whom Louis made his way, and passing down stairs gained the street. He was well acquainted with the different streets, and made his way quickly, though with not enough haste to attract attention, through an alley, across the canal, through the German settlement, and by an indirect route to Avondale, where he knew the sexton of the colored burying ground. About five minutes after he left the court-room his absence was discovered, and created a great sensation. The marshal cried, "Louis is gone!" and made a rush for the door and down stairs, followed by his supporters to search for the fugitive who had slipped through their fingers. Louis' friends were all delighted, of course. . . . A vigorous search was made for Louis by the marshal and the pro-slavery party, but he could not be found.

I, and other abolitionists, learning of his whereabouts, decided that he was not safe on the outskirts of the city, and the following night we disguised him in woman's apparel, brought him into the city, and took him to the house of one of his colored friends, on Broadway, near Sixth Street. He was placed in an upper room and the door locked, and here he remained about a week. . . .

*Reminiscences of Levi Coffin* (Cincinnati, 1876), pp. 550-552.

## The Christiana Riot

[*Slaveholder Gorsuch, accompanied by United States Marshal Kline and a posse of 15 to 20 men, rode into Christiana, Pennsylvania in the morning of September 11, 1851. They had come to recapture two of Gorsuch's slaves but they ran into the Negro Vigilance Committee of William Parker. He was hiding the runaways in his house. Parker describes what happened as the United States Marshal entered his house and came up the stairs, followed by others of the posse.*]

. . . I met them at the landing, and asked "Who are you?"

The leader, Kline, replied, "I am the United States Marshal."

I then told him to take another step, and I would break his neck.

He again said, "I am the United States Marshal."

I told him I did not care for him nor the United States. At that he turned and went downstairs. . . .

I told them all not to be afraid, nor to give up to any slaveholder, but to fight until death.

"Yes," said Kline, "I have heard many a Negro talk as big as you, and then have taken him; and I'll take you."

"You have not taken me yet," I replied; "and if you undertake it you will have your name recorded in history for this day's work." . . .

While they were talking, I came down and stood in the doorway, my men following behind. . . .

"Old man, you had better go home to Maryland," said Samuel [Thompson, Gorsuch's slave].

"You had better give up, and come home with me," said the old man.

Thompson took Pinckney's gun from him, struck Gorsuch, and brought him to his knees. Gorsuch rose and signalled to his men. Thompson then knocked him down again, and he again rose. At this time all the white men opened fire, and we rushed upon them; when they turned, threw down their guns, and ran away. We, being closely engaged, clubbed our rifles. We were too closely pressed to fire, but we found a good deal could be done with empty guns. . . .

When the white men ran, they scattered. I ran after Nathan Nelson, but could not catch him. I never saw a man run faster. . . .

The riot, so called, was now entirely ended. The elder Gorsuch was dead; his son and nephew were both wounded, and I have reason to believe others were,—how many, it would be difficult to say. Of our party, only two were wounded. . . .

---

William Parker, "The Freedman's Story," *Atlantic Monthly*, Vol. 17 (March, 1866), pp. 283-288.

## *The Attempt to Free Anthony Burns, 1854*

[*Boston's Negro and white abolitionists—those that believed in direct action—were determined to free a slave being held prisoner in a Boston courthouse. Reverend Thomas Wentworth Higginson, who spearheaded the attack, tells the story.*]

. . . Mingling with the crowd, I ran against Stowall, who had been looking for the axes, stored at a friend's office in Court Square. He whispered, "Some of our men are bringing a beam up to the upper stairway." Instantly he and I ran round and grasped the beam; I finding myself at the head, with a stout [strong] Negro opposite me. The real attack had begun.

What followed was too hurried and confusing to be described with perfect accuracy of details, although the main facts stand out vividly enough. Taking the joist up the steps, we hammered away at the southwest door of the Court-House. It could not have been many minutes before it began to give way. . . . There was room for but one to pass in. I glanced instinctively at my black ally. He did not even look at me, but sprang in first, I following. . . . We found ourselves inside, face to face with six or eight policemen, who laid about them with their clubs, driving us to the wall and hammering away at our heads. Often as I had heard of clubbing, I had never before known just how it felt, and to my surprise it was not half so bad as I had expected. I was unarmed, but had taken boxing lessons at several different times . . . but hands were powerless against clubs, although my burly comrade wielded his lustily. . . . I did not know that I had received a severe cut on the chin, whose scar I yet carry, though still ignorant how it came. Nor did I know till next morning . . . that, just as the door sprang open, a shot had been fired, and one of the marshal's deputies, a man named Batchelder, had been killed. . . .

There had been other fugitive slave rescues in different parts of the country, but this was the first drop of blood actually shed. In all the long procession of events which led the nation through the Kansas struggle, past the John Brown foray, and up to the Emancipation Proclamation, the killing of Batchelder was the first act of violence. It was, like the firing on Fort Sumter, a proof that war had really begun. . . .

[*Although the attempt to free Anthony Burns failed, a few months after his return to the South the young slave was purchased by Northern abolitionists. He became a minister in Canada.*]

T. W. Higginson, "Cheerful Yesterdays," Vol. 79, *Atlantic Monthly* (March, 1897), pp. 350-352.

# Harriet Tubman Leads a Raid in Troy, New York

[*Harriet Tubman, who had rescued many from slavery in the South, was ready to defy the Fugitive Slave Law in the North. With a crowd numbering in the thousands, she helped free Charles Nalle in 1859. Martin Townsend, Nalle's white lawyer, describes the scene.*]

When Nalle was brought from Commissioner Beach's office into the street, Harriet Tubman, who had been standing with the excited crowd, rushed . . . to Nalle, and running one of her arms around his manacled arm, held on to him without even loosening her hold through the more than half-hour's struggle . . . to the dock, where Nalle's liberation was accomplished. In the *mêlée* she was repeatedly beaten over the head with policemen's clubs, but she never for a moment released her hold. . . .

True, she had strong and earnest helpers in her struggle, some of whom had white faces as well as human hearts. . . . But she exposed herself to the fury of the sympathizers with slavery, without fear, and suffered their blows without flinching. Harriet crossed the river with the crowd, in the ferry-boat, and when the men who led the assault upon the door of Judge Stewart's office were stricken down, Harriet and a number of other colored women rushed over their bodies, brought Nalle out, and putting him in the first wagon passing, started him for the West.

Sarah Bradford, *Harriet, The Moses of Her People* (New York, 1886), pp. 126-127.

## "A Successful Farce"

[*Southern bitterness toward Northerners who obstructed the Fugitive Slave Law is shown in this editorial in the Augusta, Georgia* Republican.]

Massachusetts owes to the South the fugitive slaves within her limits; efforts have been made to get several of them back. We lost the two Crafts and Shadrach, and recovered Sims. A faithful execution of the law indeed! . . . Sims was the fugitive slave of Mr. Potter, beyond dispute; yet the case was kept in court, and before a commissioner, for a whole week. It was necessary to guard him with a heavy police [guard] in the third story of the Court House. The building was surrounded by a barricade of chains, and hundreds of the military had to be kept on guard to prevent his forcible rescue. The whole case looks more like a successful farce than anything else. Look at some of the incidents. Mr. Fletcher Webster is imprisoned, Marshal Tukey is held to bail in the sum of a thousand dollars; Mr. Bacon and Mr. De Lyon, the agents of Mr. Potter, were arrested on a charge of conspiracy to kidnap, and had to give bail to the amount of $10,000—one of the agents narrowly escaped being struck on the head by a Negro named Randolph. . . . This is faithful execution of the law! . . . It was such an execution of it as will prevent nineteen persons out of twenty from attempting to rescue their slaves at all. . . .

Austin Bearse, *Reminiscences of Fugitive-Slave Law Days in Boston* (Boston, 1880), p. 30.

## *Voting in Kansas in 1856*

[*Settlers poured into Kansas during the 1850's, but not all who came intended to stay. Each election day proslavery "Border Ruffians" entered the state from Missouri merely to vote. They sought to make Kansas a slave state, but they failed, for Kansas finally entered the Union as a free state in 1861 and it was the first state to arm Negroes for the Union. The following passage is from the report of a Congressional Committee which had witnessed an election in Kansas in 1856.*]

On the 28th of March, persons from Clay, Jackson, and Howard Counties, Mo., began to come into Tecumseh [the 3rd election district], in wagons, carriages, and on horseback, armed with guns, bowie-knives, and revolvers; and with threats, they encamped close by the town, and continued camping until the day of election. . . . On the morning of the election, before the polls were opened, some 300 or 400 Missourians, and others were collected in the yard . . . where the election was to be held, armed with bowie-knives, revolvers, and clubs. They said they came to vote, and whip the damned Yankees, and would vote without being sworn [as duly qualified voters]. Some said they came to have a fight, and wanted one. . . . Threats were made against the Free-state men. In the afternoon the Rev. Mr. Gispatrick was attacked and driven off by a mob. . . .

. . . a large majority, four to one, of the actual settlers of that district were Free State men, and there cannot be the least doubt that if none but the actual settlers of the district had voted at that election, the Free State candidate would have been elected. The number of legal votes in the district, according to the census-return, was 101. The total number of votes cast was 372, and . . . we are satisfied that not over 40 legal votes were cast at that election. . . .

Wm. A. Howard and John Sherman, *Report of the Congressional Committee*, Presented in the House of Representatives on Tuesday, July 1, 1856 (New York, 1856), p. 8.

# *Senator Charles Sumner Is Beaten in the Senate*

[*On May 22, 1856, Senator Charles Sumner, a New England abolitionist, spoke in the Senate about the war in "bleeding Kansas." He
blamed slaveholders and named some of his Senate colleagues by name.
The next day, as Senator Sumner sat writing at his desk, he was beaten
unconscious with a cane wielded by Representative Preston Brooks of
South Carolina. The following passages from three editorials in Virginia newspapers illustrate the Southern reaction to the incident.*]

[The Richmond Whig] A glorious deed! a most glorious
deed!! Mr. Brooks, of South Carolina, administered to Senator Sumner, a notorious Abolitionist, from Massachusetts, an effectual and
*classical* caning. We are rejoiced. The only regret we feel is that Mr.
Brooks did not employ a Slave-whip, instead of a stick. We trust the
ball may be kept in motion. Seward and others should catch it next.

[The Petersburg Intelligencer] We entirely concur with *The
Richmond Whig*, that if thrashing is the only remedy by which the
Abolitionists can be controlled, that it will be well to give Senator
William H. Seward a double dose at least every other day until it
operates freely on his political bowels.

[The Richmond Examiner] Good!—good!!—very good!!! The
Abolitionists have been suffered to run too long without collars.
They must be lashed into submission. Sumner, in particular, ought
to have nine-and-thirty [lashes] early every morning. . . . Senator
Wilson . . . [is] absolutely dying for a beating. Will not somebody take him in hand? . . . If need be, let us have a caning or
cowhiding every day.

---

George W. Carleton, *The Suppressed Book About Slavery* (New York, 1864), pp.
368-369.

## Abraham Lincoln Sees No Peaceful End of Slavery

[*It has often been said that Lincoln was slow to realize the full meaning of slavery's dangers to the country. He had once said that he did not remember a time when he was not against slavery—but many have felt that he came to this understanding only after years of war. Yet, in this letter written in 1855, he appears to have clearly understood the violent course that the slave power would take. His prophecy that the Czar of Russia would free his serfs long before the South did took place in 1860, the year of his election.*]

Hon. Geo. Robertson, Lexington, Ky.

My Dear Sir: . . . [you] once spoke of "the peaceful extinction of slavery" and used other expressions indicating your belief that the thing was, at some time, to have an end. Since then we have had thirty-six years of experience; and this experience has demonstrated, I think, that there is no peaceful extinction of slavery in prospect for us. . . . On the question of liberty, as a principle, we are not what we have been. When we were the political slaves of King George, and wanted to be free, we called the maxim that "all men are created equal" a self-evident truth; but now when we have grown fat, and have lost all dread of being slaves ourselves, we have become so greedy to be *masters* that we call the same maxim "a self-evident lie." The Fourth of July has not quite dwindled away; it is still a great day for burning fire-crackers!

That spirit which desired the peaceful extinction of slavery has itself become extinct with the *occasion* and *men* of the Revolution. . . . The Autocrat of all the Russians will resign his crown and proclaim his subjects free republicans, sooner than will our American masters voluntarily give up their slaves.

Our political problem now is, "Can we as a nation continue together *permanently—forever*—half slave, and half free?" The problem is too mighty for me. . . .

John G. Nicolay and John Hay, *Abraham Lincoln*, Vol. I (New York, 1890), pp. 390-391.

# The Raid of John Brown's Men

*[John Brown's band of Negroes and whites struck terror in the hearts of slaveholders. With courage and resolution, Brown and his men faced the gallows in Virginia. John Copeland, one of the Negroes in the band, wrote this letter to his brother shortly before his execution.]*

I am not terrified by the gallows, which I see staring me in the face, and upon which I am soon to stand and suffer death for doing what George Washington was made a hero for doing. . . . While, for having lent my aid to a general no less brave, and engaged in a cause no less honorable and glorious, I am to suffer death. Washington entered the field to fight for the freedom of the American people —not for the white man alone, but for both black and white. The blood of black men flowed as freely as that of white. . . . It was a sense of the wrongs which we have suffered that prompted that noble but unfortunate Captain Brown and his associates to attempt to give freedom to a small number, at least, of those who are now held by cruel and unjust laws, and by no less cruel and unjust men. . . . I fully believe that not only myself, but also all three of my poor comrades who are to ascend the same scaffold (a scaffold already made sacred to the cause of freedom by the death of that great champion of human freedom, Captain John Brown), are prepared to meet our God.

Richard J. Hinton, *John Brown and His Men* (New York and London, 1894), pp. 509-510.

*[The high regard in which Negroes held John Brown is seen in this report of his execution in a Negro magazine.]*

This execution, which took place Dec. 2 at 11:15 A.M., was in the highest degree imposing and solemn, and without disturbance of any kind. Lines of patrols and pickets encircled the field for ten miles around, and five hundred troops were posted about the gallows. . . .

On leaving the jail, John Brown had on his face an expression of calmness and serenity characteristic of the patriot who is about to die with a living consciousness that he is laying down his life for the good of his fellow creatures. . . .

As he stepped out of the door, a black woman, with a little child in her arms, stood near his way. . . . He stopped for a moment in his course, stooped over, and with the tenderness of one whose love is as broad as the brotherhood of man, kissed the child affectionately. . . .

---

"The Execution of John Brown," *The Anglo-African Magazine*, Vol. 1 (December, 1859), p. 398.

# 9

# *The Civil War*

THE South Carolina troops who manned the big guns facing Fort Sumter asked old Edmund Ruffin, a Virginia slaveholder and hater of Yankees, if he would like the honor of firing the first shot. That evening he wrote in his diary: "Of course I was highly gratified by the compliment and delighted to perform the service—which I did. The shell struck the fort. . . . The firing then proceeded." Ruffin had no idea that his action would lead to the end of the slavery he had so long defended. Few Americans did.

### *The War to Preserve the Union, 1861–1863*

American Negroes immediately answered President Lincoln's call for 75,000 volunteers to suppress the rebellion but were turned away. One hundred and fifteen Negro students from Wilberforce University rushed to enlist. "We were told," recalled Richard Cain, who became a South Carolina Congressman after the war, "that this was a white man's war and that the Negro had nothing to do with it." When Jacob Dodson, who had explored the West with Kit Carson and John C. Frémont, offered to raise a force of 300 other Negroes to defend Washington, D.C., he was turned down by Secretary of War Simon Cameron.

From the beginning, President Lincoln made clear that his central purpose was to preserve the Union. He assured North and South he would not meddle with slavery. While Negroes and abolitionists called for an end to slavery and the use of Negro soldiers, Lincoln was concerned with keeping the loyalty of the four slave states that had remained in the Union. He also knew that most Northerners would not support a war fought to end slavery.

Although Lincoln had long opposed slavery, he had also favored sending Negroes "back to Africa" for he did not believe that the two races could live in peace in America. By the end of the war, he had modified this view considerably.

To prevent slavery from becoming an issue in the conflict, the President and the War Department ordered Union generals to return slaves who were coming into their lines. General George McClellan announced he would crush any slave revolts that took place in his sector. He also ordered the Hutchinson family of folk-singers out of his camp because of the antislavery songs they sang to the troops.

*Contrabands pour into Union lines. The approach of the bluecoats was the sign for a general slave stampede from the plantation. Slaves in the four loyal slave states simply took their own liberty as the war progressed. Many former slaves ended up in the Union Army and Navy.*

When John Frémont tried to liberate slaves in Kentucky and General Hunter tried to enlist ex-slaves in the Union Army, Lincoln brought both actions to a halt.

But the slavery issue would not die. Black men, women, and children kept entering Union lines seeking freedom. They insisted that the bluecoats were their friends long before emancipation became a Union policy.

The Union soldier, trapped behind Confederate lines, found the slaves to be of invaluable assistance. "The Negroes were fairly jubilant at being able to help genuine Yankees," wrote John Ransom, a Union private. He described how a few Negroes led him and his buddies through a Confederate fortress one night, "actually stepping over the sleeping rebels." Said another Union soldier: "To see a black face was to find a true heart."

The Union spy system relied heavily upon information supplied by former slaves. Allen Pinkerton, chief of the Union Secret Service, wrote that he "found the Negroes of invaluable assistance" from the beginning of the war. John Scobel, a Mississippi slave, became one of Pinkerton's most trusted agents, repeatedly crossing into Confederate territory to bring back military information.

An outstanding example of help to the Union forces was provided by Robert Smalls, the Negro pilot of a Confederate gunboat,

*The crew of the* Planter. *The pilot, Robert Smalls,*
*later met with President Lincoln.*

the *Planter*. In May, 1862 Smalls and his slave crew sailed the ship out of Charleston harbor and surrendered it to the Union fleet. "I thought the *Planter* might be of some use to Uncle Abe," he explained. Smalls and his crew were rewarded by Congress for their brave exploit and Smalls was asked to Washington to meet President Lincoln. Smalls became one of many Negro ship pilots, mostly former slaves, who served the Union Navy. When the Union flag was again raised over Fort Sumter in April, 1865 it was the *Planter*, with Smalls at the helm, that brought more than 2,000 Negroes to the ceremony. "Their appearance was warmly welcomed and their joy seemed to be unbounded," wrote William Lloyd Garrison, an honored guest at the occasion. After the war, Smalls served five terms as a South Carolina Congressman.

The closer the bluecoats came to the plantations, the more difficult it became for masters to control their slaves. Slave patrols were doubled during the war, but discontent continued to grow. Forty slaves were killed in Mississippi for plotting a rebellion. Others took to the woods to form guerrilla bands. Most, however, waited for the approach of the federal troops. Union General Rufus Saxton told of the resistance of Negroes as bluecoats captured the Sea Islands in 1861:

> They [the slaveholders] tried to take their Negroes with them but they would not go. They shot down their Negroes in many instances because they would not go with them. They tied them behind their wagons, and tried to drag them off; but the Negroes would not go. The majority of Negroes remained behind and came into our lines.

These slaves soon established their own schools, tended the soil, built roads and homes for a community of thousands. They later formed the First South Carolina Volunteers, the first slave regiment to go into action against the Confederacy.

The Union policy toward the slaves slowly began to change. On May 23, 1861 General Ben Butler of the Union Army was holding three slaves who had fled to Fortress Monroe after they had been forced to build Confederate defenses. When a Confederate officer came to get them, Butler refused to give them up. Since they had been used by the enemy he considered them in the same light as captured guns or ammunition—*contraband of war*. With that phrase Butler began the official freeing of slaves.

News of liberty always traveled fast among slaves—in two months, Butler's post had 900 "contrabands" working for the Union Army. Soon these ex-slaves were performing most of the various services needed around the army camps. Many tried to get the blue-coats to teach them the magic of reading and writing.

## The War to End Slavery, 1863–1865

Before the year 1862 was half over, President Lincoln saw the need for a further change in Union policy on slavery. He told a member of his Cabinet that he had "come to the conclusion that it was a military necessity, absolutely necessary for the salvation of the nation, that he must free the slaves. . . ." By the time he issued the Emancipation Proclamation on January 1, 1863, Negro regiments in Louisiana, Missouri, and South Carolina had clashed with their former masters.

*Even before the Emancipation Proclamation, Negroes were fighting Confederates. In 1862 the First South Carolina Volunteers met and drove back an attack by Confederate soldiers and their bloodhounds.*

The new policy meant that the White House doors were open for the first time to Negro visitors and advisers. Frederick Douglass was invited several times "to talk with, and even to advise, the head man of a great nation." Although the two often disagreed, their friendship and respect for each other grew with each meeting. When Douglass tried to enter the White House for Lincoln's Second Inaugural reception, he was seized by two policemen. Thirty seconds after the President was informed of this, however, Douglass was ushered into the East Room and reported this conversation with the President.

> Taking me by the hand, he said, "I am glad to see you. I saw you in the crowd today, listening to my inaugural address; how did you like it?"
>
> I said, "Mr. Lincoln, I must not detain you with my poor opinion, when there are thousands waiting to shake hands with you."
>
> "No, no," he said, "you must stop a little, Douglass; there is no man in the country whose opinion I value more than yours. I want to know what you think of it?"
>
> I replied, "Mr. Lincoln, that was a sacred effort."
> "I am glad you liked it!" he said. . . .

The Emancipation Proclamation opened the United States armed forces to Negroes, slave and free. Before the war ended, 200,-000 entered the army and navy. "Brothers! The hour strikes for

*Negro troops in North Carolina liberating slaves.*

us. . . ." wrote a New Orleans Negro paper in both French and English. Said Frederick Douglass: "The day dawns—the morning star is bright upon the horizon." Wrote abolitionist poet Whittier: "It is great to live in such times."

## The Negro Soldier

Many in the North and South were surprised to find that Negroes, especially those who had been slaves, made good soldiers. "The idea of their doing any serious fighting against white men is simply ridiculous," said one Southern newspaper. The reports from the battlefields soon ended the laughter. In more than 200 battles, they fought bravely and won praise from both friends and enemies. Twenty Negroes won the Medal of Honor, American's highest military honor. At Milliken's Bend Negro troops faced an attacking force of Texans twice the size of their own. Though recently inducted into the army and largely untrained, the colored troops defended their position. *Harper's Weekly* reported some early battles in these words:

*Sergeant William H. Carney, one of the twenty Negro Medal of Honor men during the Civil War, took part in the battles to recapture Fort Sumter.*

> At Helena, they bore the brunt of the fighting, and defeated a superior force of the enemy. At Port Hudson, they led . . . General Bank's unsuccessful attack upon the place, and left half of their number on the field. At Charleston, the colored regiment from Massachusetts, led by the heroic Colonel Shaw, was placed in the front, and sacrificed itself to make a way for the white troops who followed. Wherever the Negroes have had a chance they have given evidence of the most exalted gallantry.

Just one year after the Emancipation Proclamation, President Lincoln wrote to General Wadsworth that the Negro troops had "heroically vindicated their manhood on the battlefield."

The contributions of the Negro soldier were remarkable in light of the disadvantages under which he served. He was placed in segregated units under white officers who were often prejudiced. (Less than a hundred Negroes were made officers.) Negro regiments were sent into battle with less training than the white regiments had received and with weapons inferior to those issued to whites. Their medical facilities were worse and their doctors fewer. They suffered greater casualties than whites for all of these reasons. For more than

*An ex-slave is transformed into a Union Soldier. More than 200,000 Negroes served in the Union Army and Navy; their courage was admired by friends, feared by foes.*

a year, the War Department paid Negro soldiers half as much as whites. Until their pay was made equal, some Negro regiments refused to accept any pay at all. However, they all continued to fight.

The worst hazard which the colored troops faced was capture by the Confederates. The South sold some into slavery and put others to death. At Fort Pillow, Tennessee, Negro troops were

*Negro infantrymen rout Confederates in Virginia, and capture their cannons. Northerners and Southerners were surprised to find that Negroes, especially ex-slaves, made courageous soldiers. Even President Lincoln had had his doubts.*

massacred after their surrender on April 12, 1864. Ransome Anderson of the United States Colored Heavy Artillery described the scene to Congress:

> Most all the men that were killed on our side were killed after the fight was over. They [the Confederates] called them out and shot them down. Then they put some in the houses, and shut them up, and then burned the houses.

When Lincoln warned the Confederacy that he would take action against their soldiers for such deeds, this brutality stopped.

The Confederacy dared not arm its slaves. When New Orleans free Negroes volunteered to fight, they were issued broomsticks instead of guns. After the city was captured by federal troops, General Butler provided these soldiers with guns and they went into action against the Confederacy.

Negro women as well as white women served the troops behind the lines and organized relief societies. Susie King was one of many Negro nurses who worked with Clara Barton tending the sick and wounded. Harriet Tubman, familiar with the South after ten years as a conductor for the Underground Railroad, led Union raids deep in Confederate territory. Mrs. Elizabeth Keckley, the White House seamstress, began a relief society for the freedmen who now poured behind Union lines or spilled over the countryside in the wake of General Sherman's march through Georgia. Northern Negroes as well as the President and Mrs. Lincoln contributed to Mrs. Keckley's Contraband Relief Society. In Nashville and other Southern cities held by Union troops, colored men and women organized their own committees for relief.

## The Home Front

The war quickened the Negroes' demands for equality in the North —and led to marked advances. After long campaigns by Negroes, Illinois and California dropped their "Black Laws" that denied Negroes equal rights. Illinois repealed a law that punished Negroes for merely entering the state. Congress voted to allow Negroes to testify in federal cases and approved the hiring of Negro mail carriers. Philadelphia Negroes continued their fight to ride the streetcars. So did Negro officers and soldiers in Washington, D.C., some of them wounded in battle.

While these advances were being made, the Northern home front exploded in anti-Negro violence. In New York City, the poorest and most ignorant whites, many of them recent Irish immigrants who blamed Negroes for the war and resented their competition for jobs, rioted for four days. Roving bands attacked and lynched Negro men, women, and children. A colored orphans' home was set ablaze. As Irish fireman led some twenty Negro children to safety, crowds yelled: "Wring the necks of the d———d Lincolnites." The entire city police force as well as United States troops had to be called to restore order and halt the murders.

## The End of the War

But the war was coming to a close. In February, 1865 Negro troops entered Charleston and the white Colonel of the 55th Massachusetts Regiment wrote of their reception:

> The few white inhabitants left in the town were either alarmed or indignant, and generally remained in their houses; but the colored people turned out *en masse*. . . . Cheers, blessings, prayers, and songs were heard on every side. Men and women crowded to shake hands with men and officers. . . . The glory and the triumph of this hour may be imagined, but can never be described. . . .

*The 55th Massachusetts Colored Infantry liberating Charleston on February 21, 1865. Colonel Charles B. Fox (riding horse) wrote: "It was one of those occasions which happen but once in a lifetime, to be lived over in memory for ever."*

In April, 1865 the Union Army advanced on General Robert E. Lee in Virginia. Colonel Samuel Armstrong, whose 8th United States Colored Troops were part of the vast army surrounding Lee, wrote:

> The rebs gave way—all was quiet, there was a rumor of surrender—we waited—other rumors came, and finally it was certain that the crucial war was over.

Edmund Ruffin, who fired the first shot of the war, heard the news of surrender. His South had lost and his slaves had gone to freedom. Ruffin took his gun and fired another shot—ending his own life.

Just before the war ended, General Ben Butler told his Negro troops: "With the bayonet you have unlocked the iron-barred gates of prejudice, opening new fields of freedom, liberty, and equality to yourselves and your race forever." The General had spoken too soon. The war was over, but the fight for rights was only beginning. When Abraham Lincoln's funeral took place in Washington, Negro troops were left out of the vast army of sorrowing soldiers and civilians who marched behind his coffin. Only after they had protested bitterly were they allowed to march with the other mourners.

*"The Union Dead" as pictured by* Harper's Weekly, *1865. President Lincoln believed that the Negro had won his right to citizenship by his wartime valor and sacrifices.*

## Negro Volunteers Are Rejected

[*Jacob Dodson had served with General Frémont on his famous explorations of the West. In this letter of April 23, 1861, addressed to Secretary of War Cameron, Dodson answers Lincoln's call for volunteers.*]

Sir: I desire to inform you that I know of some three hundred of reliable colored free citizens of this City, who desire to enter the service for the defence of the City.

I have been three times across the Rocky Mountains in the service of the Country with Frémont and others.

I can be found about the Senate Chambers, as I have been employed about the premises for some years.

Yours respectfully,

Jacob Dodson,

(Colored)

[*Mr. Dodson received this reply. It was dated April 29, 1861.*]

Sir: . . . I have to say that this Department has no intention at present to call into the service of the government any colored soldiers.

Simon Cameron

Secretary of War

Elon A. Woodward, ed., *The Negro in the Military Service of the United States*, Vol. II (Washington: National Archives, 1888), pp. 803, 807.

## Runaways and Union Troops

[*It was government policy that runaway slaves coming into army lines were to be returned to their masters, but this Congressional investigation found that some Union troops refused to return the slaves. In this passage, General Daniel E. Sickles is being questioned.*]

*Q.* We have been directed by the House of Representatives to inquire into the treatment of contrabands coming within your lines. What has been the custom of dealing with them in your division . . . ?

*A.* . . . My own practice has been, when contrabands come into my lines from Virginia, crossing the river, to examine them and obtain what information was practicable. When I found them intelligent and well behaved I have retained them in camp, sometimes in the quartermaster's department, sometimes in [the] charge of suitable persons near my headquarters, that they might be employed as scouts and guides . . . [and] when no objection has been made they have been employed, in a few instances, by officers as servants. . . .

. . . In September and October last, and perhaps as late as November, in two or three instances, orders came from the headquarters of the army of the Potomac, directing that such and such persons—naming them—claiming to have slaves within one of my camps . . . should be permitted to search the camp and reclaim their slaves. I addressed a communication . . . stating that such steps would be likely to lead to disorder and mischief in the camps; because in several instances the sympathies of the men had been excited by seeing slaves, reclaimed under such circumstances, very harshly treated. . . .

*Q.* Was that communication sent to General McClellan?

*A.* Yes, sir. . . .

*Q.* You spoke of the barbarous treatment these men [the slaves] had received sometimes when they had been surrendered; what can you state about that more than you have already stated?

*A.* Lieutenant Colonel Benedict reported to me one or two instances that had come under his notice, where Maryland owners had obtained possession of their slaves, and would immediately set to work flogging them in view of the troops; and the result would be that the soldiers would go out and rescue the Negro, and in some instances would thrash the masters. . . . It was a regiment of excellent soldiers, but they were resolute, desperate men; they were all firemen of New York City—the 2nd regiment of Fire Zouaves—and they came to the conclusion . . . that they would not permit any man to come within their lines upon a similar mission. . . .

*Q.* You spoke of some orders of General Hooker directing that certain men who were disloyal should be permitted to go into [your] camp and search for their men.

*A.* Some of them were disloyal.

*Q.* Was any inquiry made as to that matter?

*A.* No, sir; not that I know of. I know that Posey [one of the slave-owners] was under arrest in Washington for some time, for using his house as a signal station for the enemy. . . .

The most valuable and reliable information of the enemy's movements in our vicinity that we have been able to get we have derived from Negroes who have come into our lines. They have been frequently employed by me as scouts, sometimes singly and sometimes in parties of two or three. Sometimes they have been sent as guides with our troops when it was not deemed proper to hazard them unattended; and they have uniformly, whether employed as scouts or guides, proved faithful. In many instances they have proved to be persons of remarkable intelligence. . . .

*Q.* Were these colored, who rendered you these services, slave or free?

*A.* All of them slaves, I presume. I will mention one instance particularly, where a colored man named Jim . . . was sent on a number of scouting expeditions, both for the army and the navy, for the Potomac flotilla and for myself. And one duty that he performed was attended with so much danger, and was performed with so much fidelity and ability, that I recommended that he should be allowed one hundred dollars for it. My recommendation was complied with, and he received that sum. That is but one of twenty services that he has rendered the government, all of more or less magnitude. . . .

*Q.* Do you know of any instance where they have been treacherous to the Union cause?

*A.* No, sir; not one. . . . They will submit to any privation, perform any duty, incur any danger. I know an instance in which four of them recently carried a boat from the Rappahannock river, passing through the enemy's pickets successfully, to the Potomac and crossed over to my camp and reported themselves there. They gave us information of the position of the enemy's force which was communicated to headquarters; a service upon which it would be difficult to fix a price. These services rendered by these men are known to the soldiers, and contribute, I presume, largely to the sympathy which they feel for them. . . .

[*Lieutenant Joseph L. Palmer, Jr. gave the following testimony.*]

Q. What do you know in relation to parties owning slaves coming into your camps after them . . . ?

A. . . . There was one case in the 5th regiment where a man named Cox claimed some slaves. He was very badly treated by the soldiers. He came there with an order from division headquarters for two or three slaves. He pointed out who they were, and undertook to take them away; but the soldiers pounced upon him and beat him severely, injuring him considerably. The officers interfered, and saw him safely out of the camp, but not until he had been considerably injured. He went away without his slaves. . . .

With our people, there was a feeling of indignation against it, from the lowest to the highest; it was the universal feeling. Some of the officers would turn away, saying to these claimants "you can take your property if you will, but I will have nothing to do with it," and then walk into their tents and pay no more attention to them. Sometimes they would allow their men to treat these people very roughly, until they were obliged to interpose to prevent their being seriously injured.

---

*Report of the Joint Committee on the Conduct of the War*, Report 108, Part III, 37th Congress, Third Session, pp. 632-645.

## Slaves Become Contraband of War

[*By calling slaves who entered his lines "Contraband of War," General Benjamin Butler took the first legal step toward the emancipation of all slaves. He describes how he first used the idea at Fortress Monroe, Virginia.*]

On the day after my arrival at the fort, May 23 [1861], three Negroes were reported coming in a boat from Sewall's Point, where the enemy was building a battery. Thinking that some information as to that work might be got from them, I had them before me. . . . The Negroes said they belonged to Colonel Mallory, who commanded the Virginia troops around Hampton, and that he was now making preparation to take all his Negroes to Florida soon, and that not wanting to go away from home they had escaped to the fort. I directed that they should be fed and set at work.

On the next day I was notified by an officer in charge of the picket line next to Hampton that an officer bearing a flag of truce desired to be admitted to the fort to see me. As I did not wish to allow officers of the enemy to come inside the fort just then and see us piling up sand bags to protect the weak points there, I directed the bearer of the flag to be informed that I would be at the picket line in the course of an hour. Accompanied by two gentlemen of my staff . . . I rode out to the picket line and met the flag of truce there. . . .

[*The Confederate officer who came to see General Butler was Major Carey.*]

. . . "I am informed," said Major Carey, "that three Negroes belonging to Colonel Mallory have escaped within your lines. I am Colonel Mallory's agent and have charge of his property. What do you mean to do with those Negroes?"

"I intend to hold them," said I.

"Do you mean, then, to set aside your constitutional obligation to return them?"

"I mean to take Virginia at her word, as declared in the ordinance of secession passed yesterday. I am under no constitutional obligations to a foreign country, which Virginia now claims to be."

"But you say we cannot secede," he answered, "and so you cannot consistently detain the Negroes."

"But you say you have seceded, so you cannot consistently claim them. I shall hold these Negroes as contraband of war, since they are engaged in the construction of your battery and are claimed as your property. The question is simply whether they shall be used for or against the Government of the United States. . . ."

Benjamin Butler, *Butler's Book* (Boston, 1892), pp. 256-257.

# The Clothesline Telegraph

*[The slaves often provided the Union Army with valuable information. This story tells of one method used to relay the information back to army headquarters.]*

There came into the Union lines a Negro from a farm on the other side of the river, known by the name of Dabney, who was found to possess a remarkably clear knowledge of the topography of the whole region; and he was employed as cook and body servant at headquarters. When he first saw our system of army telegraphs, the idea interested him intensely, and he begged the operators to explain the signs to him. They did so, and found that he could understand and remember the meaning of the various movements as well as any of his brethren of paler hue.

Not long after, his wife, who had come with him expressed a great anxiety to be allowed to go over to the other side as servant to a "secesh [secessionist] woman." . . . The request was granted. Dabney's wife went across the Rappahannock, and in a few days was duly installed as laundress at the headquarters of a prominent rebel General. Dabney, her husband, on the north bank, was soon found to be wonderfully well informed as to all the rebel plans. Within an hour of the time that a movement of any kind was projected, or even discussed, among the rebel generals, Hooker knew all about it. He knew which corps was moving, or about to move, in what direction, how long they had been on the march, and in what force; and all this knowledge came through Dabney, and his reports always turned out to be true.

Yet Dabney was never absent, and never talked with the scouts, and seemed to be always taken up with his duties as cook and groom about headquarters.

How he obtained his information remained for some time a puzzle to the Union officers. At length, upon much solicitation, he unfolded his marvellous secret to one of our officers.

Taking him to a point where a clear view could be obtained at Fredericksburg, he pointed out a little cabin in the suburbs near the river bank, and asked him if he saw that clothes-line with clothes hanging on it to dry. "Well," said he, "that clothes-line tells me in half an hour just what goes on at Lee's headquarters. You see my wife over there; she washes for the officers, and cooks, and waits around, and as soon as she hears about any movement or anything going on, she comes down and moves the clothes on that line so I can understand it in a minute. That there gray shirt is Longstreet; and when she takes it off, it means he's gone down about Richmond. That white shirt means Hill; and when she moves it up to the west end of the line, Hill's corps has moved up stream. That red one is Stonewall. He's down on the right now, and if he moves, she will move that red shirt." . . .

As long as the two armies lay watching each other on opposite banks of the stream, Dabney, with his clothes-line telegraph, continued to be one of the promptest and most reliable of General Hooker's scouts.

John Truesdale, ed., *The Blue Coats* (Philadelphia, 1867), pp. 132-134.

## Lincoln Decides on Emancipation

[*In his diary, Gideon Wells, Lincoln's Secretary of the Navy, noted the first time that the President spoke of emancipation.*]

On Sunday, the 13th of July, 1862, President Lincoln invited me to accompany him in his carriage to the funeral of an infant child of Mr. Stanton. Secretary Seward and Mrs. Frederick Seward were also in the carriage. . . . It was on this occasion and on this ride that he first mentioned to Mr. Seward and myself the subject of emancipating the slaves by proclamation in case the rebels did not cease to persist in their war on the Government and the Union, of which he saw no evidence. He dwelt earnestly on the gravity, importance, and delicacy of the movement; said he had given it much thought, and had about come to the conclusion that it was a military necessity, absolutely essential for the salvation of the nation, that we must free the slaves or be ourselves subdued, etc., etc. This was, he said, the first occasion where he had mentioned the subject to anyone . . . and before separating, the President desired us to give the subject special and deliberate attention, for he was earnest in the conviction that something must be done. It was a new departure for the President, for until this time, in all our previous interviews, whenever the question of emancipation or the mitigation of slavery had been in any way alluded to, he had been prompt and emphatic in denouncing any interference by the General Government with the subject. . . . But the reverses before Richmond, and the formidable power and dimensions of the insurrection, which extended through all the slave States and had combined most of them in a confederacy to destroy the Union, impelled the Administration to adopt extraordinary measures to preserve the national existence. . . .

John G. Nicolay and John Hay, *Abraham Lincoln, A History*, Vol. VI (New York, 1890), pp. 121, 122.

## *The Georgia Sea Islands Celebrate Emancipation*

[*The following two descriptions are of the Emancipation Day celebration that took place at the Sea Island headquarters of Colonel Thomas Wentworth Higginson's First South Carolina Volunteers on January 1, 1863. The first section is by Charlotte Forten, the young Negro schoolteacher who was working on the island, and the second is by Colonel Higginson himself.*]

The celebration took place in the beautiful grove of live-oaks adjoining the camp. It was the largest grove we had seen. I wish it were possible to describe fitly the scene which met our eyes as we sat upon the stand, and looked down on the crowd before us. There were the black soldiers in their blue coats and scarlet pantaloons, the officers of this and other regiments in their handsome uniforms, and crowds of lookers-on,—men, women, and children, of every complexion, grouped in various attitudes under the moss-hung trees. . . .

Charlotte Forten, "Life on the Sea Islands," Part II, *Atlantic Monthly*, Vol. 13 (June, 1864), pp. 668-669.

[*Thomas Wentworth Higginson, the white commander of the First South Carolina Volunteers, describes the celebration's climax.*]

. . . the colors were presented to us by the Rev. Mr. French, a chaplain who brought them from the donors in New York. All this was according to the programme. Then followed an incident so simple, so touching, so utterly unexpected and startlingly, that I can scarcely believe it on recalling, though it gave the key-note to the whole day. The very moment the speaker had ceased, and just as I took and waved the flag, which now for the first time meant anything to these poor people, there suddenly arose, close beside the platform, a strong male voice (but rather cracked and elderly), into which two women's voices instantly blended, singing, as if by an impulse that could no more be repressed than the morning note of the song-sparrow,—

> My Country, 'tis of thee,
> Sweet land of liberty,
> Of thee I sing!

People looked at each other, and then at us on the platform, to see whence came this interruption, not set down in the bills. Firmly and irrepressibly the quavering voices sang on, verse after verse; others of the colored people joined in; some whites on the platform began, but I motioned them to silence. I never saw anything so electric; it made all other words cheap; it seemed the choked voice of a race at last unloosed. Nothing could be more wonderfully unconscious; art could not have dreamed of a tribute to the day of jubilee that should be so affecting; history will not believe it; and when I came to speak of it, after it was ended, tears were everywhere. . . . Just think of it!—the first day they had ever had a country, the first flag they had ever seen which promised anything to their people, and here, while mere spectators stood in silence, waiting for my stupid words, these simple souls burst out in their lay [song], as if they were by their own hearths at home! When they stopped, there was nothing to do for it but to speak, and I went on; but the life of the whole day was in those unknown people's song.

Thomas Wentworth Higginson, *Army Life in a Black Regiment* (Boston, 1882), pp. 40-41.

## *The First Slave Regiment*

[*Thomas Wentworth Higginson fought against slavery long before the war. He led an attack on a Boston jail to free a captured fugitive, Anthony Burns, and worked in the Underground Railroad. He fought in the Kansas civil war against the proslavery forces and was a sponsor of John Brown's raid on Harpers Ferry.*

*Here Colonel Higginson writes about his experience as commander of the First South Carolina Volunteers, the first official regiment of ex-slaves.*]

. . . I had always had so much to do with fugitive slaves, and had studied the whole subject with such interest, that I found not much to learn or unlearn as to this one point. Their courage I had before seen tested; their docile and lovable qualities I had known; and the only real surprise that experience brought me was in finding them so little demoralized. . . .

. . . In almost every regiment, black or white, there are a score or two of men who are naturally daring, who really hunger after dangerous adventures, and are happiest when allowed to seek them. Every commander gradually finds out who these men are, and habitually uses them; certainly I had such, and I remember with delight their bearing, their coolness, and their dash. Some of them were Negroes, some mulattoes. One of them would have passed for white, with brown hair and blue eyes, while others were so black you could hardly see their features. These picked men varied in other respects too; some were neat and well-drilled soldiers, while others were slovenly, heedless fellows,—the despair of their officers at inspection, their pride on a raid. They were the natural scouts and rangers of the regiment; they had the two-o'clock-in-the-morning courage, which Napoleon thought so rare. The mass of the regiment rose to the same level under excitement, and were more excitable, I think, than whites, but neither more nor less courageous. . . .

. . . I do not remember ever to have had the slightest difficulty in obtaining volunteers, but rather in keeping down the number. . . . There were more than a hundred men in the ranks who had voluntarily met more dangers in their escape from slavery than any of my young [white] captains had incurred in all their lives. . . .

. . . As to the simple general fact of courage and reliability I think no officer in our camp ever thought of there being any difference between black and white. . . .

. . . They had more to fight for than the whites. Besides the flag and the Union, they had home and wife and child. They fought with ropes round their necks, and when orders were issued that the officers of colored troops should be put to death on capture, they took a grim satisfaction. It helped their *esprit de corps* immensely. With us, at least, there was to be no play-soldier. Though they had begun with a slight feeling of inferiority to the white troops, this compliment substituted a peculiar sense of self-respect. And even when the new colored regiments began to arrive from the North my men still pointed out this difference,—that in case of ultimate defeat, the Northern troops, black or white, would go home, while the First South Carolina must fight it out or be re-enslaved. . . .

. . . Inexperienced officers often assumed that, because these men had been slaves before enlistment, they would bear to be treated as such afterwards. Experience proved the contrary. The more strongly we marked the difference between the slave and the soldier the better for the regiment. One half of military [duty] lies in obedience the other half in self-respect. A soldier without self-respect is worthless. Consequently there were no regiments in which it was so important to observe the courtesies and proprieties of military life as in these. I had to caution the officers to be more than usually particular in returning the salutations of the men . . . and on no account to omit the titles of the non-commissioned officers. . . .

. . . All now admit that the fate of the Confederacy was decided by Sherman's march to the sea. Port Royal was the objective point to which he marched, and he found the Department of the South, when he reached it, held almost exclusively by colored troops. Next to the merit of those who made the march was that of those who held open the door. That service will always remain among the laurels of the black regiments.

Thomas Wentworth Higginson, *Army Life in a Black Regiment* (Boston, 1882), pp. 243-263.

## Lincoln Defends Emancipation

[*In this letter dated August 26, 1863, President Lincoln gives his views on freeing the slaves and using them as soldiers. He is answering a letter by a man opposed to these policies.*]

I know, as fully as one can know the opinions of others, that some of the commanders of our armies in the field, who have given us our most important successes, believe the emancipation policy and the use of the colored troops constitute the heaviest blow yet dealt to the rebellion, and that at least one of these important successes could not have been achieved when it was but for the aid of black soldiers. . . .

You say you will not fight to free Negroes. Some of them seem willing to fight for you—but no matter. Fight you, then, exclusively to save the Union. I issued the proclamation on purpose to aid you in saving the Union. Whenever you shall have conquered all resistance to the Union, if I shall urge you to continue fighting, it will be an apt time then for you to declare you will not fight to free Negroes. I thought that in your struggle for the Union, to whatever extent the Negroes should cease helping the enemy, to that extent it weakened the enemy in his resistance to you. Do you think differently? I thought that whatever Negroes can be got to do as soldiers leaves just so much less for white soldiers to do in saving the Union. Does it appear otherwise to you? But Negroes, like other people, act upon motives. Why should they do anything for us, if we will do nothing for them? If they stake their lives for us, they must be prompted by the strongest motive, even the promise of freedom. And the promise, being made, must be kept. . . .

Peace does not appear so distant as it did. I hope it will come soon, and come to stay; and so come as to be worth the keeping in all future time. . . . And then there will be some black men who can remember that with silent tongue, and clenched teeth, and steady eye, and well-poised bayonet they have helped mankind on [to] this great consummation; while I fear there will be some white ones unable to forget that with malignant heart and deceitful speech they strove to hinder it.

John G. Nicolay and John Hay, *Abraham Lincoln, A History*, Vol. VII (New York, 1904), pp. 382-384.

## *The Battle of Milliken's Bend, Louisiana*

[*On Sunday morning, June 6, 1863, a little over 1,000 Negro troops, who had been so recently recruited that they still had not been taught the use of their weapons, were surprised in camp by a rebel force of about 2,000 men. An eyewitness makes this report.*]

. . . a force of about one thousand Negroes and two hundred men of the Twenty-third Iowa . . . was surprised in camp by a rebel force of about two thousand men. Before [their] colonel was ready, the men were in line, ready for action. As before stated, the rebels drove our force toward the gunboats, taking colored men prisoners and murdering them. This so enraged them that they rallied and charged the enemy more heroically and desperately than has been recorded during the war. It was a genuine bayonet charge, a hand-to-hand fight, that has never occurred to any extent during this prolonged conflict. Upon both sides men were killed with the butts of muskets. White and black men were lying side by side, pierced by bayonets, and in some instances transfixed to the earth. In one instance, two men, one white and the other black, were found dead, side by side, each having the other's bayonet through his body. If facts prove to be what they are now represented, this engagement of Sunday morning will be recorded as the most desperate of this war. . . . it was a contest between enraged men: on the one side from hatred to a race; and on the other, desire for self-preservation, revenge for past grievances, and the inhuman murder of their comrades. One brave man took his former master prisoner, and brought him into camp with great gusto. A rebel prisoner made a particular request, that *his own* Negroes should not be placed over him as a guard. Dame Fortune is capricious! His request was *not* granted. Their mode of warfare does not entitle them to any privileges.

George W. Williams, *History of the Negro Race in America*, Vol. II (New York, 1883), pp. 326-327.

## Sergeant William Carney Wins the Congressional Medal of Honor at Fort Wagner

[*On July 18, 1863, the 54th Massachusetts Volunteers—first Negro regiment from the North—distinguished themselves in their attack on Fort Wagner, off the South Carolina coast. In this letter, written on October 15, 1863, Colonel M. S. Littlefield forwards to the Governor of Massachusetts an eyewitness report of Sergeant William Carney's heroism.*]

When the Sergeant arrived to within about one hundred yards of the fort—he was with the first battalion, which was in the advance of the storming column—he received the regimental colors, pressed forward to the front rank, near the Colonel [Shaw], who was leading the men over the ditch. He says, as they ascended the wall of the fort, the ranks were full, but as soon as they reached the top, "they melted away" before the enemy's fire "almost instantly." He received a severe wound in the thigh, but fell only upon his knees. He planted the flag upon the parapet, lay down on the outer slope, that he might get as much shelter as possible; there he remained for over half an hour, till the 2nd brigade came up. He kept the colors flying until the second conflict was ended. When our forces retired he followed, creeping on one knee, still holding up the flag. It was thus that Sergeant Carney came from the field, having held the emblem of liberty over the walls of Fort Wagner . . . and having received two very severe wounds, one in the thigh and one in the head. Still he refused to give up his sacred trust until he found an officer of his regiment.

When he entered the field hospital, where his wounded comrades were being brought in, they cheered him and the colors. Though nearly exhausted with the loss of blood, he said: "Boys, the old flag never touched the ground."

Of him as a man and soldier, I can speak in the highest term of praise.

---

George W. Williams, *History of the Negro Race in America*, Vol. II (New York, 1883) pp. 330-331.

# A Sailor Is Awarded the Navy Medal of Honor

[*This is the Navy Medal of Honor citation for a Negro seaman.*]

[*Joachim Pease, Seaman*] Served as seaman on board the U.S.S. *Kearsarge* when she destroyed the *Alabama* off Cherbourg, France, 19 June 1864. Acting as loader during this bitter engagement, PEASE exhibited marked coolness and good conduct and was highly recommended by his divisional officer for gallantry under fire. [General Order 45, Dec. 31, 1864]

---

The United States Navy, *Medal of Honor, 1861-1949*, p. 43, n.d., n.p.

# Negro Troops in Battle

[*This is a description of the first battle of the Negro troops commanded by General Hinks. The battle took place near Petersburg, Virginia, in June, 1864.*]

. . . The Rebel cannon opened. The sons of Africa did not flinch, but took their positions with deliberation. They had been slaves; they stood face to face with their former masters, or with their representatives. The flag in front of them waving in the morning breeze was the emblem of oppression; the banner above them was the flag of the free. . . .

The Rebels were on a knoll in the field, and had a clear sweep of all the approaches. The advancing troop must come out from the woods, rush up the slope, and carry it at the point of the bayonet, receiving the tempest of musketry and canister.

Hinks deployed his line. At the word of command the colored men stepped out from the woods, and stood before the enemy. They gave a volley, and received one in return. Shells crashed through them, but, unheeding the storm, with a yell they started up the slope upon the run. They received one charge of canister, one scathing volley of musketry. Seventy of their number went down, but the living hundreds rushed on. The Rebels did not wait their coming, but fled towards Petersburg, leaving one of the pieces of artillery in the hands of their assailants, who leaped over the works, turned it in a twinkling, but were not able to fire upon the retreating foe, fleeing in consternation towards the main line of entrenchments two miles east of the city.

The colored troops were wild with joy. They embraced the captured cannon with affectionate enthusiasm, patting it as if it were animate, and could appreciate the endearment.

"Every soldier of the colored division was two inches taller for that achievement," said an officer describing it. These regiments were the Fifth and Twenty-Second United States colored troops, who deserve honorable mention in history.

Charles Carleton Coffin, *Four Years of Fighting* (Boston, 1866), p. 356.

# Sherman's Armies March Through North Carolina

[*General Sherman's march to the sea was joined by many thousands of slaves anxious to leave the plantations. Sherman's aide, Major George E. Nichols, talked to one of these families in Fayetteville, North Carolina.*]

As in other parts of the South which we have visited, the masters have run away, taking with them all the able-bodied slaves; but the Negroes who were able escaped, and have returned to join our column. . . .

An intelligent old quadroon woman, whose mother, eighty-six years of age, sat near, and who was surrounded by her daughters and grandchildren—four generations in one group—said to me today:

"There, sir, are my two sons-in-law. Yesterday morning their master tried to take them away, offering them their freedom if they would go into the army voluntarily; but they knew better than that. They never would fire a gun against the Federals."

"No," interposed one of the young men; "I would not fight for the man who is my master and my father at the same time. If they had forced me into the army, I would have shot the officer they put over me the first time I got a chance."

The old grandmother, who, with her family, spoke with no trace of the Negro dialect, continued:

"No, sir; the slaves know too well what it means; they'd never put muskets in the slaves' hands if they were not afeared that their cause was gone up. They are going to be whipped; they are whipped now. . . ."

"Indeed, sir," they all broke out with one accord, "if we can only get to any place where we can be free, and able to work for ourselves, we shall be thankful."

---

Brevet Major George Ward Nichols, *The Story of the Great March* (New York, 1865), pp. 236-239.

## Demand for a Soldier's Pay

[*Corporal James Henry Gooding of the 54th Massachusetts Colored Regiment wrote this letter to protest the fact that Negro soldiers received less pay than whites. His regiment refused to accept any pay for 18 months until the War Department stopped this discrimination. By the time the pay was equalized, however, Corporal Gooding was dead. Captured in battle, he died in Andersonville prison.*]

Morris Island, Department of the South, September 28, 1863.

Your Excelency Abraham Lincoln:
Your Excelency will pardon the presumtion of an humble individual like myself, in addressing you, but the earnest Solicitation of

my Comrades in Arms, besides the genuine interest felt by myself in the matter is my excuse, for placing before the Executive head of the Nation our Common Grievance: On the 6th of the last Month, the Paymaster of the department informed us, that if we would decide to receive the sum of $10 (ten dollars) per month, he would come and pay us that sum [white soldiers were paid $13]. . . . Now the main question is, Are we *Soldiers* or are we LABOURERS. We are fully armed, and equipped, have done all the various Duties, pertaining to a Soldiers life, have conducted ourselves, to the complete satisfaction of General Officers, who were, if any, prejediced *against* us, but who now accord us all the encouragement, and honour due us: have shared the perils, and Labour, of Reducing the first stronghold, that flaunted a Traitor Flag: and more, Mr. President, Today, the Anglo Saxon Mother, Wife, or Sister, are not alone, in tears for departed Sons, Husbands, and Brothers. The patient Trusting Decendants of Africs Clime, have dyed the ground with blood, in defense of the Union, and Democracy. Men too your Excellency, who know in a measure, the cruelties of the Iron heel of oppression, which in years gone by, the very Power, their blood is now being spilled to Maintain, ever ground them in the dust. But When the war trumpet sounded o'er the land, when men knew not the Friend from the Traitor, the Black man laid his life at the Altar of the Nation,—and he was refused. When the Arms of the Union, were beaten, in the first year of the War, And the Executive called [for] more food, for its ravaging maws, again the black man begged, the privelege of Aiding his Country in her need, to be again refused. And now, he is in the War: and how has he conducted himself? Let their dusky forms, rise up, out of the mires of James Island, and give the answer. Let the rich mould around Wagners parapets be upturned, and there will be found an Eloquent answer. Obedient and patient, and Solid as a wall are they, all we lack, is a paler hue, and a better aquaintance with the Alphabet. Now your Excellency We have done a Soldiers Duty. Why cant we have a Soldiers pay? . . .

We appeal to You, Sir: as the Executive of the Nation, to have us Justly Dealt with. The Regt, do pray, that they be assured their service will be fairly appreciated, by paying them as american Soldiers, not as menial hierlings. Black men You may well know, are poor, three dollars per month, for a year, will supply their needy Wives, and little ones, with fuel. If you, as Chief Magistrate of the Nation, will assure us, of our whole pay, we are content, our Patriotism, our enthusiasm will have a new impetus, to exert our energy more and more to Aid Our Country. Not that our hearts ever flagged, in Devotion, spite the evident apathy displayed in our behalf, but We feel as though, our Country spurned us, now we are sworn to serve her.

Please give this a moments attention.

Letter of Corporal James Henry Gooding to President Abraham Lincoln (Washington: National Archives, War Records Office), pp. 1-4.

# Harriet Tubman Leads a Raid

[*Famous for her abolitionist activities, Harriet Tubman, an ex-slave, volunteered to serve in the Union Army.*]

General Hunter asked her at one time if she would go with several gun-boats up the Combahee River, the object of the expedition being to take up the torpedoes placed by the rebels in the river, to destroy railroads and bridges, and to cut off supplies from the rebel troops. She said she would go if Colonel Montgomery was to be appointed commander of the expedition. Colonel Montgomery was one of John Brown's men, and was well known to Harriet. Accordingly, Colonel Montgomery was appointed to the command, and Harriet, with several men under her . . . accompanied the expedition. Harriet describes in the most graphic manner the appearance of the plantations as they passed up the river; the frightened Negroes leaving their work and taking to the woods, at sight of the gun-boats; then coming to peer out like startled deer, and scudding away like the wind at the sound of the steam-whistle. . . . But the word was passed along by the mysterious telegraphic communication existing among these simple people, that these were "Lincoln's gun-boats come to set them free." In vain, then, the drivers used their whips in their efforts to hurry the poor creatures back to their quarters; they all turned and ran for the gun-boats. They came down every road, across every field, just as they had left their work and their cabins; women with children clinging around their necks, hanging to their dresses, running behind, all making at full speed for "Lincoln's gun-boats." Eight hundred poor wretches at one time crowded the banks, with their hands extended toward their deliverers, and they were all taken off upon the gun-boats, and carried down to Beaufort.

Sarah Bradford, *Harriet, The Moses of Her People* (New York, 1886), pp. 99-100.

## Susie King Taylor and the Union Army

[*Ex-slave Susie K. Taylor married a soldier and went to work for the army wherever she could be of help. She was one of thousands of Negro women, free or slave, who served as nurses, teachers, and cooks.*]

I taught a great many of the comrades in Company E. to read and write, when they were off duty. Nearly all were anxious to learn. My husband taught some also when it was convenient for him. . . .

About four o'clock, July 2 [1864], the charge was made. The firing could be plainly heard in camp. I hastened down to the landing and remained there until eight o'clock that morning. When the wounded arrived, or rather began to arrive, the first one brought in was Samuel Anderson of our company. He was badly wounded. Then others of our boys, some with their legs off, arm gone, foot off, and wounds of all kinds imaginable. They had to wade through creeks and marshes, as they were discovered by the enemy and shelled very badly. A number of the men were lost, some got fastened in the mud and had to cut off the legs of their pants, to free themselves. The 103d New York suffered the most, as their men were very badly wounded.

My work now began. I gave assistance to try to alleviate their sufferings. I asked the doctor at the hospital what I could get for them to eat. They wanted soup, but that I could not get; but I had a few cans of condensed milk and some turtle eggs, so I thought I would try to make some custard. . . . This I carried to the men, who enjoyed it very much. My services were given at all times for the comfort of these men. I was on hand to assist wherever needed. I was enrolled as company laundress, but I did very little of it, because I was always busy doing other things through camp, and was employed all the time doing something for the officers and comrades.

Susie King Taylor, *Reminiscences of My Life in Camp* (Boston, 1902), pp. 21, 34-35.

# The Colored Troops Take Over Charleston, South Carolina

[*On February 17, 1865, the 55th Regiment of Massachusetts Volunteers marched triumphantly into the rebel city singing "Babylon Is Falling," and the "Battle-Cry of Freedom." A few days later war correspondent Charles Coffin described them, their reception, and their duties.*]

While dining we heard the sound of drums and a chorus of voices. Looking down the broad avenue we saw a column of troops advancing with steady step and even ranks. It was nearly sunset, and their bayonets were gleaming in the level rays. It was General Potter's brigade, led by the Fifty-Fifth Massachusetts,—a regiment recruited from the ranks of slavery. Sharp and shrill the notes of the fife, stirring the drum-beat, deep and resonant the thousand voices singing their most soul-thrilling war-song,—

*"John Brown's body lies a mouldering in the grave."*

Mingling with the chorus were cheers for Governor Andrew [of Massachusetts] and Abraham Lincoln!

They raised their caps, hung them upon their bayonets. Proud their bearing. They came as conquerors. Some of them had walked those streets before as slaves. Now they were freemen,—soldiers of the Union, defenders of its flag.

Around them gathered a dusky crowd of men, women, and children, dancing, shouting, mad with very joy. Mothers held up their little ones to see the men in blue, to catch a sight of the starry flag, with its crimson folds and tassels of gold. . . .

Up the avenue, past the citadel, with unbroken ranks, they marched, offering no insult, uttering no epithet, manifesting no revenge, for all the wrongs of centuries heaped upon them by a people now humbled and at their mercy. . . .

The deepest humiliation to the Charlestonians was the presence of Negro soldiers. They were the provost guard [Military Police] of the city, with their head-quarters in the citadel. Whoever desired protection papers or passes, whoever had business with the marshal or the general commanding the city, rich or poor, high-born or low-born, white or black, man or woman, must meet a colored sentinel face to face and obtain from a colored sergeant permission to enter the gate. They were first in the city, and it was their privilege to guard it, their duty to maintain law and order.

A Rebel officer who had given his parole, but who was indiscreet enough to curse the Yankees, was quietly marched off to the guard-house by these colored soldiers. It was galling to his pride, and he walked with downcast eyes and subdued demeanor.

Charles Carleton Coffin, *Four Years of Fighting* (Boston, 1866) pp. 481-482.

## A New Life for Slaves

[*When the Union Army and Navy freed the slaves of the Georgia and South Carolina Sea Islands, Charlotte Forten, a free Negro from New England, was one of many teachers who came to help the slaves learn new ways. Her description gives us a picture of her own feelings as well as those of the freedmen.*]

Christmas night, the children came in and had several grand shouts. They were too happy to keep still.

"Oh, Miss, all I want to do is to sing and shout!" said our little pet, Amaretta. And sing and shout she did, to her heart's content.

She read nicely, and was very fond of books. The tiniest children are delighted to get a book in their hands. Many of them already know their letters. The parents are eager to have them learn. . . .

They are willing to make many sacrifices that their children may attend school. One old woman, who had a large family of children and grandchildren, came regularly to school in the winter, and took her seat among the little ones. She was at least sixty years old. Another woman—who had one of the best faces I ever saw—came daily, and brought her baby in her arms. . . .

While writing these pages I am once more nearing Port Royal . . . . I shall dwell again among "mine own people." I shall gather my scholars about me, and see smiles of greeting break over their dusk[y] faces. My heart sings a song of thanksgiving, at the thought that even I am permitted to do something for a long-abused race, and aid in promoting a higher, holier, and happier life on the Sea Islands.

Charlotte Forten, "Life on the Sea Islands," Part II, *Atlantic Monthly*, Vol. 13 (June, 1864), pp. 667-676.

## *The Death of President Lincoln*

[*America's Negro population was particularly shocked at the tragic death of the President. They were shocked, too, to learn that they would not be included in the funeral procession—until they strongly protested. Frances Ellen Watkins Harper, a widely known Negro poet, expressed the feelings of many in this letter written a few days after the assassination.*]

Sorrow treads on the footsteps of the nation's joy. A few days since the telegraph thrilled and throbbed the nation's joy. To-day a nation sits down beneath the shadow of its mournful grief. Oh, what a terrible lesson does this event read to us! . . . Well, it may be in the providence of God this blow was needed to intensify the nation's hatred of slavery, to show the utter fallacy of basing national reconstruction upon the votes of returned rebels, and rejecting loyal black men. . . . Moses, the meekest man on earth, led the children of Israel over the Red Sea, but was not permitted to see them settled in Canaan. Mr. Lincoln has led [us] up through another Red Sea to the table land of triumphant victory, and God has seen fit to summon for the new era another man. . . . Let the whole nation resolve that the whole virus shall be eliminated from its body; that in the future slavery shall only be remembered as a thing of the past that shall never have the faintest hope of resurrection.

William Still, *The Underground Rail Road* (Philadelphia, 1872), pp. 766-767.

# 10

# *Presidential Reconstruction*

THE bullet that killed Abraham Lincoln brought deep sadness to the nation and great fear to the Negro population. For Lincoln represented the end of slavery and great hope for future progress. Although the war had ended, and slavery had been abolished by the Thirteenth Amendment to the Constitution, many in the South could not and would not accept the new situation. As the freedman reached for a new job, land, education, and a home, he found "a hundred cuffs for one helping hand," according to one visitor in the South.

### *The Freedmen's Bureau*

Before the New England school mistresses arrived to help, or the government had thought of a Freedmen's Bureau to assist, former slaves had built schools, churches, and meeting halls and had gone to work on their master's abandoned lands. Seventeen Negro carpenters built houses and schools, and teachers were giving lessons before the arrival of the New England volunteers to the Georgia Sea Islands.

It was the Freedmen's Bureau, however, that organized all efforts at education and aid for the former slaves. General Oliver Howard, who had fought at Gettysburg and marched through Georgia with General Sherman, was placed in charge by Secretary of War Stanton. "Mr. Stanton held out to me a great basketfull of papers, saying: 'There is your bureau, General, take it.' I took my

*Returning soldiers are discharged at Little Rock, Arkansas.*

bureau and walked out with it. I think now that God led me and
assigned that work to me." In the five years of its existence, the bureau built 4,300 schools and hired 3,300 teachers. It began Howard,
Fisk, Storer, and Hampton universities. It provided courts, hospitals,
and relief to whites and Negroes alike. The whites took greater advantage of its services than did the Negroes. "We have fed with government charity rations sixty-four white to one colored person," reported a Bureau official in the upper South.

The schools established by the freedmen and the Bureau were
a great success. General Samuel Chapman Armstrong, who began
Hampton Institute to train teachers for the schools, was one of many
idealistic Northerners who came South to help. "I begin," he said,
"in a humble way, a more patriotic, more difficult work than fighting
for my country." Negro teachers, such as Charlotte Forten of Philadelphia, came South to teach as early as 1862. Miss Forten insisted
that her pupils hear about famous Negroes in history as well as
white heroes.

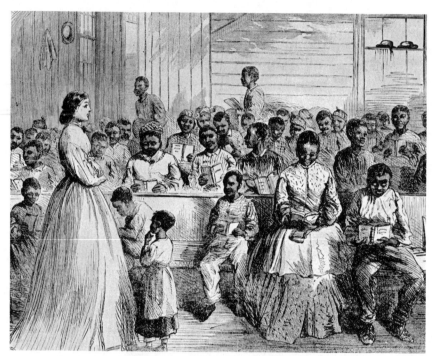

*A New England "carpetbagger" teacher instructs a Vicksburg, Mississippi school for beginning readers. Schools and teachers were a consistent target for anti-Negro violence. It was the growing competence and knowledge of the Negro that many Southern whites feared. An educated or intelligent Negro was considered "uppity" or dangerous.*

To an agent of the Freedmen's Bureau, J. W. Alvord, the success of the schools was apparent in the scene he witnessed in 1866 in North Carolina: "A child six years old, her mother, grandmother and great-grandmother, the latter over 75 years of age . . . commenced their alphabet together and each one can read the Bible fluently." In 1866 a white Tennessee official reported: "The colored people are far more zealous in the cause of education than the whites. They will starve themselves, and go without clothes, in order to send their children to school."

In its five years of operation, the Freedmen's Bureau gave out barely a million acres of land in the South while the government was giving out hundreds of millions of acres to homesteaders in the West. And almost all the Freedmen's Bureau land had to be returned to the original owners when they received their pardons from President Johnson. Without his own land, the Negro's opportunity to be independent of white control was worthless. As long as he could be fired for voting as he pleased or dispossessed from his rented farm by a landlord for the same reason, the Negro could not fight effectively for his rights.

This land question was of first importance to most poor Southerners, Negro and white. After traveling through the countryside of South Carolina, Richard Cain told the state Constitutional Convention of 1868 that the South, like the North, needed "a system of small farms." If the poor "possess lands they have an interest in the soil, in the State, in its commerce, its agriculture, and in everything pertaining to the wealth and welfare of the State." Another Negro delegate, Francis L. Cardoza, a brilliant economist, demanded the breaking up of the plantations as the best hope of democracy. But nothing this radical was done. Many years later Frederick Douglass said that this failure left the Negro "on his knees."

## President Johnson's Efforts

Throughout the South the Negro was on the move, and the whites reacted with unreasoning hatred. Carl Schurz, a brilliant German immigrant, toured the South at the President's request, in 1865 and 1866, to report on conditions. "Wherever I go—the street, the shop, the house, the hotel, or the steamboat—I hear the people talk in such a way as to indicate that they are yet unable to conceive of the Negro as possessing any rights at all." Schurz found that whites who were honorable in dealing with other whites "will cheat a Negro without feeling a single twinge of their honor. To kill a Negro, they do not deem murder. . . ."

More than cities and farms had to be rebuilt in the South. The relationship between master and slave which whites accepted as natural would prove harder to remove than the debris of war. "I never did a day's work in my life, and I don't know where to begin," said a Mississippi planter. Another former slaveholder rushed into the office of a Union general and said he expected "an outbreak at any moment" by the freedmen. When the General asked him how he knew of the revolt, he said that an 18-year-old ex-slave woman who still worked for him had refused to take a whipping. "Now this is an intolerable state of affairs," he concluded. Southern Judge Samuel Spencer reported many attacks by whites on colored men "*because they have been in the* [Union] *Army*." General Clinton Fiske described the young whites of Nashville, Tennessee: "You see young men standing on street corners with cigars in their mouths and hands in their pockets, swearing Negroes won't work." And the General added, "In this city, it is the Negroes who do the hard work."

By mid-February, 1866 a delegation of Negro leaders called on President Johnson at the White House to ask his views on civil rights and on freedmen voting. That very week ex-rebel soldiers in Kentucky (still in uniform) were robbing freedmen after the town marshal had taken away the guns of returning Negro soldiers. An officer of the Freedmen's Bureau wrote from the upper South, "I am powerless to accomplish anything without soldiers."

President Johnson, after shaking hands with the Negro delegation which included Frederick Douglass, George T. Downing of Rhode Island, and Illinois philanthropist John Jones, made clear that he opposed any federal laws to protect freedmen. He preferred to leave the matter to the states—anything else, he felt, "will commence a war of races." He suggested that Negroes migrate from the South and opposed any idea that they had a "natural" right to vote. He scoffed at the idea of Frederick Douglass that the poor whites and Negroes would build a new party and bring democracy to the South. The delegation left knowing full well that in returning the freedmen to the control of the Southern states, the President was delivering them into the hands of their old enemies.

*In 1866 Frederick Douglass and other Negroes asked President Johnson to protect Negroes' voting rights as the surest protection for all their other rights. He refused, telling Douglass that Negro rights were a state matter.*

*Cartoon showing President Andrew Johnson falsely promising a Negro vet-
eran his protection. At this very moment Negroes in New Orleans and Memphis were massacred as they tried to assert their rights. Johnson, a Southern
poor white, resented both slaveholders and Negroes.*

President Johnson's stand of denying federal protection to the
Negro and accepting the right of Southern states to handle the problem in their own way was the beginning of a fatal course that would
cripple Negro progress for almost a century. As Frederick Douglass
charged that day in President Andrew Johnson's office: "You en-
franchise your enemies and disenfranchise your friends."

The President's policies encouraged those in the South who
sought to return the Negro to a new slavery. Colonel York, one of the
federal government's officers in the South, reported that after the
President's talk with the Negro leaders "outrages upon the Freedmen, have greatly increased." Before the summer of 1866 was half
over, anti-Negro riots in Memphis and New Orleans had left hundreds of Negroes dead or wounded. General Sheridan said of the
New Orleans riot: "It was an absolute massacre."

The President's use of his pardoning power was also hurting

the freedman. In pardoning many Confederate leaders, Johnson returned their land to them. Much of this land had been given or sold to the freedmen by the United States Army and they had no intention of giving it up. At James Island, off the coasts of Georgia and South Carolina, planters attempting to reclaim their former property were driven back three times. They were "surrounded by fierce black faces and leveled guns, captured, and not permitted to regain their boat." Their lives were spared only because a government official was with them.

General Saxton, commanding the United States Department of the South, wrote to Congress in protest: "The faith of the government has been pledged these freedmen to maintain them in the possession of their homes, and to break its promise in the hours of its triumph is not becoming to a just government." He pleaded in vain for Congress to buy the land and leave it in the hands of the freedmen. "On some of the islands," he wrote, "the freedmen have established civil governments with constitutions and laws, with all the different departments for schools, churches, building roads, and other improvements." But in spite of all protests the land was restored to the original owners.

Even before President Johnson's policy was known in the South, the slaveholders had begun their own comeback campaign. For a while it appeared that they had won the peace after losing the war. Soon after the Confederate surrender, "Black Codes" were passed in every Southern state returning the freedman to the control of his former master. Under these laws Negroes were denied civil rights and were required to have a white employer or face arrest for vagrancy. Freedmen could also be arrested for "insulting" remarks or for "being impudent" to whites.

But the jails were never full—for the prisoners were soon rented out (their former masters getting first choice) to work off their jail sentences in labor. Members of the 74th United States Colored Infantry were arrested the day after they were mustered out of the Army because they did not have employment certificates. In some places freedmen were not allowed to enter skilled trades, own property, enter a town without a pass, or possess a gun. The North began to wonder just which side had won the war.

After securing control of the state governments, Southerners next moved back to the national capital. The first Southerners elected to Congress after the war included 58 Confederate Congressmen, 6

Confederate Cabinet members, 9 Confederate army officers, and Confederate Vice-President Alexander H. Stephens. If President Johnson was not unhappy, Congress was and it refused to seat the Southerners. In 1866 a Mississippi planter admitted that the Confederates had moved too soon.

> Yes, it was unwise, *at this time. We showed our hand too soon.* We ought to have waited till the troops were withdrawn, and our representatives admitted to Congress; then we could have had everything our way.

## A Soldier Asks for the Vote

*[John Cajay of the 11th United States Colored Heavy Artillery was one of many men who felt that the Negro's courage on the battlefield entitled him to the vote. He wrote this letter to a Negro newspaper on June 5, 1865 from Louisiana.]*

. . . I see, as peace and reconstruction make their progress, the predominant feeling, which [kept] . . . us from rising upon a level with other citizens, shows itself more plainly as the rebellion is being brought to a close. If we did not merit this suffrage, or had done anything detrimental to the good of the country, then I would think such proceedings were just; but when we have done all we could to help sustain the government, and assisted, with other loyal citizens, to crush this rebellion, I think it no more than right that we should have the rights of suffrage. . . .

. . . These self same people who are opposed to our right [to vote], are those who have been tutored from their cradles to look upon the Negro as their inferior, and are taught to persecute us. . . .

*The Anglo-African Magazine,* August 5, 1865, p. 1.

*[President Abraham Lincoln had written in January, 1864.]*

How to better the condition of the colored race has long been a study which has attracted my serious and careful attention; hence I think I am clear and decided as to what course I shall pursue . . . regarding it as a religious duty, as the nation's guardian of these people who have so heroically vindicated their manhood on the battlefield, where, in assisting to save the life of the republic, they have demonstrated in blood their right to the ballot. . . .

*The Liberator,* December 29, 1865.

# The Aspirations of Free Men

[*In the months following the end of the Civil War, Negroes met in Southern states to formulate their plans and desires as free men. The group that met at the First Baptist Church of Norfolk, Virginia, on December 1, 1865, drew up these resolutions.*]

. . . we are a peaceable and law abiding people and that the stories so industriously circulated against us That we are contemplating and preparing for insurrection and riotous and disorderly proceedings are vile falsehoods designed to provoke acts of unlawful violence against us. . . .

. . . we have faith in God and our Country and in the justice and humanity of the American people for redress of all our grievances but that we will not cease to importune and labor in all lawful and proper ways for equal rights as citizens until finally granted.

. . . we appoint [a committee] to proceed to Washington to urge upon Congress such legislation as will secure to the lately rebellious states a republican form of Government and the consequent protection to ourselves of life, liberty, and property and of the granting to our people in those states of the right to testify in the Courts and of equality of suffrage the same as to white citizens. That said committee be empowered to represent us before the Freedmen's Bureau at Washington . . . to secure if possible the selection and nomination . . . of the local agents by the Freedmen themselves. . . .

---

Freedmen's Bureau files (Washington, National Archives), R.G. 92.

# When Freedom Came

[*In late 1861 thousands of slaves were freed when Union forces captured Port Royal, South Carolina. President Lincoln directed Edward L. Pierce to handle their problems. After the Negroes were provided with food and clothing, Pierce established schools. He visited the schools and reported this conversation with one class of children.*]

"Children, what are you going to do when you grow up?"

"Going to work, Sir."

"On what?"

"Cotton and corn, Sir."

"What are you going to do with the corn?"

"Eat it."

"What are you going to do with the cotton?"

"Sell it."

"What are you going to do with the money you get for it?"

One boy answered in advance of the rest,—

"Put it in my pocket, Sir."

"That won't do. What's better than that?"

"Buy clothes, Sir."

"What else will you buy?"

"Shoes, Sir."

"What else are you going to do with your money?"


There was some hesitation at this point. Then the question was put,—

"What are you going to do Sundays?"

"Going to meeting."

"What are you going to do there?"

"Going to sing."

"What else?"

"Hear the parson."

"Who's going to pay him?"

One boy said,—"Government pays him;" but the rest answered, —"We's pays him."

"Well, when you grow up, you'll probably get married, as other people do, and you'll have your little children; now what will you do with them?"


There was a titter at this question; but the general response came,—

"Send 'em to school, Sir."

"Well, who'll pay the teacher?"

"We's pays him."

One who listens to such answers can hardly think that there is any natural incapacity in these children to acquire, with maturity of years, the ideas and habits of good citizens.

Edward L. Pierce, "The Freedmen at Port Royal," *Atlantic Monthly*, Vol. 12 (September, 1863), pp. 306-307.

## *"I Never Before Saw Children So Eager to Learn"*

[*This is how Charlotte Forten, one of many Negro teachers who went South to teach the ex-slaves, describes her first days of teaching school on the Georgia Sea Islands.*]

. . . I never before saw children so eager to learn, although I had had several years' experience in New-England schools. Coming to school is a constant delight and recreation to them. They come here as other children go to play. The older ones, during the summer, work in the fields from early morning until eleven or twelve o'clock, and then come to school, after their hard toil in the hot sun, as bright and as anxious to learn as ever.

Of course there are some stupid ones, but these are in the minority. The majority learn with wonderful rapidity. Many of the grown people are desirous of learning to read. It is wonderful how a people who have been so long crushed to the earth . . . can have so great a desire for knowledge, and such a capacity for attaining it. . . .

After the lessons, we used to talk freely to the children, often giving them slight sketches of some of the great and good men. Before teaching them the *John Brown* song, which they learned to sing with great spirit, Miss T. told them a story of the brave old man who had died for them. I told them about Toussaint [L'Ouverture, the Negro liberator of Haiti], thinking it well they should know what one of their own color had done for his race. They listened attentively, and seemed to understand. . . .

Charlotte Forten, "Life on the Sea Islands," *Atlantic Monthly*, Vol. 13 (March, 1864), p. 591.

## Ideas That Did Not Die with the Confederacy

[*Southerners explain how they feel about Negroes.*]

[*In 1865 a Mississippi planter speaks to a Northern visitor.*] "We can't feel towards them as you do; I suppose we ought to, but it isn't possible for us. They've always been our owned servants, and we've been used to having them mind us without a word of objection, and we can't bear anything else from them now. If that's wrong, we're to be pitied sooner than blamed, for it's something we can't help. I was always kind to my slaves. I never whipped but two boys in my life, and one of them I whipped three weeks ago."

"When he was a free man?"

"Yes; for I tell you that makes no difference in our feeling towards them. I sent a boy across the country for some goods. He came back with half the goods he ought to have got for the money. . . ."

J. T. Trowbridge, *The South* (Hartford, 1866), pp. 291-292.

[*Reuben Davis, cousin of Confederate President Jefferson Davis.*] I think the world is made up of various grades of life. I think the Negro is about two degrees below the white man. . . .

I think the Negro is by nature dishonest; I think the Negro is by nature destitute of all ideas of virtue, and I think the Negro is capable of being induced to commit any crime whatever, however violent, especially if he was encouraged by bad white men. . . . I don't think he can ever be civilized to the extent that the white man has been civilized. . . .

*Mississippi in 1875*, Senate Report 527, Part II, 44th Congress, First Session (Washington, 1875), p. 1064.

## A Northern Visitor Views the Southern Problem

[*Sidney Andrews, a white Northerner, toured the South at the close of the Civil War, and gave his impressions.*]

. . . the whites seem wholly unable to comprehend that freedom for the Negro means the same thing as freedom for them. They readily enough admit that the Government has made him free, but appear to believe that they still have the right to exercise over him the old control. . . .

. . . it is a cruel slander to say that the [Negro] race will not work, except on compulsion. I made much inquiry, wherever I went, of great numbers of planters and other employers, and found but very few cases in which it appeared that they had refused to labor reasonably well, when fairly treated and justly paid. Grudgingly admitted to any of the natural rights of man, despised alike by Unionists and Secessionists, wantonly outraged by many and meanly cheated by more of the old planters, receiving a hundred cuffs for one helping hand, and a thousand curses for one kindly word,—they bear themselves toward their former masters very much as white men and women would under the same circumstances. . . . They grope in the darkness of this transition period, and rarely find any sure stay for the weary arm and the fainting heart. Their souls are filled with a great, but vague longing for freedom; they battle blindly with fate and circumstance for the unseen and uncomprehended, and seem to find every man's hand raised against them. What wonder that they fill the land with restlessness!

---

Sidney Andrews, "Three Months Among the Reconstructionists," *Atlantic Monthly*, Vol. 17 (February, 1866), pp. 244-245.

## General Swayne Reports on Texas

[*United States General W. Swayne reported on Texas reconstruction and the problems of freedom for people of both races.*]

The entire crop raised in Texas—cotton, corn, sugar, and wheat—was gathered and saved by the 1st of December. Most assuredly no white man in Texas had anything to do with the gathering of the crops, except perhaps to look on and give orders. Who did the work? The freedmen, I am well convinced, had something to do with it; and yet there is a fierce murmur of complaint against them everywhere that they are lazy and insolent. . . .

Two-thirds of the freedmen in the section of the country which I traveled over have never received one cent of wages since they were declared free. A few of them were promised something at the end of the year, but instances of prompt payment of wages are very rare.

I saw freedmen east of the Trinity River who did not know that they were free until I told them. There had been vague rumors circulated among them that they were to be free on Christmas day, and that on New Year's there was to be a grand division of all the property, and that one-half was to be given to the black people. . . .

Public speakers in different portions of the State declared and insisted that the only object the Yankees had in continuing the war was to free the Negroes, and that if the southern people were beaten, all the lands and property would be taken from them and given to the blacks, and that the poor whites and rich people alike would be enslaved. It is not strange that the freedmen hearing this matter talked of publicly for four years by men of influence and standing should finally believe there was some truth in it. . . .

*Report of the Joint Select Committee to Inquire into the Condition of Affairs in the Late Insurrectionary States*, 42nd Congress, Second Session, 1872.

# The Rebel Spirit Lives On

[*President Andrew Johnson did everything he could to win the good will of the white Southerners. At the same time he allowed Southerners to deny justice to the freedmen—as can be seen in these two reports of the Florida Freedmen's Bureau.*]

[*Andrew Mahoney from Lake City, Florida, May 1, 1866.*] . . . the system here is when a freedman is found guilty of a crime for stealing he is fined and if he cannot pay the fine, his services are sold to the highest bidder for the shortest period of time, this is according to the Law of the State and there is no other means of punishing Criminals. In my district there are a great many freed people suffering such sentences throughout this part of the State. . . .

The blessings of Freedom have neither made them [the Negroes] vain nor indolent, on the Contrary—as it naturally should, for they are not so unappreciative, or benighted as their late groveling condition would seem to warrant the belief, it has infused into them a feeling of manliness, and enterprising industry, which, if properly nurtured will raise them as far above their late condition, as in that condition they were beneath Free-men, in a marvelously short time.

[*T. W. Osborn from Tallahassee, Florida, May 8, 1866.*] We have unfortunately had some cases of personal violence in the State. One freedman in Madison Co. killed by a white man. The murderer has made his escape without arrest. One freedman shot in Alachua County by a white man who was arrested and afterwards released from the guard by an armed mob. Other cases of violence have occurred. . . .

The freed people are working well throughout the State and the agricultural prospects of the State are now excellent. Vagrancy among the colored people is almost unknown, and no assistance is required by them. . . .

The schools are in a prosperous condition and have thus far been successfully conducted. . . .

[*Mr. Osborn did report, however, that the children in a Bureau school were attacked by the children from a white school for singing* Rally Round the Flag (*a Union Army song*) *and other patriotic songs.*]

Office of the Adjutant General, Letters Received, Vol. IV (Washington: National Archives, War Records Office, 1866).

## *Trouble for the Freedmen's Bureau in Kentucky*

[*Lieutenant-Colonel York reports on the difficulties he faces in 1866 as an agent for the Freedmen's Bureau.*]

. . . the rampant disloyalty of the people in that portion of the State [Livingston County], seems to demand immediate attention. The enemies of the Gov't, acting under a misapprehension of the action of President Johnson, have recently been more violent in denouncing the Bureau, and I am convinced that outrages upon the Freedmen, have greatly increased, from the same cause.

Mr. Furman, who was sent from this office to investigate the Bucker case, passed several days in Livingston and Lyons Counties, and reports that the Union people are alarmed by the fierce demonstrations of the rebels, who·openly denounce the Freedmen's Bureau, and seek in every way to harass the Union people, and illtreat and oppress the Freedmen—that meetings are called ostensibly to endorse the President [Andrew Johnson], but in reality to denounce the Gov't. . . . In this place the same malignant spirit of disloyalty is held in check, only by the presence of the military. During the present week the windows of the Freedmen's School house have been broken by parties unknown. . . . I have been indicted by the Grand Jury of McLenacken Co. upon a charge of having furnished false passes to slaves, and the Sheriff has a warrant to arrest me and confine me in the Co. jail in default of my giving bail in the sum of Five Hundred Dollars. . . . I would respectfully request instruction as to the action most proper in this case.

. . . it is with pleasure that I report the condition of the old [Negro] people in this place as steadily improving. All they require is an opportunity and proper encouragement to become good and useful citizens.

Office of the Adjutant General, Letters Received, Vol. IV (Washington: National Archives, War Records Office, 1866).

## The Freedmen's Bureau Courts

[*The Freedmen's Bureau brought the South a new kind of justice based on neither wealth nor color. A Northern visitor describes a few hours in a court established by the Freedmen's Bureau.*]

The freedmen's court is no respecter of persons. The proudest aristocrat and the humblest Negro stand at its bar on an equal footing. . . .

A great variety of business is brought before the Bureau. Here is a Negro-man who has printed a reward offering fifty dollars for information to assist him in finding his wife and children, sold away from him in times of slavery: a small sum for such an object, you may say, but it is all he has, and he has come to the Bureau for assistance. . . . Yonder is a white woman, who has been warned by the police that she must not live with her husband because he is black, and who has come to claim protection in her marriage relation, bringing proof that she is really a colored woman. . . . Yonder comes an old farmer with a stout colored boy, to get the Bureau's sanction to a contract they wish to make. "Pull off your hat, Bob," says the old man; "you was raised to that"; for he was formerly the lad's owner. . . . He is very grateful for what the officers do for him, and especially for the good advice they give the boy. "I'll do well by him, and larn him to read, if he'll do well by me."

As they go out, in comes a powerful, short-limbed black in tattered overcoat. . . . He has made a crop; found everything—mules, feed, implements; hired his own help,—fifteen men and women; managed everything; by agreement he was able to have one half; but, owing to an attempt to swindle him, he has had the cotton attached and now it is not on his account he has come, but he is owing his men wages, and they want something for Christmas, which he thinks reasonable, and he desires the Bureau's assistance to raise three hundred dollars. . . . "For I'm bound," he says, "to be liberal with my men."

Here is a boy, who was formerly a slave, to whom his father, a free man, willed a sum of money, which the boy's owner borrowed, giving his note for it, but never repaid,—for did not the boy and all that he had belong to his master? The worn and soiled bit of paper is produced; and now the owner will have that money to restore, with interest. Lucky for the boy that he kept that torn and dirty scrap carefully hidden all these years! . . .

J. T. Trowbridge, *The South* (Hartford, 1866), pp. 340-344.

# Defending the Night School

[*Throughout Reconstruction, the freedmen tried as best they could to defend themselves, their families, their white friends, and their property. This 1866 letter by Brevet Captain C. M. Hamilton describes how Negroes in Marianna, Florida met threats against their school and their white teacher.*]

The night school has been frequently disturbed. One evening a mob called out of the school house, the teacher, who on presenting himself was confronted with four revolvers, and menacing expressions of shooting him, if he did not promise to quit the place, and close the school.

The freedmen promptly came to his aid, and the mob dispersed.

About the 18th or 19th of the month, I was absent . . . when quite a formidable disturbance took place at this school. The same mob threatened to destroy the School that night, and the freedmen learning this, assembled at their . . . place of instruction in a condition of self-defence.

I understand that not less than forty colored men armed to protect themselves, but the preparations becoming known to the *respectable rowdies*, they only maneuvered about in small squads, and were
wise enough to avoid a collision.

It is to be lamented that such bitterness and anarchy should
exist, and on my return I discountenanced the movement, even on the
part of those who only sought self-protection. Yet I am gratified to
report that the result of this affair has been quite salutary on the
disposition of the people, for it seems to have infused a terror into
them, and they now see the fearful necessity for *law* to rule, instead
of mobs and riots.

---

Office of the Adjutant General, Letters Received, Vol. IV (Washington: National
Archives, War Records Office, 1866).

## *"The President . . . Seemed to Forget"*

[*President Johnson used his pardoning power to restore the rights of
former Confederates. He also returned their land—which had been
given to the freedmen. A Northern visitor in Hampton, Virginia described the changes which were taking place.*]

I found it a thrifty village, occupied chiefly by freedmen. The
former aristocratic residences had been replaced by Negro huts.
. . . There was an air of neatness and comfort about them which
surprised me, no less than the rapidity with which they were constructed. One man had just completed his house. He told me that it
took him a week to make the poles for it and bring them from the
woods, and four more days to build it.

A sash-factory and blacksmith's shop, shoemakers' shops and
stores, enlivened the streets. The business of the place was carried
on chiefly by freedmen, many of whom were becoming wealthy, and
paying heavy taxes to the government.

Every house had its wood-pile, poultry and pigs, and little garden devoted to corn and vegetables. Many a one had its stable and
cow, and horse and cart. The village was surrounded by freedmen's
farms, occupying the abandoned plantations of recent Rebels. The
crops looked well, though the soil was said to be poor. Indeed, this
was by far the thriftiest portion of Virginia I had seen.

In company with a gentleman who was in search of laborers, I made an extensive tour of these farms, anxious to see with my own eyes what the emancipated blacks were doing for themselves. I found no idleness anywhere. Happiness and industry were the universal rule. I conversed with many of the people, and heard their simple stories. They had but one trouble: the owners of the lands they occupied were coming back with their pardons [from the President] and demanding the restoration of their estates. Here they [the freedmen] had settled on abandoned Rebel lands, under the direction of the government, and with the government's pledge, given through its [Army] officers, and secured by an act of Congress, that they should be protected in the use and enjoyment of those lands for a term of three years, each freedman occupying no more than forty acres, and paying an annual rate to the government not exceeding six per cent. of their value. Here, under the shelter of that promise, they had built their little houses and established their humble homes. What was to become of them? On one estate of six hundred acres there was a thriving community of eight hundred freedmen. The owner had been pardoned unconditionally by the President, who, in his mercy to one class, seemed to forget what justice was due to another.

J. T. Trowbridge, *The South* (Hartford, 1866), pp. 220-221.

# 11

# *Congressional Reconstruction*

TO some in Congress, it was obvious that radical measures were necessary to halt disloyalty in the South and to protect the rights of the freedmen. Two abolitionists, Thaddeus Stevens in the House and Charles Sumner in the Senate, led the "Radicals" of Congress to enact new laws. Over the vetoes of President Johnson, Congress passed legislation that provided for military control of the South, gave equal rights to Negroes, and canceled the rights of ex-Confederate leaders. The battle over Reconstruction resulted in the unsuccessful attempt to remove the President from office. By a single Senate vote, Andrew Johnson kept the Presidency.

In the South "Radical Reconstruction" led to the beginning of a new social order. The freedmen's right to vote was protected by the Fourteenth and Fifteenth Amendments to the Constitution. In an 1864 letter to General Wadsworth of New York, President Lincoln had said that he felt that Negro soldiers "have demonstrated in blood their right to the ballot, which is but the human protection of the flag they have so fearlessly defended." Congressman Thaddeus Stevens saw the vote of freedmen as absolutely necessary to protect their rights and keep the South loyal. "If it be just," he said, "it should not be denied; if it be necessary, it should be adopted; if it be punishment to traitors, they deserve it." Although the overwhelming majority of ex-slaves could neither read nor write, neither could many white Southern voters or the European immigrants who voted in large Northern cities.

*Outside the doors of Congress, Negroes celebrate passage of the Fourteenth Amendment granting them citizenship and equality. After Reconstruction the Amendment was not enforced.*

Now Negroes and poor whites began rebuilding their state governments. They drew up new constitutions, approved the Fourteenth and Fifteenth Amendments, returned their states to the Union, and elected men to Congress. Although Negro voters outnumbered whites in several states, they never sought to control any government at any time. Though Negroes held offices from local sheriff to state governor, they were always willing to support white candidates. One Negro, P. B. S. Pinchback, served 43 days as Governor of Louisiana when the white Governor was removed by impeachment.

*P. B. S. Pinchback*

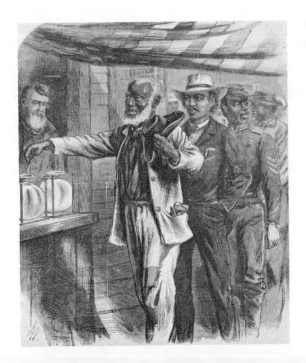

*Under the protection of the Fourteenth Amendment and federal troops Southern Negroes began to vote. Negroes helped draw up new state constitutions in each Southern state. Only South Carolina's Constitutional Convention had a majority of Negroes; Louisiana's had an equal number of Negroes and whites. Whites predominated in all others.*

At South Carolina's Constitutional Convention Negroes played a decisive role—there were 76 of them among the 131 delegates. Among the delegates were such brilliant and educated Negroes as Francis Cardoza and Robert B. Elliott, both educated at British universities. But it was another Negro college graduate and delegate, Reverend Richard Cain, who proclaimed the great purpose of the convention.

*Reverend Richard Cain was one of several college-educated Negroes to take part in South Carolina's Constitutional Convention of 1868 and in the government that developed from it. He was twice elected to the United States Congress.*

> I want a constitution that shall do justice to all men. I have no prejudices and feel above making any distinctions. . . . I hope we will take hold high upon the highway of human progress. . . . I want to see internal improvements, the railroads rebuilt, and, in fact, the whole internal resources of the State so developed that she shall be brought back more happy and prosperous than she ever was.

The Constitution drawn up by the Negroes and whites of the state of South Carolina brought the great reforms of the North to the South. Louis F. Post, who was to serve Woodrow Wilson for eight years as Assistant Secretary of Labor, was present in South Carolina and recalled:

> By every truly democratic test, that Negro-made constitution of South Carolina stands shoulder high above the white man's Constitution which it superseded.

The state lowered the taxes on the poor, abolished imprisonment for debt, granted voting rights to all regardless of property or race. The state's first public school system was established. Women were granted greater rights than ever before. Presidential electors were chosen directly by the people. Courts, county governments, hospitals, and charitable and penal institutions had to be built or reorganized.

Years later Negro Congressman Joseph Rainey, a former slave who escaped during the Civil War, pointed with pride to the justice of the South Carolina Constitution:

*Congressman Joseph Rainey of South Carolina.*

> Our convention which met in 1868, and in which Negroes were in a large majority . . . adopted a liberal constitution, securing alike equal rights to all citizens, white and black, male and female, as far as possible. Mark you, we did not discriminate, although we had a majority. Our constitution towers up in its majesty with provisions for the equal protection of all classes of citizens.

In Mississippi, too, "a state government had to be organized from top to bottom" and this "important task was splendidly, creditably, and economically done," reported Negro leader John R. Lynch, later Mississippi's lone Negro Congressman.

Vast political changes were taking place from Virginia to Texas. Edward King, a Northern writer touring the South in 1873, who had many anti-Negro prejudices, found their contributions to government remarkable for a people just released from slavery. In Virginia he found that Negro officeholders often had a "ludicrous" manner of speech, "but it was evident that all were acting intelligently." He visited a city council meeting and found it "as well conducted as that of any Eastern city." In Arkansas he found Negro officials "of excellent ability." In Florida he found that the State Superintendent of Education was a colored "gentleman of considerable culture and capacity."

In Mississippi and South Carolina King saw large numbers of Negro officials among the higher and lower officers of the states. He noted them in Natchez managing city affairs in "a very satisfactory" manner. In South Carolina King found that "the President of the Senate and the Speaker of the House, both colored, were elegant and accomplished men, highly educated, who would have creditably presided over any commonwealth's legislative assembly." As King stood in the library of the state university, two Negro Senators were enrolling in the law classes. "I was informed that dozens of members were occupied every spare moment outside of the sessions in faithful study."

*A Negro policeman in South Carolina in 1873. During Reconstruction there were Negro sheriffs, mayors, judges, and representatives in the South.*

A new day had dawned in the South. In Natchez, Mississippi (which had a Negro mayor) black and white children played together in the streets. Louisiana School Superintendent Thomas Conway described school integration: "The children were simply kind to each other in the school-room as in the streets and elsewhere! . . ."

*Negro and white children play together during Reconstruction. Children were always willing to break racial barriers.*

But 99 per cent of the Southern schools remained segregated. Negro parents knew that school integration would lead to the closing of schools. They accepted education on a segregated level rather than this dread possibility.

Concluding the 1873-1874 session of the South Carolina legislature, the Negro Speaker of the House, S. J. Lee, thanked the men of both races who had made it a success. He admitted that the group was little skilled in government but stated that they sincerely sought to serve the best interests of the state. He pointed out how they had reduced the debt from 20 to 6 million dollars, and said that they, "in a large degree, regained the confidence of the public." Turning to the future, he said: "The first thing necessary for us to do is to secure as much intelligence as we can. Intelligence, is *the* power, the controller of a nation's fate, and that we must secure at all hazards." He pointed with great pride to growing numbers of schools and the increasing number of "competent, well-trained teachers." New scholarships at the university were established for the poor and "the people are becoming daily more enlightened." "The colored people . . . are progressive and thrifty, and striving to educate themselves, and thereby become worthy and prosperous citizens." He ended by thanking them for electing him Speaker. "I felt my inexperience and the heavy responsibility resting upon me. I have tried, and I hope successfully, to be impartial and just. If sometimes I failed," Mr. Lee admitted, "attribute it rather to the head than the heart. . . ."

*South Carolina legislators. For several years Negroes were a majority of the members of the state's lower house. Whites continued to control the senate, courts, governorship, and most local offices.*

## The Negro in Congress

From 1870 to 1901 22 Negroes served their states as Congressmen. Southern Negroes sat in every Congress from the 41st to the 56th, with one exception. Although half of them were former slaves, the group included brilliant men and superb orators. Republican Presidential candidate James G. Blaine, who served with many of these men, said of their abilities:

> The colored men who took seats in both the Senate and the House did not appear ignorant or helpless. They were as a rule studious, earnest, ambitious men whose public conduct . . . would be honorable to any race.

None of them, pointed out one former Confederate leader, had ever been touched by the corruption that had reached so many men in the

THE FIRST COLORED SENATOR AND REPRESENTATIVES.
In the 41ˢᵗ and 42ⁿᵈ Congress of the United States.

A Currier and Ives print of seven of the fourteen Negro Congressmen who served during Reconstruction (1870-1876).

federal government during this era of easy money and low public morality.

Half of the Negro Congressmen were college-educated men, and several held college degrees. Robert Smalls, who served five full terms as a South Carolina Congressman, was the war hero who had delivered a Confederate gunboat to the Union Navy. All of the men were vitally interested in protecting the new rights of the freedmen and battled long hours for passage of civil rights laws. The interest of Negro Congressmen in civil rights often stemmed from their own bitter experiences on trains or in restaurants. Jefferson Long, Georgia's only Negro Congressman, spoke from personal experience against violence during elections. While seven of his supporters were shot in street fighting one Election Day, Long hid in a church belfry. These Congressmen also demanded protection for the many whites in the South who faced violent attack for defending equality.

The 22 Negro Congressmen (two were Senators from Mississippi) took an interest in a wide range of issues besides civil rights. As loyal Republicans they supported higher tariffs to protect American industry. Some favored soldier's pensions, internal improvements, and federal aid to education. Mississippi Senator B. K. Bruce was one of the very few members of Congress to defend the American Indians from unfair government laws and the Chinese immigrants from the exclusion policies which most Congressmen wanted adopted. On February 15, 1879 Bruce presided over the United States Senate.

*Senator B. K. Bruce of Mississippi. A former runaway slave, Bruce once received six votes for the Republican Vice-Presidential nomination and was considered for a post in President Garfield's cabinet. He was appointed Register of the Treasury and his signature on all United States paper money made it valid.*

## The Violent End of Reconstruction

The downfall of the Negro-white governments of the South was inevitable since Negroes had few guns, little land, and less government protection. Organized violence was the main weapon of those who sought to restore the old order.

Masked night riders such as the Ku Klux Klan sprang up everywhere to terrorize Negro voters and their white supporters. The main Klan targets were Negro officials, teachers, and successful farmers. When freedmen "made good money and had a good farm, the Ku Klux went to work and burned 'em down," recalled one

Negro. In 1869 a Louisiana agent of the Freedmen's Bureau reported: "*Driving the freedmen from their crop* and seizing it themselves when it is grown, is a complaint against the planters that comes to us from every quarter." Cane Cook of Georgia was beaten senseless by his landlord in 1869 when he tried to argue with him about his share of the crop. Each year, along with the "generous yield of nature, so welcome, so needed, so widespread, come, too, reports of injustice, outrage, violence, and crime," wrote a United States official.

The 25,000 troops assigned to control the South—and guard the entire Mexican border—were not able to halt the Klan attacks. While some officers did their best others made only token efforts. Striking at night, masked, and on fast horses, the Klan picked off the most competent and daring of the Negro leaders. No courts convicted the Klan leaders. "We are in the hands of murderers," wrote 300 Vicksburg voters in 1875. "They say they will carry this election either by ballot or bullet." Negroes who were ready to fight back often had been stripped of their weapons by white sheriffs, or were too poor to afford guns. Abraham Burriss appealed to Governor Ames of Mississippi: "But give us guns and we will show the scoundrels that colored people *will fight*." After 30 Negroes were massacred at Meridian, Mississippi in 1871, Congress passed a law to end the Ku Klux Klan menace, but other organizations sprang up at once to take the Klan's place.

Negroes reacted to the mounting violence in many ways. Negro militia companies were formed, some sponsored by the state governments. Others warned of the consequences of meeting violence with violence. Reverend Charles Ennis of Georgia explained the problem:

> We have no protection at all from the laws of Georgia. . . . A great many freedmen have told me that we should be obliged to rise and take arms and protect ourselves, but I have always told them this would not do; that the whole South would then come against us and kill us off, as the Indians have been killed off. I have always told them the best way was for us to apply to the Government for protection, and let them protect us.

The attacks on Negro and white teachers and schools for freedmen did not cease. Samuel Allen, a Negro teacher, was attacked by a mob in 1869 because he had "committed a great wrong; I had kept a

*Anti-Negro violence was designed to prevent Negroes from holding office, voting, and attending schools. Federal troops seemed powerless to halt the violence.*

Sunday school. . . ." Allen fought off the mob with a saber and fled to the woods. An Alabama teacher was warned to "dismiss the school immediately or prepare yourself . . . and you had better move instanter." When a mob in Marianna, Florida called a white teacher out of his Negro school, "the freedmen came promptly to his aid, and the mob dispersed," reported a United States Army captain. When the mob returned the next night "forty colored men armed to protect themselves" and drove the mob off without firing a shot. In all Southern states, schools were set ablaze and teachers beaten or forced to leave the state.

Weapons more subtle than violence were used against the reconstruction governments. Their enemies charged them with fraud or misuse of public funds. Corruption of public officials during the postwar period reached into all levels of government; city, state, and federal. This was the era of the Credit Mobilier scandal, the Whiskey Ring, the salary grab, and the Tweed Ring. In New York the Tweed Ring stole $100,000,000 while it ran the city government.

*Cartoonist Thomas Nast pictures the corruption of New York's Tweed Ring which ran New York City in 1867. It was an era of corruption in local, state, and national governments, including the Negro-white governments of the South. Though in on "the take" Negroes received less than their former masters, railroad interests, carpetbaggers, and former Confederates. But those who sought the elimination of Negroes from Southern governments heaped the blame on them for all corruption.*

Members of President Grant's Cabinet fled the country to escape prosecution for the misuse of public funds.

The Reconstruction governments of the South also were often unable to halt those who sought to use governmental power for personal gain. While public funds were misused by the Reconstruction governments, the Negro participants did not inaugurate this practice. As a matter of fact, they benefited least from it. Corrupt Northern Carpetbaggers and Southern Scalawags and Democrats were able to steal far more than the freedmen. Moreover, the Tweed Ring in New York managed to steal more money than all the Reconstruction governments combined.

Those seeking to restore Southern "white supremacy" exaggerated the corruption and incompetence of Negro lawmakers. Their real enemies were the many successful and competent Negro farmers, merchants, and lawmakers who disproved their concept of white superiority.

White Southerners who supported the Reconstruction governments were termed "Scalawags" and Northerners who came

*Reverend Henry M. Turner, elected to the Georgia Legislature, was denied his seat by the white lawmen. Toward the end of his life Turner came to believe that Negroes would be better off in Africa than in America.*

South to join them were called "Carpetbaggers." Scalawags, Carpetbaggers, and "radical" Negroes could not find jobs easily. Wives and children of Republican Negroes were insulted or refused service by doctors or stores. Since there was no secret ballot, Mississippi papers printed the names of Republican voters in 1875 so that they could be fired from their jobs or beaten. In Lafayette County, Negroes had to wear Democratic badges or face beatings.

Voting booths were secretly moved on Election Day or guarded by masked riders. When all else failed, the Republican votes were given to the Democrats by election officials. In Georgia, the state legislature simply refused to seat the many elected colored representatives. A furious Senator, Henry M. Turner, shouted, "I am here to demand my rights, and to hurl thunderbolts at the men who would dare to cross the threshold of my manhood." But it was of no use and Turner and the others were refused entrance. (One hundred years later Georgia legislators twice denied Julian Bond, a Negro, his seat in the legislature. He was finally seated by order of the United States Supreme Court.)

By 1876 only three Southern states—Florida, Louisiana, and South Carolina—had Reconstruction governments. The fate of the Southern freedmen was finally sealed as part of the "deal" that gave the 1876 Presidential election to Rutherford B. Hayes. When it first appeared that he had lost to the Democrat, Tilden, Hayes said "I don't care for myself; and the [Republican] party, yes, and the country, too, can stand it; but I do care for the poor colored man of the South." But a few weeks later he announced that he was convinced that "absolute justice and fair play to the Negro" could be gotten best "by trusting the honorable and influential whites." On Hayes's Inauguration Day, whites in Hamburg, South Carolina attacked and killed scores of Negro residents.

Although some colored men were elected to office during the following generation, for the vast majority of freedmen the democracy of Reconstruction was over—and with it the schools and public facilities that had been opened to colored men, women, and children. President Grant looked at the government of Mississippi and said it "is governed today by officials chosen through fraud and violence such as would scarcely be credited to savages, much less to a civilized and Christian people."

In 1875 a tall, muscular Negro farmer had stood before Senator George Boutwell of Massachusetts and demanded that something be done about the continued murder of his people. He was considering killing the Klan leaders responsible, saying "We could do it in a night." "No," answered the Senator, "we intend to protect you." The promise was never kept.

For the black man and for the South the result was tragedy. The torch of democracy that had burned brightly for a short while was extinguished. And Southerners would live—from that day until this—in the darkness of tyranny, poverty, and ignorance.

*Congressman Robert Brown Elliott speaking in favor of the 1875 Civil Rights Bill. Elliott was answering Alexander H. Stephens, former Vice-President of the Confederacy. The law passed, only to be declared unconstitutional in 1883 by the Supreme Court.*

## The South Carolina Constitutional Convention of 1868: "Should Race or Color Be Mentioned?"

[*Negro delegates B. F. Randolph and F. L. Cardoza argue for the inclusion of a section saying: "Discrimination on account of race or color in any case whatsoever shall be prohibited. . . ."*]

*Mr. B. F. Randolph.* . . . In our Bill of Rights, I want to settle the question forever. . . .

*Mr. C. P. Leslie.* I would ask the delegate if it would not have been a little better for his theory if the Scriptures had added "without distinction of race or color."

*Mr. B. F. Randolph.* If the gentleman will tell me why Congress saw fit to say "all men are created equal," I may answer his question.

*Mr. B. F. Whitmore.* . . . We discussed this matter in Committee, and the determination arrived at was not to introduce the word color in the Bill of Rights. . . . The colored man was a citizen, his rights had been declared, and I propose to defend those rights whenever called upon. . . .

*Mr. F. L. Cardoza.* It is a patent fact that, as colored men, we have been cheated out of our rights for two centuries, and now that we have the opportunity, I want to fix them in the Constitution in such a way that no lawyer, however cunning or astute, can possibly misinterpret the meaning. If we do not do so, we deserve to be, and will be, cheated again. . . .

---

*Proceedings of the Constitutional Convention of South Carolina*, Vol. I (Charleston, 1868), pp. 353-355.

# The South Carolina Constitutional Convention of 1868: "Land and Freedom"

[*Here Reverend Richard Cain and Francis L. Cardoza give their views of the poor white's and the Negro's need for land. Cardoza stresses the basic importance of breaking up the plantations and distributing small farms to the landless. Born free in Charleston, in 1837, Cardoza had studied at the University of Glasgow as well as in London and Edinburgh. In 1865 he returned to South Carolina after two years as a minister in Connecticut. He speaks first.*]

. . . What is the main cause of the prosperity of the North? It is because every man has his own farm and is free and independent. Let the lands of the South be similarly divided. . . . We will never have true freedom until we abolish the system of agriculture which existed in the Southern States. It is useless to have any schools while we maintain this stronghold of slavery as the agricultural system of the country. . . . If they [the lands] are sold, though a few mercenary speculators may purchase some, the chances are that the colored man and the poor [white] man would be the purchasers. I will prove this . . . by facts. About one hundred poor colored men of Charleston met together and formed themselves into a Charleston Land Company. They subscribed for a number of shares at $10 per share, one dollar payable monthly. They have been meeting for a year. Yesterday they purchased some 600 acres of land for $6,600 that would have sold for $25,000 or $50,000 in better times. . . . This is only one instance of thousands of others that have occurred in this city and State. . . .

[*Delegate Richard Cain, born free in Virginia and educated at Wilberforce University, agreed.*]

. . . I believe the possession of lands and homesteads is one of the best means by which a people is made industrious, honest and advantageous to the State. . . . I have gone through the country and on every side I was beseiged with questions: How are we to get homesteads, to get lands. . . . Give these men a place to work, and I will guarantee before one year passes, there will be no necessity for the Freedmen's Bureau. . . .

. . . what we need is a system of small farms. Every farmer owning his own land will feel he is in possession of something. It will have a tendency to settle the minds of the people in the State and settle many difficulties. . . .

*Proceedings of the Constitutional Convention of South Carolina*, Vol. I (Charleston, 1868), pp. 117, 379-380.

## The South Carolina Constitutional Convention of 1868: "Schools and Education"

[*The delegates debated whether to make school attendance compulsory and whether or not to integrate the schools. Each of the Negro delegates who offers his opinion here later represented his state in Congress—with the exception of Mr. Cardoza, who served for eight years as Secretary of State and Secretary of the Treasury of South Carolina.*]

*Mr. R. C. De Large.* . . . This section proposes to open these schools to all persons, irrespective of color, to open every seminary of learning to all. Heartily do I endorse the object, but the manner in which it is to be enforced meets my most earnest disapproval. . . . The schools may be opened to all, under proper provisions in the [State] Constitution, but to declare that parents "shall" send their children to them whether they are willing or not is, in my judgment, going a step beyond the bounds of prudence. . . .

*Mr. A. J. Ransier.* . . . Civilization and enlightenment follow fast upon the footsteps of the schoolmaster; and if education must be enforced to secure these grand results, I say let the compulsory process go on. . . .

*Mr. F. L. Cardoza.* . . . We only compel parents to send their children to some school, not that they shall send them with the colored children; we simply give those colored children who desire to go to white schools, the privilege to do so.

*Mr. R. H. Cain.* . . . To do justice in this matter of education, compulsion is not required. I am willing to trust the people. They have good sense, and experience itself will be better than all the force you can employ to instill the idea of duty to their children. . . .

*Mr. R. B. Elliott.* . . . [Another speaker] has said this law is to force the white and colored children into the public schools together. The only question is whether children shall become educated and enlightened, or remain in ignorance. This question is not white or black, united or divided, but whether children shall be sent to school or kept at home. If they are compelled to be educated, there will be no danger to the Union, or a second secession of South Carolina. . . .

---

*Proceedings of the Constitutional Convention of South Carolina*, Vol. II (Charleston, 1868), pp. 685-704.

# Progress and Corruption in Mississippi

[*Henry W. Warren graduated from Yale in 1865 and headed South, serving first as a school teacher in Tennessee and later as a plantation owner and Speaker of the Mississippi Legislature. He describes the functioning of the Negro-white Mississippi government he observed.*]

. . . From the first there were plenty of Confederate generals and colonels in the Legislature. The manner of the blacks to the whites was habitually civil, and something of the slave's deference to the white man remained. I think the legislation was generally of reasonably good character. I knew positively of but little corruption. That there was some corruption and more extravagance, I have no doubt. But I have served in the Massachusetts Legislature, and I think the Southern State was but little worse than the Northern. The Negro members, though with some able and honest leaders of their own, like Bruce and Lynch, followed largely the prominent white men. . . . A "carpet-bagger" I hardly ever met, though no doubt there were some—but the name was given to all Northerners. As to expense, you must remember that the State had to be completely rehabilitated. The war had ruined everything; public buildings were destroyed or dilapidated; and under military rule things had simply been kept going. Everything had to be reconstructed. The slaves had become citizens, and that doubled the number to be provided for. There had been practically no public schools, and they were set up throughout the State. Taxes had fallen largely on slave property, now they came on land. So it was inevitable that there should be an increase in taxation . . . . In those years there was immense progress on the part of the Negroes,—political discussion was educational. I think if the Federal government had provided better school education, and had protected the voters at the polls, all might have gone well. That there was more or less extravagance on the part of the Legislature is not to be denied. So there is in Massachusetts. . . .

George S. Merriam, *The Negro and the Nation, A History of American Slavery and Enfranchisement* (New York, 1906), pp. 338-340.

## *The Purposes of the Ku Klux Klan*

[*The objectives of the Klansmen did not include the murder or removal of all Negroes from the South. Their purpose was to keep the Southern Negro ignorant and under white control. The sworn testimony of two Negroes, one a state Senator from Mississippi and the other a teacher in North Carolina, indicates the aims of the KKK in the early 1870's.*]

[*State Senator Robert Gleed of Mississippi*] Well, sir, we have thought from their organization and from other indications we have had, that the . . . purposes of the [Klan] organization have been to remand the colored men of the country to as near a position of servitude as possible, and to destroy the Republican Party if possible; it has been, in other words, political. . . .

Do you think one of the objectives of the Ku Klux organization in its various visits has been to break down the growing spirit of independence in the black man?

Yes, sir; and to establish white supremacy in the South, and to destroy the republican party. . . .

*Testimony Taken by the Joint Select Committee to Inquire into the Condition of Affairs in the Late Insurrectionary States*, Mississippi, Vol. II (Washington, 1872), p. 722.

[*Samuel Allen, a teacher who beat off a Klan raid*] They [the Klansmen] said I had committed a great wrong; I had kept a Sunday-school which I was forbidden to do. They told me that this thing of teaching . . . was something they did not allow; that the church they belonged to never sanctioned any such thing; that it was not sanctioned by the neighborhood or the country and it must not be done, and finally they told me it should not be done and when I proceeded on with the Sunday-school, they said to me, "We gave you orders to stop, and you have continued against our orders; now you have got to stop."

*Report on the Alleged Outrages in the Southern States by the Select Committee of the Senate* (Washington, 1871), p. 49.

## The Power of the Ku Klux Klan

[*Throughout Reconstruction, masked groups such as the Klan had power which was greater than their numbers would indicate and influence that reached into every part of local and state government. Colonel George W. Kirk of the North Carolina state troops gave this picture of Klan power in his state.*]

. . . I have spoken of their having the law and the courts all on their side. The juries were made up of Ku-Klux, and it was impossible for any of the loyal people to get justice before the courts. Not less than fifty or sixty persons have been killed by the Ku-Klux in the State, besides some three or four hundred whippings, and there has never been a man convicted that I have heard of. Out of all those that I arrested, against whom there was as good proof as could possibly be given, enough to convict anybody before twelve honest men, I do not think one has ever been tried. They know very well when they commit these depredations that they will be cleared, and it just makes it that much worse for the loyal people. If they prosecute them for debt or for anything else they fail. Colored men cannot get justice, cannot get their hard earned money. They agree to give them part of the crop, and about the time of the harvest they charge them with something and run them off. They dare not say a word. . . .

*Report on the Alleged Outrages in the Southern States by the Select Committee of the Senate* (Washington, 1871), p. 10.

## *Teaching School in Georgia in 1870*

[*This report of an agent of the Freedmen's Bureau, J. K. Lewis, indicates the continuing attack on Negro education during this period.*]

In one half of the state there is little opposition to their schools and the respectable citizens give them their countenance and support. In many counties however there is still great bitterness of feeling against the schools and all those engaged in the work and bands of K.K.K. armed and disguised men, have committed most atrocious outrages. About the last of November Mr. R. H. Gladdings who has been teaching . . . at Greensboro, Green Co. was driven away. The man with whom he boarded (a white man) was taken out of his house in the night and unmercifully whipped and Mr. Abram Colby (colored) a member-elect of the legislature and one of Mr. Gladdings strong supporters in the school work, was taken out of his house and beaten nearly to death. Mr. Gladdings was warned to leave and appealed to the Mayor for protection to prevent any outrage upon him, he was therefore obliged to leave. . . . Notwithstanding these difficulties the school work goes on with increased efficiency. The freemen pay more liberally than ever toward the support of their schools.

*Office of the Adjutant General, Letters Received* (Washington: National Archives, War Records Office, 1870).

## *"His Intense Zeal for Education"*

[*R. A. Seely, an official of the Freedmen's Bureau, wrote this report, in 1870, about an incident that occurred in his region.*]

On the fourth of October the [school] house was completely destroyed by fire, nothing being saved but a few benches, and the Sunday School Library. . . .

The fire was undoubtedly the work of an incendiary as it occurred at midnight and no fire had been kindled within the building. . . . The total loss was not less than ten thousand dollars.

It would be difficult for any one who does not know the poverty of the freedman and his intense zeal for education to conceive the disheartening effect of such a calamity upon the poor people who had denied themselves every luxury, and with unprecedented liberality had given one half their wages, week after week, for the construction of this house for themselves and their children. But words of cheer and friendly counsel were not wanting. And, thanks to the elastic temperament of the African, the general despondency soon gave way to new and more vigorous effort. And the work was re-commenced with resolution as firm as before. And with means and purposes broader than ever.

---

*Office of the Adjutant General, Letters Received* (Washington: National Archives, War Records Office, 1870).

## *Lawmakers Go to College*

[*Edward King, a white Northerner, visited the South Carolina legislature in 1873 and wrote this revealing description of the changes taking place.*]

The House, when I visited it, was composed of eighty-three colored members, all of whom are Republicans, and forty-one whites; the Senate consisted of fifteen colored men, ten white Republicans, and eight white Democrats. The President of the Senate and the Speaker of the House, both colored, were elegant and accomplished men, highly educated, who would have creditably presided over any commonwealth's legislative assembly. . . . The little knot of white Democrats, massed together in one section of the hall, sat glum and scornful amid the mass of black speakers. . . . There are men of real force and eloquence among the Negroes chosen to the House but they are the exception. In the Senate there was more decorum and ability among the members. Several of the colored senators spoke exceedingly well, and with great ease and grace of manner; others were awkward and lacked refinement. . . .

I visited the University a day or two after the revolution caused there by the entrance of the first colored student, the Secretary of State himself. In the library . . . I saw the book from whose lists the white students had indignantly erased their names when they saw the Secretary's round, fair script beneath their own. The departure of the old professors and scholars was the signal for a grand onward movement by the blacks, and a great number entered the preparatory and law schools. They have summoned good teachers from the North, and are studying earnestly. . . . While I was in the library a coal black senator arrived, with two members of the House, whom he presented to the head of the faculty as desirous of entering the law class. I was informed that dozens of members were occupied every spare moment outside of the sessions in faithful study. . . .

Edward King, "The Great South," *Scribner's Monthly*, Vol. 8 (June, 1874), pp. 156-158.

## A Negro Congressman Denounces Segregation

[*Mississippi Negro Congressman John R. Lynch describes to Congress the indignities he suffered on an official trip to Washington. Lynch was born a slave in 1847. He began school in Natchez as soon as federal troops freed his family. He was elected speaker of the Mississippi House when he was 22, and was then elected to three terms in the United States Congress.*]

. . . Think of it for a moment; here am I, a member of your honorable body, representing one of the largest and wealthiest districts in the State of Mississippi, and possibly in the South; a district composed of persons of different races, religions, and nationalities; and yet, when I leave my home to come to the capital of the nation, to take part in the deliberations of the House and to participate with you in making laws for the government of this great Republic, . . . I am treated, not as an American citizen, but as a brute. Forced to occupy a filthy smoking-car both night and day, with drunkards, gamblers, and criminals; and for what? Not that I am unable or unwilling to pay my way; not that I am obnoxious in my personal appearance or disrespectful in my conduct; but simply because I happen to be of a darker complexion. If this treatment was confined to persons of our own sex we could possibly afford to endure it. But such is not the case. Our wives and our daughters, our sisters and our mothers are subjected to the same insults and to the same uncivilized treatment. . . . The only moments of my life when I am necessarily compelled to question my loyalty to my Government or my devotion to the flag of my country is when I read of outrages having been committed upon innocent colored people and . . . when I leave my home to go travelling.

Mr. Speaker, if this unjust discrimination is to be longer tolerated by the American people . . . then I can only say with sorrow and regret that our boasted civilization is a fraud; our republican institutions a failure; our social system a disgrace; and our religion a complete hypocrisy. . . .

*The Congressional Record*, Vol. II, Part V, 43rd Congress, First Session, p. 4783.

## A Negro Senator Defends Himself

[*Many of the Negroes elected to Congress during Reconstruction were kept from taking their seats for long periods of time. They were often challenged by their Democratic opponents, and some were never able to take their seats in Congress. One of these was P. B. S. Pinchback, the famous Louisiana politician who served briefly as Governor of that state. In this speech, given in 1873 while his case was under consideration by the Senate, he defended his election and record. Although he was not seated, the Senate paid him his Senator's salary.*]

. . . several Senators (I hope they are not Republicans) think me a very bad man. If this be true I fear my case is hopeless, for I am a bad man in the eyes of the democracy [and] weak-kneed Republicans. But of what does my badness consist [?] I am bad because I have dared on several important occasions to have an independent opinion. I am bad because I have dared at all times to advocate and insist on exact and equal justice to all Mankind. I am bad because having colored blood in my veins I have dared to aspire to the United States Senate, and I am bad because your representatives dared express the will of the people rather than obey the will of those who thought they were the peoples' Masters, when they elected me.

Friends I have been told that if I dared utter such Sentiments as these in public that I certainly would be Kept out of the Senate, all I have to say in answer to this, is that if I cannot enter the Senate except with bated breath and on bended knees, I prefer not to enter at all. . . .

P. B. S. Pinchback, *Pinchback's Handwritten Manuscript: Notes for a Speech*, from Howard University's Moorland Collection (Washington, 1873).

# Final Report to the South Carolina House of Representatives, 1874

*[Speaker S. J. Lee gives this report to the Negro and white members of the House at the close of the regular session.]*

We have been condemned and maligned; our motives have been misconstrued, and our actions [too]. . . ; but notwithstanding the malignity of our enemies, every right thinking person must perforce admit that we have done well. While we are . . . perhaps, very little skilled in the science of government, many good and laudable enactments have emanated from us, and . . . we have sought in every instance to subserve all personal interests to those of the State. . . .

We cannot hide the fact that many things in our midst need pruning and reforming, but *we* can effect it. . . . We, as a people, are blameless of misgovernment. It is owing to bad men, adventurers, persons who, after having reaped millions from our party, turn traitors and stab us in the dark. Ingratitude is the worst of crimes, and yet the men we have fostered, the men we have elevated and made rich, now speak of our corruption and . . . charge us with every conceivable crime. They lay everything at our doors, and seek by letters, published in northern journals, to ruin our credit and blacken our prospects abroad. . . .

Permit me, now, to refer to our increased educational advantages. It is very pleasing, gentlemen, to witness how rapidly the schools are springing up in every portion of our State, and how the number of competent, well-trained teachers are increasing. . . . Our State University has been renovated and made progressive. New Professors, men of unquestionable ability and erudition, now fill the chairs once filled by men who were too aristocratic to instruct colored youths. A system of scholarships has been established that will, as soon as it is practically in operation, bring into the University a very large number of students. . . . The State Normal School is also situated here, and will have a fair attendance of scholars. We have, also, Claflin University, at Orangeburg, which is well attended, and progressing very favorably; and in the different cities and large towns of the State, school houses have been built, and the school master can be found there busily instructing the "young idea how to shoot." The *effects* of education can also be perceived; the people are becoming daily more enlightened; their minds are expanding, and they have awakened, in a great degree, from the mental darkness that hitherto surrounded them. . . .

*Journal of the House of Representatives of the State of South Carolina, for the Regular Session of 1873-1874* (Columbia, 1874), pp. 549-553.

## A Mississippi Election: Vote Stealing

[*D. J. Foreman, a Negro Republican leader, had 300 Republican voters and only 47 Democrats in his district. He explains to a Senate Committee, in 1875, how the district went to the Democrats.*]

. . . we held meetings but we did not hold them publicly. We used to go into the swamps to hold them, and we had a house off the road where we could meet, with no lamps or anything.

*Q.* What did you do at those meetings?

*A.* We would meet for the purpose of discussing what we were going to do at the election.

*Q.* What did you propose to do at the election?

*A.* Some said not to go to the polls; some said they would go; some said they were afraid to go, and some said they were not, and they would go if they got killed. . . .

*Q.* Are your people armed generally [?]. . . .

*A.* No, sir; they are poorly armed. . . .

*Q.* When did you first know what the result was [in the 1875 election]?

*A.* I met Bazelius, clerk of the election, the next morning coming from Vicksburgh, and I asked him what was the result of the election. He told me: "We beat you badly yesterday." I says, "No, you didn't; you polled forty-seven votes." He says, "It was you polled forty-seven votes, and we polled three hundred. You all voted democratic votes." . . .

*Q.* Do you know anything more about what took place at the election?

*A.* [The whites] . . . met the colored people, and would not allow them to come with arms; and the white people kept on theirs, and that scared the colored people. . . .

*Q.* And the democrats carried their arms?

*A.* Yes, sir; and Mr. Henderson told me that I would have to shut my mouth; and I told him that I thought they were going to let us have a fair election; and they said it was a fair election, only the fuss I was making. I told him I was making a fuss for something; that I thought as they did not allow colored people to bring their arms, that they ought not to have theirs.

---

*Mississippi in 1875*, Senate Report 527, Part II, 44th Congress, First Session (Washington, 1876), pp. 1380-1383.

# A Mississippi Election: Violence

[*The election of 1875 in Mississippi was the scene of bloody massacres of Negro voters and their white friends. These letters to the Republican Governor, Adelbert Ames, picture the mounting threats that were received and the violence that took place as Election Day approached. The first letter is from Senator Charles Caldwell, a fearless Negro Republican leader, who was assassinated a few months later by his political enemies.*]

. . . The intimidation and threatening of colored voters continues uninterrupted, and with as much system, determined purpose, and combination of effort as if it were a legitimate means of canvassing and the chief one to be relied on in controlling the colored element. . . .

In behalf of the people whom I represent, I appeal to your excellency for the protection which the laws of the State guarantee to every citizen regardless of party or race.

[*Letter from 300 Vicksburg Negro voters.*] . . . we are intimidated by the whites. We wants to hold meetings, but it is impossible to do so; if we does, they will say we are making an invasion on the city and come out [to] kill us. When we hold church meetings, they breakes that up; our lives are not safe in our houses. Now we ask you who shall we look to for protection. . . . We are in the hands of murderers. There will not be peace here until troops come to unarm them. . . .

[*Letter of H. W. Lewis of Columbia, Mississippi.*] Dear Sir: Everything in this and adjoining counties is up to fever heat. The 24-pound cannon thunders forth every night. The brass band accompanies the democratic speakers, together with about 50 hot-headed young men, and assassination and bloodshed are openly encouraged. Our voters are very much overawed, and [we] fear we cannot get out more than one-half of them. If troops could be sent here, even a "corporal's guard," it would act like magic, and we would sweep everything in this part of the State. As it is, it looks as though we should lose everything. . . .

If anything can be done, I know you will do it. If not, we shall do the best we can and try to meet the issue bravely.

[*Letter from a group of Negro Republicans.*] Dear Governor: We here give you notice that the white people of this towne have jest received, by express from New Orleans, three boxes of guns and also some boxes of pistols for the porpus of a riot in this place, while we have not got a gun or do not want any desturbemenst, and we asks you for our protection or helpe some way or erther, knowing that you are our govnor and the only help for us. Please give us some helpe, we ask agin. . . .

[*William Canly writes from De Soto County.*] Governor Ames, DEAR SIR: We, as Republicans of the State of Mississippi, do ask you to tell us whether we are to be murdered by the whites of the State or not, without protection at all. . . .

. . . the whites are allowed to have war guns among us in time of peace, and we call all such as that unjust.

Now, when we was registering [to vote], I saw Mr. Jim Chamberlin turn away some men who was 23 years of age. Is that equal? No sir. . . . White men who were to young to work on the public roads could register. I call all such as that fraud.

[*A white Republican wrote this letter after the election had been held.*] Our election has been *broken* up by armed White-Leaguers. This morning, long before the opening of the polls in this city, the

White-Leaguers came, cavalry, infantry, and artillery, and they drove the colored men before them, and compelled them to fly for their lives. No colored man was allowed to vote unless he voted the democratic ticket. They openly declared that if any republican tried to go to the polls they would shoot him down. . . .

We have been slumbering on a volcano for ten days, but to-day it culminated at the ballot-box. It is no longer with them the number of votes but the number of guns.

"Documentary Evidence," *Mississippi in 1875*, Senate Report 527, Part II, 44th Congress, First Session (Washington, 1876), pp. 19-56.

# 12

# An Age of Invention and Industrial Growth

THE Civil War had swept away the obstacles to America's industrial growth. Congress was no longer dominated by slaveholders who voted down high tariffs, grants to railroads, and other measures for the protection or advancement of business. The hard-driving industrialist became the hero of the new age. The abolitionist was a man of the past and many who had had sympathy for the slave now showed little interest in the freedman.

The new change in interest could be clearly seen in the actions of the federal government. Rutherford B. Hayes had served as a volunteer lawyer for fugitive slaves before the Civil War. Now, as President, he withdrew the last federal troops from the South, ending all protection of the freedmen. Instead of defending Negro rights with federal troops, Hayes and other Presidents used them to break strikes of railroad workers.

The Fourteenth Amendment to the Constitution, designed to shield the rights of freedmen, was used, instead, to protect corporations. Federal courts ruled that when the Amendment stated that no state could "deprive any person of life, liberty, or property" this meant corporations as well as people. In the years that followed, the nation's industrial concerns received all the protection from the Amendment that the Negroes of the South were being denied.

In an age of greed, the kind of men who cornered the United States gold market also stole the pennies that ex-slaves had deposited in the Freedmen's Bank. Money, after all, was money, and the only trick was getting it. There was little sentiment in these times, and even less concern, for the powerless. You had to be strong to survive, and if you were not, your troubles meant little. Those who did survive built a powerful industrial and commercial nation. Their raw materials included the brain power of America's inventive minds, and the powerful arms and skills of its factory workers.

## Inventors and Inventions

To meet the needs of faster communication and transportation, American companies sought out the best inventive minds. Many Negroes were among those who produced electrical, mechanical, and telephonic equipment. Before the turn of the 19th century Negroes had patented hundreds of inventions. They produced everything from new kinds of elevators and photographic and telegraphic equipment to refrigerators, golf tees, and modern bathroom fixtures. They became part of the inventive thrust needed to feed the industrial revolution.

Elijah McCoy, the son of runaway slaves, played a prominent role in the development of transportation and factory machinery. In 1872 McCoy, educated in Scotland as a mechanical engineer, invented a lubricating cup that fed oil to parts of a machine while it was in operation. This made it possible for locomotives, steam boilers, and factory machinery to be oiled without interrupting their operations. Inventor McCoy received more than 75 patents for his various devices.

*Elijah McCoy, son of runaway slaves, held many patents. His lubricating cup was the first "real McCoy."*

*Lewis Howard Latimer assisted Bell and Edison.*

Lewis Howard Latimer, who worked with both Alexander Graham Bell and Thomas Edison, was born to a poor Boston family in 1848. To help support the family, and at the same time further the cause of emancipation, he sold copies of William Lloyd Garrison's *The Liberator* on the streets. When he was 16, Latimer joined the United States Navy and served aboard the U.S.S. *Massasoit* during the Civil War. After the war, he returned to Boston where he began work as an office boy in a company of patent lawyers. He rose to the position of chief draftsman for the firm.

Around the year 1876 Latimer, then an expert electrical engineer and draftsman, met Alexander Graham Bell. Some of the people who knew Latimer in the early days said: "It was Latimer who executed the drawings and assisted in preparing the applications for the telephone patents of Alexander Graham Bell."

He left Bell a few years later to join the United States Electric Lighting Company at Bridgeport, Connecticut where, with the noted inventor Hiram S. Maxim, he invented an incandescent electric light and supervised the building of manufacturing plants in New York, Philadelphia, and Canada.

In 1884 Latimer joined the engineering staff of the Edison Electric Light Company. He worked for Edison for many years, becoming the only Negro member of the famous Edison Pioneers, a group of people who had worked with Edison before 1885. In 1890 he wrote a book explaining, to the general public, the use and workings of the electric light. Latimer also proved invaluable to the legal department of the Edison Company. Since he had usually drawn the original plans for Edison inventions, he was the company's star witness in patent cases that reached the courts. After he retired, Latimer published a volume of his poetry and gave more of his time to the study of literature.

Granville T. Woods directed his inventive talents toward improvements in the railroad and electrical industries. He invented a telegraph system that made it possible to send messages between moving trains, thus reducing the danger of accidents. His invention of an automatic air brake brought greater safety to the nation's railroads. Woods also contributed to the development of the "third rail" used in electrical railroads.

He invented devices which he sold to Bell, Edison, and Westinghouse. In two patent cases against the Edison Company, Woods was able to prove that he had had earlier rights to inventions claimed by Edison. After the second court victory, Thomas Edison offered Woods a position, which he turned down, preferring to be his own boss. In 1888 the *American Catholic Tribune* called Woods "the greatest electrician in the world." Though this would be hard to prove, it indicates that, though Woods is unknown today, he was highly thought of in his own time.

Unlike Granville T. Woods, Jan Matzeliger never received the recognition due an important inventor. In 1883, when he was thirty

*Granville T. Woods invented devices purchased by Bell, Westinghouse, and Edison.*

*Jan Matzeliger, inventor of the machine that revolutionized the shoe industry and made Lynn, Massachusetts the shoe capital of the world. Government experts, baffled by his patent drawings, sent a specialist to examine the machine. Matzeliger died young and poor after working ten years to develop his device.*

years old, he invented a machine which combined so many steps that it practically manufactured an entire shoe in one operation. A slender, erect young man, Matzeliger was well liked in his town of Lynn, Massachusetts. Neighbors found him cheerful and "quick to see the funny side of things," and a Lynn editor found him "a man not only of wonderful mechanical ability, but a man of equally wonderful energy and tenacity of purpose." The machine he devised became the basis for the multimillion-dollar growth of the United Shoe Company, which bought the invention. Yet Matzeliger sold it for very little and, like many other inventors, died a poor man, at the age of 36.

The complete story of the early Negro inventors cannot be told because prejudice has blurred the picture. When inventors found that many people would not accept their devices when it was learned they were Negroes, some concealed their identities. A naval cadet who left Annapolis because of racial prejudice, Henry E. Baker, Assistant Examiner of the United States Patent Office for many years, conducted a long and careful investigation of the matter. Although he found proof difficult to obtain in many cases, he turned up some 800 to 1,200 patents that were taken out by men he identified as colored—before the year 1913.

In 1900 Henry Baker published his first findings in four giant volumes which included the actual drawings and plans submitted to the Patent Office by colored inventors prior to the turn of the century. Baker's findings are highly instructive because the Negro's contribution to America's early achievements in science and invention has been almost totally neglected.

# The Colored Inventor
## A RECORD OF FIFTY YEARS
By HENRY E. BAKER, Assistant Examiner United States Patent Office

*Title of a booklet by Henry E. Baker describing hundreds of inventions developed by Negroes just fifty years after Emancipation.*

Baker's list includes these inventions patented by Negroes before 1900: a jet-propulsion balloon; a railroad crossing switch; an electric lamp; a self-setting animal trap; a telephone system; combination cotton seed planter and fertilizer distributor; letter box; window cleaner; gauge; guitar; printing press; lifesaving device for ships; folding chair; fountain pen; safety gate for bridges; a spring gun; a rapid-fire naval gun; bicycle; steam boiler.

The most noted Negro inventor of the modern period was Garrett A. Morgan. On July 25, 1916 an explosion in Tunnel Number Five, 228 feet below Lake Erie, trapped a dozen men. Morgan was summoned to the scene with his newly invented gas mask. Putting on his mask, Morgan entered the gas-filled tunnel and rescued a number of the men. In 1923 Morgan invented the traffic light which straightened out the disorder of crowded city streets in the age of the automobile. A complicated device with a simple purpose, the invention has saved many lives from that day to this.

*Garrett A. Morgan.*

## Great Fortunes

No Negroes amassed great fortunes equal to those of John D. Rockefeller, J. P. Morgan, or Andrew Carnegie. But the first American woman to become a millionairess by her own efforts was the daughter of ex-slaves. In 1905 Madam C. J. Walker, an orphan at six and a former laundry worker, developed a hair conditioner for Negro women. Since whites ignored this market she also developed other cosmetics which were specifically designed for colored women. In a few years, the Madam C. J. Walker Manufacturing Company in Indiana was a vast industry and included a school to train salesmen and saleswomen. Before Madam Walker died in 1919 at the age of 51, she built a school for girls in West Africa, provided it with a $100,000 grant, and gave a good deal of money to charity. Madam Walker's $250,000 mansion on the Hudson River, with its gold-plated piano and a $60,000 pipe organ, was one of the showplaces of wealthy Westchester County during this "gilded age."

Charles C. Spaulding also followed the "rags to riches" trail. He entered the insurance business in 1898 and accepted a 65 cents commission on a $40 life insurance policy. A few days later the customer died, and Spaulding and his partners paid the policy out of their own pockets. Undismayed, Spaulding had to work harder than before to make a success of the business.

> When I came into the office in the morning, I rolled
> up my sleeves and swept the place as a janitor. Then
> I rolled down my sleeves and was an agent. And later
> I put on my coat and became general manager.

When he died in 1952, Spaulding's small concern had amassed $200 million in assets and policies, and by 1967 about 35 Negroes were millionaires.

In an age of fierce competition and deep-seated prejudice, the most successful Negro businesses and banks resulted from cooperative efforts. Some were sponsored by churches, for in American Negro life the house of worship was often a bulwark against all storms and an aid in all aspects of life. Early in the 20th century, Mrs. Maggie L. Walker of Virginia built a church-sponsored insurance business into a thriving enterprise. Mrs. Walker organized youth clubs and fostered interracial work with white women's clubs. Her outstanding contribution to her state and to tolerance was noted by Governor E. Lee Trinkle at a public meeting in 1925: "If the State of Virginia had done no more, in fifty years with funds spent on the education of Negroes than educate Mrs. Walker, the State would have been amply repaid for its outlay and efforts."

*Andrew J. Beard invented a device for coupling railroad cars. Before the automatic coupler, railroad workers had to place a pin between cars as they moved together, and were often injured or killed. Beard received $50,000 for this invention.*

## Labor and Unions

It is not known whether John Henry of the famous folk song was a man of flesh or myth. But his race with a steam drill has come to symbolize man's attempt to resist the power of machines. Gigantic John Henry, according to the song, beat the machine—but died in the attempt. The worker in industrial society needed greater protection against the machine than his own arms. Some saw unions as one way to meet the new challenge. This type of organization was also the workers' response to the employer who now had so many workmen he rarely knew their names or skills.

A few months after the end of the Civil War, New Orleans Mayor Kennedy looked on as levee workers struck for higher pay. "They marched up the levee in a long procession, white and black together." But, said the mayor, when the strikers tried to prevent others from taking over their jobs, "the police promptly put a stop to their proceedings."

Most workmen in the postwar period faced severe competition and the determined opposition of their employers. The government usually took the employer's side against unions. To achieve any success, workers knew that they must be united. But this was difficult. The color prejudice that had separated black workers from white ones during slavery continued to divide them after freedom. As late as 1934, in Pennsylvania, a Negro steel worker said, "The jobs whites won't touch—we get them."

The early national unions tried to unite all workers, regardless of color. In 1866 the National Labor Union invited Negroes to join. Isaac Myers of Baltimore, the outstanding Negro labor leader of the time, assured the 1869 convention of the National Labor Union: "The white laboring men have nothing to fear from the colored laboring men. We desire to have the highest rate of wages that our labor is worth. . . ." Myers stressed, "American citizenship for the black man is a complete failure if he is proscribed from the workshops of the country." After the speech a majority of the delegates voted to accept Negroes—but in separate locals.

Isaac Myers had no choice but to begin a separate organization. By the end of 1869 he assembled 200 delegates at the first convention of the National Colored Labor Union. These unionists spoke for the income tax, women's rights, cooperative associations, and the unity of all workers regardless of color or belief. The following year Myers entered the South to organize workers of both races. He pleaded that to win success "the white and colored mechanics must come together and work together." But white unions still refused to accept Negro members. The Negro unions were too weak to bargain effectively with employers. Gradually Republican politicians used these unions for their own publicity purposes. In 1872 Myers' National Colored Labor Union admitted this when it said of the Republican Party: "By its success, we stand; by its defeat we fall." It soon fell.

The Knights of Labor, formed as a secret union in 1869, also made an effort to unite all workers. It opened its doors to "men and women of every craft, creed and color." With the help of Negro organizers, its Negro membership soon skyrocketed to 60,000. Southern states passed laws against the new union and drove its organizers out of the South. In 1887 George and Henry Cox were among the leaders of 10,000 Negro and white workers who went out on strike against Louisiana sugar plantations. The strike was violently crushed and the Negro brothers were among the score of union leaders killed.

At the first meeting of the American Federation of Labor in 1881, Negro delegate Jeremiah Grandison warned the others that "it would be dangerous to skilled mechanics to exclude from the organization the common laborers." He pointed out that these men could be used to replace skilled men on strike. President Samuel Gompers and his new A.F. of L. paid no attention to Grandison's warning and ignored the unskilled workers in favor of the skilled craftsmen.

Although the unions of the A.F. of L. claimed to be open to all, Negroes were rarely accepted as members. Some were allowed to form segregated locals which had little power. Just as Grandison had predicted, this exclusion led Negro workers to take work for less than union pay. When they did this Samuel Gompers scornfully called them "cheap men."

The only important Negro A.F. of L. union of this early period came into being in August, 1925. It was called the Brotherhood of Sleeping Car Porters and it chose Asa Philip Randolph to be its President. A tall, scholarly man, Randolph was respected for his knowledge of history and economics as well as his abilities as an editor and public speaker. He rejected all efforts of the employers to frighten or bribe him and soon won pay increases for his 8,000 members. His union became part of the A.F. of L. and Randolph became the first Negro to hold a seat on its executive board, a position he used to prod union leaders who discriminated against minorities.

*Labor leader A. Philip Randolph, most noted Negro union leader in American history. His long battle against discrimination in unions and employment included a planned march on Washington. It was canceled when President Franklin D. Roosevelt issued an executive order establishing America's first Fair Employment Practices Commission to hear complaints of job discrimination in concerns doing government work.*

Despite isolated incidences of progress few Negroes were in unions by 1900. Of 22,000 Negro carpenters, only 1,000 were union members. White workers often tried to drive Negroes off jobs, and many strikes occurred in the North and South when Negroes were hired to work alongside whites. Oscar DePriest, a Kansas painter who later became the North's first Negro Congressman, carried a pistol to warn those trying to drive him off jobs.

Even those Negroes who had skills that were appreciated when they were slaves found little use for them in freedom. Discriminatory laws and customs gradually eliminated Negroes from the skilled trades. And whites refused to accept Negro apprentices. The A.F. of L., by accepting only skilled laborers, thus automatically excluded the vast majority of Negro workers, without even resorting to discrimination.

By keeping Negroes out of unions, the white workers turned them into competitors instead of allies. Employers were quick to seize on this division and they used Negro strike breakers during labor conflicts. The famous Homestead Strike of 1892 and 1919 steel strike were won by employers, partly in this way. Many Negroes were able to break into certain industries only when the white workers went out on strike and they were offered the jobs.

Although the temptation to take a decent job was great, many Negroes stubbornly resisted being used as strikebreakers. In 1901 when 300 Birmingham Negroes were brought to Chicago to break a steel strike, many of them attended the meeting called by the whites to protest strikebreaking. Negro leader Henry Taylor told the meeting: "There is not a man in our party who will work . . . under a gun or in another's place. We don't want to fill strikers' places and we won't under guard." His men kept the pledge.

In several places, and even during strikes, Negro and white workers proved themselves capable of unity—even in the Deep South. For example, the New Orleans Dock and Cotton Council's 72 union members included an equal number of Negro and white union delegates. Its top officers were rotated so that each group would have a turn at running this central union body. When a strike of 10,000 of these workers hit New Orleans at the turn of the century, the president of the Negro longshoremen, E. S. Swan, commented: "The whites and Negroes were never before so strong cemented in a common bond and in my 39 years of experience on the levee, I never saw such solidarity." The strikers won their demands.

Before it was crushed, a 1908 strike in Birmingham, Alabama

*Learning by doing at Hampton College, 1900. Negro and Indian students gained a variety of industrial skills by working and building at the college. Ironically this emphasis upon industrial education came when white artisans were forcing Negroes from the skilled trades. Nevertheless, most Negro colleges continued to emphasize this type of education. (Collection, The Museum of Modern Art, New York. Gift of Lincoln Kirstein.)*

showed that a remarkable degree of unity between Negro and white mine workers was possible. They struck for a union shop and to oppose a wage cut. For two months these 20,000 laborers held out against the opposition of local police, state troops, bombings, and a lynching. According to a Birmingham reporter, they attended meetings at which "Negroes as well as whites bore red flags, and black men were among the principal speakers." But they were finally beaten down by overwhelming force.

A New York union of street workers laid down their tools and went home when Negro members were treated unfairly by the company. "Unless you give us a written guarantee to recognize all the members of our union, black as well as white," none would work, a white member told the company. The company gave in.

In most places, however, the prejudice against the Negro

worker kept him from joining unions or receiving the support of white workers. The A.F. of L. also discriminated against Oriental workers in clearly racist terms. In a booklet written in 1908 Samuel Gompers and other A.F. of L. leaders called for the exclusion of Oriental laborers from America by law or, if necessary, "by force of arms." The booklet added: "The yellow man found it natural to lie, cheat, and murder and ninety-nine out of every hundred Chinese are gamblers." An Oriental, it continued, leaves his job at the end of a day and "joyfully hastens back to his slum . . . and an atmosphere of horror."

At this same point in American history reporter Ray Stannard Baker visited an Indianapolis hod-carriers union which was controlled by Negroes, even though it did include a number of white workers. When some of the Negro members bullied a white worker, other Negro members reported this to the union. Several workmen were warned about their behavior and one Negro left the job when he was fined. The union then went on with its work of building a clubhouse for all of its members.

If other unions had been able to solve—or more to the point, had wanted to solve—the problems of discrimination this easily, the history of American racial relations might have been vastly different. And so might have been the history of American labor.

# Granville T. Woods, Electrical Inventor

[*In the age of invention that followed the Civil War, Granville T. Woods played an important part. He devised a system of communication between moving trains, but is best known for his invention of an automatic air brake. This article about Woods appeared in* Cosmopolitan Magazine *in 1895.*]

Mr. Woods has taken out some thirty-five patents in various countries and has many still pending. He is the inventor of a telephone which he sold to the Bell Telephone Company, and of a system of telegraphing from moving railway trains, which was successfully tried on the New Rochelle branch of the New Haven road in 1885. Three years ago, an electric railway system of his invention was operated at Coney Island [New York]. It had neither exposed wires, secondary batteries, nor a slotted way. The current was taken from iron blocks placed at intervals of twelve feet between the rails, in which, by an ingenious arrangement of magnets and switches, the current was turned on to the blocks only as they were successively covered by the cars.

The most remarkable invention of Mr. Woods is for the regulation of electric motors. In almost all applications of electric power it is necessary at times to control the speed of the motors without changing the loads or disturbing the voltage at the source of supply. This has usually been done by introducing large dead resistances in series with the motors. These quickly become hot, and are extremely wasteful of electricity. Mr. Woods has, by his improvements, reduced the size of these resistances, so as to materially lessen the losses by them, and to remove other objectionable features. . . .

Certain features of this invention are now involved in interference proceedings in the United States Patent Office with five rival inventors. Of these, only one had the invention perfected to the extent of using a dynamotor. . . . The proceedings, however, showed that Woods completely developed his invention when there was no prior model to guide him, and when the others were at most only taking the preliminary steps which led them years later in the same direction. . . .

When a boy of ten, Mr. Woods was set to work at bellows blowing in an Australian railroad repair shop. He soon made himself familiar with all its departments, and with his spare earnings engaged private instruction from the master mechanic of the establishment. At the age of sixteen, Woods was brought by his parents to America, and he became a locomotive engineer on the Iron Mountain road, in Missouri. Later, he secured a position as engineer on the British steamer "Ironsides," and in 1880 established a repair shop of his own in Cincinnati.

Mr. Woods has a remarkably thorough knowledge of the intricate mathematics of electricity, and of legal practice respecting inventions. . . .

S. W. Balch, *Cosmopolitan Magazine*, Vol. 18 (April, 1895), pp. 761-762.

# A Member of the Edison Pioneers

[*Lewis H. Latimer was the only Negro member of the Edison Pioneers, that early group of inventors who worked with Thomas Edison. When Latimer died on December 11, 1928, the Edison Pioneers issued this statement about his life and contribution to the field of invention.*]

Mr. Latimer was born at Chelsea, Mass., September 4th, 1848. . . . At the age of 16 he enlisted in the Naval service of the Federal Government, serving as a "landsman" on the U.S.S. *Massasoit* from which he was honorably discharged in 1865, when he returned to Boston and secured employment as an office boy in the office of Messrs. Crosby and Gould, patent solicitors. In this office he became interested in draughting and gradually perfected himself to such a degree as to become their chief draughtsman. . . . It was Mr. Latimer who executed the drawings and assisted in preparing the applications for the telephone patents of Alexander Graham Bell. In 1880 he entered the employ of Hiram S. Maxim, Electrician of the United States Electric Lighting Co., then located at Bridgeport, Connecticut. It was while in this employ that Mr. Latimer successfully produced a method of making carbon filaments for the Maxim electric incandescent lamp, which he patented. His keen perception of the possibilities of the electric light and kindred industries resulted in his being the author of several other inventions. . . . In 1884 he became associated with the Engineering Department of the Edison Electric Light Company. . . .

He was of the colored race, the only one in our organization, and was one of those to respond to the initial call that led to the formation of the Edison Pioneers, January 24, 1918. Broadmindedness, versatility in the accomplishment of things intellectual and cultural, a linguist, a devoted husband and father, all were characteristic of him, and his genial presence will be missed from our gatherings.

Lewis Howard Latimer, "Statement of the Edison Pioneers," December 11, 1928.

# A Negro Congressman Speaks of Black Inventors

[*George H. Murray, a former slave who was an orphan by Emancipation time, managed to educate himself and spent two years at South Carolina University, until all Negroes were expelled in 1876. In 1892 he was elected to the United States Congress where he championed the causes of free silver and Negro education. On August 10, 1894 he told his white colleagues in the House of Representatives of Negro progress, even in the difficult field of invention.*]

We have proven in almost every line that we are capable of doing what other people can do. We have proven that we can work as much and as well as other people. We have proven that we can learn as well as other people. We have proven that we can fight as well as other people, as was demonstrated in the late [Civil] war. There are still, however, traducers and slanderers of our race who claim that we are not equal to others because we have failed to produce inventors. . . .

. . . I hold in my hand a statement prepared by one of the assistants in the Patent Office, showing the inventions that have been made by colored men within the past few years. . . .

This statement shows that colored men have taken out patents upon almost everything, from a cooking stove to a locomotive. Patents have been granted to colored men for inventions and improvements in the workshop, on the farm, in the factory, on the railroad, in the mine, in almost every department of labor, and some of the most important improvements that go to make up that great motive power of modern industrial machinery, the steam engine, have been produced by colored men. . . .

. . . Mr. Speaker, the colored people of this country want an opportunity to show that the progress, that the civilization which is now admired the world over, that the civilization which is now leading the world, that the civilization which all the nations of the world look up to and imitate—the colored people, I say, want an opportunity to show that they, too, are part and parcel of that great civilization. . . .

Mr. Speaker, in conclusion I ask the liberty [of] appending to my remarks the statistics to which I referred.

There was no objection.

*[Congressman Murray then submitted the list of 92 patents. Eight of them were patents which he held.]*

*The Congressional Record*, 53rd Congress, Second Session, p. 8382.

## The Demands of Free Laborers, 1865

*[Shortly after Emancipation, Negroes united to demand better working conditions. Richmond, Virginia tobacco workers drew up this demand.]*

*Richmond September 18, 1865* Dear Sirs We the Tobacco mechanicks of this city and Manchester is worked to great disadvantages. In 1858 and 1859 our masters hiered us to the Tobacconist at a price ranging from $150 to $180. The Tobacconist furnished us lodging food and clothing. They gave us tasks to performe. all we made over this task they payed us for. We worked faithful and they paid us faithful. They then gave us $2 to $2.50, and we made double the amount we now make. The Tobacconist held a meeting, and resolved not give more than $1.50 cts. per hundred, which is about one days work—in a week we make 600 lbs apece with a ste[a]mer. This weeks work then at $1.50 amounts to $9—the steamers wages is from $4 to $4.50 cts. which leaves from $5 to $4.50 cents per week about one half what we made when slaves. Now to Rent two small rooms we have to pay from $18 to 20. We see $4.50 cts or $5 will not more then pay Rent say nothing about food clothing medicin Doctor Bills. Tax and Co. They say we will starve through laziness that is not so. But it is true we will starve at our present wages. . . . give us a chance. . . . It is impossible to feed ourselves and family—starvation is Cirten unless a change is brought about.

*Tobacco Factory Mechanicks of Richmond and Manchester*

J. T. Trowbridge, *The South* (Hartford, 1866), pp. 230-231.

# Keynote Address at the First Colored National Labor Convention

[*Some two hundred Negro delegates gathered to unite Negro labor in 1869. The principal address was made by John M. Langston who later became professor of law and a Dean at Howard University, United States Minister to Haiti and the Dominican Republic, and Virginia's only Negro Congressman.*]

The laboring class of any community, educated and united, constitute its strength. . . .

Among the colored men of this country there is no small amount of industrial capacity, native and acquired. All over the South and among the colored people of the North, workmen in gold, silver, brass, iron, wood, brick, mortar, and the arts, are found doing skillfully and at usual wages the most difficult tasks in their several departments of labor. . . . As illustrating this statement, it may be appropriately mentioned that perhaps the most accomplished gunsmith among the Americans is a black man, an ex-slave of North Carolina. . . . It is perhaps true, too, that the most finished cabinet-maker and blacksmith of our country is of the same class. And it is said to be the fact that the most valuable invention given us by the South, the cotton plough (the patentee of which formerly resided in Mississippi), was the creature of a slave's genius. . . .

Of the pilots and engineers running steamboats on the different rivers of this State, many of the very best are colored men. It is said that the two most trustworthy pilots in North Carolina are freedmen; one of whom is running a steamboat on Cape Fear river, and the other across Albermarle sound, and on the Chowan and Blackwater rivers. The former is paid $15 per month more than any other pilot on the river, because of his superior ability. The engineer on the boat run by this pilot, is also a freedman, and is said to be one of the best in the State.

. . . one of the most interesting sights which it was my good fortune to witness while in the State, was the building of a steamboat on Cape Fear river by a colored shipbuilder, with his gang of colored workmen. . . .

With a voting power under our present and just system of reconstruction of seven hundred and fifty thousand electors, and an actual laboring force of three millions, out of [a Negro population of] four millions and a quarter . . . we are an element in the industry of the country of importance, value, and power.

. . . our mottoes are liberty and labor, enfranchisement and education! The spelling-book and the hoe, the hammer and the vote, the opportunity to work and to rise . . . we ask for ourselves and our children. . . .

---

*Proceedings of the Colored National Labor Convention Held in Washington* (Washington, 1870), pp. 16-18.

## The Negro Mechanics of Atlanta

[*Discrimination against Negroes by employers and unions had become a pervasive policy by the turn of the century. In the spring of 1902 seniors from Atlanta University investigated the conditions of Negro artisans of their city. This is the report of one of them, H. H. Pace.*]

The first person from whom I obtained any real information was a brickmason who received me cordially and who was inclined to talk. . . . He was a Union man and said that colored brickmasons were well received by the white unions "if they knew their business," although the initiation fee was larger for colored men and the sick and death benefits much smaller for them than for whites. I next saw a machinist who lived in a tumble down house in a rather poor locality. But he said he owned the house. I found a carpenter who was almost totally despondent. He couldn't get work. . . .

The next thing of particular interest to me was a gang of men, white and black, at work upon ten or twelve three-room houses. The person in charge of the work was a colored man who gave his name and address as Tom Carlton, Edgewood, Georgia. He talked to me himself but refused to let me talk to his employees. . . . He said he could join the white union now, they were after him every day to do so. But he wouldn't, because once awhile back when he was working for wages he was refused admission. . . .

Of the whole number questioned . . . all had worked at some time or did work sometimes with whites in the same work. The painters said that the white painters were not very friendly disposed toward them, and did not allow them to join their union under any circumstances. The plumbers were under somewhat the same ban.

Not one of the artisans in my territory had been to a trade school. Nearly every one simply "worked awhile under a first-class brickmason" or "carpenter," etc. Several had learned their trades during slavery and followed them ever since. . . . None answered "Yes" to the question of any "higher training."

The most interesting bit of information in regard to color discrimination was obtained from a colored fireman on the Southern Railway. He said the Company refused to sign a contract and wage scale with his union but did sign one with the white union. Moreover, he said:

> If I take a train from here to Greenville, S.C., I get for that trip $2.60, the white engineer gets $6.00. But if that same train had the same engineer and a *white* fireman, the engineer would get his $6.00 just the same but the fireman would get $3.25. He gets 65 cts. more for doing the same work I do. . . .

W. E. Burghardt Du Bois, ed., *The Negro Artisan* (Atlanta, 1902), p. 115.

## Some Unions Broke the Color Bar

[*In 1900 only 32,000 Negroes were in unions. The United Mine Workers alone had 20,000 of these. Secretary Pearce of the UMW described integration in his union to a United States Industrial Commission in 1900.*]

As far as we are concerned as miners, the colored men are with us in the mines. They work side by side with us. They are members of our organization; can receive as much consideration from the officials of the organization as any other members, no matter what color. We treat them that way. . . . there is only one particular objection, and that is they are used to a great extent in being taken from one place to another to break a strike. . . .

[*A Florida Negro organizer for another union.*]

The Negroes in this city have no need to complain, as the white men work, smoke, eat and drink together with them, meet in Central Union and hold office together. I organized and installed the Central Union, as General Secretary, and I am a Negro, and have held the same [office] for two elections and was elected by the whites, who are in a majority. . . .

[*Although Negro Pullman porters and dining-car waiters formed successful unions, it was not until the formation of the CIO that significant numbers of Negroes were admitted to the protection of the most powerful unions.*]

W. E. Burghardt Du Bois, ed., *The Negro Artisan* (Atlanta, 1902) pp. 161, 177.

## The Emergence of a Negro "Upper Class"

[*In 1895 W. E. B. Du Bois received his Ph.D. from Harvard: it made him the fifth Negro to receive a doctorate in America. A Negro upper class of wealth and education was developing even in the South, as this report by Massachusetts reformer Samuel Barrows shows.*]

. . . two aristocracies are appearing in the colored race,—the aristocracy of culture and the aristocracy of wealth. Fortunately, at present, in the younger generation culture and prosperity are moving together. The colored man's standard of wealth is relatively much smaller than that of the white man. There are no Negro millionaires that I know of; but there is growing up a class of men with fortunes ranging from $15,000 to $100,000. . . .

There are conspicuous cases of individual prosperity in nearly all the large centers and in the agricultural districts. Thus, in Montgomery, Alabama, a colored barber, originally a slave, his accumulated property amounting to $75,000 or $100,000. An ex-slave in Mississippi has bought one of the plantations that formerly belonged to Jefferson Davis. The colored people of Maryland are said to possess property to the amount of $9,000,000. . . .

Samuel J. Barrows, "What the Southern Negro Is Doing for Himself," *Atlantic Monthly*, Vol. 67 (June, 1891), p. 810.

# The National Negro Business League

*[In 1900 Booker T. Washington, noting the rising number of Negro business concerns and wishing to unite them for mutual gain, organized the National Negro Business League. Within five years there were more than 100 chapters. The resolution passed in 1905 that led to the formation of the Colorado Springs, Colorado chapter, indicates the goals of the organization.]*

Whereas, we believe that the time has come for the colored people to enter more largely into business pursuits by means of individual as well as co-operative efforts as the surest and most speedy way to gain earnings from invested capital, and to afford employment for our race, and for the further purpose of stimulating our people in this community to engage in such industrial pursuits as may be practical and possible, therefore be it

Resolved, That we form a local business league . . . and invite the cooperation of all who desire to better the material condition of our people in this city.

Resolved, That we take steps to present the wonderful undeveloped agricultural and mineral resources of Colorado to desirable colored citizens who may be induced to settle in this state, bring with them capital, brains and pluck for the purpose of seeking permanent homes and helping to develop the natural resources of this state.

---

Newspaper clipping, *Booker T. Washington Papers* (Washington: Library of Congress Manuscript Collection), Box 847.

# 13

# *The Last Frontier*

LIFE in the West was dangerous until settlers filled in the last open spaces and law and order came to stay. Mobs calling themselves vigilantes often made laws and executed men they decided were guilty of crimes. Federal troops and marshals did their best to keep the peace, suppress the Indians, and prevent the outlaws from killing or terrorizing the law-abiding settlers who poured into the territories.

Many Negroes were among these farmers and riders of the last frontier. The typical trail crew of eight that drove cattle up the Chisholm Trail to Kansas after the Civil War included two or three Negro cowboys. Some had come West as slaves and were cowboys before they became free men. Thousands of others headed West after emancipation, seeking a new and free life where skill would count more than skin color. Some came to live by the law; others rode in to break it.

Black and white cowboys shot it out on the streets of Dodge City and Abilene. The first man shot in Dodge was a cowboy named Tex, an innocent bystander to a fight—and he was a Negro. The first man arrested in Abilene was not innocent—and he was a Negro. His black and white trail crew were so infuriated by his arrest that they shot up the town and staged Abilene's first jail break to rescue their buddy.

Even the good and the young had to be ready for a life of danger and death on the frontier. Although Jack Hardy, a Negro boy of 13, had never seen Indians, he managed to outwit the Comanche

*A soldier is helped to safety during
an Indian attack.*

tribe that had captured him. He acted with such coolness and self-
assurance that the tribe made him a member and presented him with
a bow and arrows. Young Hardy waited until the first opportunity
and then made his escape.

Britton Johnson, a tall, former slave, was known far and wide
in Texas for his physical strength and courage and, mainly, for being one of the best shots on the Texas frontier. In 1864 a Comanche raiding party attacked his settlement, killing Johnson's young
son and several other people. The Comanche carried off his wife,
his three other children, and several white settlers. Johnson's plan for
reuniting his family called for him to enter the Indian camp and gain
the tribe's confidence by volunteering as a warrior.

Johnson was accepted by the tribe, since they needed new warriors badly. One night he helped his wife, children, and the white
prisoners escape. His trouble with the Comanche, however, did
not end there.

In 1871 Johnson and a few other Negro cowboys were attacked
by 25 Comanche on the Texas plains. Johnson directed the men to
kill their horses and use their bodies as breastworks. But the Indians
repeatedly rode through the cowboys' defenses and picked the men
off one by one. When Johnson found that he was the only one still
alive, he gathered all the guns and loaded them during lulls in the
battle so that he could pour a rapid fire into the attacking Indians. He

faced charge after charge before he was finally cut down. A settler who found his body counted 173 shells near it.

Most of those who came West had neither the skill nor the bravery of Britton Johnson. Some were just simple people looking for a home and good farming land which they could call their own. Nancy Lewis and her husband rode to Denver by joining their covered wagon to the wagon team of Sisler and Saur in 1865. The couple, both former slaves, had met and married at Fort Leavenworth, Kansas and came West seeking freedom and adventure. Years later Mrs. Lewis would recall all the fun she had had but would regret not getting an education.

The rough life of the West created a number of wild men who lived by their own law. One of these was a former slave called Nat Love, but better known as "Deadwood Dick." He claimed that he had ridden with Billy the Kid and Frank and Jesse James and that he had known Buffalo Bill and Bat Masterson.

In his 1907 autobiography, Nat Love wrote of his many adventures on the frontier. He was adopted by an Indian tribe, rode 100 miles in twelve hours on an unsaddled horse, and tried to rope and steal a United States Army cannon. His good friend Bat Masterson got him out of that scrape. Love told how he rode into a Mexican saloon and ordered two drinks—one for him and one for his horse.

*Nat Love won the title of "Deadwood Dick" at an 1876 rodeo. He claimed his good friends Billy the Kid and Frank and Jesse James were "misunderstood" men, not criminals.*

Whether in town or out on the range, Love lived a life of wild fun and had amazingly good luck. "While our money lasted," he wrote of a trip into Dodge City, "we could certainly enjoy ourselves in dancing, drinking, and shooting up the town." Even the dangers of the plains were fun to him. "Horses were shot from under me, men killed around me, but always I escaped with a trifling wound at the worst."

In 1890, the year the United States Census showed that the last frontier had closed, Nat Love left the wild life of the cowboy for a peaceful berth on the railroad—as a Pullman porter. He did not see the "Iron Horse" as his enemy, or regret leaving the range.

It would be incorrect to conclude from the story of Nat Love's life that cowboys were always lucky men or accurate shots. In 1869 a Negro cowboy named Ben and his white buddies went after a group of Indians who had stolen their horses. Ben was so angry that he charged alone into their village and shot it out with the Indian mounted on his horse. Only Ben's horse was killed.

The West had its share of men who killed neither by accident nor as a result of a fight. They were the desperadoes who robbed banks and trains, or jumped claims, or shot people down in cold blood. Some of these, such as Billy the Kid and Cherokee Bill, were mass murderers. Cherokee Bill was similar to Billy the Kid in almost everything but skin color. Both young men killed without regard to whether or not their victims were armed. Both died before they reached the age of 21. Cherokee Bill told the happy crowd that turned out to see him swing at the end of a rope that he had no last words. He said that he had come to die for his crimes and not to make a speech.

## The Men Who Tamed the West

For many years the uneasy peace in the Western territories was kept by the United States Army, which included Negro units—the 9th and 10th Cavalries and the 24th and 25th Infantries. They were stationed at various times from the Rio Grande to the Canadian border. They fought bandits as well as Apaches, Sioux, and Comanche. They took the field against Billy the Kid, Geronimo, Crazy Horse, and a Negro chief of the Apaches named John Horse. During the Indian wars, fourteen of these black soldiers won the nation's highest military decoration, the Congressional Medal of Honor. A unit of 61

*The determined soldiers of the 24th Infantry spent many years defending the West against outlaws and Indians. Two of the men won the Congressional Medal of Honor for fighting on against bandits although they were severely wounded.*

members of the 10th Cavalry survived 86 hours without water on the Texas plains. And by 1877, West Point had graduated its first Negro officer, Henry O. Flipper of Georgia, who was assigned to the 10th Cavalry.

The black troopers of the 9th and 10th Cavalries constituted a fifth of all the United States mounted troops assigned to protect the

*Ninth Cavalry troops ride to the rescue. This sketch is by the noted artist Frederick Remington. This unit had a reputation for arriving just in the nick of time to rescue settlers or other soldiers—but they have never appeared in any cowboy movie of the old West.*

frontier. They were commanded by white officers who considered the assignment a professional honor. Lieutenant John J. Pershing led the 10th in Montana, in the charge up San Juan Hill, in the Philippines, and during the punitive expedition into Mexico in 1916— and was nicknamed "Blackjack" Pershing. "We officers of the 10th Cavalry," recalled the tough, emotionless Pershing, "could have taken our black heroes in our arms."

10TH CAVALRY

Isaiah Dorman rode into fame and death with General George Custer at the Little Big Horn. For many years Dorman had served as a courier for the War Department in the Dakota territory. In May of 1876 General Custer requested that Dorman be assigned to his command "and report for duty to accompany the expedition as Interpreter" into Montana. Dorman may have been part Sioux, which would explain his ability to serve as interpreter.

On June 25 and 26 Dorman was among the 264 men who fought and died with Custer. For reasons never made clear, the Sioux did not scalp and mutilate Dorman as they did the white soldiers.

In April 1875 Pompey Factor, Indian Scout with the 24th Infantry, won the Medal of Honor for heroically defending a small party of United States' troops against thirty Indians near the Pecos and Rio Grande rivers in Texas. It was not until 1965 that research uncovered the fact that Factor was a Negro, one of many who had joined the Seminoles.

During the period of Reconstruction and extending into the 1890's, Negro Texans were among those elected to the state legislature. They worked to protect cattlemen and build a more prosperous state. In 1870 a former slave named Richard Allen devised the Texas pension law for veterans. As chairman of the Committee on Roads and Bridges of the Texas legislature, Representative Allen helped link his vast state with a system of bridges and roads.

Negro legislator Alexander Asberry sponsored a law to protect the grazing herds of cattle by holding the railroads responsible for cattle run down by their trains.

State Senator G. T. Ruby's bill was directed against lawlessness in the Lone Star State. Another of Ruby's resolutions provided for a survey of the vast resources of the state. This led to the uncovering of important mineral deposits as well as rich new lands for farming.

State Senator Matt Gaines also worked hard for Texas. He proposed granting tax exemptions to libraries, schools, and churches. Concerned with the protection of the unfortunate, he sought to have the state assume responsibility for its mentally ill. Gaines and the other Negro legislators battled long and hard but without success against the laws that segregated Negro students from whites in Texas schools.

## Helping the Red Man

In the days when it was generally agreed that "the only good Indian is a dead Indian," the Negro college at Hampton was the first to open its doors, in 1879, to more than a hundred "redskins." An eager young ex-slave, Booker T. Washington, was placed in charge of this unique experiment to prove that Indians could and should be educated. They finally gave up their blankets, long hair, and peace pipes for books, workshops, and the new fields of knowledge which the college offered them. The experiment was a success.

When Mr. Washington took one of his Indian students to the nation's capital, he found a strange color line. Aboard the steamboat the Indian was admitted to the dining room, while he was not. And in Washington a hotel manager accepted the pupil but not the teacher.

*Indian orchestra at Hampton College, 1900. Acceptance of Indians at Hampton and defense of their rights by Negro Congressmen Bruce of Mississippi and Hyman of South Carolina came during the period when most whites felt "the only good Indian is a dead Indian." (Collection, The Museum of Modern Art, New York. Gift of Lincoln Kirstein.)*

## The "Exodus of 1879"

The same year that Indians were admitted to Hampton, a former slave named Benjamin "Pap" Singleton led a vast migration of Southern Negroes to the West. This "Exodus of 1879" was one of the most dramatic invasions of settlers that the West has ever known. Thousands upon thousands of poor Negro farmers organized committees, contributed their savings, and hired agents to arrange the trip West. In torn and tattered clothing, with their few belongings on their backs, they poured into Kansas. They were searching for liberty and opportunity and fleeing a brutal oppression. One settler told a Congressional investigating committee why they left: "The whole South—every State in the South—had got into the hands of the very men that held us as slaves. . . . We said there was no hope for us and we better go."

This ragged band often found a helping hand. The Governor of Kansas received a delegation of 100 in 1879 and told them what they could expect by way of help in his state. A Freedman's Relief Association was organized. An eyewitness reported that "temporary shelter was speedily provided for them; food and the facilities for cooking it were furnished them in ample measure." Many whites in Kansas provided the "Exodusters" with jobs and homes.

Not all of the "Exodusters" were warmly welcomed into communities. A group of 150 persons from Mississippi was driven out of Lincoln, Nebraska. A Denver, Colorado paper reported that who arrived there "found that the owners of houses would not rent to them." But both prominent Negroes of the town and sympathetic whites built and sold them small houses.

The refugees from the South who poured into Nebraska built a number of small communities. But earlier, in 1867, when the state joined the Union, Negroes were told to stay away from the polls in Nebraska City and were threatened with guns and knives when they came to vote in Omaha. By the 1880's, however, Negroes were among those graduating from Nebraska high schools and serving in the state legislature. David Patrick of Aurora carried the mail by Pony Express to Fort Kearny and Tom Cunningham was a police officer in Lincoln. Dr. M. O. Ricketts, an ex-slave, graduated with honor from the University of Nebraska College of Medicine in 1884. The doctor was twice elected to the state legislature and five other Negroes followed in his footsteps to the state house.

Negroes contributed to the growth of the West throughout its last frontier days. A crew of 300 Negro laborers worked on the Union Pacific Railroad along with the Irish, German, and Chinese laborers. Emmett J. Scott of Houston published the *Texas Freeman* and W. J. Harding served in the Wyoming legislature. Charles Pettit served as a United States Deputy Marshal in Wichita, Kansas. Some Negroes built hotels and others built laundries. One of the best-known pioneers of Denver, Colorado, was Ed Sanderlin, a barber who became a rich man and whose funeral was attended by the remaining pioneers of both races. Other unknown black men "struck it rich" as gold prospectors.

A Negro cowboy named Williams taught Theodore Roosevelt how to break in a horse, while another named Clay taught comedian Will Rogers the art of roping. Others, far too numerous to mention, helped tame the West and found there a greater measure of equality than in the places from which they had come.

## The Farmers' Rebellion

The prosperity which the Civil War brought to the farmer began to end with the surrender of General Robert E. Lee. The farmer's economic troubles went from bad to worse as he waited for prices to rise. Debts came due, railroads and banks raised their rates, and as prices dropped, farmers obtained the money which they so desperately needed by taking out mortages on their homesteads. In Kansas the number of mortgages increased 300 per cent in the seven years following 1880. And the seven-year period was capped with the most devastating winter and broiling summer in the history of the Great Plains. The depressions of 1873 and 1893 drove the farmers even closer to desperation as they saw their friends and neighbors lose their homes and land to creditors.

In the South cotton prices began a rapid decline after the war. By 1868 the price of cotton had fallen from one dollar a pound to twenty-five cents. By 1894 the price was down to 5 cents.

Throughout the South, the sharecropping system grew. The poor whites and Negroes worked a landlord's acreage for a part of the crop. The landlord kept the records of the sharecropper's expenses and often falsified the record to keep him in never-ending debt. The average sharecropper, white or Negro, had little chance before the law. But the Negro sharecropper had even less chance than the white, because he had to face white sheriffs, judges, and juries.

*Convict road gangs in North Carolina, 1910. The wagons were the homes of Negro convicts who were moved from place to place to do labor for the state. Bloodhounds, whips, and guns were part of the control system over the prisoners.*

Very often the sharecropper was not even free to move. An illiterate Arkansas farmer by the name of Steve Green tried to leave the Saddler land around 1913 when his rent was raised from five dollars an acre to nine. Saddler said to the Negro sharecropper, "Green, didn't I tell you that if you didn't work on my farm that there was not room enough in Crittenden County for you and me to live." Saddler then drew his gun and pumped three shots into Green. The sharecropper limped into his house and returned the fire with his Winchester. Then he fled. He finally got to Chicago where police held him at the request of Arkansas officials but he was not returned to Arkansas. As he explained, "the colored people of Chicago had heard the story and got out a writ of habeas corpus." Few were as lucky as Steven Green.

A large number of Negroes lived under a system of peonage. One of its victims told how it worked:

> I am not an educated man. I will give you the peonage system as it is practiced here in the name of the law.
>
> If a colored man is arrested here and hasn't any money, whether he is guilty or not, he has to pay just

the same. A man of color is never tried in this country. It is simply a farce. Everything is fixed before he enters the courtroom. I will give you an illustration of how it is done:

I was brought in a prisoner, to go through the farce of being tried. The whole of my fine may amount to fifty dollars. A kindly appearing man will come up and pay my fine and take me to his farm to allow me to work it out. At the end of the month I find that I owe him more than I did when I went there. The debt is increased year in and year out. You would ask, "How is that?" It is simply that he is charging you more for your board, lodging, and washing than they allow you for your work, and you can't help yourself either . . . because you are still a prisoner. . . .

One word more about peonage. The court and the man you work for are always partners. One makes the fine and the other one works you and holds you, and if you leave you are tracked with bloodhounds and brought back.

## The Populists

During the post-Civil War years farmers united to fight their common enemies. At first they formed separate groups, the whites fearing that advances for the Negro would be at their expense. A colored Farmers' Alliance reached a million members by 1890. That year the white Farmers' Alliance invited the Negro group to a joint meeting in Florida. A Kansas farmer reported "the former slave owner and the former slave shook hands warmly."

From Kansas, south to the Rio Grande, Negroes and whites responded to the call of the People's or Populist Party. Negro Populists in Texas served on the party's executive committee from 1891 to 1900. One reported that "colored people are coming into the new party in squads and companies. They have colored third-party speakers and are organizing colored clubs." A delegate named Watson told the Texas Populist convention of 1892, "I am an emancipated slave of this state" and "my interest is yours and yours mine."

That same year 92 Negroes were seated as delegates to the Populist National Convention. Populist Ignatius Donnelly predicted the party's victories "would wipe out the color line in the South."

An important Populist contribution to American democracy was its ability to unite Negro and white farmers in the South. The Populist candidate for President in 1892, James B. Weaver, rode into Raleigh, North Carolina, in a parade of 350 Negro and white horsemen. Tom Watson, a white Georgia Congressman, told Negro and white farmers: "You are kept apart that you may be separately fleeced of your earnings. You are made to hate each other because upon that hatred is rested the keystone of the financial despotism which enslaves you both." A Negro preacher named H. S. Doyle made sixty-three speeches for Watson despite many threats against his life. In one town a large group of armed white farmers massed to protect Doyle from violence.

The Populists specifically appealed to Negro voters by their willingness to nominate Negro candidates and their demand for a secret ballot and an end to the convict-lease system. The secret ballot would protect the Negro voter from intimidation by his employer or other whites. The convict-lease system made slaves of Negro workers and there were ten Negroes to every white victim of this forced-labor device.

The Populist convention of 1896 bitterly debated the idea of merging with the Democrats behind William Jennings Bryan. Reporter Henry Demarest Lloyd wrote, "The most eloquent speeches made were those of the whites and blacks explaining to the convention what the rule of the Democrats meant in the South." A Negro delegate from Georgia, Lloyd reported, "told how the People's Party alone gave full fellowship to his race, when it had been abandoned by the Republicans and cheated and betrayed by the Democrats." While the Populists voted to support Bryan for President, they nominated Tom Watson for Vice-President. Seconding Watson's nomination, a Negro delegate said, "He has made it possible for the black man to vote according to his conscience in Georgia." But with the defeat of the Populists and Democrats by Republican William McKinley, the Populist Party began to decline.

The most noted Negro politician during the Populist era was George H. White, a college graduate who held law degrees from several universities. This former slave served six years in the North Carolina legislature and eight years as a state prosecuting attorney. In 1896 and in 1898 Negro and white voters of his state elected him to Congress despite widespread anti-Negro violence.

In Congress and out Representative White sought to advance the industrial and agricultural interests of his state. As Congres-

*Congressman George Henry White, who sponsored America's first anti-lynching bill, served North Carolina from 1897 to 1901. He spoke for Negro rights during a time of maximum oppression, in which the public conscience rested in deep slumber.*

sional interest turned to Cuba and the war with Spain, he warned his colleagues "the nation must care for those at home as well as abroad." The problem of racial injustice, he told Congress, must be met. "You will have to meet it. You have got this problem to settle, and the sooner it is settled the better it will be for all concerned. I speak this in all charity. I speak this with no hostility."

At every opportunity Congressman White denounced discrimination "by constitutional amendment and State legislation" or "by cold-blooded fraud and intimidation." He pointedly asked Congress, "How long will you sit in your seats and hear and see the principles that underlie the foundations of this Government sapped away little by little?"

Representative White repeatedly drew the applause of his Congressional colleagues for his pointed speeches and biting humor. The only Negro in Congress for two terms, White never forgot that he spoke "as the sole representative for nine million people." He attacked every form of discrimination from the use of anti-Negro jokes to the mounting number of lynchings. "We ask and expect a chance in legislation, and we will be content with nothing else," he told Congress, and insisted that the Constitutional amendments protecting Negro rights be enforced. On January 20, 1900, he introduced the first Congressional bill to make lynching a federal crime. Petitions poured into White's office from all over the country supporting his bill, but it never came to a vote.

In his last speech, Representative White reminded Congress that his antilynching bill "still sweetly sleeps" in the committee to which it was referred. He entered a last plea for "the life, the liberty, the future happiness" of his people. The Negroes were, he reminded all, "a rising people" and would in time send other men to the United States Congress.

Violence and intimidation were the main methods used to drive the remaining Negro Populists out of their offices. In North Carolina, where the Populist campaigns had led to the election of many Negroes, one newspaper screamed in 1898 about "NEGRO CONGRESS-MEN, NEGRO SOLICITORS, NEGRO REVENUE OFFICERS, NEGRO COL-LECTORS OF CUSTOMS, NEGROES in charge of white institutions . . . NEGRO MAGISTRATES trying white women and white men, white convicts chained to NEGRO CONVICTS, and forced to social equality with them." "It is time for the shotgun to play a part, and an active one in the elections," said another opponent of Negro rights. A bloody riot in Wilmington, North Carolina drove out Negro officeholders and many plain citizens. This massacre became the background of Negro novelist Charles W. Chestnutt's moving book *The Marrow of Tradition*. But the Wilmington riot was not the final stage of the "white supremacy" campaign. In 1900 the North Carolina Constitution was amended to include a poll tax, a literacy test, and a "grandfather clause" that denied the suffrage to Negroes.

The defeat of the Populists led to a systematic repression of the South's Negro population. From 1890 to 1910 Southern states restricted the right to vote to whites. And it was during this same period that most of the segregation laws were passed. Many of the white Populists, such as Tom Watson, turned on the Negro with a fury. Watson blamed the Negroes for Populist defeats and backed every effort to deprive them of the right to vote. Watson stayed on in politics, using his bigotry to attract the votes of fellow white Georgians. His hate campaign was extended to Catholics and Jews. Early in the 20th century, Watson was calling Catholic priests "murderers" and cheering the action of a Georgia mob which had lynched an innocent Jewish man. By the time Watson died in 1922, he was a bitter racist and a United States Senator from Georgia. The Ku Klux Klan sent an eight-foot cross of roses to his funeral.

*Young Dr. George Washington Carver aids students working in his Tuskegee laboratory.*

## The Farmers' Scientist

The greatest single benefit to Southern agriculture after the Civil War came from the gentle hands of George Washington Carver. A slave boy who had once been exchanged for a horse, Dr. Carver gained national fame because of his scientific research at Tuskegee Institute.

After long years of experimentation and investigation, Dr. Carver found more than three hundred and fifty uses for the Southern crops of peanuts, sweet potatoes, and pecans. He traveled through the Alabama countryside to bring his knowledge to farmers of both races. The Crown Prince of Sweden spent three weeks at the side of the Tuskegee scientist, watching him make things grow and discovering new ways of making them more useful to man. Henry Ford provided a laboratory in which Carver might expand his work and visited him there regularly. His students remember the great scientist as a kindly teacher who "would never embarrass you or get angry in public." Many years before Dr. Martin Luther King asked his followers to meet hatred with love, Dr. Carver said, "No man can drag me down so low as to make me hate him."

*Dr. George Washington Carver at work in his laboratory in the 1940's.*

For many years Dr. Carver worked for the United States Government. At one time he was called before Congress and given fifteen minutes to explain his work, for no one thought that talk about peanuts or sweet potatoes need take any longer. His talk so aroused the interest of the Congressmen that he was allowed almost two hours in which to finish. Many of his findings were published by the Department of Agriculture for the use of farmers everywhere.

When Dr. Carver died in 1943, President Franklin D. Roosevelt and Vice-President Henry A. Wallace led the nation in paying respect to the great scientist.

## Nat Love, "Deadwood Dick," Cowboy

[*A few years after the Civil War, Nat Love, fifteen years old and a former slave, rode into the West seeking adventure. He found it and wrote about it in* The Life and Adventures of Nat Love, *published in 1907. His boastful tales are as believable as those told by Davy Crockett, Daniel Boone, Jim Beckwourth, and earlier Western hands and tall-tale spinners. Nat Love tells how he won the title of Deadwood Dick on July 4, 1876 in Deadwood City.*]

. . . Our trail boss was chosen to pick out the mustangs from a herd of wild horses just off the range, and he picked out twelve of the most wild and vicious horses that he could find.

The conditions of the contest were that each of us who were mounted was to rope, throw, tie, bridle and saddle, and mount the particular horse picked for us in the shortest time possible. The man accomplishing the feat in the quickest time [was] to be declared the winner.

It seems to me that the horse chosen for me was the most vicious of the lot. Everything being in readiness, the "45" cracked and we all sprang forward together, each of us making for our particular mustang.

I roped, threw, tied, bridled, saddled, and mounted my mustang in exactly nine minutes from the crack of the gun. The time of the next nearest competitor was twelve minutes and thirty seconds. This gave me the record and championship of the West, which I held up to the time I quit the business in 1890, and my record has never been beaten. It is worthy of passing remark that I never had a horse pitch with me so much as that mustang, but I never stopped sticking my spurs in him and using my quirt on his flanks until I proved his master. Right there the assembled crowd named me Deadwood Dick and proclaimed me champion roper of the western cattle country.

[*Nat Love fights off an Indian attack single-handedly on October 4, 1876.*]

. . . I was riding along alone when all at once I heard the well-known Indian war whoop and noticed not far away a large party of

Indians making straight for me. They were all well mounted and they were in full war paint, which showed me that they were on the war path, and as I was alone and had no wish to be scalped by them I decided to run for it. . . . I turned in my saddle every once in a while and gave them a shot by way of greeting, and I had the satisfaction of seeing a painted brave tumble from his horse and go rolling in the dust every time my rifle spoke. . . . Reaching Yellow Horse Canyon, I had about decided to stop and make a stand when one of their bullets caught me in the leg, passing clear through it and then through my horse, killing him. Quickly falling behind him I used his dead body for a breast work and stood the Indians off for a long time, as my aim was so deadly and they [had] lost so many that they were careful to keep out of range.

But finally my ammunition gave out, and the Indians were quick to find this out, and they at once closed in on me, but I was by no means subdued, wounded as I was and almost out of my head, and fought with my empty gun until finally overpowered. When I came to my senses I was in the Indians' camp. [And of course Deadwood Dick escaped again.]

---

Nat Love, *The Life and Adventures of Nat Love, by Himself* (Los Angeles, 1907), pp. 73, 93, 98-99.

## Fighting Off a Bandit Ambush

[*The Arizona sun beat down on a small detachment of Negro soldiers of the 24th Infantry and 9th Cavalry as they moved across the plains from Fort Grant to Fort Thomas guarding the Army paymaster, Wham, and his strong box. A large gang of outlaws had placed a boulder in their path and waited in ambush. The paymaster describes what happened when the soldiers investigated the boulder blocking the road.*]

They were nearly all at the boulder when a signal shot was fired from the ledge of rocks about fifty feet above to the right, which was instantly followed by a volley, believed by myself and the entire party to be fifteen or twenty shots.

A sharp, short fight, lasting something over thirty minutes, ensued during which time the . . . officers and privates, eight of whom were wounded, two being shot twice, behaved in the most courageous and heroic manner. . . .

Sergeant Brown, though shot through the abdomen did not quit the field until again wounded, this time through the arm.

Private Burge who was to my immediate right, received a bad wound in the hand, but gallantly held his post, resting his rifle on his fore-arm and continuing to fire with much coolness, until shot through the thigh and twice through the hat.

Private Arrington was shot through the shoulder, while fighting from this same position.

Privates Hams, Wheeler, and Harrison were also wounded, to my immediate left, while bravely doing their duty under a murderous cross-fire. . . .

The brigands fought from six well-constructed, stone forts; the arrangments seemed thorough, the surprise complete. . . .

I was a soldier in Grant's old regiment, and during the entire war it was justly proud of its record of sixteen battles and of the reflected glory of its old Colonel, the "Great Commander," but I never witnessed better courage or better fighting than shown by these colored soldiers, on May 11, 1889, as the bullet marks on the robber positions to-day abundantly attest.

---

"Letter of J. W. Wham," *Medal of Honor File of Sergeant Benjamin Brown* (Washington: War Records Office, National Archives, 1889).

## Senator Bruce Demands Justice for Indians

[*B. K. Bruce escaped from slavery during the Civil War and moved to Mississippi during Reconstruction. There he became a teacher and a wealthy landowner, entered politics, and was elected to the United States Senate in 1874. His long fight for democratic rights included a defense of open immigration and of Indian rights. During a Senate debate on the Indian, which took place on April 7, 1880, Bruce took the floor to denounce the American policy "that has kept the Indian a fugitive and a vagabond, that has bred discontent, suspicion, and hatred in the mind of the red man. . . ."*]

Our Indian policy and administration seem to me to have been inspired and controlled by a stern selfishness, with a few honorable exceptions. Indian treaties have generally been made as the condition and instrument of acquiring the valuable territory occupied by the several Indian nations, and have been changed and revised from time to time as it became desirable that the steadily growing, irrepressible white races should secure more room for their growth and more lands for their occupancy; and wars, bounties, and beads have been used . . . for the purpose of temporary peace and security for the whites, and as the preliminary to further aggressions upon the red man's lands, with the ultimate view of his expulsion and extinction from the continent. . . .

Now, sir, the Indian is a physical force; a half million of vigorous, physical, intellectual agents ready for the plastic hand of Christian civilization, living in a country possessing empires of untilled and uninhabited lands. The Indian tribes, viewed from this utilitarian stand-point, are worth preservation, conservation, utilization, and civilization, and I believe that we have reached a period when the public sentiment of the country demands such a modification in the Indian policy, in its purposes, and in its methods, as shall save and not destroy these people.

---

*The Congressional Record*, 46th Congress, Second Session, pp. 2195-2196.

# Private Johnson's Story of Bravery Against the Ute Indians

[*Private Henry Johnson describes his action against the Ute Indians, which won him the Congressional Medal of Honor at Milk River, Colorado, in October, 1879.*]

[I] was on guard as Sergeant of the Guard, on or about the day and night of October 5th 1879, during which time there was almost continual firing from the enemy [Ute Indians] upon our men; that we had fortified ourselves into small pits known as rifle pits, and that the Indians outnumbered the soldiers by at least ten to one.

During the morning of the date above mentioned, [I] came out of the pit in which [I] had been fortified and went over to other pits to give necessary instruction to some of the members of [my] guard, during which time [I] was exposed to the fire from the Indians who were very near and at easy range of [me].

Some of Major Thornburg's men had been wounded, and were suffering from want of water, and that [I] was one of the party of men who formed a skirmish line by order of Capt. F. Dodge 9th

Cavalry and fought their way to the Creek (Milk River) for water for the wounded and themselves.

---

Deposition of Henry Johnson, Troop K, 9th Cavalry, August 14, 1890 (Washington: National Archives, War Records Office).

## *The 9th Cavalry Battles the Apaches*

[*Subduing Geronimo's Apaches was part of the work of the 9th Cavalry, "United States Colored Troops." The actions of the three soldiers cited below won them the Congressional Medal of Honor.*]

I take pleasure in certifying as an eye-witness to gallant conduct on the part of Sergeant Thomas Boyne, Troop L, 9th Calvalry, in action with hostile Apaches [in] New Mexico, May 29th, 1879.

I was bringing in a wounded man with a few men, was surprised by the Indians, my horse killed and was corralled by the hostiles. Sergeant Boyne commanded a detachment sent to my assistance, flanked, and gallantly charged the Indians driving them off.

*Henry L. Wright*

Lieut. 9th Cavalry

This soldier [Moses Williams] rallied the detachment when his commanding officer was dismounted and unable to reach them; he skillfully conducted the right flank in a running fight of three or four hours; his keen-sightedness in discovering the Indians in hiding probably prevented the command from falling into a trap; and his coolness, bravery, and unflinching devotion to duty in standing by his commanding officer in an exposed position under heavy fire from a large party of Indians was undoubtedly the means of saving the lives of at least three of his comrades.

*Joseph B. Doe*

Asst. Secretary of War

. . . While the detachment under my command was making a mounted charge to relieve Lt. Valois—whom the Indians had almost completely surrounded, having killed ten (10) of his horses, and wounded several of his men—the horse of Pvt. Burton, became un-manageable and was carrying him directly into the Indians' line;—to avoid this Pvt. Burton dropped out of the saddle when within about one hundred yards from the enemy's position, and lay prone—and inactive. As the Indians were constantly keeping up a heavy fire, I presumed of course he had been struck. . . . Pvt. Burton—whom we all supposed to be dead—called to us not to leave him. I immediately called for a volunteer to go to his assistance, but Pvt. Walley had anticipated me and galloping rapidly over to where Pvt. Burton was lying, quickly dismounted, assisted him in the saddle, and mounting behind him joined the Troop in the most unconcerned manner. The Indians having observed the movement opened a concentrated fire on them and it is a source of mystery to me how they escaped unhurt—considering the shortness of the range.

I might add numerous minor instances of Pvt. Walley's gallantry and bravery on this and other Campaigns for he was always to the front, ready, willing and anxious to do his full duty—and even more—but I will content myself in the above, adding that during a period of nearly two (2) years, while under my immediate command —whether in the garrison or field—I always found Pvt. Walley a thoroughly reliable, trustworthy, and efficient soldier . . . and I have always heard him spoken of in terms of praise by my brother officers. . . .

*Geo. R. Burnett*

1st Lt. 9th Cavalry

---

*Medal of Honor Records of Sergeant Thomas Boyne, Sergeant Moses Williams, and Private Augustus Walley* (Washington: National Archives, War Records Office).

# The 10th Cavalry Spends 3½ Days Without Water

[*Lieutenant Charles L. Cooper of the 10th Cavalry describes his Negro unit's 86-hour period without water on the Staked Plains of Texas.*]

. . . we were to make a supply camp at some convenient point, and manoeuvre from there in pursuit of depredating Indians, as also to protect settlers who are rapidly populating this region of the country. . . .

[After several days of trailing a group of Indians the troops were] lost on the Staked Plains, without water and no prospects of getting any, as we did not know which way to go for it, and from our experience we knew the greater part of the country was "dry as a bone."

In the meantime our men had been dropping from their horses with exhaustion, as we had been nearly two days without water, and we were retarded greatly in endeavoring to keep the men together. . . . [By the next day] the men were almost completely used up, and the captain and I were not much better. Our men had dropped back, one by one, unable to keep up with us; their tongues and throats were swollen, and they were unable even to swallow their saliva—in fact, they had no saliva to swallow, that is if I judge of their condition from my own. My tongue and throat were so dry that when I put a few morsels of brown sugar, that I found in my pocket, into my mouth, I was unable to dissolve it in order to swallow it. During this time while lying on the ground, one of my private horses showed signs of exhaustion, staggered, and fell; so, in order to relieve the men, I had his throat cut, and the blood distributed among them. The captain and I drank heartily of the steaming blood. . . .

This, our fourth day without water, was dreadful. . . . Men gasping in death around us; horses falling dead to the right and left; the crazed survivors of our men fighting each his neighbor for the blood of the horses. . . . We left camp at 8 o'clock at night, and travelled until about 3 the next morning. . . . The captain and I travelled some five miles . . . and finally reached Double Lake, completely exhausted. We found there six of the men of our company, whom we had missed, and immediately started them out with canteens of water for their suffering comrades. Our loss on the trip was four men died from thirst [out of 61]. . . .

*The Daily Tribune*, September 8, 1877 (Washington National Archives, War Records Office).

# Defending the Wagon Train Against the Sioux

[*The Sioux wars in the Dakotas often involved units of the 9th Cavalry. Corporal William O. Wilson won the Congressional Medal of Honor for the action described here by his commanding officer.*]

On the morning of December 30, 1890, the wagon train of the Battalion 9th Cavalry, on route from White River, South Dakota, to Pine Ridge Indian Agency, South Dakota, with Troop D, 9th Cavalry, under my command as escort, was attacked at the crossing of Cheyenne Creek, near Pine Ridge S.D. Deeming it necessary to communicate with the Battalion Commander, Major Guy V. Henry, 9th Cavalry, then at Pine Ridge Agency, and inform him of the attack, two Indian Scouts were asked to take a message to the Agency, and declined to do so when Corporal William O. Wilson, Troop I, 9th Cavalry, who was on duty with the wagon train and on the skirmish line, volunteered to take the message, and did so successfully, although Indians could be seen plainly endeavoring to cut him off from reaching the Agency.

John S. Loud

Captain 9th Cavalry

---

*Medal of Honor Records of Corporal William O. Wilson* (Washington: National Archives, War Records Office).

# A Southern Exodus Reaches Kansas

[*In 1879 a vast migration of Southern Negroes, fleeing cruel oppression, poured into Kansas. An eyewitness describes the scene.*]

One morning in April, 1879, a Missouri steamboat arrived at Wyandotte, Kansas, and discharged a load of colored men, women and children, with divers barrels, boxes, and bundles of household effects. It was a novel, picturesque, pathetic sight. They were of all ages and sizes . . . ; their garments were incredibly patched and tattered, stretched, and uncertain; . . . and there was not probably a dollar in money in the pockets of the entire party. The wind was eager, and they stood upon the wharf shivering. . . . They looked like persons coming out of a dream. And, indeed, such they were . . . for this was the advance guard of the Exodus.

Soon other and similar parties came by the same route, and still others, until, within a fortnight, a thousand or more of them were gathered there at the gateway of Kansas—all poor, some sick, and none with a plan of future action. . . .

The case was one to appeal with force to popular sympathy. . . . So temporary shelter was speedily provided for them; food and facilities for cooking it were furnished them in ample measure. . . . Then came more of them. The tide swelled daily. . . .

The closing autumn found at least 15,000 of these colored immigrants in Kansas. Such of them as had arrived early in the spring had been enabled to do something toward getting a start, and the thriftier and more capable ones had made homestead-entries and contrived, with timely aid, to build cabins; in some cases, small crops of corn and garden vegetables were raised. . . .

. . . Numerous cabins of stone and sod were constructed while the cold season lasted; . . . in many cases, the women went to the towns and took in washing, or worked as house-servants . . . while the men were doing the building. Those who could find employment on the farms about their "claims", worked willingly and for small wages, and in this way supported their families, and procured now and then a calf, a pig, or a little poultry; others obtained places on the railroads, in the coal-mines, and on the public works at Topeka. Such as got work at any price, did not ask assistance; those who were compelled to apply for aid did it slowly, as a rule, and rarely came a second time. Not a single colored tramp was seen in Kansas all winter; and only one colored person was convicted of any crime. . . .

. . . their savings are not remarkable, to be sure, but they are creditable, and not to be lightly passed over. The wonder is that they have anything whatever to show for . . . twelve months of hand-to-mouth hardship and embarrassment.

Henry King, "A Year of the Exodus in Kansas," *Scribner's Monthly*, Vol. 8 (June, 1880), pp. 211-215.

## Counting the Negro Vote

[*A visitor to the South tells how Negroes continued to vote after Reconstruction despite the violence and fraud practiced on them by their enemies.*]

In Southern Alabama, prominent leaders in democratic [party] politics said that in the "black districts" it was common to have, at each place of holding elections, two ballot-boxes, one for white voters, and the other for the Negroes. . . . If the blacks are present, and likely to vote in such numbers as to "threaten the overthrow of society," or give cause of alarm to the leading white citizens, the offered vote of some ignorant Negro is challenged. The gangway is filled behind him by a long line of Negroes, pressing forward in single file, and impatient to vote. The Negro selected to be challenged is always one who lives in a distant part of the township or district. Somebody is dispatched to summon witnesses from his neighborhood, or some other cause of delay is discovered. . . . Of course the other Negroes cannot vote until this case is decided. It comes to an end by and by, and the conclusion which is at last reached is, usually, that the challenged Negro has the right to vote, and his ballot is accepted. . . . When the hour for the closing of the polls arrives there has not been sufficient time for the full Negro republican [party] vote to be polled. . . .

"But," I often inquired, "what if the Negroes should become tired of this enforced waiting, and, understanding its purpose, should push forward, and demand that their votes shall be received?"

"Then," answered my informants, significantly, "there is a collision. The Negroes are the attacking party, and of course they will be worsted." . . .

In Southern Alabama and in Mississippi influential and prominent Democrats said to me: "Some of our people, some editors especially, deny that the Negroes are hindered from voting; but what is the good of lying? They *are* interfered with, and we are obliged to do it, and we may as well tell the truth."

---

J. B. Harrison, "Studies in the South," *Atlantic Monthly*, Vol. 50 (July, 1882), pp. 103-104.

## The First and Dearest Rights of Negro Farmers

[*Negro Representative Thomas E. Miller of South Carolina was a college graduate and lawyer before he entered Congress. In 1891 he told the House of Representatives what Southern Negro farmers needed most.*]

There are other things more important to us [than holding office]. First is the infernal lynch law. That is the thing we most complain of. It is a question whether when we go to work we will return or not. Second, they have little petty systems of justices who rob us of our daily toil, and we cannot get redress before the higher tribunals. Third, we work for our task-masters, and they pay us if they please, for the courts are so constructed that Negroes have no rights if these rights wind up in dollars and cents to be paid by white task-masters. . . .

Yes, gentlemen, we want office but the first and dearest rights the Negro of the South wants are the right to pay for his labor, his right of trial by jury, his right to his home, his right to know that the man who lynches him will not the next day be elected by the State to a high and honorable trust, his right to know that murderers shall be convicted and not elected to high office. . . .

*The Congressional Record*, Vol. 22, Part II, 51st Congress, Second Session, p. 1216.

## A Negro Populist Vows: We Will Return

[*In his farewell speech of January 29, 1901, Representative George H. White of North Carolina, the last Negro Congressman from the South, notified his fellow members that "one day we will break the bonds" for "we are climbing!" His speech is a superb summary of the Negro's accomplishments in the first 35 years of freedom.*]

. . . we have reduced the illiteracy of the race at least 45 per cent. We have written and published near 500 books. We have nearly 300 newspapers, 3 of which are dailies. We have now in practice over 2,000 lawyers and a corresponding number of doctors. We have accumulated over $12,000,000 worth of school property and

about $40,000,000 worth of church property. We have about 140,-
000 farms and homes, valued at in the neighborhood of $750,000
000, and personal property valued at about $170,000,000. We have
raised about $11,000,000 for educational purposes, and the property
per capita for every colored man, woman, and child in the United
States is estimated at $75.

We are operating successfully several banks, commercial en-
terprises among our people in the Southland, including 1 silk mill
and 1 cotton factory. We have 32,000 teachers in the schools of the
country; we have built, with the aid of our friends, about 20,000
churches, and support 7 colleges, 17 academies, 50 high schools, 5
law schools, 5 medical schools, and 25 theological seminaries. We
have over 600,000 acres of land in the South alone. The cotton produced, mainly by black labor, has increased from 4,669,770 bales in
1860 to 11,235,000 in 1899. All this we have done under the most
adverse circumstances. We have done it in the face of lynching,
burning at the stake, with the humiliation of "Jim Crow" cars, the
disfranchisement of our male citizens, slander and degradation of our
women, with factories closed against us, no Negro permitted to be
conductor on the railway cars, whether run through the streets of our
cities or across the prairies of our great country, no Negro permitted
to run as engineer on a locomotive, most of the mines closed against
us. Labor unions—carpenters, painters, brick masons, machinists,
hackmen, and those supplying nearly every conceivable avocation for
livelihood have banded themselves together to better their condition,
but, with few exceptions, the black face has been left out. The Negroes are seldom employed in our mercantile stores. At this we do not
wonder. Some day we hope to have them employed in our own stores.
With all these odds against us, we are forging our way ahead, slowly
perhaps, but surely. You may tie us and then taunt us for a lack of
bravery, but one day we will break the bonds. You may use our labor
for two and a half centuries and then taunt us for our poverty, but let
me remind you we will not always remain poor. You may withhold
even the knowledge of how to read God's word and learn the way
from earth to glory and then taunt us for our ignorance, but we
would remind you that there is plenty of room at the top, and we are
climbing. . . .

This, Mr. Chairman, is perhaps the Negroes' temporary farewell to the American Congress; but let me say, Phoenix-like he will
rise up some day and come again. These parting words are in behalf
of an outraged, heart-broken, bruised, and bleeding, but God-fearing

people, faithful, industrious, loyal people—rising people, full of potential force. . . .

The only apology that I have to make for the earnestness with which I have spoken is that I am pleading for the life, the liberty, the future happiness, and manhood suffrage of one-eighth of the entire population of the United States. [Loud applause.]

*The Congressional Record*, 56th Congress, Second Session, pp. 1636-1638.

# 14

# *Reformers Meet the Problems of the Machine Age*

FOR many citizens, the most important products of America's factories were the social problems created by this new industrial power. Immigrants just off the boats from Europe and Asia, and migrants fresh from the farms of the countryside, poured into the cities that began to spread out around the factories. In the last decades of the 19th century America changed from a nation of tiny towns and small farms to one of large cities. The stresses and strains were enormous. In Atlanta, Georgia schools, 4 out of 14 white children and 5 of every 7 Negro children had no seats or desks. Crowded cities led to slums and crime. Unemployment, strikes, and depressions hurt both workmen and businessmen. Poverty lived down the street or across the railroad tracks from fabulous wealth.

## *The Great Reformers*

Reformers pointed out the problems of industrialism that had to be faced and solved. Men and women wanted security for their families, decent places in which to live, good schools for their children with playgrounds nearby. Women wanted the right to vote. Immigrants wanted to enter the country and share in the opportunity that America promised. Negroes wanted the same pay, education, and rights that others received. Frederick Douglass said, before the Civil War, "I . . . would scorn to demand for my race a single right or privilege that I would not freely grant to you."

Long before the Civil War, Douglass' words and actions had made clear his interest in underprivileged and oppressed people everywhere. "I am not only an American slave, but a man, and as such, am bound to use my powers for the welfare of the whole human brotherhood." In a speech on patriotism, Douglass said: "My sympathies are not limited by my relation to any race. I can take no part in oppressing and persecuting any variety of the human family. Whether in Russia, Germany, or California, my sympathy is with the oppressed, be he Chinaman or Hebrew." Douglass' newspaper fought for the rights of "the Indian, Mongolian, Caucasian."

In an age that looked on Orientals and Indians as inferior or dangerous people, several Negro Congressmen of the Reconstruction period spoke out for fair treatment of these persecuted groups. John O'Hara of North Carolina asked the government to provide relief for the Cherokees and Senator B. K. Bruce of Mississippi demanded, in 1880, that the government deal justly with all Indian tribes. Bruce also told the Senate he could not vote for a law that restricted the immigration of Orientals: "Representing as I do a people who but a few years ago were considered essentially disqualified from enjoying the privileges and immunities of American citizenship . . . I shall vote against this bill."

In the long but ultimately successful campaign to extend the right to vote to women, Negro leaders had always played a part. In 1848 Frederick Douglass had led the fight, at the first women's rights convention, to pass the first resolution demanding that women be allowed to vote. Congressman Alonzo J. Ransier of South Carolina was an active campaigner for women's rights. William E. B. Du Bois, writing in *The Crisis* in 1919, called on "every black voter in the State of New York" to "cast his ballot in favor of woman suffrage" and all other Negroes "should do the same thing." When a 1913 women's rights parade in Washington, D.C. was heckled by males in the crowd, one of the women noted that the city's Negroes "were quiet and respectable" and seemed "sorry for the indignities which were incessantly heaped upon us." She concluded, "I thank them in the name of all the women for their kindness."

*Frederick Douglass, one of America's greatest reformers, battled for human rights until the day he died. His crusades for women's rights, universal peace, and equal rights for all took him all over America and Europe.*

Protection of American civil liberties had long been an interest of many important Americans. "To suppress free speech," said Frederick Douglass, "is a double wrong. It violates the rights of the hearer as well as those of the speaker." William E. B. Du Bois deplored the denial of rights to Sacco and Vanzetti, two Italian immigrants. When they were tried for murder in 1921, and put to death in 1927, many people all over the world were convinced that they were found guilty only because they were radicals and foreigners. "We who are black," wrote Du Bois, "can sympathize with Sacco and Vanzetti and their friends more than other Americans. We are used to being convicted because of our race and opinions." As the Irish struggled to be free of English rule, Du Bois wrote: "God speedily grant the ultimate freedom of Ireland."

James Weldon Johnson, who was famous as both a poet and a diplomat, joined in the campaign "in behalf of minority groups and in the fight for free speech." Later he became a leader in the American Civil Liberties Union, as did Asa Philip Randolph, President of the Brotherhood of Sleeping Car Porters.

## The Urban Reformers

Many newcomers to the cities were oppressed by poverty, slums, and crime. These vast problems drew the attention of such reformers as Jane Addams, Lillian Wald, Jacob Riis, and Negro reformers as well. As early as 1865, a Negro relief society in Nashville, Tennessee provided aid to starving people without regard to color. When the Negro public schools of Atlanta became too crowded, Negro parents formed a private school that housed almost a thousand students. By 1913 Negroes supported a hundred orphanages in the United States. Negro "law and order" leagues to curb crime and regulate saloons functioned in parts of Georgia and Texas.

But the problems created by urban living were not then, and have not been yet, easily solved—especially for Negroes, since they faced discrimination as well as crowding and poverty.

The Negroes who came North during the late nineteenth century faced a color line in housing. Jacob Riis, the Danish immigrant who became a New York reporter during the 1880's, wrote a description of how landlords restricted Negroes to certain sections of the city in 1890. "Where he permits them to live, they go; where he shuts the door, stay out. By his grace they exist at all in certain localities." Riis found this "despotism . . . deliberately assigns to the defenceless Black that level for the purpose of robbing him. . . ."

Dr. George E. Haynes, a New York scholar who had long

*Frances Ellen Watkins Harper, an early Negro reformer. As a teenager she helped slaves escape to Canada. As an adult she was a popular poet and speaker for temperance and women's rights.*

studied the problems of urban living, sought to reduce the crowding and poverty of the Negro people in the many industrial centers of the North and South. He knew that violence and fear lived in every ghetto. In 1911 Dr. Haynes, together with other Negro and white reformers, organized the Urban League to improve the health, housing, job opportunities, and recreation of city Negroes. A believer in racial harmony as a means of achieving progress for people of both races, Dr. Haynes explained the goals of the Urban League: "INTER-RACIAL COOPERATION was the basic principle on which the organization was to develop. White people were to be asked to work WITH Negroes for their mutual advantage and advancement rather than working for them as a problem." Today the Urban League, with Whitney Young, Jr. as its director, continues the war against poverty and discrimination in American cities.

## The Era of Jim Crow

In 1894 a crusading Seattle editor named Horace Cayton called on all citizens to unite for progress and "smoke the pipe of everlasting peace." The young Negro expressed his patriotism thus:

> Let there be one flag and one country for all manner of man that swears allegiance thereto. Let America be for Americans, without color or race distinctions cutting any figure in the contest.

Cayton's voice went unheard because he lived during the "Jim Crow" era.* This was the name given to the thousands of state laws, city ordinances, and local customs, whose impassable color line kept the Negro from opportunities which were open to whites.

*Thomas Rice dressed as the stage character "Jim Crow."*

---

* The phrase Jim Crow dates to 1830. Thomas Rice, a famous white entertainer, walked out of his Baltimore theater to observe a marvelous Negro singer-dancer performing in the alley. Rice "borrowed" the man's dance routine and costume and enlarged on the song he was singing. He made the words famous all over the world—"wheel about, turn about, dance jest so—every time I wheel about I shout Jim Crow!" While whites found the character created by Rice funny and cute, Negroes found it hateful. Like another white invention, "Uncle Tom," which Negroes used to describe a man afraid to stand up for his rights, Negroes used "Jim Crow" to mean the many kinds of discrimination they faced in America.

In the period from 1890 to 1910, each Southern state wrote into law (often into their Constitutions) the many devices which kept black men and women from enjoying the privileges of citizens and the rights of men.* And in the 1896 Plessy vs. Ferguson case, the United States Supreme Court laid down the "separate but equal" doctrine when it ruled that laws segregating people because of their race did not violate the United States Constitution. This ruling was to stand as the law of the land until 1954.

From the time Mr. Homer Plessy was arrested for taking a seat in a "white" train until our own time, Negroes have been forced to live under a variety of humiliating Southern laws. Oklahoma segregated phone booths and Mississippi segregated Coca-Cola machines. In Atlanta, a Negro witness was not allowed to swear to tell the truth on the same copy of the Bible that white witnesses used. In Birmingham, Alabama Negroes and whites faced a penalty of six months in prison if they "did play together or in company with each other in any game of cards or dice, dominoes, or checkers."

The schools of the South were totally segregated. But Florida thought it also necessary to segregate the textbooks for its Negro and white pupils while the books were in storage. Washington, D.C. Negroes found they could not bury their dead dogs in the same dog cemetery that whites used.

The Negro who faced the Southern court found a special kind of injustice. If a Negro committed a crime against a white, he received exaggerated newspaper coverage and the full penalty of the law. Often, innocent men, because of their color, were accused of crime. And if a white committed a crime against a Negro the punishment (if the case was ever brought to court) was mild. Even if a Negro committed a crime against a Negro, Southern courts thought so little of Negro life and property that his punishment was often a light one! For many years lynch mobs, often led by "respectable" white citizens, killed an average of almost two Negroes a week. The victims were often seized from the hands of the law, sometimes with the assistance of sheriffs and jailers. A study of this massive crime shows that Southern mobs preferred to burn their victims; Northern and Western mobs preferred hanging.

*In 1886 August Tolton became the first American Negro to be ordained a Catholic priest. A son of slaves, Tolton had worked from dawn to dusk in a tobacco factory for 12 years.*

---

* In 1883 the Supreme Court struck down the last of the civil rights laws (1875) passed by Congress after the Civil War. That same year Emma Lazarus, daughter of Jewish immigrants from Poland, wrote her stirring poem for the Statue of Liberty: "Give me your tired, your poor, your huddled masses yearning to breathe free. . . ."

The Negro in the North found his opportunities restricted by custom rather than by law. A white writer in 1912 admitted that in Ohio "the Negro has nothing resembling equality with the white man." Neighborhoods, schools, unions, and public facilities were silently segregated. Jackie Robinson, who lived in Pasadena, California during the 1920's, recalled: "We saw movies from segregated balconies, swam in the municipal pool only on Tuesdays, and were permitted in the YMCA on only one night a week. Restaurant doors were slammed in our faces." Robinson's example would open the door of Big League baseball to other Negro baseball players.

The intensity of anti-Negro feeling at the turn of the century can be measured by the many newspaper predictions that the race was dying. The Peoria, Illinois, *Journal* of December 3, 1899, headlined: RACE PROBLEM IS DISAPPEARING. STATISTICS SHOW NEGRO RACE WILL EVENTUALLY DISAPPEAR.

*During the time when lynching and race riots were common in the North and South, a grandfather points out the Liberty Bell to his grandchildren.*

During this era of Jim Crow the Negro was degraded in magazines, newspapers, nursery rhymes, popular songs, cartoons, movies, and jokes. He was referred to as "dangerous," "stupid," "humorous," or "childlike." In 1887, a South Carolina white wrote: "Southerners will call a Negro 'Senator Smith,' or 'Sheriff Smith,' or 'Colonel Smith,' to escape addressing him as 'Mr. Smith.'" A St. Louis Bible society published a book entitled *The Negro a Beast* which tried to prove that a person of color had no soul. It sold thousands of copies. The Negro of this time had powerful enemies and few friends.

## Resistance to Jim Crow

One of the heroic leaders of early battles against discrimination was Miss Ida Wells. At 14 she had to bring up her four younger brothers and sisters. She did so and also put herself through college. She started her campaign against lynching in Tennessee at the age of 19. Her articles in the Memphis *Free Speech* exposed the mounting number of lynchings. Miss Wells, always a forceful as well as an attractive woman, carried two pistols for protection. In 1892 she published information showing that the lynching of three successful Negro grocers was the work of their white competitors. Her press was wrecked and she was driven from Memphis but she carried her crusade to Northern cities and to Europe. In 1898 she led a delegation of women and Congressmen to President McKinley to protest the lynching of a Negro postmaster. "We refuse to believe this country, so powerful to defend its citizens abroad, is unable to protect its citizens at home," she told the President. Nothing was done, however. In 1909 she became a founder of the NAACP and continued her campaign until her death in 1931.

*Ida B. Wells devoted her life to the fight against lynching and discrimination. She became a founding member of the NAACP.*

Negroes, despite the danger, often took determined actions to halt Jim Crow practices. On the evening of May 12, 1871, a young boy launched a "sit-in" aboard a segregated Louisville horse-drawn streetcar. Screaming white teenagers cursed him, and eventually dragged him from the car. When the youth finally fought back, he was arrested. In the days that followed, other Negroes—mostly young men—entered streetcars and sat stony and silent in the face of abuse. When drivers walked off the cars, these men who staged the 1871 "sit-ins" sometimes drove the cars from stop to stop. The Louisville company, in the face of mounting violence and opposition, agreed to integrate their street railway. They said "it was useless to try to resist . . . the claim of Negroes to ride in the cars."

Reporter Ray Stannard Baker told how the appearance of segregated streetcars in Savannah, Georgia, caused "violent protestations on the part of Negroes and a refusal by many of them to use the cars at all." In the years between 1898 and 1906 Negro boycotts took place in New Orleans, Mobile, and Houston but they were generally unsuccessful. The whites had all the power and the Negroes lacked economic independence and strong organizations. These would come a half-century later.

In 1883 Negro conventions were held in Kentucky, Arkansas, South Carolina, and Texas to protest against the denial of civil rights. Editor T. Thomas Fortune told his people to "fight fire with fire," and added, "It is time to face the enemy and fight inch by inch for every right he denies us."

Despite threats of violence and murder itself, Negroes in the South elected officials in various states until the turn of the century. In 1890, 16 Negro legislators served in the Louisiana assembly. Negroes served in Congress until 1901. Famous Negro politicians such as Congressman George White and P. B. S. Pinchback (Governor of Louisiana for 43 days during Reconstruction) continued to demand an end to violence and segregation.

In the Deep South Negroes used a variety of means to defend their rights during this period of maximum repression. Negroes in Liberty County, Georgia had two representatives in the state legislature in 1899. That same year a thousand armed Negroes of the

*P. B. S. Pinchback continued to fight discrimination long after prejudice forced him from high office in Louisiana.*

*Alexander Crummel, a runaway slave who became a noted minister, author, and scholar. In 1897 he organized first meeting of the American Negro Academy to develop scholarly studies of Negro life. The brilliant intellects of the Academy sought to destroy the myth that the Negro was inferior.*

county liberated farmer Henry Delegal, who had been arrested for dating a white woman. Delegal and his army hid in the great Okefenokee swamp while the governor sent regiments of state militia after him and white newspapers pleaded: "There has never been the slightest danger that Henry Delegal would be lynched." Until matters were settled peacefully, Georgia residents trembled with the thought of a bloody race war. Two years later a Negro conference in Alabama, concerned with the growing danger of violence, passed this resolution:

> Regardless of how others may act, we urge upon our race a rigid observance of the law of the land, and that we bear in mind that lawlessness begets crime and hardens and deadens not only the conscience of the law-breaker, but also the conscience of the community.

The outnumbered Negroes had good cause to reject violence. From 1892 to 1901 Negroes were lynched at the rate of three or four a week. Usually the victims were the most forthright spokesmen of their people or common citizens who were murdered to crush the fires of discontent. Some Negro leaders simply disappeared from their homes—probably the victims of lynchers. The white South had no use for black leaders.

Successful Negroes such as Dr. Daniel Hale Williams often used their personal good fortune to help others. This fair-skinned, red-headed young doctor founded the first interracial hospital in America, Provident Hospital in Chicago. He also started a school to train Negro nurses since they were not permitted to enter white nursing schools. In 1893, by performing the first successful open-heart operation in history, Dr. Williams became world famous. President Grover Cleveland appointed him head of the Freedmen's Hospital in Washington, D.C. Throughout the rest of his life, Dr. Williams continued to make medical history and to battle against the color line which denied equality to his people.

## Booker T. Washington and His Age

During the era of Jim Crow laws the Negro was forced to live a life apart from the American mainstream. A white reporter in the 1880's was told by a Negro businessman that he "got the respect of whites . . . by his ability and by making money . . . [and] he had ceased to expect that the colored race would get it any other way." Reporter Ray Stannard Baker, after investigating conditions in the

*An 1866 Negro orphan home in Memphis, Tennessee. Negro organizations for self-help and self-improvement pre-date the United States Constitution. Exclusion from white organizations usually forced Negroes to build their own mutual benefit societies.*

cities of the South in 1909, concluded: "The struggle of the races is becoming more and more rapidly economic." In Illinois and in Oklahoma, Negroes formed their own towns to escape persecution and to prove that they could successfully manage their own affairs.

A philosophical ex-slave named Booker T. Washington carried this economic approach to the problems of his people much further. He became the leading spokesman of Negro vocational education and a living example of the heights which a Negro could reach in an era of savage repression.

Washington had taught himself to read after working all day in a West Virginia salt mine. He worked his way through Hampton Institute and then became the first President of Alabama's Tuskegee Institute. At Tuskegee he taught his students the importance of self-reliance, hard work, saving, and learning a trade. He proudly pointed out to visitors that most of the college's buildings had been built by the students themselves.

On a hot afternoon in September, 1895, Booker T. Washington came to the attention of the entire country. A skillful orator, Washington was asked to speak at the Negro exhibit at the Atlanta Exposition. Introduced by Governor Bullock of Georgia, Booker T. Washington called on his people to work hard for, and to accept, the friendship of the Southern white. In an age when the persecution of

*Booker T. Washington.*

Negroes was fierce and unrelenting, the young educator offered a program to appease the white man. He said Negroes would not join unions or cause strikes. He emphasized that "the wisest among my race understand" that seeking "social equality is the extremest folly." Washington asked for help to secure better education for his people and offered in return this acceptance of segregation: "In all things that are purely social we can be as separate as the fingers, yet one as the hand in all things essential to mutual progress."

The speech was an immediate success. Governor Bullock "rushed across the platform and took me by the hand," and "I received so many and such hearty congratulations that I found it difficult to get out of the building." A letter of praise soon came from President Grover Cleveland.

Booker T. Washington made important white friends—Presidents Roosevelt and Taft and industrialists Andrew Carnegie and John D. Rockefeller. He soon became the main channel through which money for any Negro educational purpose came, and he was able to build many schools for his people. He was consulted by Presidents on matters relating to Negro progress and was asked which Negroes should receive appointments to government posts. Thus, Booker T. Washington became a bridge between his oppressed people and the white world.

*Monument to Booker T. Washington who founded Tuskegee in 1881. From 1895 to 1915 (when he died) practically all funds for Negro education passed through his hands. He was welcomed by presidents and kings but could not vote in Alabama.*

As a leader during the period of maximum oppression, Washington's successes and failures cannot be measured by his efforts alone. During the time he rose to prominence lynchings of Negroes had reached three or four a week, and the Negro Congressional representation dwindled to one a session (and none after 1901). "We have got to be patient and long suffering," he told Alabama farmers at the turn of the century.

But Booker T. Washington's views were immediately challenged by other Negroes. President John Hope of Atlanta University publicly asked: "If we are not striving for equality, in heaven's name for what are we living. . . . Yes, my friends, I want equality. Nothing else." For many Negroes, Booker T. Washington's compromises had gone too far. Later, Washington himself would realize that his appeasement had not gained any new rights for his people and he would secretly finance those who fought for an end to segregation. In his last article he said that segregation did nothing for the Negro but hold him back.

## The Drive for Full Civil Rights

As it became increasingly clear that Booker T. Washington's program could not lead, even eventually, to civil rights, some prominent Negroes looked for another approach and a new leader. In 1903 Dr. William E. B. Du Bois challenged the basic ideas of Washington in his book *The Souls of Black Folks*. A short, soft-spoken historian and sociologist, Dr. Du Bois had been the first Negro to graduate from Harvard with a Ph.D. degree. He offered a program remarkably similar to the programs of today's civil rights leaders. His first demands were for equal political rights for his people. He pointed out that Washington "practically accepts the alleged inferiority of the Negro races," and "withdraws many of the high demands of Negroes as men and American citizens."

There were similarities as well as differences between the two men. Du Bois himself knew this: "Actually Washington had no more faith in the white man than I do." Washington's theory, however, was: "When your head is in the lion's mouth, use your hand to pet him." Each man sought to advance the cause of his people but by different means. Wrote Du Bois:

So far as Mr. Washington preaches Thrift, Patience, and Industrial Training for the masses, we must hold up his hands and strive with him. . . . But so far as Mr. Washington apologizes for injustice, North or South, does not rightly value the privilege and duty of voting . . . and opposes the higher training and ambition of our brighter minds,—so far as he, the South, or the Nation does this—we must unceasingly and firmly oppose them.

Both Du Bois and Washington were strong-willed, energetic men who overcame mountains of prejudice to gain success. Each man had a commanding influence on masses of Negroes. Washington did it through his mastery of oratory and a clear writing style; Du Bois through historical studies, poetry, novels, lectures, essays, articles, and philosophical discussions. Washington sought to advance the Negroes by pacifying whites; Du Bois, by assailing their ears with protests and demands.

Du Bois began to gather other reformers to plan a more militant attack on discrimination. In 1905 they met at Niagara Falls, Canada. (The hotels on the New York side of the border would not accept them.) The following year, they met at Harpers Ferry where fiery old John Brown had led whites and Negroes in his 1859 assault on slavery.

Tragic events were soon to give the Du Bois "Niagara movement" important white support. In 1908 bloody anti-Negro rioting exploded in Springfield, Illinois. Negroes were killed within a few blocks of where Abraham Lincoln had once lived. William English Walling, a German-Jewish reporter, who went to investigate the story for his paper, described its horrifying details. He told his readers that the "spirit of Lincoln . . . must be revived." On the 100th anniversary of Lincoln's birth, a group of white reformers, including Walling, called for resistance against anti-Negro attacks. Du Bois and his group were invited to play an important part in the organization that was formed—The National Association for the Advancement of Colored People (NAACP).

*Dr. W. E. B. Du Bois.*

The list of NAACP supporters reads like a roster of the noted reformers of this period (1909). Among the whites were writers Lincoln Steffens, Ray Stannard Baker, and William Dean Howells; reformers Lillian Wald, Jane Addams, Mary White Ovington, and Rabbi Stephen S. Wise; and educator John Dewey. Among the famous Negroes were educators Mary Church Terrell and Mary Mc-

Leod Bethune, crusader Ida Wells, philosopher William E. B. Du Bois, and churchmen Archibald H. Grimké and Alexander Walters.

The NAACP attacked discrimination on a broad front. Its staff of Negro and white lawyers stood ready to defend those accused of crimes merely because of their color. Their first case involved a New Jersey Negro arrested for murder. "There was no evidence against him," recalled NAACP leader Mary White Ovington, "but he was black and had been near the scene of the crime." The NAACP won his release. Within ten years the NAACP lawyers were winning significant cases before the United States Supreme Court.

The NAACP did not operate only on the legal front. Beginning in 1910 it published *The Crisis* magazine. Under the editorship of Du Bois its pages stressed Negro accomplishments and publicized the practices of discrimination. Negro poets were often given their first audience through the pages of *The Crisis*. In 1914 the NAACP announced it would award the Spingarn Medal to the outstanding Negro of each year. By 1921, the NAACP had conducted a campaign to have an antilynching law passed by Congress. The law did pass the House by a two-to-one vote only to be talked to death by Southern Senators.

In 1920 the NAACP hired a blond, blue-eyed young man as an investigator. His name was Walter White and despite his appearance he was a Negro and proud of it. Because of his looks, however, he was able to investigate activities that no Negro had ever witnessed. In ten years he investigated 41 lynchings and eight race riots. He met Klansmen, attended their meetings, and was once sworn in as a sheriff's deputy in Oklahoma. "Now you can go out and kill" any Negro "you see," another deputy told him, "and the law'll be behind you." But even with the evidence that White collected at the peril of his life, and photographs of the actual murderers at the particular scenes, no convictions were possible in the South.

It is interesting to note that the editorial page of the first issue of *The Crisis* was largely devoted to a discussion of the evils of school segregation. "This is wrong," wrote editor Du Bois, "and should be resisted by black men and white." It would be no accident of history that one of the greatest reforms in American history—desegregation of the schools—would be carried to the United States Supreme Court in 1954, and won by three NAACP lawyers.

## *Jim Crow Follows Cadet Smith to West Point*

[*By the 1870's Jim Crow was reaching into every part of American life, in the North as well as the South. J. W. Smith was the first Negro to enter the United States Military Academy at West Point. What happened to him there is told by Smith himself, and by David Clarke, a white educator who helped the young recruit. Smith was finally forced out. On June 15, 1877, however, another cadet, Henry O. Flipper of Georgia became the first Negro to graduate from West Point.*]

[*David Clarke.*] Smith was a member of my household, and was the most truthful and correct boy in all his habits and deportment that I ever saw. He went [to West Point], and God only knows how much he has suffered from the day he trod that ground. . . . I have been there three times to look after him. He would have left in July had it not been for me. I had an interview with President [U.S.] Grant. . . . He said, "Don't take him away; the battle might as well be fought now as any time." So he was permitted to stay. Scarcely has a day passed when he has not been assaulted by words, or blows inflicted, to force him to do something for which they might expel him. . . .*

---

* *New National Era*, January 26, 1871, p. 2.

[*Cadet J. W. Smith writes to a friend.*] Your kind letter should have been answered long ere this, but really I have been so harassed with examinations and insults and ill treatment of these cadets that I could not write or do anything else scarcely. I passed the examination all right, and got in, but my companion Howard failed and was rejected. Since he went away I have been lonely indeed. And now these fellows appear to be trying their utmost to run me off, and I fear they will succeed if they continue as they have begun. We went into camp yesterday, and not a moment has passed since then but some one of them has been cursing and abusing me. . . . It is just the same at the table, and what I get to eat I must snatch for like a dog. I don't wish to resign if I can get along at all; but I don't think it will be best for me to stay and take all the abuses and insults that are heaped upon me. . . .**

---

** *The New Era*, July 14, 1870, p. 1.

[*News account of a further incident.*] The case of the colored cadet Smith who has been on trial before a court-martial at West Point for breaking a cocoanut dipper over the head of another cadet named Wilson has been closed. . . . He appears to have been too prompt in breaking the cocoa-nut dipper over cadet Wilson's head: but that member doubtless represented to him for the time the collective heads of the white cadets who had subjected him to humiliating ill treatment. . . .†

† *New National Era*, November 3, 1870, p. 2.

## An 1879 Plea for Federal Aid to Education

[*On January 23, 1879, Congressman Richard Cain of South Carolina, completing his second term in the House of Representatives, spoke for federal aid to education.*]

. . . This Government can do no greater deed than to dedicate a part of the revenues accruing from the sale of public lands to the education of the people. There are millions of the citizens of this Republic who will not receive that education which everyone ought to have to make them worthy citizens unless the Government shall secure it to them. This should not be left entirely to the States, because they will not fully do this work.

. . . Education in the South will be more effective than a standing army. Educate the masses of the people and you open up the means for their higher and grander development. . . . but I also believe famine should be provided for before you expect schoolhouses.

*The Congressional Record*, 45th Congress, Third Session, p. 688.

## The Demands of Nashville's Black Middle Class

[*In 1886 a group of Negro businessmen told white writer Charles D. Warner what rights they expected as Americans.*]

. . . They were all solid, sensible business men, and all respected as citizens. They talked most intelligently of politics, and freely about social conditions. In regard to voting in Tennessee there was little to complain of; but in regard to Mississippi, as an illustration, it was an outrage that . . . the colored Republican vote did not count. What could they do? Some said that probably nothing could be done; time must be left to cure the wrong. Others wanted the Federal government to interfere, at least to the extent of making a test case on some member of Congress that his election was illegal. . . .

Finally I asked this intelligent company . . . "What do you want here in the way of civil rights that you have not?" The reply from one was that he got the respect of the whites just as he was able to command it by his ability and by making money, and, with a touch of a sense of injustice, said he had ceased to expect that the colored race would get it in any other way. Another reply was—and this was evidently the deep feeling of all:

> We want to be treated like men, like anybody else, regardless of color. We don't mean by this social equality at all. . . . We want the public conveyances open to us according to the fare we pay; we want privileges to go to hotels and to theatres, operas and places of amusement. We wish you could see our families and the way we live; you would then understand that we cannot go to the places assigned us in concerts and theatres without loss of self-respect. . . .

Charles Dudley Warner, "The South Revisited," *Harper's New Monthly*, Vol. 74 (March, 1887), p. 640.

## Self-Help in the South

[*Samuel J. Barrows, a New England reformer, traveled 3,500 miles through the South to investigate what Southern Negroes were doing for themselves.*]

. . . The Negroes are showing their awakened and eager interest in education by the zeal with which they are embracing their opportunities. Everywhere I found in colleges, normal institutes, and district schools fresh, live interest. In some sections, the eagerness of the colored people for knowledge amounts to an absolute thirst. In Alabama, the state superintendent of education, a former Confederate major, assured me that the colored people in that State are more interested in education than the whites are. Nothing shows better this zeal for education than the sacrifices made to secure it. President Bumstead, of Atlanta University, asks: "Where in the history of the world have so large a mass of equally poor and unlettered people done so much to help themselves in educational work?" This challenge will long remain unanswered. The students of Atlanta University pay thirty-four per cent of the expenses of that institution. A letter from the treasurer of Harvard College informs me that about the same proportion of its expenses is paid from tuition fees. . . . It must be remembered, also, that at Harvard tuition fees and other expenses are mostly paid by parents and guardians; at Atlanta they are paid by the students themselves, and to a large degree by personal labor. . . .

Another remarkable illustration is furnished by the Tuskegee Normal School. This institution was started in 1881 by a Hampton graduate, Mr. Booker T. Washington, on a state appropriation of $2000. It has grown from 30 pupils to 450, with 31 teachers. During the last year 200 applicants had to be turned away for want of room. Fourteen hundred acres of land and fourteen school buildings form a part of the equipment. . . . All the teachers are colored. Of the fourteen school buidings, eight have been erected, in whole or in part, by the students. . . .

One of the most important results of the excellent work done by Hampton, Atlanta, and Tuskegee is seen in the radiating influence they exert through the country in stimulating primary education. . . . In a district of Butler County, Alabama, the children formed a "one cent society." They brought to the teacher a penny a day. About thirty dollars was raised to buy land, and the school-teacher, a colored girl, helped to clear it and burn the brush. . . . In Lee County, the people "supplement" for an assistant teacher. One district school which I visited, eighteen miles from Tuskegee, taught by a graduate of its institute, well illustrated the advantage of industrial education. Having learned the carpenter's trade at the normal school, he was able, with the help of his pupils, to build a fine new schoolhouse. . . .

The interest in education is seen also in the self-denial and sacrifice which parents make to keep their children at school. This sacrifice falls chiefly on the mothers. . . . "I know mothers," said a student [at Tuskegee], "who get three dollars a month, and out of that pay one dollar for the rent, and yet send their children to school." To

do this they will wash all day and half the night. Said a colored clergyman in Chattanooga:

> Sometimes, when I go about and see how hard many
> of these mothers work, I feel almost inclined to say,
> "You ought to keep your child at home"; but they hold
> on with wonderful persistence. Two girls graduated
> from Atlanta University. Their mother had been wash-
> ing several years to keep them in school. She came up
> to see them graduate. She was one of the happiest
> mothers I ever saw.

At Selma University, some of the students walk for ten to fifteen
miles a day in going to and from the university. . . .

The colored people do more towards taking care of their unfortunate classes than is generally realized. . . . The colored orphan
asylum established by Mrs. Steele in Chattanooga is, I am told, the
only Protestant colored orphan asylum south of Washington. What,
then, becomes of orphan children? They are adopted. I have met
such children in many homes, and their love and respect for their
foster parents refute the charge that the Negro is incapable of gratitude. . . .

In other respects the colored people have developed a laudable
disposition to take care of their own poor. In addition to the Odd
Fellows, Masons, and Knights of Pythias, benevolent and fraternal
organizations are multiplying. The city churches are feeling a new
impulse to such work. Brotherhoods, Good Samaritan societies, and
mutual benefit organizations are established. Members of these organizations are allowed a regular stipend when sick. In New Orleans,
the colored people have started a widow's home, and have collected enough money to buy a piece of ground and put up a respectable building. In Montgomery, I visited the Hale Infirmary, founded
by the late Joseph Hale and his wife, leading colored citizens. It is a
large two-story building, especially designed by the son-in-law of the
founder for hospital purposes. . . .

. . . All that has been attempted in this article is to give such
indications and evidence as can readily be obtained by one who
travels through the South, on this mission, with his eyes and ears
open.

---

Samuel J. Barrows, "What the Southern Negro is Doing for Himself," *Atlantic
Monthly*, Vol. 57 (June, 1891), pp. 810-815.

# "*Justice Is Not Dead in the Republic*"

[*As Southern states stripped their Negro citizens of the right to vote, Negro leaders warned their followers of the dangers of these steps. One of their leaders, Louisiana ex-Governor P. B. S. Pinchback, made the following speech on the subject.*]

. . . Those laws not only deprive the colored citizens of "privileges and immunities" enjoyed by all other citizens in those States . . . but they impose a humiliating and degrading separation against, and a brand of inferiority upon, not only the colored people residing in said States, but upon every member of the entire race if they should have occasion to visit or pass through one of those States. It is an insult and a wrong which should be resisted by the whole race with every lawful means at its command. First and most important step in that direction in my opinion, is to secure a decision on the merits of the case from the Supreme Court of the United States as to the constitutionality of the so-called Constitutions recently arbitrarily and fraudulently adopted in several Southern States, under which wholesale disfranchisement is imposed upon the race solely on account of color. . . .

It is noticeable that wherever colored men have been deprived of the ballot, unjust class legislation has speedily followed, race antagonism has been intensified, and lawlessness and outrage against the race increased.

This is a grave condition. . . . It is truly said that eternal vigilance is the price of liberty. It will not do for you and me and others of the race who are not now under the immediate shadow of these unjust laws to be indifferent. It is the whole race which is assailed, and the whole race should protest against and oppose these wrongs to the last. . . . Our cause is just and must prevail if we manfully, earnestly, and judiciously appeal to the heart and conscience of the American people for redress of our grievances. Justice is not dead in the Republic. . . .

---

Speech delivered at a testimonial. Manuscript in P. B. S. Pinchback files, Howard University Moorland Collection. (No date is indicated, but mention of campaigning for McKinley places it between 1896 and 1900.)

## Booker T. Washington's "Atlanta Compromise"

[*The year 1895 was one of important changes in American Negro life. Militant leader Frederick Douglass died early in the year. The Supreme Court was considering the case of Mr. Homer Plessy, a Negro who had violated the Jim Crow railroad laws. (The Plessy decision in 1896 would make segregation legal in America for the next fifty-eight years.) Lynchings were increasing and Southern states were rewriting their constitutions to eliminate Negro rights. At this moment in history Booker T. Washington tried to conciliate the whites and act as mediator between them and the Negro people. His 1895 speech at Atlanta brought him instant approval by most whites and even many Negroes.*]

. . . To those of my race who depend on bettering their condition in a foreign land or who underestimate the importance of cultivating friendly relations with the Southern white man, who is their next-door neighbor, I would say: "Cast down your bucket where you are"—cast it down in making friends in every manly way, of the people of all races by whom you are surrounded.

Cast it down in agriculture, mechanics, in commerce, in domestic service, and in the professions. . . . Our greatest danger is that in the great leap from slavery to freedom we may overlook the fact that the masses of us are to live by the productions of our hands, and fail to keep in mind that we shall prosper in proportion as we learn to dignify and glorify common labour and put brains and skill into the common occupations of life; shall prosper in proportion as we learn to draw the line between the superficial and the substantial, the ornamental gewgaws of life and the useful. No race can prosper till it learns that there is as much dignity in tilling a field as in writing a poem. It is at the bottom of life we must begin, and not at the top. Nor should we permit our grievances to overshadow our opportunities.

To those of the white race . . . were I permitted I would repeat what I say to my own race: "Cast down your bucket where you are." Cast it down among the eight millions of Negroes whose habits you know, whose fidelity and love you have tested in days when to have proved treacherous meant the ruin of your firesides. Cast down your bucket among these people who have, without strikes and la-bour wars, tilled your fields, cleared your forests, builded your rail-roads and cities, and brought forth treasures from the bowels of the earth. . . . Casting down your bucket among my people, helping and encouraging them as you are doing on these grounds, and to education of head, hand, and heart, you will find that they will buy your surplus land, make blossom the waste places in your fields, and run your factories. While doing this, you can be sure in the future, as in the past, that you and your families will be surrounded by the most patient, faithful, law-abiding, and unresentful people that the world has seen. As we have proved our loyalty to you in the past, in nursing your children, watching by the sick-bed of your mothers and fathers, and often following them with tear-dimmed eyes to their graves, so in the future, in our humble way, we shall stand by you with a devotion that no foreigner can approach, ready to lay down our lives, if need be, in defence of yours, interlacing our industrial, commercial, civil, and religious life with yours in a way that shall make the interests of both races one. In all things that are purely social we can be as separate as the fingers, yet one as the hand in all things essential to mutual progress.

There is no defence or security for any of us except in the high-est intelligence and development of all. If anywhere there are efforts tending to curtail the fullest growth of the Negro, let these efforts be turned to stimulating, encouraging, and making him the most useful and intelligent citizen. Effort or means so invested will pay a thousand per cent interest. These efforts will be twice blessed—"blessing him that gives and him that takes." . . .

Nearly sixteen millions of hands will aid you in pulling the load upward, or they will pull against you the load downward. We shall constitute one-third and more of the ignorance and crime of the South, or one-third its intelligence and progress; we shall contribute one-third to the business and industrial prosperity of the South, or we shall prove a veritable body of death, stagnating, depressing, retard-ing every effort to advance the body politic. . . .

The wisest among my race understand that the agitation of questions of social equality is the extremest folly, and that progress in the enjoyment of all the privileges that will come to us must be the result of severe and constant struggle rather than of artificial forc-ing. No race that has anything to contribute to the markets of the world is long in any degree ostracized. It is important and right that all privileges of the law be ours, but it is vastly more important that we be prepared for the exercises of these privileges. The opportunity to earn a dollar in a factory just now is worth infinitely more than the opportunity to spend a dollar in an opera-house.

. . . I pledge that in your effort to work out the great and intricate problem which God has laid at the doors of the South, you shall have at all times the patient, sympathetic help of my race. . . .

Booker T. Washington, *Up from Slavery* (New York, 1901), pp. 218-225.

# Dr. William E. B. Du Bois Answers
# Booker T. Washington

[*In his famous book*, The Souls of Black Folks, *written in 1903, Negro scholar Dr. William E. B. Du Bois answered Booker T. Washington.*]

. . . in the history of nearly all other races and peoples the doctrine preached . . . has been that manly self-respect is worth more than lands and houses, and that a people who voluntarily surrender such respect, or cease striving for it, are not worth civilizing.

In answer to this, it has been claimed that the Negro can survive only through submission. Mr. Washington distinctly asks that black people give up, at least for the present, three things,—

First, political power,
Second, insistence on civil rights,
Third, higher education of Negro youth,—

and concentrate all their energies on industrial education, the accumulation of wealth, and the conciliation of the South. . . . As a result of this tender of the palm-branch, what has been the return? In these years [since Booker T. Washington's Atlanta speech] there have occurred:

1. The disfranchisement of the Negro.
2. The legal creation of a distinct status of civil inferiority.
3. The steady withdrawal of aid from institutions for the higher training of the Negro.

These movements are not, to be sure, direct results of Mr. Washington's teachings; but his propaganda has, without a shadow of doubt, helped their speedier accomplishment. . . .

[Negroes] do not expect that the free right to vote, to enjoy civic rights, and to be educated, will come in a moment; they do not expect to see the bias and prejudices of years disappear at the blast of a trumpet; but they are absolutely certain that the way for a people to gain their reasonable rights is not by voluntarily throwing them away and insisting that they do not want them; that the way for a people to gain respect is not by continually belittling and ridiculing themselves; that on the contrary, Negroes must insist continually, in season and out of season, that voting is necessary to proper manhood, that color discrimination is barbarism, and that black boys need education as well as white boys. . . .

So far as Mr. Washington preaches Thrift, Patience, and Industrial Training for the masses, we must hold up his hands and strive with him. . . . But so far as Mr. Washington apologizes for injustice, North or South, does not rightly value the privilege and duty of voting, belittles the emasculating effects of caste distinctions, and opposes the higher training and ambition of our brighter minds — . . . we must unceasingly and firmly oppose them. By every civilized and peaceful method we must strive for the rights which the world accords to men, clinging unwaveringly to those great words which the sons of the [Founding] Fathers would fain forget: "We hold these truths to be self-evident: That all men are created equal; that they are endowed by their Creator with certain unalienable rights; that among these are life, liberty, and the pursuit of happiness."

---

W. E. Burghardt Du Bois, *The Souls of Black Folks* (Chicago, 1903), pp. 51-59.

# The Mission of the Meddler

[*In both the North and the South a popular way of attacking reformers was to call them "do-gooders" or "meddlers," and to try to make them appear as "crack-pots" or freaks. In a magazine article, Mary Church Terrell, an 1883 graduate of Oberlin College and first president of the National Association of Colored Women, defends "the meddler."*]

Everybody who has tried to advance the interests of the human race by redressing wrongs or by inaugurating reforms has first been called a meddler. An acknowledged philanthropist or public benefactor may be defined as a meddler, whose labors have been crowned with success. . . .

In the United States there is an imperative need of meddlers today—active, insistent, and fearless meddlers who will spend their time investigating institutions, customs, and laws whose effect upon the citizens of any color or class is depressing or bad. The crying need of the whole wide world is meddlers. In Great Britain, Ireland is waiting for a large number of the aggressive, humane kind to appear. In Russia the dumb, driven cattle made in the image of God, but reduced to the level of brutes are in sore need of the meddler who has here a great and glorious work to perform. . . . In Russia and Germany and elsewhere as well the Jew needs the service of the meddler, who shall ask why the narrow and vicious of all races and creeds are permitted to pursue and persecute a people whose ability and whose virtues are so conspicuous and whose hand is raised against none.

. . . In the United States there is an imperative need of a host of meddlers who will . . . go so far as "to interfere officiously" if need be, where corruption of any kind is apparent and the transgression of the law is clear.

[*Shortly before her death, Mrs. Terrell was still one of America's important meddlers. In 1953 at the age of 89, she led a group into a restaurant in Washington, D.C. to protest its refusal to serve Negroes. The group was arrested but finally won their case in court.*]

Mary Church Terrell, "The Mission of the Meddler," *The Voice of the Negro*, Vol. 2 (August, 1905), pp. 566-567.

# *Time to Denounce Lynchings*

[*In 1894, two years after she was driven out of Memphis for publishing information exposing those who had taken part in a lynching, fiery young Ida Wells published* A Red Record. *It was the first book to document the crime of lynching. This was her conclusion.*]

362 / EYEWITNESS: *The Negro in American History*

. . . We demand a fair trial by law for those accused of crime, and punishment by law after honest conviction. No maudlin sympathy for criminals is solicited, but we do ask that the law shall punish all alike. We earnestly desire those that control the forces which make public sentiment to join with us in the demand. Surely the humanitarian spirit of this country which reaches out to denounce the treatment of Russian Jews, the Armenian Christians, the laboring poor of Europe, the Siberian exiles, and the native women of India— will not longer refuse to lift its voice on this subject. If it were known that the cannibals or the savage Indians had burned three human beings alive in the past two years, the whole of Christendom would be roused, to devise ways and means to put a stop to it. Can you remain silent and inactive when such things are done in our own community and country? Is your duty to humanity in the United States less binding?

Ida B. Wells, *A Red Record* (Chicago, 1894), p. 97.

# Congressman White Introduces
# the First Antilynching Bill

[*Here are two versions of the same news story. One is by Congressman Griggs of Georgia, the other is by George White of North Carolina. As a result of the acceptance of the first version, a Negro named Hose was lynched. Representative White in his version not only shows that Griggs's facts may have been incorrect but also that it is essential for those accused of crime to have their day in court and a trial by jury and not be subject to mob violence. Then Congressman White introduced the first antilynching bill into the United States Congress.*]

[*Representative Griggs, white.*] . . . A little family a few miles from the town of Newman were at supper in their modest dining room. The father, the young mother, and the baby were seated at the table. Humble though it was, peace, happiness, and contentment reigned in that modest house. A monster in human form, an employee on the farm [Hose], crept into that happy little home and with an ax knocked out the brains of that father, snatched the child from its mother, threw it across the room out of his way, and then by force accomplished his foul purpose. . . .

[*Representative White, Negro.*] The other side of this horrible story portrays a very different state of affairs. A white man, with no interest in Hose or his victim, declares upon oath that Hose did not commit this atrocious crime charged against him, but was an employee of Cranford [the husband], and had importuned him for pay due him for labor. This incensed his employer, who rushed upon Hose with a gun. Hose seized an ax and killed Cranford instantly, in self-defense, and then fled to the woods with the greatest possible speed. I do not vouch for either side of this story, but only refer to it to show the necessity for trying all persons charged with crime, as the law directs. . . .

I tremble with horror for the future of our nation when I think what must be the inevitable result if mob violence is not stamped out of existence and law once more permitted to reign supreme.

To the end that the National Government may have jurisdiction over this species of crime [lynching], I have prepared and introduced the following bill. . . .

> A bill for the protection of all citizens of the United States against mob violence, and the penalty for breaking such laws [death].

*The Congressional Record*, 56th Congress, First Session, pp. 2151-2153.

# Dr. Du Bois Writes to a Negro Schoolgirl, 1905

[*The great scholar took time out from his important work to tell a schoolgirl how vital it is for everyone to take part in American life.*]

I wonder if you will let a stranger say a word to you about yourself? I have heard that you are a young woman of some ability but that you are neglecting your school work because you have become hopeless of trying to do anything in the world. I am very sorry for this. How any human being whose wonderful fortune it is to live in the 20th century should under ordinarily fair advantages despair of life is almost unbelievable. And if in addition to this that person is, as I am, of Negro lineage with all the hopes and yearnings of hundreds of millions of human souls dependent in some degree on her striving, then her bitterness amounts to a crime.

There are in the United States today tens of thousands of colored girls who would be happy beyond measure to have the chance of educating themselves that you are neglecting. If you train yourself as you easily can, there are wonderful chances of usefulness before you: You can join the ranks of 15,000 Negro women teachers, of hundreds of nurses and physicians, of the growing number of clerks and stenographers, and above all of the host of homemakers. Ignorance is a cure for nothing. Get the very best training possible and the doors of opportunity will fly open before you as they are flying before thousands of your fellows. On the other hand every time a colored person neglects an opportunity, it makes it more difficult for others of the race to get such an opportunity. Do you want to cut off the chances of the boys and girls of tomorrow?

Herbert Aptheker, ed., *A Documentary History of the Negro People in the United States*, Vol. II (New York: The Citadel Press, 1951), p. 864. Reprinted by permission.

## A Jim Crow Stage Version of Negro History

[*The Jim Crow era produced a caricature of the Negro and his part in American history. Books, plays, and, later, movies ridiculed his accomplishments and held him up to scorn. The Clansman was a famous play that made heroes of the Ku Klux Klan and villains of the Negro lawmakers of the Reconstruction South. This is a review of the play by a Negro magazine in 1905. In several cities Negroes successfully had the play banned because it provoked racial conflict—but The Clansman later became the famous movie Birth of a Nation.*]

. . . To our way of thinking, Mr. Thomas Dixon, Jr., is one of those men walking about who should be incarcerated in a madhouse. Surely the man's mind is unhinged. . . . Mr. Dixon's two most prominent books, *The Clansman* and *The Leopard's Spots* are both manuals of deviltry and barbarism. They are full of wild, raging mobs and secret bands of marauders. It is the first time our public morals have been so low as to do open honor to anarchy. . . . A Negro is shown pursuing a little white girl for violent and unholy purposes. . . . The play was hissed in Richmond. In Columbia the whole performance was amid thunderous applause and hisses. . . . At Bainbridge . . . a mob, fired by the scenes in *The Clansman*, broke into a jail and lynched a Negro charged with murder. In Alabama an organization known as "The Sons of the Clansmen" has been formed among the young whites. . . . Dr. Len G. Broughton, of [Atlanta], declared that:

"The whole show is a disgrace to Southern manhood and womanhood. . . . The devil of selfish greed is back of it all. It is doing the Negro harm and corrupting the people of our own race. It is un-Christian; it is un-American; it is unsound, and it is unsafe."

. . . Rev. Richard Carroll, a Negro minister, witnessed the play by invitation at Columbia. He says, "From the beginning to the end the Negro was represented as a brute, a beast and a demon from hell. . . . It is the forerunner of much bloodshed and anarchy." . . .

*The Voice of the Negro*, Vol. II (December, 1905), p. 836.

## *The Riot That Stirred America's Conscience*

[*The bloody anti-Negro rioting in Lincoln's home town of Springfield, Illinois, in 1908, was to lead to the formation of the National Association for the Advancement of Colored People (NAACP). This article, by reporter William E. Walling, and his question at the end, "What large and powerful body of citizens is ready to come to the Negro's aid?" also brought about the NAACP.*]

"Lincoln freed you, we'll show you where you belong," was one of the cries with which the Springfield mob set about to drive the Negroes from town. The mob was composed of several thousand of Springfield's white citizens, while other thousands, including many women and children, and even prosperous business men in automobiles, calmly looked on, and the rioters proceeded hour after hour and on two days in succession to make deadly assaults on every Negro they could lay their hands on, to sack and plunder their houses and stores, and to burn and murder on favorable occasion. . . .

On the morning after the first riot I was in Chicago and took the night train for Springfield, where I have often visited and am almost at home. On arriving in the town I found that the rioting had been continued thruout the night, and was even feared for the coming evening, in spite of the presence of nearly the whole militia of the State. Altho we visited the Mayor, military headquarters, the leading newspaper, and some prominent citizens, my wife and I gave most of our attention to the hospital, the Negro quarters and the jail.

We at once discovered, to our amazement, that Springfield had no shame. She stood for the action of the mob. She hoped the rest of the Negroes might flee. She threatened that the movement to drive them out would continue. I do not speak of the leading citizens, but of the masses of the people, of workingmen in the shops, the storekeepers in the stores, the drivers, the men on the street, the wounded in the hospitals. . . .

On Sunday, August 16th, the day after the second lynching, a leading white minister recommended the Southern disfranchisement scheme as a remedy for *Negro* ( ! ) lawlessness, while all four ministers who were quoted in the press proposed swift "justice" for *the Negroes*, rather than recommending true Christianity, democracy, and brotherhood to the whites. Even the Governor's statement of the situation, strong as it was on the whole, was tainted in one place with a concession to Springfield opinion. He said that Burton, the first Negro lynched, was killed after he had incensed the crowd by firing into it to protect his home from incendiaries. But when Burton's home was attacked there had already been considerable shooting between the blacks and the whites. Moreover, according to his daughters, men had entered the house and threatened him with an axe and other weapons, while his firing of buckshot at random into a mob is by no means necessarily a murderous procedure. The Governor made, then, an understatement of the character of the mob, suggesting that the Negroes had lost their heads and were accepting the mob's challenge to war. It is probable that Burton was defending not his home, but his life.

Besides suggestions in high places of the Negro's brutality, criminality and unfitness for the ballot we heard in lower ranks all the opinions that pervade the South. . . . In fact, this went so far that we were led to suspect the existence of a Southern element in the town, and this is indeed the case. . . . Even the famous Kate Howard [leader of the mob who later killed herself] had received her inspiration, she told us, from the South. . . .

If the new Political League succeeds in permanently driving every Negro from office; if the white laborers get the Negro laborers' jobs; if masters of Negro servants are able to keep them under the discipline of terror as I saw them doing at Springfield; if white shopkeepers and saloonkeepers get their colored rivals' trade . . . ; if white miners can force their Negro fellow workers out and get their positions by closing the mines [to Negroes], then every community indulging in an outburst of race hatred will be assured of a great and certain financial reward, and all the lies, ignorance and brutality on which race hatred is based will spread over the land. . . .

Either the spirit of the abolitionists, of Lincoln and of Lovejoy, must be revived and we must come to treat the Negro on a plane of absolute political and social equality, or Vardaman [Governor of Mississippi] and Tillman [Senator of South Carolina] will soon have transferred the race war to the North. . . .

The day these methods become general in the North every hope of political democracy will be dead. . . .

Yet who realizes the seriousness of the situation, and what large and powerful body of citizens is ready to come to their aid?

William E. Walling, "The Race War in the North," *The Independent*, Vol. 65 (September 3, 1908), pp. 529-534.

## An All-Negro Town in 1908

[*During the Jim Crow era, some Negroes sought a measure of independence and self-government by forming their own towns. For a time, some of these towns achieved a degree of stability and prosperity. A white college president describes the Negro town of Brooklyn, Illinois.*]

This municipal colonization of Afro-Americans apparently affords a striking refutation of the oft-repeated claim that Negroes are born to follow and never to lead—for it seems to have progressed to a degree of unusual prosperity, and its possibilities are yet only to be estimated. The executive heads boast, and county officials have been heard to say, that there is less crime, even fewer violations of the "city code," within the confines of this little corporation than in many of the larger towns of mixed population. . . .

Whites, as well as blacks, who have watched the place grow to its present population of 1,900, agree that a spirit of perfect harmony prevails there in every business walk; that the Negroes are law-abiding to an extreme, self-supporting, honest, and proud of their achievements. . . .

The town has an annual income, from all sources, amounting to more than $10,000, and may levy additional assessments for needed improvements. The present policy is not to incur needless expense. . . .

The mere handful of whites—probably fifty in number—who have habitation in the place live in evident peace with their colored brothers. There is never any race riot or even discord, but they have no voice in the municipal government other than to walk up to the polls each succeeding year and cast their ballots for chosen leaders. Only once . . . was a white man chosen to town office. That was several years ago, when an unpopular Negro was nominated to represent his ward. The citizens banded together and elected his [white] opponent by an overwhelming majority. . . .

Business is conducted by the Negro merchants in Brooklyn much the same as in any other place of like population, where the inhabitants depend upon their weekly or monthly wage to provide for their families. Accounts are run at the different stores and payments met with remarkable promptness. . . .

The labor element find employment at $1.50 to $2 a day, and, as the larger proportion own their homes, where they raise vegetables and poultry, their lot is far from a hard one.

At the head of the administration is Burton Franklin Washington. . . . While, in his opinion, it would be better to have complete isolation from the white race, he realizes that there will always be an element to invade the towns, and says there should never be any prejudice of the blacks against the minority. "There is none here," he said, "and there never will be. As an instance of the perfect harmony which has always existed in Brooklyn, a white man here shot and seriously wounded a respectable colored citizen without apparent cause. The assailant was locked up in our town jail, and, altho the injured men hovered between life and death for many days, there was no attempt at violence upon the prisoner. We give the few whites that are here the same show that we have ourselves, if they are determined to stay with us. We pay their school teacher $80 a month, furnish them adequate police protection, and look after their interests as well as it can be done with our means." . . .

The picture is simply a case of the bottom rail being on top, where fate, fortune or whatever it may be termed has brought Afro-Americans together . . . and placed the whites under their control in a peaceable, satisfactory manner of living.

Iverson B. Summers, "A Negro Town in Illinois," *The Independent*, Vol. 65 (August 27, 1908), pp. 464-469.

# 15

# America Enters the Twentieth Century

ON a warm day in 1877 the new United States Minister to the Republic of Haiti arrived at the Presidential Palace at Port au Prince to present his credentials. For the next eight years John Mercer Langston of Virginia, a former slave who had become head of Howard University's Law School, worked to build better relations between his country and the small Negro nation. His careful studies of the island's economy enabled American exporters to penetrate the British and French monopoly on Haitian commerce. In a short time American calicoes appeared in Haitian shop windows and Americans were drinking Haitian coffee. Langston, along with Frederick Douglass and historian George W. Williams, was among the eight Negro diplomats who served their nation in foreign capitals before the Spanish-American War.

*Diplomat John Mercer Langston was one of the many Negro diplomats assigned to Haiti and Liberia after the Civil War.*

### The Spanish-American War

American interest in the Caribbean islands, as well as those in the Atlantic and the Pacific, grew out of the industrial expansion that followed the Civil War. Interest in Cuba stemmed from American investments in its plantations as well as concern for a people savagely mistreated by its Spanish rulers.

The sinking of the battleship *Maine* in Havana harbor, with a loss of 160 white and Negro sailors, brought a furious response from

Americans. For months the public had been aroused by sensational news stories printed in American papers of events in Cuba. Often the stories were entirely or partially false—but they sold newspapers. Although it was never proved that Spain was responsible for the explosion aboard the *Maine*, the newspapers claimed Spain was guilty and demanded an invasion of Cuba. Congress quickly passed a Declaration of War. George White of North Carolina, the only Negro Congressman, strongly supported the action.

Thousands of Americans rushed to enlist as soon as war was declared. Mississippi's ex-Congressman John M. Lynch, who in 1884 had been elected temporary chairman of the Republican National Convention, was one of the more than 100 Negroes commissioned as officers during the emergency. At the outset of the war there was only one Negro graduate of West Point still on active duty, Colonel Charles Young. In the ten-week war all four Negro regiments of the regular Army saw action, as did Colonel Young. As early as June 30, 1898 four privates of the 10th Cavalry were

*Troop C, 9th Cavalry, leading the charge up San Juan Hill. From a painting by Fletcher C. Ransom. Some historians claimed that Negro cavalrymen saved the Rough Riders from defeat.*

awarded the Congressional Medal of Honor for bravery in Cuba. The citations for Dennis Bell, Fitz Lee, William Tompkins, and George Wanton read: "Voluntarily went ashore in the face of the enemy and aided in the rescue of his wounded comrades; this after several previous attempts at rescue had been frustrated."

Fighting alongside the Rough Riders and Teddy Roosevelt at San Juan Hill were units of the 9th and 10th Cavalries. An eyewitness described how the Negro troopers "started the charge, and, with the Rough Riders, routed the Spaniards, causing them to retreat in disorder, leaving their dead and wounded behind."

John "Blackjack" Pershing was in command of the 10th Cavalry on the historic charge. He recalled it with pride:

> White regiments, black regiments, regulars and rough Riders, representing the young manhood of the North and South, fought shoulder to shoulder, unmindful of whether commanded by an ex-Confederate or not, and mindful only of their common duty as Americans.

Rough Rider Frank Knox, who served as Secretary of War during World War II, recalled:

> I joined a troop of the Tenth Cavalry and for a time fought with them shoulder to shoulder, and in justice to the colored race I must say that I never saw braver men anywhere. Some of those who rushed up the hill will live in my memory forever.

In the battle at El Caney, Negro units distinguished themselves. T. C. Butler, Private in the 25th Infantry, was the first to enter the blackhouse and capture the Spanish flag. But a white officer from another command who entered after Private Butler made him give it up. However, Butler tore off a piece of the flag to show his black comrades. After the battle one white Southerner said, "I've changed my opinion of the colored folks, for of all the men I saw fighting, there were none to beat the Tenth Cavalry and the colored infantry at Santiago, and I don't mind saying so."

For his actions in the battle, Sergeant Edward L. Baker won the Congressional Medal of Honor. He "gallantly assisted in the rescue of the wounded from in front of the lines and under heavy fire of the enemy."

The decisive defeat of the Spanish gave the United States a vast new empire of dark-skinned people. Despite American success in

*A trooper of the 10th Cavalry, which served in the Philippines. Men of the 10th became America's first machine-gun experts, perfecting techniques of indirect and overhead fire. The best white officers sought to command them. One of the lucky ones was John J. Pershing, who always said: "I am proud" to be "a member of that intrepid organization of the Army which has always added glory to the military history of America—the 10th Cavalry."*

bringing modern health, sanitation, and education to the new possessions, many resented American control. Soldiers, including Negro units, were part of the Army kept in the colonies that stretched from Puerto Rico in the Atlantic to the Philippines in the Pacific.

Many Americans were opposed to their country becoming a colonial power. Very few issues have divided the American people as this one did. An Anti-imperialist League was supported by such important Americans as former President Grover Cleveland and Mark Twain. No group was as disturbed by the new turn of events as were the Negroes. They feared that the mistreatment which they received would be extended to millions of dark-skinned people in these new American possessions. Lewis Douglass, a hero of the Civil War and a son of Frederick Douglass, said bitterly in 1898: "It is a sorry, though true, fact, that wherever this government controls, injustice to dark races prevails."

As the United States Army fought a three-year war to suppress the rebellion in the Philippines, led by a young Filipino named Aguinaldo, many Negroes compared Aguinaldo's battle for independence with their own fight for rights in America. Kelly Miller, a brilliant defender of the rights of his people, said:

> The Negro would show himself unworthy of the rights which he claims should he deny the same to a struggling people under another sky. . . . The pill of

imperialism may be sugar-coated to the taste, but the Negro swallows it to his own political damnation.

Negro Congressman George White changed his views of our new role in the world. He denounced the American businessmen who seized the Hawaiian government (as did President Grover Cleveland). But after the Spanish-American War he told Congress how he "very cheerfully" supported "the recent war for liberating a very much oppressed" Cuba. He noted that the country had always given a "helping hand to the oppressed, to the outraged—I mean, of course, without the borders of the United States." And in the same speech he demanded American "acquisition of all of the territory that is within our grasp as a result of that war." He insisted, however, "The nation must care for those at home as well as those abroad."

## Claiming the North Pole

While there was disagreement among Americans about their nation becoming a colonial power, all rejoiced at news of the discovery of the North Pole by men of three races.

*Matt Henson, first man to stand atop the world, reached the North Pole on April 6, 1909. Twice he had saved Robert Peary's life. He won a hundred-dollar bet with a naval officer who claimed no Negro could reach the Pole and return with all his fingers and toes. However, Henson lost 35 pounds and was exhausted for weeks.*

*Inspired by Henson's courage, Herbert Frisby made twenty-one Arctic trips in twenty-two years. He wanted to show up his teacher who said, "Henson was the first Negro to get to the Pole and you can bet he'll be the last!" Frisby has devoted his life to securing recognition for the part Henson played in the Peary expeditions. Frisby's house, "The Igloo," is on a quiet street in Baltimore, Maryland.*

On a sub-zero arctic day in early April, 1909 Matt Henson and the Eskimo guides of Commander Robert E. Peary's expedition reached the top of the world. The small party built an igloo and waited for the Commander to arrive and confirm Henson's calculations that indicated they were at the top of the world. In less than an hour an exhausted Peary arrived and confirmed the fact.

"Plant the Stars and Stripes over there, Matt—at the North Pole," directed Peary. It was a victory which the two men had tried desperately to accomplish during seven previous expeditions. Peary had met Henson in a Washington clothing store, where the young Negro had been employed as a clerk. Henson became far more than a companion to Peary during their 23 years of joint exploration. Henson learned the Eskimo language and became an expert in the many skills needed for survival in the Arctic. Donald MacMillan, another member of the Peary expedition, recalled that:

> He [Henson] was the most popular man aboard the ship with the Eskimos. He could talk their language like a native. He made all the sledges which went to the Pole. He made all the stoves. Henson, the colored man, went to the Pole with Peary because he was a better man than any of his white assistants. . . .

As Matt Henson planted the American flag at the North Pole, he turned to his Eskimo companions and called upon them to join with Peary and himself in three hearty cheers. "Three cheers rang out on the still, frosty air, our dumb dogs looking on in puzzled surprise," Henson later recorded in his book *A Negro Explorer at the North Pole* which was published in 1912.

In 1945 Congress awarded Henson a medal for "outstanding service to the Government of the United States in the field of science," and a decade later President Eisenhower honored Henson at the White House. After another decade the state of Maryland placed a plaque in his memory in the state house—the first time a Negro was so honored in the South.

## The "Progressive Years"

A pistol shot ushered in the "progressive years" between the turn of the century and the First World War. A crazed assassin fired at President William McKinley as he stood smiling and shaking hands at the Pan-American Exposition in Buffalo, New York. The next man in line to shake hands, a six-foot-six, college-educated Negro waiter named Parker seized the assassin before he could escape, and turned him over to the police. In a week McKinley was dead and "Teddy" Roosevelt was sworn in as the new President. This energetic young reformer, who promised all Americans a "Square Deal," dominated American political life for the next dozen years.

Three months after he entered the White House, President Roosevelt invited Booker T. Washington to visit him for a conference. There was nothing unusual in this since the Negro educator had often been consulted by Presidents. At the White House the President and Washington had dinner. This meal made more history than any other since the first Thanksgiving. Southern newspapers exploded in anger. Wrote the *New Orleans Times Democrat:* "When Mr. Roosevelt sits down to dinner with a Negro he declares that the Negro is the social equal of the white man." Another paper screamed: "White men of the South, how do you like it? . . . White women of the South, how do you like it?"

For perhaps the only time in his life, the impulsive and fearless Roosevelt did not fight back. He said nothing. Later he wrote to a friend that the dinner "was a mistake." While Roosevelt and President Taft after him continued to meet with Booker T. Washington, neither of them ever ate with him again and both Presidents made greater efforts to win the support of white Southerners than Republicans had ever done before. Both refused to speak out forcefully against the many lynchings that took place during their terms in office.

At the same time Roosevelt and Taft appointed two of the foremost Negro lawyers of the day to posts in the federal government. William H. Lewis, who had graduated from Amherst College where he was captain of the football team and an outstanding orator, was appointed Assistant Attorney General of the United States, the first Negro to reach a sub-Cabinet post. Harvard graduate Robert Terrell was made a municipal judge in Washington D.C.

James Weldon Johnson, poet and for eight years an American diplomat, reported that both Presidents Roosevelt and Taft listened to a "Black Cabinet" on Negro matters. This group was composed of "colored men who held important federal positions in the capital," its chief spokesman being Booker T. Washington. A handful of jobs was provided for Negroes by the Republican Party from Reconstruction until the election of Wilson. These included diplomatic posts in

Haiti and Liberia, Recorder of Deeds in Washington, Auditor of the Navy Department, Register of the Treasury, Collector for the Port of Washington, and a post as Assistant Attorney General. These positions carried little power. They were largely ceremonial and enabled Republican politicians to claim that they had helped to elevate the Negro.

For the majority of colored men and women of the South, however, the years of Roosevelt and Taft were not progressive. In 1903 the Governor of North Carolina announced "I am proud of my state" because "we have solved the Negro problem." He then explained: "We have taken him out of politics and have thereby secured good government. . . ." Governor James Vardaman of Mississippi told a cheering audience in Poplarville of his determination to keep Negroes from voting: "How is the white man going to control the government? . . . If it is necessary every Negro in the state will be lynched; it will be done to maintain white supremacy." He also suggested that the Fifteenth Amendment to the Constitution "ought to be wiped out. We all agree on that. Then why don't we do it?"

During the years at the turn of the century, many Southern states also sought to reduce the education of Negroes to a bare minimum. Governor Vardaman explained that "this education is ruining our Negroes. They're demanding equality." By 1912 a white school superintendent in the South reported:

> There has never been any serious attempt in this state to offer adequate educational facilities for the colored race. The average length of the term for the state is only four months. . . . [Some schools have] as many as 100 students to the teacher; no attempt is made to do more than teach the children to read, write, and figure, and these subjects are learned very imperfectly.

One year later, Senator Cole Blease of South Carolina announced, "God Almighty never intended he [the Negro] should be educated."

Negroes were losing faith in President Theodore Roosevelt. In 1906 President Roosevelt dishonorably discharged from the United States Army an entire battalion of Negro troops stationed in Brownsville, Texas. The men, who had been insulted and even struck by the townspeople, were charged with shooting up the town and killing one man. Roosevelt acted after a military court failed to establish who the guilty soldiers were, but held, "We know they were Negro soldiers." Before this incident the unit's military record had been considered superb. Senator Joseph B. Foraker of Ohio defended the troops, saying: "They ask no favors because they are Negroes, but only justice because they are men." But the President refused to soften the soldiers' penalties.

When the 1912 election came around, Negro voters were deserting both Republican Taft and "Progressive" Roosevelt. Taft had told Negroes that they should be content to remain farmers and Roosevelt's Progressive Party ignored their hopes and even excluded them from many Southern delegations to the national convention. Many Negro leaders looked to the tall Princeton University president, Woodrow Wilson, as a more sympathetic leader—even though he was both a Southerner and a Democrat. Wilson was elected President of the United States when Taft and Roosevelt split the Republican vote in 1912. Black and white voters looked forward with enthusiasm to what Wilson called his "New Freedom" for America.

## Wilson and the New Freedom

Americans found Wilson to be a dynamic President. He convinced Congress to pass new laws to regulate interstate trade, control monopolies, and tax incomes. Another law protected seamen from brutal treatment aboard American ships. The Negro, however, found the New Freedom to be as empty for him as the Square Deal had been. President Wilson had even restored segregation to the Treasury and Post Office departments. Partitions were put up to separate Negro and white clerks.

Booker T. Washington visited the capital in 1913 and remarked, "I have never seen the colored people so discouraged and bitter as they are at the present time."

Those Negro leaders who supported Wilson in 1912 were denounced by their followers. They had told their people that Wilson meant to keep his campaign promise that "they may count upon me for absolute fair dealing," and "for everything by which I could assist in advancing the interests of their race."

Led by Monroe Trotter, the stocky and energetic editor of the Boston *Guardian*, a group of Negro leaders visited President Wilson in 1913 to complain about his segregation of government employees. The President told them, "Segregation is not humiliating but a benefit, and ought to be so regarded by you gentlemen." When Trotter pointed out that colored and white clerks had worked side by side in the federal government for half a century, Wilson became angry. "Your manner offends me," he told the editor. "I was thunderstruck," recalled Trotter and replied, "You misinterpret my earnestness for passion." But it was clear that the President would not alter his policy. The delegation left sadder but wiser. Fast-moving events soon diverted everyone's attention to Europe.

## World War I

When Congress declared war against the Central Powers in April, 1917, American Negroes were among the first to volunteer and serve. More than 100,000 went overseas as stevedores, artillerymen, machine gunners, and infantrymen. The first two Americans to win France's Croix de Guerre for bravery were Negroes Henry Johnson of Albany, New York and Needham Roberts of Trenton, New Jersey. By themselves these two men smashed a German surprise attack and virtually wiped out the raiding party.

*Sergeant Henry Johnson (holding flowers) receives a postwar New York tickertape welcome honoring his bravery in fighting off a German unit of twenty men. His buddy, Private Needham Roberts, was in another car.*

At the outbreak of the war, Colonel Charles Young, the highest ranking Negro officer in the Army, was forced into retirement by "high blood pressure." To establish his fitness for active duty, Young mounted his horse and rode from Ohio to Washington, D.C., and back. He was not permitted to return to active duty, however, until four days before the Armistice was signed.

The Negro combat regiments were assigned to the French and fought in many of the important battles of the war, including the Marne defense and the Meuse-Argonne offensive. They captured important towns and strategic objectives and entered Germany as part of the French army of occupation. Despite German efforts to win them over by propaganda leaflets reminding them of the conditions they faced back home in the United States, not a single Negro deserted. Four entire Negro regiments were awarded the Croix de Guerre and the 369th spent 191 days on the firing line, more time than any other American regiment. A young white officer named Harry Truman observed that the Negro units that were allowed to have Negro officers were even more effective than those with white officers. When he became President of the United States, he took steps to insure that Army officers would be chosen for merit, not color, and it was under his administration, in 1948, that the armed forces were officially integrated.

*A few of the Negro soldiers who earned the French Croix de Guerre wearing their medals. Most Negroes in France, however, were assigned to service units rather than fighting units.*

On the home front as well as the fighting front Negroes backed the nation's war effort. Thousands of Southern Negroes poured into Northern industrial centers. Charles Knight, at the Bethlehem Steel plant in Maryland, broke the world's record for driving rivets in steel ships. A Negro crew in Pennsylvania broke the world's record for driving piles. Dr. George E. Haynes and Emmett J. Scott were brought to Washington by the Wilson administration to serve the nation's war effort. Dr. Haynes was made head of the Department of Negro Economics of the Department of Labor. Scott was a special assistant to the Secretary of War, advising on matters affecting the morale of Negro soldiers and civilians. He toured Army camps and brought complaints to the attention of the government.

During the war to "make the world safe for democracy," Negroes did not neglect their own fight for equality. Three months after the United States declared war 15,000 Negroes conducted a silent parade in New York City. They carried signs to protest the continued lynchings and the race riots in American cities. One read "MR. PRESIDENT, WHY NOT MAKE AMERICA SAFE FOR DEMOCRACY?" The NAACP led a successful campaign to have the Army train Negroes as officers—but the Army insisted that they be trained separately from whites. By 1917, the Negro officer-training center at Des Moines, Iowa graduated more than 600 captains and lieutenants.

*New York City Silent Parade. Organized by the NAACP in 1917, it protested lynchings and race riots as the United States entered World War I "to make the world safe for democracy."*

*In 1917 some 64 members of the 24th Infantry were tried for murder after a battle with Houston citizens.*

The resistance of Negro soldiers to discrimination brought about several dramatic incidents on the home front. When the 8th Illinois Regiment, stationed in Newport News, Virginia, refused to accept segregation aboard the town's streetcars, it was quickly sent overseas. In Houston, Texas, Negro soldiers of the famed 24th Regiment bitterly resented the insulting jeers of the townspeople and the assaults of the local police. Some of the infantrymen seized arms and shot it out with the police and white citizens, killing 17. Thirteen of the soldiers were sentenced to death, 40 others were given life imprisonment and further prosecutions were planned. The condemned men were denied the right of appeal to the Secretary of War or the President. Only the determined action of the NAACP halted further prosecutions. James Weldon Johnson led other Negro leaders in a delegation that convinced the President to halt all other actions against the men.

After the Armistice General Pershing addressed the much-decorated 92nd Division as it prepared to leave France. "I want you officers and soldiers of the 92nd Division to know that the 92nd Division stands second to none in the record you have made since your arrival in France. . . . The American public has every reason to be proud of that record. . . ." Earlier in the war Robert S. Abbott, Negro owner of the *Chicago Defender*, told his readers, "The colored soldier who fights side by side with the white American in the titanic struggle now raging across the sea will hardly be begrudged a fair chance when the victorious armies return." Abbott had spoken too soon, too optimistically.

While President Woodrow Wilson was in Paris trying to bind the world together in a treaty that would end war forever, another American labored in Paris for the unity and peace of the world. William E. B. Du Bois organized the first meeting of the world's colored peoples. Delegates from 15 countries and colonies attended. Colored men from Atlanta, Georgia talked of peace and brotherhood with delegates from Capetown, South Africa. This "Pan-African" movement would grow to great power in our own time, uniting the many people of color throughout the world.

# *The 25th Infantry Captures El Caney*

*[The Spanish-American War marked America's emergence as a world power. Four Negro units of the regular Army were among the American troops who saw action. When the 25th Infantry was sent to Cuba, it had already served in Texas, Minnesota, the Dakotas, Montana, and Mexico. When they left Missoula, Montana, to go off to war, Easter services in all churches were postponed so that the whole town could bid them farewell. Here is Negro Sergeant-Major Frank W. Pullen, Jr.'s story of the end of the historic battle of El Caney that began at dawn, July 1, 1898, and of the capture of Santiago, Cuba.]*

Finally, late in the afternoon, our brave Lieutenant Kinnison said to another officer: "We cannot take the trenches without charging them." Just as he was about to give the order for the bugler to sound "the charge" he was wounded and carried to the rear. The men were then fighting like demons. Without a word of command, though led by that gallant and intrepid Second Lieutenant J. A. Moss, 25th Infantry, some one gave a yell and the 25th Infantry was off, alone to the charge. The 4th U.S. Infantry, fighting on the left, halted when those dusky heroes made the dash with a yell which would have done credit to a Comanche Indian. No one knows who started the charge; one thing is certain, at the time it was made excitement was running high; each man was a captain for himself and fighting accordingly. Brigadier Generals, Colonels, Lieutenant-Colonels, Majors, etc., were not needed at the time the 25th Infantry made the charge on El Caney, and those officers simply watched the battle from convenient points, as Lieutenants and enlisted men made the charge alone. It has been reported that the 12th U.S. Infantry made the charge, assisted by the 25th Infantry, but it is a recorded fact that the 25th Infantry fought the battle alone, the 12th Infantry coming up after the firing had nearly ceased. Private T. C. Butler, Company H, 25th Infantry, was the first man to enter the blockhouse at El Caney, and took possession of the Spanish flag for his regiment. An officer of the 12th Infantry came up while Butler was in the house and ordered him to give up the flag, which he was compelled to do, but not until he had torn a piece off the flag to substantiate his report to his Colonel of the injustice which had been done to him. Thus, by using the authority given him by his shoulder-straps, this officer took for his regiment that which had been won by the hearts' blood of some of the bravest, though black, soldiers of Shafter's army. . . .

A word more in regard to the charge. It was not the glorious run from the edge of some nearby thicket to the top of a small hill, as many may imagine. This particular charge was a tough, hard climb, over sharp, rising ground, which, were a man in perfect physical strength, he would climb slowly. Part of the charge was made over soft, plowed ground, a part through a lot of prickly pineapple plants and barbed-wire entanglements. It was slow, hard work, under a blazing July sun and a perfect hailstorm of bullets, which, thanks to the poor marksmanship of the Spaniards, "went high." . . .

On July 14th it was decided to make a demonstration in front of Santiago, to draw the fire of the enemy and locate his position. Two companies of colored soldiers (25th Infantry) were selected for this purpose, actually deployed as skirmishers and started in advance. General Shafter, watching the movement from a distant hill, saw that such a movement meant to sacrifice those men, without any or much good resulting, therefore had them recalled. Had the movement been completed it is probable that not a man would have escaped death or serious wounds. When the news came that General Toral had decided to surrender, the 25th Infantry was a thousand yards or more nearer the city of Santiago than any regiment in the army, having entrenched themselves along the railroad leading into the city. . . .

*Frank W. Pullen, Jr.*

Ex-Sergeant-Major 25th U.S. Infantry.
Enfield, N.C., March 23, 1899

---

Edward A. Johnson, *History of Negro Soldiers in the Spanish-American War* (Raleigh, 1899), pp. 29-32.

## Paul Lawrence Dunbar, Poet

[*One of America's most famous poets at the turn of the century was Paul Lawrence Dunbar, the son of fugitive slaves. Although most of his popular poems were light and amusing dialect stories of Negroes, he was capable of writing serious poems about Negro life in America, such as "We Wear The Mask."*]

### We Wear The Mask.

We wear the mask that grins and lies,
It hides our cheeks and shades our eyes,—
This debt we pay to human guile;
With torn and bleeding hearts we smile,
And mouth with myriad subtleties.

Why should the world be over-wise,
In counting all our tears and sighs?
Nay, let them only see us, while
   We wear the mask.

We smile, but, O great Christ, our cries
To thee from tortured souls arise.
We sing, but oh the clay is vile
Beneath our feet, and long the mile;
But let the world dream otherwise,
   We wear the mask!

---

Paul Lawrence Dunbar, *Lyrics of Lowly Life* (New York, 1899), p. 167.

## Imperialism and the Negro

[*As the United States extended its sovereignty to areas of darker peoples in other parts of the world, many American voices, white and Negro, were raised in opposition to this policy. One of the Negro voices raised against it was that of Kelly Miller, brilliant writer, graduate of Harvard, and Dean of Howard University's College of Arts and Sciences.*]

The welfare of the Negro race is vitally involved in the impending policy of imperialism. . . .

. . . the United States is attempting to force . . . an alien government upon a unanimously hostile and violently unwilling people. Acquiescence on the part of the Negro in the political rape upon the Filipino would give ground of justification to the assaults upon his rights at home. The Filipino is at least his equal in capacity for self-government. The Negro would show himself unworthy of the rights which he claims should he deny the same to a struggling people under another sky. He would not only forfeit his own weapon of defense, but his friends would lose theirs also. For how, with consistency, could the despoilers of the brown man's rights in Manila, upbraid the nullifiers of the black man's rights in Mississippi? The pill of imperialism may be sugar-coated to the taste, but the Negro swallows it to his own political damnation. . . .

The whole trend of imperial aggression is antagonistic to the feebler races. It is a revival of racial arrogance. It has ever been the boast of the proud and haughty race or nation that God has given them the heathen for their inheritance and the uttermost parts of the earth for their possession. . . . Will the Negro stultify himself and become part of the movement which must end in his own humiliation?

Whatever may happen, the Negro should adhere to the principles of the great Declaration [of Independence]. Of this instrument he has been the chief beneficiary; and whatever others may do, he should follow the light that has led him safe thus far on the road to American citizenship. Though all men should forsake it, yet should not he.

---

Kelly Miller, "The Effect of Imperialism Upon the Negro Race," *Howard's American Magazine*, Vol. 5 (October, 1900), pp. 87-92.

# First Men at the North Pole

*[On April 6, 1909, America's flag was planted on another frontier. This is how Matthew Henson, Negro guide and assistant to Commander Robert E. Peary, described the day of success to Lowell Thomas.]*

We had been travelling eighteen to twenty hours out of every twenty-four. Man, that was killing work! Forced marches all the time. From all our other expeditions we had found out that we couldn't carry food for more than fifty days, fifty-five at a pinch. . . .

We used to travel by night and sleep in the warmest part of the day. I was ahead most of the time with two of the Eskimos. . . .

The morning of April sixth I found we were in the middle of hummock ice. I calculated about how far I had come, and I said to myself, "If I'm not on the Pole, I've crossed it, so I don't have to go no further." And I said to my Eskimos: "We're going to camp here. Make an igloo."

Commander Peary was forty-five minutes behind. He came up to us as we were building the igloo and he says, "Well, my boy, how many miles have we made today?" And I answers, "Too many, Commander; I think we crossed the Pole." So the Commander got out his notebook and figured a bit and he says, "I guess you're right."

As a matter of fact, for about a mile or so I must have been going south instead of north. When you're up there, any direction you walk away from the Pole is south.

---

Lowell Thomas, "First at the Pole," *This Week*, April 2, 1939. Reprinted from *This Week* magazine. Copyright 1939 by the United Newspapers Magazine Corporation. Reprinted by permission of the author.

# The Beliefs of the First Man to Stand Atop the World

*[Matthew A. Henson, who became the first man to stand atop the world when he reached the North Pole on April 6, 1909, kept this credo in his lecture notes.]*

Great ideals are the glory of man alone. No other creature can have them. Only man can get a vision and an inspiration that will lift him above the level of himself and send him forth against all opposition or any discouragement to do and to dare and to accomplish wonderful and great things for the world and for humanity. . . . There can be no conquest to the man who dwells in the narrow and small environment of a groveling life, and there can be no vision to the man the horizon of whose vision is limited by the bounds of self. But the great things of the world, the great accomplishments of the world, have been achieved by men who had high ideals and who have received great visions. The path is not easy, the climbing is rugged and hard, but the glory at the end is worth while. . . .

*Lecture Notes of Matthew A. Henson* (Baltimore, Henson Collection, Soper Library, Morgan State College).

## Moving North to Jobs, 1910–1920

[*The Great War in Europe brought prosperity to America's factories—located mostly in Northern cities. From 1910 to 1920 more than half a million Southern Negroes moved northward, attracted by the opportunity for better jobs and homes. This letter from a Mississippi mechanic indicates the great desire to come North—and the Southern efforts to halt the exodus. The "Mr. Abbott" referred to is the Negro owner of the Chicago* Defender *who encouraged the migration.*]

Granville, Mississippi, May 16, 1917

Dear Sir: This letter is a letter of information of which you will find stamp envelop for reply. I want to come north some time soon but I do not want to leve here looking for a job where I would be in dorse all winter. Now the work I am doing here is running a guage edger in a saw mill. I know all about the grading of lumber. I have been working in lumber about 25 or 27 years. My wedges here is $3.00 a day 11 hours a day. I want to come North where I can educate my 3 little children also my wife. Now if you cannot fit me up at what I am doing down here I can learn anything any one els can. also there is a great deal of good women cooks here would leave any time all they want is to know where to go and some way to go. please write me at once just how I can get my people where they can get something for their work. There are women here cookeing for $1.50 and $2.00 a week. I would like to live in Chicago or Ohio or Philadelphia. Tell Mr. Abbott that our pepel are tole that they can not get anything to do up there and they are being snatched off the trains here in Greenville and a rested but in spite of all this, they are leaving every day and every night 100 or more is expecting to leave this week. Let me here from you at once.

---

Emmett J. Scott, "Letters of Negro Migrants of 1916-1918," *Journal of Negro History*, Vol. 4 (July, 1919), p. 435, published by the Association for the Study of Negro Life and History, Inc. Reprinted by permission.

## *President Wilson and Segregation*

[*Soon after he became President, Woodrow Wilson segregated Washington's federal employees. In November, 1913, a Negro delegation protested this action. A year later they returned to receive the President's answer. Editor Monroe Trotter of the Boston* Guardian *speaks for the delegates.*]

[*Mr. Monroe Trotter.*] Mr. President, we are here to renew our protest against the segregation of colored employees in the departments of our National Government. We [had] appealed to you to undo this race segregation in accord with your duty as President and with your pre-election pledges to colored American voters. We stated that such segregation was a public humiliation and degradation, and entirely unmerited and far-reaching in its injurious effects. . . .

[*President Woodrow Wilson.*] The white people of the country, as well as I, wish to see the colored people progress, and admire the progress they have already made, and want to see them continue along independent lines. There is, however, a great prejudice against colored people. . . . It will take one hundred years to eradicate this prejudice, and we must deal with it as practical men. Segregation is not humiliating but a benefit, and ought to be so regarded by you gentlemen. If your organization goes out and tells the colored people of the country that it is a humiliation, they will so regard it, but if you do not tell them so, and regard it rather as a benefit, they will regard it the same. The only harm that will come will be if you cause them to think it is a humiliation.

[*Mr. Monroe Trotter.*] It is not in accord with the known facts to claim that the segregation was started because of race friction of white and colored [federal] clerks. The indisputable facts of the situation will not permit of the claim that the segregation is due to the friction. It is untenable, in view of the established facts, to maintain that the segregation is simply to avoid race friction, for the simple reason that for fifty years white and colored clerks have been working together in peace and harmony and friendliness, doing so even through two [President Grover Cleveland] Democratic administrations. Soon after your inauguration began, segregation was drastically introduced in the Treasury and Postal departments by your appointees.

[*President Woodrow Wilson.*] If this organization is ever to have another hearing before me it must have another spokesman. Your manner offends me. . . . Your tone, with its background of passion.

[*Mr. Monroe Trotter.*] But I have no passion in me, Mr. President, you are entirely mistaken; you misinterpret my earnestness for passion.

*The Crisis,* Vol. 9 (January, 1915), pp. 119-120. Reprinted by permission.

## *Trouble with Mexico, 1916*

[*Just prior to World War I, American-Mexican relations became strained. Mexican bandits crossed into American territory and United States troops crossed into Mexico in pursuit of them. One of the most famous incidents of this time was the battle between Negro 10th Cavalry troops and Mexicans on June 21, 1916. Lance Corporal John A. Jeter, Jr., who took over command when his white officers were killed or wounded, describes the scene.*]

. . . The [Mexican] General informed Captain Boyd [in charge of troops K and C of the 10th Cavalry] that if he attempted to pass he would be compelled to fire upon him. Captain Boyd replied that "that made no difference as he intended to go through and was going to make the attempt." The General and his staff then returned to their troops; Captain Boyd returned to his troop. . . . After I joined the troop the command was given "Prepare to fight on foot, Action right." . . . We advanced between 25 and 50 yards toward the Mexican line when they opened fire upon us. We all fell prone and Captain Boyd gave the command "Commence firing." After two or three seconds, he gave the command to rush from the right. After the second rush, the Captain said he was shot. They opened on us at 200 yards with two machine guns. I shot one of the machine gun operators; this put the gun out of action. After the Captain said he was shot, he said "jump them, boys, jump them." About the same time Sergeant Winrow remarked that he was shot but said it was not serious and for us to go ahead. . . . We drove practically everything in front of us up to the town. . . .

Deposition of Lance Corporal John Jeter, Jr. (Washington: National Archives, War Records Office, June 27, 1916). This deposition was recorded by Colonel Charles Young, highest ranking Negro officer in the United States Army at the time.

# American Intervention in Latin America

[*In the last decade of the 19th century and the early decades of the 20th century, American interest in Latin America grew to the point of military occupation of various countries. The purpose of this "big stick" or "dollar diplomacy" was to protect American business interests in Latin America or control the nations near our Panama Canal. United States control of the Negro Republic of Haiti lasted from 1915 to 1934. It was investigated by Negro poet and diplomat James Weldon Johnson, formerly United States Consul to Venezuela, Nicaragua, and the Azores. This is part of Johnson's report.*]

To know the reasons for the present political situation in Haiti, to understand why the United States landed and has for five years maintained military forces in that country, why some three thousand Haitian men, women, and children have been shot down by American rifles and machine guns, it is necessary, among other things, to know that the National City Bank of New York is very much interested in Haiti. It is necessary to know that the National City Bank controls the National Bank of Haiti . . . and that Mr. R. L. Farnham, vice-president of the National City Bank, is virtually the representative of the State Department in matters relating to the island republic. . . .

. . . since July 28, 1915, American military forces have been in control of Haiti. These forces have been increased until there are now somewhere near three thousand Americans under arms in the republic. From the very first, the attitude of the Occupation has been that it was dealing with a conquered territory. Haitian forces were disarmed, military posts and barracks occupied, and the National Palace was taken as headquarters for the Occupation. After selecting a new and acceptable president for the country, steps were at once taken to compel the Haitian government to sign a convention in which it virtually foreswore its independence. . . .

. . . brutalities and atrocities on the part of American marines have occurred with sufficient frequency to be the cause of deep resentment and terror. Marines talk freely of what they "did" to some Haitians in the outlying districts. . . . I often sat at tables in the hotels and cafes in company with marine officers and they talked before me without restraint. I remember the description of a "caco" hunt by one of them; he told how they finally came upon a crowd of natives . . . and how they "let them have it" with machine guns and rifle fire. . . .

Perhaps the most serious aspect of American brutality [is shown in the remarks of an American officer who said] . . . "The trouble with this whole business is that some of these people with a little money and education think they are as good as we are," and this is the keynote of the attitude of every American to every Haitian. Americans have carried American hatred to Haiti. They have planted the feeling of caste and color prejudice where it never before existed. . . .

If the United States should leave Haiti today [1920], it would leave more than a thousand widows and orphans of its own making, more banditry than has existed for a century, resentment, hatred, and despair in the heart of a whole people, to say nothing of the irreparable injury to its own tradition as the defender of the rights of man.

James Weldon Johnson, "Self-Determining Haiti," *The Nation*, Vol. 111 (August 28, 1920 and September 4, 1920), pp. 236-237, 266-267. Reprinted by permission.

# The Negro Silent Parade of July 28, 1917

[*Soon after the United States entered World War I, 15,000 Negroes marched down Fifth Avenue to protest the continued lynchings and discrimination faced by them. While they marched in silence their message of protest was expressed by their signs and in this leaflet which they distributed to the crowds of spectators.*]

We march because by the grace of God and the force of truth the dangerous, hampering walls of prejudice and inhuman injustices must fall.

We march because we want to make impossible a repetition of Waco, Memphis, and East St. Louis [anti-Negro riots] by arousing the conscience of the country, and to bring the murderers of our brothers, sisters, and innocent children to justice.

We march because we deem it a crime to be silent in the face of such barbaric acts.

We march because we are thoroughly opposed to Jim Crow cars, segregation, discrimination, disfranchisement, lynching, and the host of evils that are forced on us. It is time that the spirit of Christ should be manifested in the making and execution of laws.

We march because we want our children to live in a better land and enjoy fairer conditions than have fallen to our lot.

*Why We March*, Leaflet.

# Behind the Lines: Discrimination in France

[*Howard H. Long, who served as an officer during the First World War, recalled the conditions imposed on himself and other Negro soldiers by the United States Army in France.*]

. . . Many of the field officers seemed far more concerned with reminding their Negro subordinates that they were Negroes than they were with having an effective unit that would perform well in combat. There was extreme concern lest the Negro soldiers be on too friendly terms with the French people. An infamous order from division headquarters . . . made speaking to a French woman a disciplinary offense. . . .

We were billeted in Joneville, Haute Marne [France], for a period of training, where the men moved freely among the populace. For no obvious reason we were moved out on the drill ground a quarter of a mile away and even the officers were forbidden to return to the village. When the townspeople came out on the following Sunday they found that the Negro soldiers had been prohibited from meeting and talking with them. . . . One officer was put under arrest, guarded by a private with fixed bayonet, because the commanding officer saw him exchange a note with a French lady across the line. . . .

Howard H. Long, "The Negro Soldier in the Army of the United States," *Journal of Negro Education*, Vol. 12 (Summer, 1943), pp. 311-312. Reprinted by permission.

## *The 369th and 371st Win the Croix de Guerre*

[*During World War I 100,000 Negroes served abroad. The 369th Regiment set a record of 191 days on the firing line without losing a foot of ground or a single prisoner. The 371st won 121 French and 27 American Distinguished Service Crosses. Both entire units won the French Cross of War with these citations.*]

[*369th Infantry . . . French croix de guerre with silver star. . . .*]
Under the command of Colonel Hayward, who although wounded, insisted on leading his regiment into combat . . . and Major Little, a real leader of men, the 369th Regiment of American Infantry, under fire for the first time, captured some powerful and energetically defended enemy positions, took the village of Sechault by main force, and brought back six cannon, mainly machine guns, and a number of prisoners.

[*371st Infantry . . . French croix de guerre with palm. . . .*]
Under the command of Colonel Miles, this regiment, with superb spirit and admirable disregard for danger rushed to the assault of a strongly defended enemy position which it captured after a hard struggle under a violent machine-gun fire. It then continued its advance, in spite of the enemy artillery fire and heavy losses, taking numerous prisoners, capturing cannon, machine guns, and important material.

*General Orders No. 11*, United States War Department (Washington: National Archives, March 27, 1924), pp. 22-23.

# 16

# *The Twenties*

IN 1919, triumphant armies of khaki-clad soldiers passed in review down New York's Fifth Avenue to the cheers of thousands of citizens crowding the sidewalks. It was generally agreed that one of the most thrilling sights and sounds was that of the 369th Colored Infantry swinging up the Avenue toward Harlem, marching to the syncopated beat of Jim Europe's blaring jazz band. Adults tapped their feet to the new sound and schoolchildren followed the solid ranks of marching men. Yet, soon after the victory parades ended, Negro soldiers like these, all over the country—in big cities and tiny towns —would be forced to defend their very lives.

## *The Growth of Intolerance*

A fearful wave of lynchings and anti-Negro violence swept the nation. Ignorant, hate-filled whites, afraid that these returned Negro soldiers would insist on fair treatment as men and as citizens, decided that now was the time "to keep them from stepping out of their place." Discharged Negro soldiers, some still in uniform, were among the victims of these rampaging white mobs.

By the summer of 1919 bloody rioting had taken place in Chicago, Illinois; Omaha, Nebraska; Longview, Texas; Washington, D.C., and Elaine, Arkansas. Negroes were dragged from streetcars, beaten on the sidewalks, or attacked in their homes.

*The 369th Regiment marches up New York's Fifth Avenue in 1919. They had learned their close-order march from the French.*

An investigator for the NAACP wrote from Arkansas: "The police and deputy sheriff either refuse to check the mobs or [they] join hands with the mobs." In Elaine, 68 Negro sharecroppers meeting in a church to form a union, were fired on by sheriff's deputies. The sheriff claimed that the people in the church had fired first, but he was never able to explain why he and his men just happened to be outside the church on the particular night the meeting was being held. A dozen Negro leaders were then arrested and afterward sentenced to death for firing back and killing one of the attackers, and 67 of the Negro farmers were sentenced to life imprisonment or long terms in prison. The church was later burned down by lynch mobs and in the reign of terror that followed "men and women were shot down in the fields like wild beasts," numbers were rounded up and "penned in stockades in Little Rock." Two whites later admitted using torture to force confessions from the Negro sharecroppers. Only after the NAACP provided lawyers and brought the facts to the public were all the defendants eventually liberated.

"The land of liberty is in danger of becoming the land of lynchers," warned Kelly Miller of Howard University. The Ku Klux Klan enjoyed a spectacular rise in membership and power during and after the war. This growth had been partly stimulated by the

1915 movie *Birth of a Nation*, which showed columns of heroic hooded Klansmen galloping through the night to save civilization.

By the time the war in Europe had ended, the Klan had extended its hate campaign to include Catholics, immigrants, Jews, Orientals, union leaders, and "radicals" of all types. Klan officials claimed a membership of 5 million, and branches were set up in Northern cities and towns. The flaming cross—the Klan's warning to all those it opposed—burned from New York to Oregon as well as in Mississippi. Klan power stretched from Maine to California and from local sheriffs to the United States Senate. It was as influential in Indiana as in Georgia. D. C. Stephenson, Grand Dragon of the half-million strong Indiana Klan, proclaimed, "I am the law in Indiana." Klan leaders became rich selling membership cards for ten dollars and special Klan regalia for six. Stephenson was said to have made two million dollars in one period of eighteen months. Klan floggings in Oklahoma in 1923 numbered 2,500.

That same year the governor of Oregon and the mayor of Portland attended a dinner for the Grand Dragon of the Oregon Klan and the governor spoke on "Americanism."

By August 8, 1925, the KKK was able to assemble 40,000 members for a parade through Washington, D.C. From midafternoon to dusk, robed men and women marched, arms folded across their chests, past the Capitol. Grim-faced Washington Negroes

*James Weldon Johnson, first Negro executive director of the NAACP, led the campaign to halt violence against Negroes by the Ku Klux Klan.*

stood in the crowds. One of them recalled, "We were ready to fight if they broke ranks. We didn't know anything about nonviolence in those days." In fact, the only violence that day was the thunderstorm that greeted the Klan effort to hold an outdoor meeting. No word came from the White House. President Calvin Coolidge was out of town that weekend. But no President in office during the entire period raised his voice against the Ku Klux Klan.

The anti-Negro violence and the rise in Klan popularity were part of a general era of racial fear and hatred that infected the country following World War I. Congress curtailed immigration. Employers began a campaign to smash unions which they claimed were being run by "foreign agitators." Newcomers to American soil were called "hyphenated Americans." After the 1917 Communist Revolution in Russia, any person with liberal or radical ideas had become "dangerous" or "subversive" in the minds of many. The Attorney-General of the United States, A. Mitchell Palmer, said that the Communists planned some revolutionary actions for May 1, 1919. Although May 1 came and went peacefully, Palmer's fear remained.

In his search for "dangerous radicals," the Attorney-General investigated "Radicalism and Sedition Among the Negroes as Reflected in Their Publications." Magazines such as the *Messenger*, *Emancipator*, *Challenge*, and *Crusader* were found to have subversive purposes, including an "openly expressed demand for social equality." In his report Palmer stated that the publications also had the wrong attitude toward race riots, lynchings, the Russian Revolution, the League of Nations, "the present Federal administration, [and] the South in general." The Attorney-General also found something sinister in the fact that the Negro magazines were written in "fine, pure English, with a background of scholarship" by highly educated men. When a Justice Department official asked the editor of *The Crisis* what the purpose of his magazine was, Dr. Du Bois replied that it was to uphold the United States Constitution and all of its Amendments.

Beginning in the 1920's a number of Negroes did become interested in radical political groups. Ben Fletcher was the only Negro among 101 leaders of the fiercely radical "Wobblies," the Industrial Workers of the World (IWW), who were sentenced to long prison terms for opposing World War I. The Socialist Party appealed to all workers and refused to see the Negro as a special group. When their executive board was asked by a group of foreign Socialists what their solution to lynching was, they answered "*socialism*." Some Socialists did not attempt to conceal their bias. Jack London, for example, said, "I am first of all a white man and only then a socialist." Yet the Socialists had many Negro intellectuals as members.

If Negroes did not respond to the Socialist program, they felt great personal warmth for Eugene V. Debs, longtime leader of the party and five times its presidential candidate. Debs was one of those sentenced to prison for opposing American participation in World War I. Sam Morre, a Negro life-termer he met in prison, said, "Gene Debs was the only Jesus Christ I ever knew." When Debs died in 1924, *Crisis* editor W. E. B. Du Bois wrote: "The death of so great a mind and so great a heart as that of Eugene Debs is a calamity to this poor nation." All through his long career Debs had refused to speak to segregated audiences, and demanded that the labor movement treat Negroes as equals. But, like the other Socialist leaders, he did not feel that the oppression of the Negro was any worse than that experienced by all workers "under capitalism."

The Communist Party advocated a special program designed to attract the Negro. Negroes, they said, should have the right to form a separate republic in those sections of the South where they are a majority of the residents. By 1928, however, there were fewer than 200 Negro Communists. Negroes, pointed out some of their leaders, had enough trouble being black without being "red" as well. But, during the acute economic distress of the depression, such illustrious Negro figures as Paul Robeson and Richard Wright were among those who found communism or socialism attractive. After many years of criticizing Communist tactics, William Du Bois, at 93, joined the American Communist party. A gesture of defiance, this action took place just before he left for Africa where he died two years later.

Among the more curious of the radical movements following World War I was the one led by a pudgy, moon-faced Jamaican Negro, Marcus Garvey. He announced himself to the American public as "The Provisional President of Africa" and toured 38 states to spread his campaigns for Negro improvement and an exodus "back to Africa." In August 1920, fifty thousand "Garveyites" paraded through New York's Harlem behind their leader who was dressed "in a dazzling uniform of purple, green, and black, with gold braid, and a thrilling hat with white plumes." More than a million joined Garvey's Universal Negro Improvement Society—most of them the poor who lived in the North's ghettos. Garvey rejected light-skinned Negroes in favor of "pure Africans"—like himself.

In his newspaper *The Negro World*, and in many speeches, Garvey preached of the need for racial pride. He said the Negro would never be free except in Africa under his own chosen leaders.

*Marcus Garvey.*

He was optimistic about the Negro takeover of Africa: "It is in the wind. It is coming. One day, like a storm, it will be here." Negro parents, schooled and unschooled, urged their children to learn all they could of the past glories of Africa and of America's black heroes. Ernestine Rose, the Jewish immigrant who became director of the branch public library in Harlem, reported an "intense interest" by Negroes "in works on the Negro, his history, race achievements, and present problems." Her Thursday night forums were packed with people asking "some of the most intelligent questions I ever heard."

Although his "black exodus" to Africa never took place, Garvey had stimulated great interest and argument. Some called him a "Jamaican jackass" and A. Philip Randolph warned Negroes that their control of Africa would not "bring liberation to Africa, for Negro exploiters and tyrants are as bad as white ones." But in 1922 the federal government stepped in after repeated complaints by Negro investors of possible fraud in the financial arrangements of Garvey's great dream—the Black Star Steamship Line.

He was indicted on charges of using the mails to defraud and brought to trial in 1923. He insisted on conducting his own defense. He did a poor job. Wrote a Negro reporter: "He convicted himself by his own admissions, his swaggering monkey-shines in the courtroom . . . and his insults to the judge and prosecuting attorney." He was sentenced to five years in prison. Garvey delayed going to the federal penitentiary at Atlanta until 1925 by legal manipulations and, after two years in prison, he was pardoned by President Coolidge and deported to Jamaica.

Because he had appealed to his people's pride in their race and history, Garvey had aroused millions. Although not a single Negro, not even Garvey himself, emigrated to Africa as a result of his work, he had stirred the hopes of many—stirred their imaginations, as no one had ever done before.

## Gangster Days in Chicago

In the decade following the outbreak of the war in Europe more than one million Negroes migrated from the South to Northern cities. Because they were just off the farms and colored, they were restricted to the worst jobs, neighborhoods, and schools. Crime grew in all city slums but Negro crime was splashed over the front pages of the newspapers. Authorities noted that while Negroes were only 9 per cent of the population, they represented 23 per cent of the prison population. They ignored the part that discrimination, even in law enforcement, played in piling up these statistics. "Negroes are more likely to be arrested on suspicion than white persons," stated Judge Kickham Scanlon of the Chicago courts. And his colleague Judge Hugo Pam said "the colored man starts with a great handicap" because there is "great prejudice" against him.

Those few Negroes who did turn to crime found that the whites had control of the most lucrative rackets. No Negro crook ever had the money or the power of an Al Capone. John "Mushmouth" Johnson was one of the few Negro racketeers to come anywhere near the "big time." He explained his career in crime in these words: "While my family went in for religion and all that, I didn't exactly fancy so much book learning and went out to see where the money grew. Some of those who know me say that I found it." By the time he died in 1907, his gambling and saloon establishments had become popular among whites, Negroes, and Orientals.

Johnson's remark to losers is still remembered: "A man that gambles had better be without money anyway. I may put it to some good use; you wouldn't know how." He made a quarter of a million dollars from his various illegal operations in this underworld which was dominated by whites. Along with other Chicago gangsters of the time, he contributed to both the Democratic and Republican parties and was tipped off well in advance about police raids.

During Prohibition, Chicago racketeers of both races made and sold bootleg liquor, gunned down their competitors in the streets, and were carted off to prison by federal agents. Some ended up in Lake Michigan wearing "cement shoes." Only a rare few lived out normally long lives as "respectable citizens" and died natural deaths.

Dan Jackson, a graduate of Lincoln University, became the leading Negro racketeer of the Roaring Twenties. He, like John "Mushmouth" Johnson, never made more than a quarter of a million dollars from his Chicago bootlegging and gambling syndicate. Jackson provided coal for the poor and often paid their rent bills. He contributed to various charities and made donations to the NAACP. Along with Al Capone's representative, he sat on the local Republican committee that picked candidates for public office. The Governor appointed Jackson to the Illinois Commerce Commission.

Jackson was himself a victim as well as an overlord of Chicago crime. He was once held up on the steps of City Hall and relieved of $25,000 in cash. It has never been explained what he was doing at City Hall with so much cash and whether he was going in or coming out. When he died in 1929 (of natural causes), he was sixty years old and under indictment. His friends on both sides of the law gave him "a grand funeral."

More than a hundred Negroes were part of Chicago's overworked police force during this prolonged crime wave. Some were among those accused of "going around collecting graft money," but most did their best to foil crime, arrest criminals, and halt graft. Like most white policemen, they were hardworking, dedicated lawmen in a lawless city.

## The Negro Renaissance

While crimes of violence scarred all the big cities, a movement of great importance to America was getting under way in New York, particularly in the Negro ghetto of Harlem. In the decade of prosperity and easy money that followed World War I, the white population had enough cash in their pockets to make a pastime out of finding new ways in which to spend it. Plays and movies boomed as they rarely had before. The dance halls around Broadway were packed to the doors by high school students and their grandparents dancing afternoon and evening to the new jazz. Although the world credited the fox trot to the famous dance team of Vernon and Irene Castle, the Castles credited bandleader Jim Europe. And the thousands who had thrilled to his jazz band's music as they marched up Fifth Avenue at the head of the 369th Colored Infantry after the war could now dance to his orchestra at the Winter Garden.

A new age had come to the American theater. At Greenwich Village's Provincetown Playhouse, a young man named Eugene

*Jim Europe's Army band brought American jazz music to France and back to New York. Vernon and Irene Castle credited Europe with teaching them the fox trot, which they taught to the world.*

O'Neill was writing plays which used the decks of oil tankers or tenements in Harlem as settings, rather than the usual fancy living rooms and gardens of the rich. Some of his plays called for Negroes in important roles and Charles Gilpin made an astonishing success in O'Neill's *Emperor Jones*, which was first produced in 1920 and filled the theater for the next four years.

On Broadway the hit of the 1921 season was a sparkling musical with an all-Negro cast, *Shuffle Along*. Its star, Florence Mills, was a tiny young lady of many talents. All America sang its lead song, *I'm Just Wild About Harry*. Virtually every year in the Twenties saw another Broadway hit with either an all-Negro cast or many Negroes featured in leading roles: *Liza*, *Running Wild* (which gave the world the Charleston dance), *Chocolate Dandies*, *Porgy*, and *Green Pastures*.

*All-American football star Paul Robeson became a famous actor and singer. His support of radical causes hurt his popularity.*

In 1924 at the Provincetown Playhouse in Greenwich Village, another young Negro actor, a husky, former All-American football star named Paul Robeson, made history in O'Neill's *All God's Chillun Got Wings*. He later played Gilpin's role in a revival of *Emperor Jones*. Robeson then won tremendous applause for his singing role in the musical hit *Showboat* on Broadway. In 1930 his fame became worldwide when he starred in a London production of Shakespeare's *Othello*.

The significance of the Negro contribution to the dramas of the Twenties was stated by critic James Weldon Johnson, himself a poet, songwriter, and novelist:

> In *Porgy* the Negro removed any lingering doubts as to his ability to do intelligent acting. In *Green Pastures* he established conclusively his capacity to get the utmost across the footlights, to convey the most delicate nuances of emotion, to create the atmosphere in which the seemingly unreal becomes for the audience the most real thing in life.

Soon whites seeking to see "Negro life," entertainers, or jazz bands began taking the short subway ride up to Harlem. They crowded the dance floors of the night clubs and enjoyed the spectacular floor shows. The white owners of Harlem's night spots responded

*As James Weldon Johnson looks on, conductor Walter Damrosch congratulates tenor Roland Hayes for winning the Spingarn Medal awarded each year by the NAACP to an outstanding Negro. Johnson was also a Spingarn Medal winner, and a noted song writer, poet, critic, and diplomat.*

by offering new and bigger clubs. The best-known of these excluded Negroes. Even W. C. Handy, composer of the *St. Louis Blues* and hundreds of other songs, accompanied by the white director of the American Society of Composers, Authors and Publishers (ASCAP), could not get into one of these clubs where Handy's music was being featured. "Harlem," complained poet Claude McKay, "is an all-white picnic ground with no apparent gain to the blacks."

But this was an exaggeration. While the average Negro received no more money in his pay envelope as a result of all this white attention, talented Negroes found a new audience. Some of the whites who had come uptown for fun returned to study and learn. A few became patrons of Negro poets, artists, novelists, and playwrights.

The three young poet-heroes of this Negro Renaissance were Claude McKay from the West Indies, Langston Hughes from Missouri, and Countee Cullen from New York. All came to stay in Harlem—as did thousands of less famous Negroes pouring up from the South. Mainly in poetry, but also in short stories, novels, and essays, these three expressed the new mood of rugged determination to overcome the Jim Crow system. "We younger Negro artists who create intend to express our individual dark-skinned selves without fear or shame," wrote Langston Hughes, a descendant of a Negro who died with John Brown and another who served as a Virginia Congressman. "If white people are pleased we are glad. If they are not, it doesn't matter."

Although the three had a sizable white audience unmatched by any Negro since Paul Lawrence Dunbar, they faced limitations that angered them. "The more truthfully we write about ourselves," said

*Langston Hughes. He preferred the parties used by Harlem's poor to raise rent money to the fancy face Harlem put on for its many white visitors during the 1920's.*

Langston Hughes, "the more limited our market becomes." And he much preferred the "rent-parties" of Harlem's poor, given to help raise rent money, to the sights and sounds of the white man's Harlem.

Sometime after the 1929 stock market crash, the Renaissance began to fade. "For how could a large and enthusiastic number of people be crazy about Negroes forever?" asked Langston Hughes. "The white people had much less money to spend on themselves, and practically none to spend on Negroes, for the depression had brought everybody down a peg or two. And the Negroes had but few pegs to fall." But between 1914 and 1924 no Negro novels had been published. In the next ten years twenty appeared.

## The Frustrating Fight for Rights

During the 1920's American Negroes battled against overwhelming odds to secure their rights and there were some outstanding successes in business. By the mid-1920's there were 25 Negro-owned insurance companies carrying policies amounting to two billion dollars. By 1928 Negroes owned 50 banks and 25 insurance companies. In New York the Black Swan Company sold 7,000 records a day. Walter H. Lee of Chicago ran a fleet of cabs.

Success in business, however, did not lead to civil rights victories, especially in the South. In Mobile, Alabama only 135 of the city's 30,000 Negroes were permitted to vote. In Birmingham it was 300 out of 80,000. Mrs. Indiana Little, a Birmingham schoolteacher, tried to organize a voter registration drive among her people in 1925. When she led them to the city hall to register, she was arrested and jailed for "disorderly conduct."

The battle for rights in the North achieved some success by 1930. In 1921 an antilynching bill passed the House of Representatives by a vote of 230 to 119, only to be filibustered to death in the Senate. But by 1930 a Negro, Oscar DePriest, sat in the United States Congress and fourteen more were in state legislatures of five Northern states and two Southern border states. The NAACP successfully led a campaign to defeat a Supreme Court nomination of President Herbert Hoover. He had asked the Senate to confirm the nomination of Judge John J. Parker who had once stated that Negroes should not vote for their own good and that of the country. Parker was defeated by a Senate vote of 41 to 39 and a Southern

*Washington, D. C. Negroes parade against the rise in postwar lynchings, part of the NAACP campaign to have Congress pass the Dyer antilynching bill. The House passed it by an overwhelming majority, but it was filibustered to death by Southern Senators.*

newspaper credited the NAACP for being the force that "broke his back."

In 1930 a Chicago Negro newspaper, the *Whip*, led a boycott of stores that did not hire Negroes. By the end of its fifth month, the boycott had led to the hiring of one thousand Negroes. Du Bois called the boycott "one tremendous and most effective weapon" and voiced the hope that "this is but the beginning."

The most dramatic affirmation of human rights took place in Detroit, shortly after Labor Day, 1925. Dr. Ossian Sweet, who had recently returned from Paris where he had studied the effect of radium with Madam Curie, purchased a home in a white neighborhood. He waited nine months for his neighbors-to-be to settle down before he moved in. But all during this time Mrs. Sweet received threatening calls predicting her death and the destruction of their new home.

On September 8, 1925, the Sweets moved in, bringing along guns, ammunition, and a few relatives and friends to stand by them in case of trouble. The first night a small crowd gathered. The next night the mob grew menacing.

At 8:25 P.M. a car filled with Negroes who had come to reinforce the Sweets arrived in front of the house. The mob charged to the door after the newcomers. "It looked like a human sea," Dr. Sweet later testified. "When I opened the door and saw the mob, I realized that I was facing the same mob that had hounded my people through its entire history. In my mind I was pretty confident of what I was up against. I had my back against the wall. I was filled with a peculiar fear, the fear of one who knows the history of my race. I knew what mobs had done to my race before."

Almost as soon as Dr. Sweet had let in his friends and shut the door on the mob, shots rang out from outside and from an upstairs window. A white man fell dead in the street. The police, who had done nothing to disperse the mob, arrested everyone in the house, including Mrs. Sweet. The entire group was charged with murder.

The NAACP hired Clarence Darrow to defend the Sweets. He faced many white witnesses who denied that there had even been a mob outside the Sweets' home that evening. Darrow pointed out that the prosecution had "put on enough witnesses who said they were there, to make a mob." He stressed that the man killed could not be "innocent" for no person in such a mob was innocent. His final point was simply that a Negro had as much right to defend his home as a white. The jury agreed and the Sweets went free. It was a historic occasion.

## *The 369th Swings* Up *Fifth Avenue*

*[The author's father was a New York City high school student during World War I. Here he tells of the memorable day on which the city welcomed home the 15th Infantry (Colored) National Guard of New York, which had become the 369th United States Infantry.]*

I was strolling up Fifth Avenue on February 17, 1919, during lunchtime, with a lot of my buddies from school, when we heard the fanfare of the bugles and the booming drums of a marching band. I can't remember if the papers had said anything about a parade. There were lots of them before, during, and after the war and, it seems to me, generally without as much advance publicity and hullabaloo as is thought necessary nowadays to guarantee record-breaking crowds. Even before the troops appeared, the sidewalks were jammed from buildings to curbs with spectators, for there was something odd about this parade right from the start. Most of the other parades came *down* Fifth Avenue—this one was moving uptown!

We soon saw why. Back from the Rhine to get the applause of their city and of Harlem were the troops known in France as the 369th U.S. Infantry, but known in New York as the Harlem Hell Fighters.

Not till many years later would I understand the reason for the great impression of steel-helmeted *power*, those of us on the sidelines got that day. The 369th was marching in a formation unfamiliar to most American troops, and certainly to the public until that day. Because the 369th had been segregated from the rest of the American forces and had served under the French command, they were marching in the extraordinarily dramatic Phalanx formation of the French Army. Shoulder to shoulder, from curb to curb, they stretched in great massed squares, thirty-five feet wide by thirty-five feet long, of men, helmets, and bayonets. Through the newly erected Victory Arch at 25th Street and Fifth, they tramped far up the Avenue in an endless mass of dark-skinned, grim-faced, heavy-booted veterans of many a French battlefield.

Then we heard the music! Somewhere in the line of march was Jim Europe and his band that the French had heard before we ever did. Major Little claims they played no jazz until they got to Harlem later that day—but if what we along the curbs heard was not jazz, it was the best substitute for it I've ever heard in my life. All I know is that my school friends and I stepped out into the middle of the street with great hordes of other spectators, and swung up Fifth Avenue behind the 369th and the fantastic sixty-piece band that was beating out those rhythms that could be heard all the way down at our end of the parade. As Major Little said later, on the "17th of February, 1919, New York City knew no color line."

## A Veteran Is Chased by a Mob

[*In Chicago, during a 1920 race riot, a Negro university student, working in a factory just outside the city, left work early, unaware of the riot that was in progress. As he was about to board a streetcar, he was attacked by about twenty young white men. He jumped into the car and they followed.*]

The motorman opened the door, and before they knew it I jumped out and ran up Fifty-first Street as fast as my feet could carry me. Gaining about thirty yards on them was a decided advantage, for one of them saw me and with the shout "There he goes!" the gang started after me. One, two, three, blocks went past in rapid succession. They came on shouting, "Stop him! Stop him!" I ran on the sidewalk and someone tried to trip me, but fortunately I anticipated his intentions and jumped into the road. . . .

Then I came to a corner where a drug-store was open and a woman standing outside. I slowed down and asked her to let me go in there, that a gang was chasing me; but she said I would not be safe there, so I turned off Fifty-first Street and ran down the side street. Here the road had been freshly oiled and I nearly took a "header" as I stepped in the first pool, but fortunately no accident happened. My strength was fast failing; the suggestion came into my mind to stop and give up or try to fight it out with the two or three who were still chasing me, but this would never do, as the odds were too great, so I kept on. My legs began to wobble, my breath came harder, and my heart seemed to be pounding like a big pump, while the man nearest me began to creep up on me. It was then that an old athletic maxim came into my mind—"He's feeling as tired as you." Besides, I thought, perhaps he smokes and boozes and his wind is worse than mine. Often in the last hundred yards of a quarter-mile that thought of my opponent's condition had brought forth the last efforts necessary for the final spurt. There was more than a medal at stake this time, so I stuck, and in a few strides more they gave up the chase. . . .

This is no place for a minister's son, I thought, and crept behind a fence and lay down among some weeds. . . .

My problem was to get home and to avoid meeting hostile elements. Temporarily I was safe in hiding, but I could not stay there after daybreak. So I decided to wait a couple of hours and then try to pass through "No Man's Land"—Halsted to Wentworth. I figured the time to be about 11:30 and so decided to wait until 1:30 or 2:00 A.M., before coming out of cover. Shots rang out intermittently; the sky became illumined; the fire bells rang, and I imagined riot and arson held sway as of the previous year. . . .

Then the injustice of the whole thing overwhelmed me—emotions ran riot. Had the ten months I spent in France been all in vain? Were those little white crosses over the dead bodies of those dark-skinned boys lying in Flanders fields for naught? Was democracy merely a hollow sentiment? What had I done to deserve such treatment? I lay there experiencing all the emotions I imagined the innocent victim of a southern mob must feel when being hunted for some supposed crime. Was this what I had given up my Canadian citizenship for, to become an American citizen and soldier? Was the risk of life in a country where such hatred existed worth while? Must a Negro always suffer merely because of the color of his skin? . . .

. . . with resources at an end, I picked up four rocks for ammunition and started out. . . .

At State and Thirty-seventh I saw two colored fellows waiting for a car and ran up to them. Putting my hands on their shoulders I said, "Gee! I'm glad to see a dark skin." . . . They assured me the "fun" was all over, and I was thankful. . . . A white man came along, and my first impulse was to jump on him and beat him up. But again reason told me he was not responsible for the actions of a gang of rowdies, and he was as innocent as I had been when set upon.

The Chicago Commission on Race Relations, *The Negro in Chicago, a Study of Race Relations and a Race Riot* (Chicago: The University of Chicago Press, 1922), pp. 481-484. Reprinted by permission.

# A Woman's View of the 1919 Riots

[*In this moving letter to the editor of* The Crisis, *a Negro woman tells why she is happy that Negroes fought back against their oppressors in the Washington, D.C. riot of 1919.*]

The Washington riot gave me the *thrill that comes once in a life time.* I . . . read between the lines of our morning paper that at last our men had stood like men, struck back, were no longer dumb driven cattle. When I could no longer read for my streaming tears, I stood up, alone in my room, held both hands high over my head and exclaimed aloud: "Oh I thank God, thank God." . . . Only colored women of the South know the extreme in suffering and humiliation.

We know how many insults we have borne silently, for we have hidden many of them from our men because we did not want them to die needlessly in our defense . . . , the deep humiliation of sitting in the Jim Crow part of a street car and hear the white men laugh and discuss us, point out the good and bad points of our bodies. . . .

And, too, a woman loves a strong man, she delights to feel that her man can protect her, fight for her if necessary, save her.

No woman loves a weakling, a coward be she white or black, and some of us have been near thinking our men cowards, but thank God for Washington colored men! All honor to them, for they first blazed the way and right swiftly did Chicago men follow [during the 1919 race riot]. They put new hope, a new vision into their almost despairing women.

God Grant that our men everywhere refrain from strife, provoke no quarrel, but that they protect their women and homes at any cost.

*A Southern Colored Woman*

---

*The Crisis,* Vol. 19 (November, 1919), p. 339. Reprinted by permission.

# Marcus Garvey: "The Negro Must Have a Country"

[*Marcus Garvey believed he was a black Moses chosen to lead his people back to Africa. In this magazine article he explained his beliefs to white Americans.*]

The Negro must have a country, and a nation of his own. If you laugh at the idea, then you are selfish and wicked, for you and your children do not intend that the Negro shall discommode you in yours. If you do not want him to have a country and a nation of his own; if you do not intend to give him equal opportunities in yours; then it is plain to see that you mean that he must die, even as the Indian to make room for your generations.

Why should the Negro die? Has he not served America and the world? Has he not borne the burden of civilization in this Western world for three hundred years? Has he not contributed his best to America? Surely all this stands to his credit, but there will not be enough room and the one answer is "find a place." We have found a place, it is Africa and as black men for three centuries have helped white men build America, surely generous and grateful white men will help black men build Africa. . . .

Let the Negroes have a Government of their own. Don't encourage them to believe that they will become social equals and leaders of the whites in America, without first on their own account proving to the world that they are capable of evolving a civilization of their own. . . .

---

Marcus Garvey, *An Appeal to the Soul of White America* (Baltimore: Soper Library, Morgan State University, 1923), n. p.

# The South During the 1920's

[*In 1929 Robert Bagnall, a Negro investigator for the NAACP, toured the South and wrote this report on conditions.*]

It is Mississippi. "*The* River" is on its annual rampage. Wastes of water spread over the landscape. Houses are submerged up to the second story. Boats have replaced automobiles and buggies. . . . At any time, any and every Negro may be impressed to save the levees. . . . Everywhere there is unrest and an atmosphere of fear and suspense. . . .

The railroad embankment runs like a ribbon flanked by the flowing waters—but as we get away from Vicksburg we find fields above ground. Looking out of my car window as my train scuttled across the state as if it feared the rising waters might engulf it, I was riveted by a scene in the field opposite me. A Negro was desperately fleeing. Behind him ran two white men. I saw the flashes of their pistols as they fired at him. All at once, he stumbled, threw up both arms and fell. In a moment he was on his feet once more. Again, the two whites running towards him blazed away, as he haltingly fled before them. My train whisked me out of sight and I shall never know whether the Negro was killed. He probably was. Who were the whites—officers or civilians? I shall never know. I scanned the papers for days afterwards but saw no word of what had happened. When I told my friend in Louisiana, he merely shrugged his shoulders and said—"Why, that was merely an incident"—a common one. "The world never hears of many things like that." In Baton Rouge they told me how Negroes dared not report whippings and lynchings. . . .

In the upper part of Louisiana—as in most places of the South —the whites believe that Chief Justice Taney's decision that "a Negro has no rights which a white man is bound to respect" yet holds. A Negro sued the parish for damages he had suffered. His was a good case. Therefore, persons close to the affairs of the parish determined to settle the matter out of court. They took him for a ride, flogged him until his clothing had been cut to ribbons and his back was in shreds, broke his arm, and ordered him never to return to the parish. The encouraging thing is that he has courage enough to continue his fight in court. I understand, too, action is to be started against his assailants whom he recognized, it is stated, as officers of the parish.

But it is "the magic city" of Birmingham which holds the prize for terrorism. There police and courts are run by that order of thugs —the Ku Klux Klan. Without provocation police shoot Negroes so frequently there, that it is no longer news. Negroes are beaten up daily for standing on the streets. Recently the police killed a school-teacher because he was standing on a corner and didn't move with sufficient alacrity at their orders.

This is a black picture but there is another side. Here and there citizens are protesting and acting against these injustices. . . . Negroes dare not speak. But now and then . . . white men both speak and act. Their numbers steadily increase. . . . Down in a college town in Tennessee white and colored college students met regularly, ate, drank, discussed, and played together—even to the extent of dancing until a nasty newspaper article frightened the authorities in their schools. . . . I know southern whites who have given up father, mother, home, and hopes of inheritance, in order to cling to their beliefs, that men and women are to be made comrades on the basis of congeniality regardless of color, "My father died in my arms without forgiving me," said one of these to me, "because of my position on race matters, but I am happy, for I have found something worthwhile in life." . . .

The most hopeful thing in the South, however, is the growing realization of colored people that without organization destined to mould public opinion, to modify laws, and to gain justice in courts and safety of life, limb and property, Negroes can have no freedom nor ending of danger. . . .

---

Robert W. Bagnall, "The Present South," *The Crisis*, Vol. 36 (September, 1929), pp. 303, 321-322. Reprinted by permission.

# *The Negro Reenters the United States Congress*

[*In 1928 Oscar DePriest of Chicago became the first Negro to be elected to Congress from the North and the first to be elected in the twentieth century. During his three terms in office, the Illinois Republican was America's only Negro Congressman. He was always aware of the fact that he represented more than the people of his district. This was clear when he took part in the Congressional debate about American occupation and treatment of Haiti, a Caribbean nation with a Negro population.*]

I . . . am very glad to see the gentlemen on the minority [Democratic] side of this House so solicitous about the condition of the black people of Haiti. I wish to God they were equally solicitous about the black people of America. We in America would like in some of the States of this country to have the right of self-determination also. The people of Haiti should have the right of self-determination under the broad principles laid down by our Constitution. . . .

This should apply to Haiti and also to every other class of people that God's sun shines on, and I am glad to see the gentlemen on the minority side of the House converted to the right way of thinking, for once in their lives, because I appreciate the condition of the black Americans, where they are denied the right of self-determination in almost every State south of the Mason and Dixon line, and I congratulate the gentlemen for starting in right in Haiti and conceding the common people the right of self-determination and hope it will spread to every State in America and that we will all enjoy the same rights and privileges.

*The Congressional Record*, Part I, 71st Congress, Second Session, pp. 912-913.

# *The "Negro Renaissance" in Harlem*

[*Poet, dramatist, novelist, and historian Langston Hughes was in his twenties when he took part in the "Negro Renaissance."*]

All of us know that the gay and sparkling life of the so-called Negro Renaissance of the 20's was not so gay and sparkling beneath the surface as it looked. . . .

It was a period when every season there was at least one hit play on Broadway acted by a Negro cast. And when books by Negro authors were being published with much greater frequency and much more publicity than ever before or since in history. It was a period when white writers wrote about Negroes more successfully (commercially speaking) than Negroes did about themselves. It was the period (God help us!) when Ethel Barrymore appeared in blackface in *Scarlet Sister Mary!* It was the period when the Negro was in vogue.

I was there. I had a swell time while it lasted. But I thought it wouldn't last long. . . . For how could a large and enthusiastic number of people be crazy about Negroes forever? But some Harlemites thought the millennium had come. They thought the race problem had at last been solved. . . . They were sure the New Negro would lead a new life from then on in green pastures of tolerance created by Countee Cullen, Ethel Waters, Claude McKay, Duke Ellington, Bojangles, and Alain Locke.

I don't know what made any Negroes think that—except that they were mostly intellectuals doing the thinking. The ordinary Negroes hadn't heard of the Negro Renaissance. And if they had, it hadn't raised their wages any. As for all those white folks in the speakeasies and night clubs of Harlem—well, maybe a colored man could find *some* place to have a drink that the tourists hadn't yet discovered.

Then it was that house-rent parties began to flourish—and not always to raise the rent either. But, as often as not, to have a get-together of one's own, where you could do the black-bottom with no stranger behind you trying to do it, too. . . .

The Saturday night rent parties that I attended were often more amusing than any night club, in small apartments where God knows who lived—because the guests seldom did—but where the piano would often be augmented by a guitar, or an odd cornet, or somebody with a pair of drums walking in off the street. And where awful bootleg whiskey and good fried fish or steaming chitterling were sold at very low prices. And the dancing and singing and impromptu entertaining went on until dawn came in at the windows. . . .

Almost every Saturday night when I was in Harlem I went to a house-rent party. I wrote lots of poems about house-rent parties, and ate thereat many a fried fish and pig's foot—with liquid refreshments on the side. I met ladies' maids and truck drivers, laundry workers and shoe shine boys, seamstresses and porters. I can still hear their laughter in my ears, hear the soft slow music, and feel the floor shaking as the dancers danced.

Langston Hughes, *The Big Sea, An Autobiography* (New York: Hill and Wang, 1963), pp. 227, 228-229, 233.

## *Trouble with the Angels*

[*One of the greatest hit shows of the Twenties was Marc Connelly's* Green Pastures. *It won the 1929 Pulitzer Prize for drama. For the first time in the history of the American theater, a Negro "Great God Almighty" and colored "Angels" were shown on the stage in a nonreligious show with music. The Negroes of Washington wrote to the show's management asking them to drop their discriminatory policies and allow Negroes to purchase tickets. When the management turned them down and the actor who played God refused to interfere, the Angels, led by a young actor named Johnny Logan, decided to strike for at least one night. Poet Langston Hughes tells of what followed.*]

Logan spent the whole day rallying the flagging spirits of his fellow actors. They were solid for the strike when he was around, and weak when he wasn't. . . .

"Listen here, you might as well get wise. Ain't nobody gonna strike tonight," one of the boys told him about six o'clock in the lobby of the colored Whitelaw Hotel. "You just as well give up. We ain't got no guts."

"I won't give up," said Logan.

When the actors reached the theatre, they found it surrounded by cops and the stage full of detectives. In the lobby there was a long line of people—white, of course—waiting to buy standing room. God arrived with motorcycle cops in front of his car. He had come a little early to address the cast. . . .

They called everybody together on the stage. The Lord wept as he spoke of all his race had borne to get where they were today. Of how they had struggled. Of how they sang. Of how they must keep on struggling and singing—until white folks saw the light. The strike would do no good. The strike would only hurt their cause. With sorrow in his heart—but more noble because of it—he would go on with the play. And he was sure his actors—his angels—his children—would, too.

The white men accompanying God were very solemn, also, as though hurt to their souls to think what their Negro employees were suffering—but far more hurt to think that they wanted to jeopardize a week's box office receipts by a strike! That would hurt everybody—*even white folks!*

All gave up but Logan. He went downstairs to fight . . . to carry through the strike. But he couldn't. Nobody really wanted to strike. . . .

The management sent two detectives downstairs to get Logan. They were taking no chances. Just as the curtain rose they dragged him off to jail—for disturbing the peace. All the other colored angels were massed in the wings for the opening spiritual when the police took the black boy out. They saw a line of tears running down his cheeks. Most of the actors thought he was crying because he was being arrested—and in their timid souls they were glad it wasn't them.

---

Langston Hughes, "Trouble with the Angels," *New Theatre*, Vol. 11, No. 7 (July, 1935), p. 7. Reprinted by permission of Harald Ober Associates.

# Dr. Du Bois Reviews Twenty Years of Progress

[*In 1929, on the 20th anniversary of the NAACP, Dr. Du Bois reviewed the gains made by his people.*]

Twenty years ago there was scarcely a reputable scientist who dared to assert the equality of the Negro race. . . . Africa was assumed to have no history and there was only one college in the United States that offered a course of study in Negro history and psychology. . . .

It was declared by all reputable authorities that the fate of the Negro race in the United States was extinction and death, and that what tuberculosis did not do, crime and inefficiency would finish. And finally, it was said by the Negroes themselves, almost unanimously, that real effective organization for the attainment of the rights of black men in America was impossible.

But we disregarded the advice of our friends. We went in for agitation. We pushed our way into the courts. We demanded the right to vote. We urged and pushed our children into college. We encouraged Negro art and literature. We studied African history and in season and out of season we declared that the colored races were destined at least to share in the heritage of the earth.

We stand today at the threshold of a new generation, with 12,000 of our children in college; with a recognized place in American literature and art; with the reappearance of the black man in Congress and, what is more important, with the emergence of an independent Negro vote. . . .

---

*Keynote address, 20th Anniversary NAACP Conference* (Washington: Library of Congress, Moorfield Storey Papers, Manuscript Collection, June 27, 1929).

# 17

# Depression and the New Deal

IN 1929 it seemed as though the prosperity and good times of the 1920's would never end. Behind the secret doors of "speakeasies" jazz bands played on. And in spite of Prohibition, Americans consumed more liquor and beer than they ever had before.

### The Depression

The stock market crash of 1929 brought America's most devastating depression to every doorstep. People were fired as factories closed. Across the nation Americans lined up for bread, milk, and jobs. Desperation born of hunger led some people to take matters into their own hands. By 1931 unemployed men, both Negro and white, entered an Oklahoma City grocery store and seized all the food they could carry. In Greenville, South Carolina 2,000 Negroes and whites marched to a local construction site to demand work. Then they sat down together to plan other actions for their economic relief. Even hooded Klansmen did not shake their unity.

The most dramatic demand for relief was the march of from 15,000 to 20,000 veterans of World War I on Washington in the spring of 1932. This Bonus Expeditionary Force (BEF) as it called itself was composed of unemployed Negro and white veterans demanding a bonus. Reporter Roy Wilkins, who later became executive director of the NAACP, toured the BEF tent camp in Washington and wrote an article about the march in *The Crisis*. While he found no discrimination, he noticed that the white veterans were bitter while "disappointment and disillusionment are an old story to the Negroes." Though these veterans did not get their bonus, they notified the government that it could not stand by while Americans starved or had no work.

The common misery of the depression helped to build a new unity among farmers, especially the mistreated sharecroppers. On a July evening in 1934, the Southern Tenant Farmer's Union was started in a dingy Arkansas schoolhouse. Old and young farmers of both races debated whether to break tradition and build one union. An old, white-haired, black sharecropper, who had seen his union wiped out in the 1919 Elaine, Arkansas massacre, rose to speak.

> We colored people can't organize without you and you white folks can't organize without us. Aren't we all brothers and ain't God the Father of us all? We live under the same sun, eat the same food, wear the same kind of clothes, work on the same land, raise the same crop for the same landlord who oppresses and cheats us both. For a long time now the white folks and the colored folks have been fighting each other and both

*A government supervisor leads a discussion on home management with a group of migratory workers. The New Deal took an interest in that part of the population that was ill-clad, ill-housed, and ill-fed.*

*A meeting of an agricultural workers' union in 1936. The pain brought on by hunger cut across racial lines and united white and black workers in the new unions of the CIO.*

of us has been getting whipped all the time. We don't have nothing against one another but we got plenty against the landlord. The same chain that holds my people holds your people too. If we're chained together on the outside, we ought to stay chained together in the union. It won't do no good for us to divide because there's where the trouble has been all the time. The landlord is always betwixt us, beatin' us and starvin' us, and makin' us fight each other. There ain't but one way for us to get him where he can't help himself and that's fer us to get together and stay together.*

* Mary White Ovington, *The Walls Came Tumbling Down* (New York: Harcourt, Brace & World, 1947), pp. 163-164. Reprinted by permission of the publisher.

After the old man sat down the farmers voted for one union for all. The common misery of economic depression had brought about a new unity.

After eight months of organizing tenant farmers, Ward Rodgers, a white organizer, reported that the Arkansas union had 10,000 members "and practically no friction over the race question." Rodgers told how Negroes were able to run meetings "as they should be run" because of the many clubs, burial societies, and organizations they had belonged to. But the white Southerners, complained the organizer, did not have this "training in correct procedures in meetings" because their only organization experience was as "members of the night-riding K.K.K." The Southern Tenant Farmers' Union and the depression had even united Klan members and Negroes!

However, when William Anderson, a nineteen-year-old Negro janitor in a white junior high school, led a voter registration drive in Greenville, South Carolina, he met with determined Klan opposition. The local Klan leader stopped Anderson as he led his people to register. The two men argued and Anderson shook his finger in the Klan leader's face. Eleven days later Anderson was arrested by police and charged with calling a white student on the phone and trying to make a date with her. He was quickly tried, found guilty, and given thirty days in jail.

The depression struck the country's Negroes with a greater force than the whites. For example, in Pittsburgh Negroes constituted 8 per cent of the population but 38 per cent of the unemployed in 1931 were Negroes. The Negro was the last to be hired, the first to be fired. He had less savings to fall back on than white workers. While all businesses suffered or went bankrupt during the depression, Negro-owned businesses were particularly hard hit because Negroes had even less money.

*A Farm Security Administration supervisor discusses the cotton crop with a Louisiana farmer. One-eighth of those receiving loans from the FSA were Negroes.*

### President Franklin D. Roosevelt and the New Deal

During this period of worldwide depression, some European nations turned to dictatorship to solve the problems of economic and social unrest. But in America, President Franklin D. Roosevelt operated within the context of the American constitutional system as he

*The New Deal President greets Dr. George Washington Carver.*

charted a course of social and economic experimentation. Much as the tragedy of the Civil War had guided Lincoln's policies, the suffering of the depression would bring forth from Roosevelt a new and fresh approach to the role of the government during a severe crisis. The President indicated the desperation of the situation when he remarked that if he were not a good President, he would be America's last President. American Negroes, who had remained Republicans since the days of Abraham Lincoln, became Roosevelt's strongest supporters. The city Negroes of the North were becoming Democrats. In 1940, Harlem's 17th Assembly District voted Democratic by a seven-to-one margin.

It was both the New Deal program of the President and his concern for the underdog that convinced the skeptical Negro population that, at long last, there seemed to be someone in the White House who might be aware of what it meant to be a Negro in the United States. Both the new President and his energetic and humanitarian wife, Eleanor, appeared to be truly concerned about the "one-third of a nation" that was poor—and this included most Negroes. Despite the anger of Southern politicians Roosevelt and his wife made no secret of their warm personal friendship with some Negroes and their interest in the cause of equal justice. By 1939 the Roosevelt administration had ordered the creation of a civil rights section in the Department of Justice. Although it received 8,000 to 14,000 complaints each year and took few actions, lynchings decreased steadily.

Immediately after he became President, Franklin D. Roosevelt began to bring outstanding Negroes into the federal government. These Negroes came to be called the "Black Brain Trust" or the "Black Cabinet." These men and women served as "racial advisers" to the many New Deal agencies. Reporter Roi Ottley found that these "intellectual workers" were "permeated with the bold thinking of the New Deal." "They are aggressively for integration," he wrote in his book *New World A'Coming*, and they succeeded in securing employment for many other Negroes. "I was frankly surprised when I was in Washington recently to see the thousands of Negroes who were working for the government and to see the variety of jobs they were doing—jobs hitherto beyond wishful thinking. Many held positions of authority and influence," continued Ottley, "and others were patiently solving technical problems as economists, lawyers, chemists, and consultants of various sorts. Hundreds were operating office machines and a few worked as secretaries to both white and Negro officials."

The two leading Negro members of the "Black Cabinet" were Robert C. Weaver and Mary McLeod Bethune. Dr. Weaver was a bright young college professor who came to Washington in the first year of the New Deal. The "Black Cabinet" usually met in his basement. He served in the Interior Department, Housing Authority, and during World War II, on the War Production Board. He earned his Ph.D. at Harvard in 1934. Under President Lyndon B. Johnson, Robert Weaver became the first Negro to be appointed to the President's Cabinet and the first man to hold the post of Secretary of Housing and Urban Development.

Mrs. Bethune was one of seventeen children born to poor ex-slave parents. With six students and $1.50, she established a Florida college for Negroes and saw it grow to the million-dollar Bethune-Cookman College. Mrs. Bethune served as an adviser to the National Youth Administration and soon became a trusted friend of the President and his wife. "I'm always glad to see you, Mrs. Bethune," President Roosevelt told her, "for you always come asking for help for others—never for yourself." Mrs. Bethune continued to work as an adviser to President Harry Truman and was one of the observers he

*Mary McLeod Bethune with her students at Florida's Bethune-Cookman College. An unusually bright and energetic person, Mrs. Bethune refused to follow segregation laws and constantly prodded the White House on matters relating to Negro rights.*

chose to attend the first meeting of the United Nations held in San Francisco in 1945.

Dr. Ralph Bunche and William Henry Hastie were two other Negroes who began their public careers during the New Deal. Dr. Bunche, a brilliant scholar and expert on the world's colonial areas, worked for the State Department. He became one of the Americans who helped plan the organization of the United Nations during World War II. Of his many awards, the most notable is the Nobel Peace Prize of 1950 which was awarded for his role in the settling of the Arab-Israeli dispute.

Dr. Hastie, who like Bunche and Weaver received his Ph.D. from Harvard, won many legal cases for the NAACP. He served the Interior Department and the Secretary of War during World War II. He was made a judge in the Virgin Islands in 1937 and, ten years later, was appointed Governor of the territory by President Harry Truman. During the war he protested the continued segregation of the armed forces by resigning from his post with the War Department.

While the Negro who suffered during the depression appreciated seeing many brown-skinned men and women being elevated to high positions in government, he himself benefited more directly from the New Deal program. By 1934, 3,500,000 Negroes were receiving relief. Others worked in forests for the Civilian Conservation Corps (CCC) or built roads, schools, and bridges for the Works Projects Administration (WPA). Despite some discrimination in relief and jobs, Dr. Weaver pointed out that "vast numbers of Negroes were enabled to retain work habits and a minimum of health as a result of federal aid."

The New Deal program meant more than just immediate relief or a job to the Negro. "To the younger Negroes, the WPA and relief mean not only aid but a guaranty that no longer must they work at any salary given them, that they are entitled—they emphasize the word—to a living wage," wrote political analyst Samuel Lubell in 1940.

*A CCC worker handles a tractor.*

*A CCC worker helps to protect the nation's forests. Two hundred and fifty thousand Negroes were among the three million CCC workers.*

The WPA provided work for artists, musicians, actors, and playwrights during the 1930's. Artist Ernest Critchlow recalled how he and "many Negro artists were aided during those times by the work assigned them by the WPA. Without that aid many of today's important artists might never have made their contributions to the nation's art." Under government grants, Negro scholars were able to research the history of their people in America and many of these studies were published so that the public might recognize the contributions Negroes made to America. Other federal funds provided salaries for Negro actors who had been unable to find work for years. Soon impressive stage productions, under the best directors in the country, were being shown to audiences in the large cities, free of charge.

When concert singer Marian Anderson was refused permission to give a concert in Constitution Hall in Washington, D.C., Secretary of the Interior Harold Ickes invited her to sing outdoors at the Lincoln Memorial. Before an audience of 75,000 that included Supreme Court justices, Cabinet officers, and Congressmen, Miss Anderson began her historic 1939 concert. She recalled that "the crowd stretched in a great semicircle from the Lincoln Memorial around

*Marian Anderson sings to 75,000 at the Lincoln Memorial on Easter Sunday, 1939. After she had been denied the right to sing in Constitution Hall because she was a Negro, Secretary of the Interior Harold L. Ickes offered her the Lincoln Memorial. Ickes had been an NAACP leader in Chicago.*

the reflecting pool onto the shaft of the Washington Monument. I had a feeling that a great wave of goodwill poured out from these people, almost engulfing me." Her program included operatic arias and folk songs, and ended with *America the Beautiful.* Twenty years later, Miss Anderson was chosen by President Dwight D. Eisenhower to serve her country as a delegate to the United Nations.

## A New Deal for Labor

An important New Deal assault on the poverty produced by the depression was the attempt to raise wages in industry. For years the Negro laborer had known the bitter truth that usually he could only get "any job that the white man cannot stand." And Negro opportunities for promotion were severely limited. A colored worker in Pennsylvania who had trained many white employees said, "I have never been promoted. I am the oldest on my job and have never been advanced and have no chance. . . . Colored are seldom promoted." Secretary of Labor Frances Perkins, America's first woman Cabinet member, indicated a new government interest in Negro labor in 1934, when she said: "A way must be found of gradually raising the living standards of the colored laborers. . . ."

The National Labor Relations Act of 1935 inspired a drive to bring the workers of mass production industries (steel, auto, rubber) into unions. A wave of union organization swept the country from coast to coast. John L. Lewis, President of the United Mine Workers Union, led a number of unions out of the American Federation of Labor (AFL) into the Congress of Industrial Organizations (CIO). Workers were welcomed into the CIO regardless of craft, sex, color, or the amount of money in their pay envelope.

Employers did their best to keep their hired help out of the new unions. They put special pressure on Negroes who signed up as union members. A unionist in Lackawanna, New York was told: "When you came here there were plenty of Mexicans and Armenians. You couldn't walk through the streets for them. Now unless you want them to come back you had better be careful." Another Negro, who became a union leader, reported: "On Friday the foreman spoke to me and said, 'You shouldn't jeopardize your job'. . . . On Saturday he asked me if I was interested in myself and I told him that I was interested in everybody, all the workers." Another Negro unionist said that his foreman "sent me after sand and gave me more work and made me do unnecessary things. . . . They have been trying to irritate me so they could fire me. I don't pay any attention to them any more. They do the same to all union members."

The CIO unions often introduced a new note of brotherhood among members. A white Chicago factory worker told how a Negro organizer "woke a lot of us up by showing how the company built up race hatred by playing on our sense of superiority." Another white unionist found that "through union activity, white and colored have known each other better. . . . They are drawn closer together on the job." A Negro worker in Pennsylvania said: "The union is breaking down prejudice and segregation. . . . There is no office in the union that is held from a colored man because of his color." In Birmingham, Alabama as well as Chicago, Illinois, Negroes were elected to high posts in mixed unions.

Many Negro laborers, long excluded from unions, were, at first, reluctant to support the labor organizations. A most difficult test of loyalty was met squarely in the 1941 Ford Motor Company strike. Negro auto workers for Ford recalled that their employer had offered

*Pickets at a 1938 Pennsylvania strike. The industrial unions of the CIO organized all the workers in a plant. For Negroes, long excluded from craft unions, this meant a first chance to be a union member.*

them jobs when few others did. When white unionists at Ford walked off the job, many Negroes remained at their posts. For a while it appeared that a labor dispute might turn into a racial conflict. But finally the Negro workers joined the strike and made it a success. An improved contract was worked out by Negro and white union leaders and the Ford officials.

## Americans React to European Dictators

Soon after Hitler's rise to power in Germany, American Negroes felt, as one expressed it, that "any individual who becomes a world menace on a doctrine of racial prejudice, bigotry, and oppression of minorities . . . is our concern." In 1933 Kelly Miller, Negro educator and writer, compared Hitler's persecution of the Jews to Klan attacks on Negroes, in an article called *Hitler—The German Ku Klux*.

The attack on the tiny kingdom of Ethiopia in 1935 aroused the world to the danger of Mussolini's fascism. Never had the Negro communities of the United States been so moved by a foreign event. They raised money and gathered medical supplies for the African nation. Emperor Haile Selassie said many years later: "We can never forget the help Ethiopia received from Negro Americans during the terrible crisis. . . . It moved me to know that Americans of African descent did not abandon their embattled brothers, but stood by us." Unfortunately, however, the democratic nations of the world and the League of Nations did not give Ethiopia the protection it needed. Haile Selassie was loudly cheered by League members when he called for "collective security" against aggressors—but nothing was done.

When the Spanish Civil War broke out a few years later, American Negroes enlisted in the International Brigades that went to Spain to fight Generalissimo Francisco Franco and his Nazi and Fascist allies. Poet and journalist Langston Hughes toured the front lines and interviewed one hundred of these colored soldiers, doctors, and nurses. "They were not professional soldiers like the Germans, or draftees like the Italians," he wrote. "They came of their own free will."

As the war danger came closer to America in the late 1930's, Negroes bitterly protested against their exclusion from the nation's defense industries. In New York City only 142 Negroes were among the 30,000 defense workers. Negro leaders repeatedly asked the President to issue an executive order opening these jobs to all.

Meetings took place but no order was forthcoming. Labor leader Asa Philip Randolph concluded: "The Administration will never give the Negro justice until they see masses—ten, twenty, fifty thousand Negroes on the White House lawn." Randolph planned what he called a "nonviolent demonstration of Negro mass power" —a march on Washington. Four days before the march was to begin, its leaders were invited to the White House to meet with the President and members of his Cabinet.

On June 25, 1941 President Franklin D. Roosevelt issued Executive Order 8802 banning discrimination in all plants working on national defense contracts. He signed this order "in the firm belief that the democratic way of life within the Nation can be defended successfully only with the help and support of all groups within its borders. . . ." For the first time since the Emancipation Proclamation, a President of the United States had issued an order protecting the rights of Negro Americans.

In less than six months every ounce of American manpower and patriotism would be needed to defend the very life of the nation.

*Joe Louis, Detroit's "Brown Bomber," meets Brig. General Benjamin O. Davis, highest ranking World War II Negro officer in the United States Army. Louis became a hero to those opposing world fascism when he knocked out the German Max Schmeling in the first round of a 1938 battle for the world heavy-weight championship. Nazis had claimed that Schmeling would easily defeat Louis, who represented an "inferior race and country." World War II again found Louis and Schmeling in opposing corners: Louis was a sergeant in the United States Army; Schmeling was a Nazi paratrooper.*

# The Desperate Voice of the Unemployed

[*As unemployment soared in the early 1930's, Negroes found that discrimination made their lot even harder than that of the whites. Southern states used the program of the Federal Emergency Relief Administration (FERA) to assist whites far more than Negroes—as these two Louisiana letters to the NAACP show.*]

[From Louisiana, Feb. 3, 1934] I am writing you asking you if you will through your honorable organization assist me in procuring work . . . or Direct relief. I have been deprived of work since Oct. 20th 1933. All because I wrote several letters to Washington asking for work. I registered with the N.R.S. about Nov. 13, 1933 and just because I wrote those letters to Washington that office refused to call me out on any job. Being denied of work so long I was forced to apply for direct relief and the woman Parrish director of the [F.]E.R.A. told me because I had quit a job in Sept. that only paid me $2.00 per week 10-to-14 hours per day and because I had written several letters to Washington reporting this office she said you will not get any direct relief here. I will show you that you cannot run this office [she said]. You have been quarrelling with this office all the year. I will show you that you can't run this office. I have explained the situation to every legal authority I knew . . . and the only thing that I can get is an answer as though I am seeking information. I am not seeking information I am seeking justice. Now since I cannot of myself get justice I am asking you to take this matter up with the legal authority of this country. I am enclosing a few letters received from Washington and New Orleans but such letters dont help me any I need food and raiment for my wife and children. I have not had one day of relief work since Oct. 20th 1933.

[From Louisiana, April 3, 1934] Only a few line to ask you to do something for us down hear in Plaquemines Parish. We have report to the [F.] E.R.A. and they dont gave us any work and dont gave relif to the colored peple. so kindly got in tutch with Washington. See why they dont gave us work and dont wont to gave relif down hear in Plaquemines Parish. . . . Bad place to recave mail. No work to make a living, no money to leave. this will bee all for today kimdly do this faver for us. . . .

---

"Some Work for the F.E.R.A.," *The Crisis*, Vol. 41 (November, 1934), pp. 330-331. Reprinted by permission.

# The Unemployed Veterans March on Washington, 1932

[*Before President Hoover was voted out of office, the depression had made millions of Americans jobless. In the spring of 1932 over 15,000 World War I veterans converged on Washington, D.C. to demand payment of a bonus. Reporter Roy Wilkins found that the Bonus Expeditionary Force (BEF) was integrated.*]

The men of the B.E.F. were come together on serious business; they had not time for North, East, South, West, black, and white divisions. The main problem was not to prove and maintain the superiority of a group, but to secure relief from the ills which beset them, black and white alike. . . .

Here they were, then, the brown and black men who had fought (some with their tongues in their cheeks) to save the world for democracy. They were scattered about in various state delegations or grouped in their own cluster of crude shelters. A lonely brownskin in the delegation from North Platte, Nebr.; one or two encamped with Seattle, Wash.; increasing numbers bivouacked with California and the northern states east of the Mississippi river; and, of course, the larger numbers with the states from below the Mason and Dixon line. . . .

At Anacostia some Negroes had their own shacks and some slept in with white boys. There was no residential segregation. . . . The Chicago group had several hundred Negroes in it and they worked, ate, slept, and played with their white comrades. The Negroes shared tasks with the whites from kitchen work to camp M.P. duty.

In gadding about I came across white toes and black toes sticking out from tent flaps and boxes as their owners sought to sleep away the day. . . .

All about were signs containing homely philosophy and sarcasm on the treatment of veterans by the country, such as: "The Heroes of 1918 Are the Bums of 1932." I believe many of the white campers were bitter and sarcastic. They meant what they said on those signs. But disappointment and disillusionment is an old story to Negroes. They were philosophic about this bonus business. . . . So, while the indifference of the government to the bonus agitation might be a bitter pill to the whites, it was nothing unusual to the Negroes. . . .

Over in one corner a white vet was playing a ukelele and singing what could have been the theme song of the camp: *In a Shanty in Old Shanty Town*. On a Sunday afternoon the camp piano was played alternately by a brown lad with a New York accent and a red-necked white boy from Florida, while a few rods away Elder Micheaux's visiting choir was giving voice, in stoptime, to a hymn, *God's Tomorrow Will Be Brighter Than Today*. Negroes and whites availed themselves of the free choice of patting their feet either outdoors to the piano or in the gospel tent to the choir. . . .

Captain A. B. Simmons, colored, who headed his company, hails from Houston, Tex. He and his men were loud in their declarations of the fair treatment they had received on the march to Washington. They were served meals in Southern towns, by Southern white waitresses, in Main Street Southern restaurants along with their white companions. They rode freights and trucks and hiked together. Never a sign of Jim Crow through Northern Texas, Arkansas, Tennessee, or Virginia. Captain Simmons attended the regular company commanders' councils and helped with the problems of administration. His fellow officers, all white Southerners, accorded him the same consideration given others of his rank.

His story was corroborated by others. A long, hard-boiled Negro from West Virginia who had just stepped out of the mess line behind a white man from Florida said: "Shucks, they ain't got time for that stuff here and those that has we gets 'em told personally." And said a cook in the North Carolina mess kitchen (helping whites peel potatoes): "No, sir, things is different here than down home."

In general assemblies and in marches there were no special places "for Negroes." The black boys did not have to tag along at the end of the line of march; there was no "special" section reserved for them at assemblies. They were shot all through the B.E.F. In the rallies on the steps of the nation's capitol they were in front, in the middle and in the rear.

Roy Wilkins, "The Bonuseers Ban Jim Crow," *The Crisis*, Vol. 39 (October, 1932), pp. 316-317. Reprinted by permission.

## Sharecroppers and the White House Door

[*Will Alexander, a white Southerner who had been a leader in inter-racial organizations since 1907, was a director of the Farm Security Administration when this incident occurred.*]

I recall so well the winter of 1935 with its sharecroppers' strike and wholesale evictions from the cotton farms of southeast Missouri. Several hundred dispossessed families, white and Negro, squatted by the highway in severe winter weather, with all but no protection. One of the leaders was a Negro preacher, himself a sharecropper, a man of limited education but native initiative.

He decided to appeal to the White House and by writing to Mrs. Roosevelt, secured an appointment. He set out in a dilapidated Ford with his wife and the nineteen-year-old daughter of one of the evicted white families. The snow was deep in the Virginia mountains; their car broke down, but a free ride brought them to Washington on the day set.

As administrator of Farm Security, I was familiar with the situation in southeast Missouri, and Mrs. Roosevelt's secretary requested me to be present. Somewhat in advance of the hour, I was seated by an usher in one of the famous reception rooms on the first floor of the White House. Soon the visitors arrived. The couple was thinly clad in the shabby clothes of sharecroppers, and chilled to the bone. Their young white companion was bareheaded, and a thin cotton coat was her only outer wrap. They had scarcely sat down when a uniformed servant came in and lighted a crackling fire laid in the hearth.

There was to be a reception later that afternoon and already there was an air of festivity with uniformed musicians from the navy assembling outside our door. When Mrs. Roosevelt came in she greeted these special guests as naturally as if they belonged to the party. The Negro preacher told the story of the people by the road-side. He was perhaps forty—small, vigorous. if awkward, in his speech. With instant directness, Mrs. Roosevelt found out what lay back of the evictions and what the government was doing. She inquired of me what further could be done, and asked to be kept abreast of developments. In the few remaining minutes, her friendly overtures elicited from the wife the story of their eleven children, and she drew out the white girl's own story of herself and her folks.

There was still give and take, back and forth, as they left the room, threading their way through the navy's musicians and the bustle of activity for the reception. The visitors had been treated with dignity; they had been identified as individuals; their problems had been reviewed with practical directness. As they went out the front door of the White House, it was unmistakably with a sense of their own worth; new faith in their country, new hope for their kind.

Will W. Alexander, "The Negro in the Nation," *Survey Graphic*, Vol. 36 (January, 1947), p. 94.

## *Light and Darkness in the Tennessee Valley*

[*In 1933 President Franklin D. Roosevelt proposed that the federal government go into the business of producing cheap electric power for a seven-state region in the Deep South. The Tennessee Valley Authority (TVA) provided jobs as well as electricity for the valley farmers. But this 1935 eyewitness picture shows that all were not sharing the benefits equally.*]

A contrast of performance with promise shows that Negroes have never been given their proportionate share of jobs on TVA projects. In addition when payrolls of Negro and white workers are contrasted even greater inequities appear. . . .

It is in seeking a reason for these inequities that one discovers overt acts of discrimination on the part of TVA officials which nullify their every pretense of impartiality. For the most part skilled work is denied Negro workers. Employment of labor is done through the TVA personnel division. Negro workers are employed by Negro assistant personnel officers under the supervision of white officials. To the Negro assistants only requisitions for unskilled work are given. Thus the assistants cannot offer skilled work to any Negro applicants. Only by currying favor with white bosses, may a Negro worker once on the job hope to rise to a higher level of pay or skilled employment. Such instances are very few. Thus at Wheeler Dam where the largest number of Negroes were employed in June 1935, only eight Negro workmen out of 1,048 then employed received as much as $1.00 an hour. There were 300 white carpenters employed on the job there, but not a single Negro. Only 12 Negroes received as much as 75 cents an hour at Wheeler Dam. . . .

A basic concept put forward by TVA officials is that electric power may be used to remove many of the drudgeries of daily life, to effect many home and farm economies, and thus make possible a better life. It is on this basis that the policy of rural electrification was supposed to have been begun in the Valley. As first steps in putting this program into operation TVA successfully negotiated for the use of its power in Tupelo, Mississippi and Athens, Alabama. In Lee County in which Tupelo is located there are 11,225 Negroes or 31.8 per cent of the population. More than 50 per cent of the persons on relief are Negro. A rural county, a large share of the Negro population is engaged in sharecropping and tenant farming. In Tupelo the Negro population lives largely in grotesque rented slum dwellings.

For Negroes the introduction of cheaper electric rates into Lee County as result of the TVA power policy has meant nothing. Landlords, whether of Negro slum dwellers in Tupelo or of Negro tenant farmers in the rural section of the county, have not found it to their advantage to wire their Negro tenants' homes at the cost of $15 to $25, when already they are squeezing all the rent possible from these tenants. . . .

[*According to a government agency the basic appliances for a family (range, water heater, and refrigerator) could be purchased for $5.33 a month. The TVA electric rates amounted to $6.98 a month.*]

It is obvious that such rates are completely out of reach of the Negro resident of Lee County. The total sum represents more nearly his total monthly cash income than any amount which he would be able to spend for electricity. Thus so far as TVA's electrification program is concerned the Negro family is still in outer darkness.

John P. Davis, "The Plight of the Negro in the Tennessee Valley," *The Crisis*, Vol. 42 (October, 1935), pp. 294, 314. Reprinted by permission.

# *"Belly Hunger" Erases the Color Line*

[*Ward H. Rodgers, a white organizer for the Southern Tenant Farmers' Union, describes the success which the Union had in uniting sharecroppers regardless of race—or even past Klan membership!*]

All too few have been the attempts in the South, or for that matter in the North, to organize labor unions which include both the Negro and white workers. The Southern Tenant Farmers' Union has from its beginning attempted to solve the difficulties of organizing across the race line. After eight months of work we now have 10,000 members, half of whom are Negro sharecroppers. During these months we have had practically no friction within the Union over the race question. Some of our best leaders are members of the Negro race. . . .

Because of his long experience in other organizations, such as churches, burial societies, fraternal organizations and the like, the Negro generally knows how to run meetings, as they should be run. Practically the only organization that the white sharecroppers have had experience in outside of the churches is the Ku Klux Klan, therefore they have not had training in correct procedures at meetings. The only explanation that I have for sharecroppers joining our interracial organization who used to show their race prejudice by being members of the night-riding K.K.K., is that they have learned that both white and Negro sharecroppers are the victims of the same system of exploitation, both Negro and white suffer from the same "belly hunger." The sharecroppers, regardless of color, have been deprived of a living which certainly they work hard enough to earn. Both races have been driven down to a low economic level of bare subexistence. The white sharecropper also is discriminated against and insulted. The word sharecropper itself has come to be used as a term of contempt. . . .

The argument against race prejudice which has been used by the organizers is: "If we organize only a Union of Negro sharecroppers then the Negroes will be evicted and white sharecroppers from the hill country or the unemployed in Memphis will take their places. If on the other hand we organize only a Union of white sharecroppers then the white men will be evicted and Negro sharecroppers from Mississippi and the unemployed in Memphis will take their places." . . .

In spite of increasing terror, the Union grows. Hundreds are joining, Negro and white sharecroppers. We now have 10,000 members, an increase of 35 per cent since January 15.

---

Ward H. Rodgers, "Sharecroppers Drop Color Line," *The Crisis*, Vol. 24 (June, 1935), pp. 168, 178. Reprinted by permission.

## A Negro in the CCC

[*The Civilian Conservation Corps offered jobs and hope to two million young people during the height of the depression. Luther C. Wandall, a New York Negro, describes his life as a CCC worker in 1935.*]

According to instructions, I went Monday morning at 8 o'clock to Pier I, North River. There were, I suppose more than 1,000 boys standing about the pier. . . .

The colored boys were a goodly sprinkling of the whole. A few middle-aged men were in evidence. These, it turned out, were going as cooks. A good many Spaniards and Italians were about. A good-natured, lively, crowd, typical of New York. . . .

. . . we answered questions, and signed papers, and then a group of us marched over to U.S. Army headquarters on Whitehall Street in charge of an Army officer.

Here we stripped for a complete physical examination. Then we were grouped into busloads. . . .

We reached Camp Dix [New Jersey] about 7:30 that evening. As we rolled up in front of headquarters an officer came out to the bus and told us: "You will double-time as you leave this bus, remove your hat when you hit the door, and when you are asked questions, answer 'Yes, sir,' and 'No, sir.'"

. . . when my record was taken at Pier I a "C" was placed on it. When the busloads were made up at Whitehall street an officer reported as follows: "35, 8 colored." But until now there had been no distinction made.

But before we left the bus the officer shouted emphatically:

"Colored boys fall out in the rear." The colored from several buses were herded together, and stood in line until after the white boys had been registered and taken to their tents. This seemed to be the established order of procedure at Camp Dix.

This separation of the colored from the whites was complete and rigidly maintained at this camp. One Puerto Rican, who was darker than I, and who preferred to be with the colored, was regarded as pitifully uninformed by the officers. . . .

We stayed at Camp Dix eight days. We were never told officially where we were going. . . .

We were taken to permanent camp on a site rich in Colonial and Revolutionary history, in the upper South. This camp was a dream compared with Camp Dix. There [was] plenty to eat, and we slept in barracks instead of tents. An excellent recreation hall, playground, and other facilities.

I am still in this camp. At the "rec" we have a radio, a piano, a store called a "canteen," a rack of the leading New York papers, white and colored, as well as some from elsewhere. There is a little library with a variety of books and magazines. All sports are encouraged. We have a baseball team, boxing squad, etc. An orchestra has been formed, and classes in various arts and crafts. . . .

During the first week we did no work outside camp, but only hiked, drilled, and exercised. Since then we have worked five days a week, eight hours a day. Our bosses are local men, southerners, but on the whole I have found nothing to complain of. The work varies, but is always healthy, outdoor labor. As the saying goes, it's a great life, if only you don't weaken! . . .

Our officers who, of course, are white, are a captain, a first lieutenant, a doctor, and several sergeants. Our athletic director is colored, as is our vocational teacher. Discipline is maintained by imposing extra duty and fines on offenders. The fines are taken only from the $5 a month which the men receive directly [the rest of the money, about $30, being sent home].

On the whole, I was gratified rather than disappointed with the CCC. I had expected the worst. Of course it reflects, to some extent, all the practices and prejudices of the U.S. Army. But as a job and an experience, for a man who has no work, I can heartily recommend it.

Luther C. Wandall, "A Negro in the CCC," *The Crisis*, Vol. 42 (August, 1935), pp. 244, 253-254. Reprinted by permission.

# The Memorial Day Massacre of 1937

[*One of the most dramatic events in the rise of the CIO's United Steel Workers Union was the Memorial Day Massacre of Sunday, May 30, 1937. A parade of strikers was driven off by police bullets outside the Republic Steel plant of Chicago. Ten workers were killed.*]

[*A Negro striker.*] On that Sunday we marched out of the plant with signs. Lots of us were singing songs and laughing. I was in the front line. All of a sudden the cops started shooting. When they started, I ran to my extreme right, then west, then I made an "L" turn to the south. All the time, bullets were going right past my face.

When I looked up I saw a guy right on top of the plant training his gun on us. I couldn't tell whether it was a machine gun, 'cause I was anxious to get out of the line of fire. I could see the police in my path, the way I was running, so I turned around toward Sam's Place. I ran to a car and started to duck into it. A bullet whizzed by and lodged right above the right fender. Boy, I shake now when I think that if I hadn't ducked I'd have been shot in the head. I finally made it into the car and was driven to Sam's Place.

[*The wife of the one Negro killed that day.*] He was told to go to the meeting that Sunday. He was on the front line and was one of the first to get hurt. I have his clothes here. You can see where he was shot in the back. His hat is bloody. He sure was beat terrible. His life was really lost for the CIO, whether he understood it or not. I do hope his loss will help others who live.

---

St. Clair Drake and Horace R. Cayton, *Black Metropolis* (New York: Harcourt, Brace & Co., 1945), pp. 322-323. Reprinted by permission.

# *A New Deal Congressman Defeats Jim Crow*

[*Congressman Arthur W. Mitchell (1934-1942) of Chicago was the first Negro Democrat elected to Congress. Born to former slaves, Mitchell later served as office boy for Booker T. Washington. When he was forced to leave a Pullman car because of his race, Congressman Mitchell took his case to the Supreme Court and won. He tells Congress the story.*]

Mr. Speaker, on April 19, 1937, I purchased a first-class round-trip railroad ticket from Chicago, Ill., to and from Hot Springs, Ark., over the Illinois Central and Rock Island Railroads via Memphis, Tenn. While travelling on this ticket between Memphis, Tenn., and Little Rock, Ark., on the morning of April 21, 1937, I was ejected from the first-class car by the conductor of the Rock Island passenger train on which I was then travelling. The reason for ejecting me was that I was riding in the body of a Pullman car in which there were riding several white passengers, the conductor claiming that the law of the State of Arkansas prohibited such an act by statute. . . .

This fight for the rights of the Negro has been a hard and expensive one, covering a period of more than 4 years. All expenses incurred in this suit have been borne by me. I think it is well to note that I, with a Negro lawyer, Richard E. Westbrooks, of Chicago, Ill., have fought the case through all of the courts. We conducted the hearing in Chicago, argued the case before the Interstate Commerce Commission and before the United States district court in Chicago. We also argued the case before the Supreme Court of the United States, this being the first and only instance where a member of our race has argued his own case before that high tribunal.

. . . The case before the Supreme Court was heard by the full court, and their decision was unanimous for me, setting aside in strong language the findings of the Interstate Commerce Commission and the decision of the United States District Court of the Northern District of Illinois.

I think I should also call attention to the fact that the Attorney General's Office, whose duty it was to appear before the Supreme Court in behalf of the Interstate Commerce Commission, not only refused to appear and argue in favor of the findings of that commission, but through . . . Francis Biddle [later an Attorney General], filed with the Supreme Court a very strong memorandum [in favor of Mitchell's complaint]. . . .

*The Congressional Record*, 77th Congress, First Session, Appendix, pp. A4294-A4297.

## A Negro Congressman Speaks for Minority Rights

[*Congressman Arthur W. Mitchell expressed his concern over the Nazi persecution of Jewish people in this letter to President Franklin D. Roosevelt of October 12, 1938.*]

As a representative of a minority group in America, an underprivileged group which has been subjected to prejudice and mistreatment from time to time, we are interested in the attitude of majority groups throughout the world toward minority groups. At the present time we are greatly disturbed because of the intolerance of certain major groups toward the Jewish people residing in European countries and wish to have our voice heard in the interest of justice and fair play for all racial groups. We believe that the same spirit of intolerance which is working so tremendously against the safety and sacred rights of the Jewish people, if permitted to go unchallenged, will manifest itself sooner or later against all minority groups, perhaps in all parts of the world. [We] request you, the highest repesentative of our Government, to use every reasonable and peaceable means at your command in securing protection for the Jewish people in this hour of sad calamity.

[*President Roosevelt answered Congressman Mitchell's telegram, saying: "I fully appreciate the concern expressed by you" and said that he would work for a national home for the Jews in Palestine.*]

*The Congressional Record*, 76th Congress, First Session, Appendix, p. A4041.

# 18

# *World Leadership in War and Peace*

IN the early morning of December 7, 1941, Japanese planes swooped out of the powder-puff clouds above Hawaii and rained destruction on the United States Naval Base at Pearl Harbor. Mess attendant Dorie Miller, a broad-shouldered young sailor who had battled his way to the boxing championship of the *West Virginia*, dropped the laundry he had been collecting and scampered on deck. In the midst of the crashing bombs and the strafing by Japanese Zeros, he pulled his wounded captain to safety. Then he sprang to action behind a machine gun and fired away at the attacking aircraft. An officer finally had to order him to leave the sinking ship.

Dorie Miller reported that he shot down six Zeros. The Navy gave him credit for four. Either way it was not a bad record for a man who never fired a machine gun until that morning. His victory was probably the only one credited to the United States that day, and Dorie Miller was America's first hero of World War II. He served as mess attendant because that, at the time, was the only position open to Negroes in the Navy. On May 7, 1942, Fleet Admiral Chester Nimitz pinned the Navy Cross on Dorie Miller "for distinguished devotion to duty, extraordinary courage, and disregard for his own personal safety. . . ."

Miller was still a messman when he went down with his new ship, *Liscome Bay*, on November 25, 1944. But his courage would help pave the way for others who wished to do more for their country than serve as messmen. And, before World War II had ended, three other Negro sailors would win the Navy Cross.

## World War II

The Japanese sneak attack on Pearl Harbor united the American people against the Axis powers of Japan, Germany, and Italy. "If Hitler wins," wrote William E. B. Du Bois in 1941, "every single right we now possess, for which we have struggled here in America for more than three centuries, will be instantaneously wiped out. . . . If the Allies win, we shall at least have the right to continue fighting for a share of democracy for ourselves." Alice Godwin, a New York Negro high school student, wrote a composition telling why she supported America's war effort. "I have been told this war is a war for liberty for everybody. That is the reason this war is important to me. . . . Each little sacrifice I make, I make joyously. It is for a new world, tomorrow, isn't it?"

From the home-front war factories to the fighting fronts of the world, Negroes contributed to allied victories. More than a million entered the armed forces and almost half of these served overseas. The men served in every branch of the armed forces, and the women

*Troops guard Rhine River bridge.*

were Army nurses, WACs, WAVEs, and SPARs. Seven thousand Negroes served as officers, taking their training along with whites. Four commanded Merchant Marine ships and thousands served in their crews. Paul Robeson, Louis Armstrong, and Lena Horne were among the many Negro entertainers to tour the Army camps with USO troupes.

One of the most striking single contributions to Allied victory came from Dr. Charles Drew. A brilliant young surgeon, Dr. Drew was in charge of the Red Cross Blood Bank before the war began, and during the war organized a system that saved countless American and Allied lives. He worked to perfect the modern blood bank system despite the fact that his own blood, because he was a Negro, would not be acceptable to an American blood bank for a long time to come. Continued criticism from Dr. Drew and thousands of others finally led to the acceptance of blood from Negroes. But it was stored separately so that it would only be used for wounded Negro servicemen, even though it might have saved the lives of white servicemen as well.

On April 1, 1950 Dr. Drew was injured in an auto accident near Burlington, North Carolina. Although he was bleeding profusely, he was turned away from the nearest "white" hospital. By the time he was taken to another hospital, the scientist had bled to death.

*Dr. Charles Drew.*

## *Military Campaigns: European Theater*

Before American troops landed in Africa, Negro engineers were sent into Liberia (a nation founded in 1819 by former American slaves) to prepare air strips. Edward Taylor, the Negro private who was the first American soldier to set foot in Africa, told the Liberians, "We are here to join hands and fight together until this world is free of tyrannical dictators." The 450th Anti-Aircraft Artillery Battalion, the first Negro unit to land in the invasion of North Africa and the first to go into combat on European soil as well, was cited by General Mark W. Clark for "outstanding performance of duty." Among those wounded in the African campaign was "Kid Chocolate," famous for his many boxing victories before the war. He lost both of his legs.

In the invasions of Sicily, Italy, and Normandy (D-Day) in France, Negro troops were among the hard-hitting American forces. During a German night raid on ships in Naples Harbor, Negro sol-

*Members of the 92nd Division pushing northward in Italy toward the Arno River, 1944.*

diers scampered on deck to man guns on the ship and on the trucks about to be unloaded. They brought down two Nazi planes and won praise from General Mark Clark who said that "their conduct was excellent. . . . The Fifth Army welcomes such men." The Negro battalion that landed at Normandy on D-Day was commended by General Dwight D. Eisenhower because it "carried out its mission with courage and determination and proved an important element to the air-defense team."

From the battles on the African desert until the final surrender of the German forces, Negro airmen struck at Axis land, sea, and air power. The 600 airmen trained at Tuskegee as pilots carried the war from Africa to France, Italy, Poland, Romania, and Germany. Eighty-eight of the pilots won the Distinguished Flying Cross in bombing and strafing missions. The 332nd Fighter Group won a Presidential Unit Citation. Together with the all-Negro 99th Pursuit Squadron, they won 800 air medals and clusters.

The highest ranking Negro officer was Colonel Benjamin O. Davis, a West Point graduate, who flew sixty missions himself and

*Benjamin O. Davis, Jr., highest ranking Negro officer in the Army today, receives his third Legion of Merit award from Secretary of the Air Force Zukert. In 1965 Davis was made Commander of all United States forces in Korea.*

won a Silver Star, Legion of Merit, Distinguished Flying Cross, and Air Medal with four Oak Leaf clusters. One of his citations read:

> For: Extraordinary achievement—in an aerial flight as a pilot of a P-47 type aircraft, led his Group on a penetration escort attack on industrial targets in the Munich area June 9, 1944. The bomber formation was attacked by more than one hundred enemy fighters near Udine, Italy. Faced with the problem of protecting the large bomber formation with the comparatively few fighters under his control, Colonel Davis so skillfully disposed his Squadron that in spite of the large number of enemy fighters, the bomber formation suffered only a few losses.

Just six months earlier, the 99th Pursuit Squadron, while protecting the Anzio beachhead, knocked down eight Nazi planes during one of the fiercest fights of the Italian campaign, a record superior to that of any other American squadron on that day.

Negro airmen, soldiers, truck drivers, and medical personnel moved across France with the liberating armies. Fifteen hundred Negro drivers moved vital supplies along the Red Ball Highway to feed General George Patton's tanks and men. In all, 22 Negro combat units served in the European theater. The 969th Field Artillery won a Distinguished Unit Citation for "outstanding courage and resourcefulness and undaunted determination. . . ." Private Ernest Jenkins of New York City won a Silver Star for knocking out an enemy gun position and capturing 15 Germans. First Lieutenant Vernon Baker of Cheyenne, Wyoming won the Distinguished Service Cross for "extraordinary heroism in action" when he knocked out three Nazi machine gun nests and killed or wounded nine Germans.

Several Negro GIs won foreign decorations. Macon H. Johnson was awarded the "Order of the Soviet Union" by a Russian General and William Green won the "Partisan Medal for Heroism" from Marshal Tito's Yugoslav government.

The first Negro Tank Battalion went into combat in Europe in 1944. This 761st Battalion of 54 tanks and 750 men served under General George S. Patton who told them, "I don't care what color you are, so long as you go up there and kill those" Germans. Patton reminded the men that "everyone has their eyes on you. . . . Don't let them down, and damn you, don't let me down." The 761st was in combat for 183 days from France through Austria and Germany.

*Easter eggs for delivery to Germany in 1945.*

They won 391 battle awards and inflicted 129,540 casualties on the enemy. They captured a German radio station at Salz and seven enemy towns (three of which they demolished), and knocked out 331 machine-gun nests. They never let Patton down.

Until the Nazis counterattacked in the bloody Battle of the Bulge in December, 1944, Negroes were confined to segregated units, many in service or noncombat units. But a reporter with a Negro Quartermaster Battalion told how they captured 49 Germans. "These soldiers went into battle untested, untrained, and came out with the praise of every commander ringing in their ears." When the Germans broke through the Bulge, the color bar was also broken. The United States Army asked for volunteers from among those serving behind the lines. "We've been giving a lot of sweat," remarked one Negro GI. "Now I think we'll mix some blood in it." Fifty-five hundred Negroes volunteered and 2,500 were accepted to fight in the

*After the Battle of the Bulge drove the Nazis back, smiling French soldiers fill the hands of American soldiers. After the battle the 2,500 Negroes who volunteered to halt the Nazi attack were returned to their segregated service units.*

United States First Army. Negro and white platoons fought side by side to drive back the fierce Nazi attack. They succeeded. After the battle, General Lanham told the volunteers: "I have never seen any soldiers who have performed better in combat than you." But segregation was restored to all units after the Germans surrendered.

## Military Campaigns: Pacific-Asiatic Theater

From December 8, 1941, when Private Robert Brooks, son of a Kentucky sharecropper, became the first American soldier of the armored force to lose his life in land warfare against the Japanese, until final victory, Negroes were an important part of the American victories in the Pacific Theater.

In the Battle of the Solomon Islands, Mess Attendant Leonard Harmon of Texas won the Navy Cross but lost his life rescuing a fellow crewman of the U.S. *San Francisco*. The Navy honored his memory by naming a destroyer escort after him.

On the Asian mainland ten thousand Negro engineers built the road from India through Burma to China and called it "The Road to Tokyo." They worked day and night, through jungles, around cliffs, over the Himalayas—and fought off Japanese patrols as they worked. Other Negro army engineers helped build the Alcan Highway in Alaska.

During the historic May, 1942, Battle of the Coral Sea, Negro aviation engineers built the landing strips in New Caledonia from which American planes smashed Japanese targets. A few months later a Negro machine-gun crew saved the vital airdrome at Milne Bay, New Guinea. Reginald Simonds and his crew manned unfamiliar machine guns as the Japanese came out of the jungle in attack formation. Simonds reported: "We knew enough to aim and keep them [the machine guns] shooting at the Japs. And I guess that's all we had to know."

Negro servicemen were part of the vast offensive that rolled back the Japanese, island by island. The 93rd Division fought at Bougainville, Treasury Islands, and the Philippines. The United

*United States troops in Bougainville patrol against the Japanese.*

*Machine-gunners of the 93rd Infantry guard the Numa-Numa trail in the South Pacific.*

States Marines admitted Negroes in 1943, breaking a color bar that had lasted throughout Marine history. Negro Marines served with distinction in the invasion of Saipan. Negro soldiers pushed into Guadalcanal and Okinawa and helped General Douglas MacArthur retake the Philippines. In April, 1944 a Negro gun crew aboard the U.S. *Intrepid* won the Bronze Star for bringing down Japanese Kamakazi planes.

As in the First World War, the second one had its share of racial clashes behind the firing lines. Walter White of the NAACP and Lester Granger of the Urban League were hired by the government to investigate various racial incidents. Granger traveled 50,000 miles to 67 Navy installations and talked with 10,000 men. "Some of the men I conferred with as individuals and in small groups. Sometimes I met with several dozen or several hundred, in recreation halls or open theatres." He reported many complaints and noted that "from month to month new progressive changes could be noted."

Walter White flew to Guam where white soldiers had hurled insults, cans, and even two grenades into Negro Army camps. After continued outrages, including the murder of a Negro GI, some Negro soldiers mounted an armed truck and headed for the white camp. They were arrested and 44 were given long prison terms. White reported that the NAACP had to "take the cases all the way to the Secretary of the Navy and the White House" to win release of the men.

In the spring of 1943 the most violent of civilian clashes exploded in Detroit, a center for war industries that had attracted many Southern Negroes and whites. In three days of rioting many Negroes were killed and injured. Federal troops had to be called in to restore order.

Just before final victory in Europe, President Franklin D. Roosevelt died. The Negro people of the United States felt a special grief, for, said Walter White, "Negro Americans made more progress toward their goal of full citizenship than under any other administration." He added: "The world has lost a great leader, a great humanitarian, and the struggling masses of common folk over the globe of every race, color, and religion, have lost a champion and friend."

## *The Postwar Battle for Rights, 1945–1954*

Most World War II veterans returned home to find too few jobs and too few homes to go around. In addition to facing these problems, the Negro veteran returned to face racial discrimination—something which he, and other soldiers, had often been told that they were fighting to destroy in Europe and Asia. It was difficult for men who had faced death to save their country to put up with the old patterns of discrimination once the foreign enemy had been defeated. Former officers bit their lips in anger when Southern police called them "boy" or abused them. Some did not bite their lips in anger, but fought back—and a few were killed.

One of the biggest problems faced by Americans of the postwar years was that of making America a land of liberty and justice for all. Many whites had returned from Europe and Asia believing that if the idea of a "master race" was wrong for our enemies, it was wrong for America too. All during and after the war, the Congress of Racial Equality (CORE) opposed discrimination in the North by nonviolent resistance. CORE members first asked owners of eating places to allow Negroes to enter. If persuasion failed, CORE members filed in, Negro and white together, and did not leave until the issue was settled. Although CORE members were arrested or beaten, they refused to resort to violence. Each Sunday during the summer of 1947, CORE members went out to picket against the segregated swimming pool at Palisades Amusement Park in New Jersey. Reported white member James Peck, "We knew in advance that we would be beaten, arrested, or both." But they finally won.

Others carried the battle for full rights to the South. Only a few months after the war had ended, more than one hundred Negro war veterans marched on the courthouse in Birmingham, Alabama to register to vote. They were turned away by white officials who claimed that the Negroes could not "interpret the United States Constitution."

One of the most spectacular gains in civil rights was accomplished by Jackie Roosevelt Robinson, an athletic college graduate. He was asked to play for the Brooklyn Dodgers baseball team but had to promise not to fight back against those who would hurl abuses at him on the diamond. For three hours Robinson and Branch Rickey of the Dodgers worked out a strategy for the baseball star that had nothing to do with playing ball. Robinson's hitting, running, and

*Jackie Robinson in a pivotal play at second base. In 1947 Robinson broke the color barrier in big league baseball—and became the National League's "Rookie of the Year." In his third season he earned the Most Valuable Player award and was eventually the first Negro elected to baseball's Hall of Fame.*

fielding soon won him a place in baseball history as well as in the hearts of millions of Americans.

The federal government, Supreme Court, and many states moved steadily toward protecting equal rights. Negroes had, naturally, resented fighting for democracy in a segregated army. After a Negro civilian group, in 1948, demanded that President Truman end segregation in the Army, Navy, and Marines, the President issued an executive order to that effect. About a year earlier, President Truman had established the President's Committee on Civil Rights, to study the problem and issue recommendations for progress. Mrs. Sadie T. Alexander and Dr. Channing Tobias were the Negro members of the group. Its report, *To Secure These Rights*, proposed "the elimination of segregation . . . from American life." By the time of the 1948 election the issue of civil rights had become a major issue dividing the Democratic Party.

The Supreme Court of the United States, throughout the New Deal, war, and postwar periods, struck down laws that denied equality to Negroes. In 1946, for example, it found unconstitutional a Virginia law that required a Negro on an interstate bus to move to the rear to make way for a white passenger. In 1950 it ruled that a Negro could not be denied a seat in the dining car of an interstate train. In 1953 the Court ruled that any "respectable well-behaved person" had a right to be served in any public place in Washington, D.C.

New York State became a leader in protecting the rights of Negro citizens. In 1945 it passed the first fair employment practices law in the nation's history. A State Commission Against Discrimination was established to enforce equal job rights. By 1950 eight states had followed New York's example, and by 1963, 22 states, including Missouri (a former slave state), had passed fair employment practice laws. In 1949 Connecticut became the first state to ban discrimination in housing.

The full integration of the armed forces occurred during the Korean War. Negro replacements were channeled into previously white units. Black men and white men fought side by side on all fronts to stem the advances of the Korean and Chinese forces. Two Negroes were among the Americans who won the Congressional Medal of Honor.

While important progress had been made toward securing equality in America, both silent and open opposition to Negro advances continued. On Christmas night, 1951, Harry T. Moore and his wife were killed by a bomb placed beneath their Florida home. Both had been leaders in the drive of the state NAACP to register more Negroes to vote. Those guilty of this crime have never been brought to justice.

Southern Negroes who fought in the integrated Army in Korea knew that their home towns would deny them a cup of coffee in a diner, or a bathroom for their children in a shopping center, or a home in a white neighborhood. Northern Negroes who returned from battle knew that the segregation of Negroes—by custom—to the worst slums and schools, and lowest-paying jobs, seemed just as strong as the segregation by law in the South. The Negro's growing pride in himself as an American and mounting anger with those who denied him his rights were moving him toward action by the 1950's.

*Frederick F. Davis, a second lieutenant during the Korean War, mans a Sabre jet.*

## *Support for the United Nations and World Peace*

Although President Franklin D. Roosevelt died before final victory over the Axis powers, he had helped to create an instrument of peace in the United Nations (UN). America offered the world organization a home and played a key role in its formation and development. President Harry Truman sent Ralph Bunche as a delegate and William E. B. Du Bois, Mary McLeod Bethune, Dr. Mordecai Johnson, and Walter White as observers to its initial meeting in San Francisco. In 1950 the President appointed Mrs. Edith Sampson, a social worker, as an alternate delegate to the United Nations for the United States. Mrs. Sampson later represented this country on the United Nation's Economic and Social Council. Other Negro delegates to represent the United States at the United Nations during later years

*Dr. Ralph Bunche, United Nations mediator, meets with his aides in Haifa, Palestine in 1948. His peace plan earned him the Nobel Peace Prize in 1950. Two other Americans have won this high honor since World War II: George C. Marshall and Martin Luther King, Jr.*

included Archibald J. Carey, Dr. Channing Tobias, Marian Anderson, and Charles Mahoney.

From its inception, American Negroes followed the proceedings of the United Nations. They rejoiced in the Declaration of Human Rights because it struck at racial injustice, and they celebrated the birth of new African nations which were emerging from European control. The colored peoples of the world—constituting a two-thirds majority of the world's population—were on the move. Negroes were justifiably proud of the record of their darker brothers throughout the world.

The most important American contributions to the United Nations during the postwar period came from Ralph Bunche, grandson of a former slave. In 1948, Bunche was sent to Palestine to mediate the tense conflict between Arabs and Jews.* His efforts were so unusually successful that, in 1950, he was awarded the Nobel Peace Prize. In 1961 Bunche wrote: "I am proud of my ancestry just as I am proud of my nationality." He still continues his efforts for world peace as a high official in the United Nations.

As America became a world leader, the existence of discrimination within its borders hurt its world position. In 1963 Secretary of State Dean Rusk put it simply when in a speech before the Senate he said: "The biggest burden we carry on our backs in our foreign relations in the 1960's is the problem of racial discrimination here at home."

President John F. Kennedy was shocked to discover that, because of their color, African ambassadors had been refused service in a restaurant on Route 40, outside Washington, D.C. The *Daily Times* of Nigeria was also angry: "By this disgraceful act of racial discrimination the United States forfeits its claim to world leadership." In the summer of 1961 the world was also told how three Negro newsmen managed to get service in a Baltimore restaurant by dressing as delegates from "Goban," a mythical African nation. They had been refused service when they entered as American Negroes. A nation that sought world leadership could not tolerate such discrimination.

---

* Walter Rex Christenberry, a Negro seaman, sought in his own way to help make Palestine the homeland for the world's Jews. He served aboard the S.S. *Ben Hecht* which was caught smuggling 623 Jews to Palestine. Christenberry explained why he volunteered to a reporter: "It was the only place where they could establish homes for all those people."

*David B. Bolen (second from right), formerly a United States Olympic sprinter, became the State Department officer in charge of Nigerian Affairs. In a visit to the Republic of Tanzania in 1966, G. Mennen Williams, Secretary of State for African Affairs (left), met with President Julius Nyerere of Tanzania (second from left) and Bolen.*

After World War II, the State Department recognized that it had few Negro representatives in foreign lands and that those few who were in foreign service were usually assigned to Negro republics such as Liberia. In 1958, President Dwight D. Eisenhower assigned Clifton R. Wharton to be ambassador to communist Romania. In 1961 he was made ambassador to Norway by President

John F. Kennedy. The young President, shortly before his assassination, appointed veteran reporter and diplomat Carl T. Rowan as ambassador to Finland. President Lyndon B. Johnson made Rowan Chief of the United States Information Service, which made him the first Negro to sit on the National Security Council.

By 1965 Negro ambassadors were serving their country at the United Nations, in the Middle East, in Europe, and in Africa. In May, 1965, President Johnson appointed Mrs. Patricia Harris ambassador to Luxembourg. She was a young Howard University professor of law whom newspapers referred to as "brainy and beautiful." Mrs. Harris was the second woman in American history to be named an ambassador.

*Ambassador Patricia R. Harris.*

# The Home Front War Against Discrimination

[*During World War II, Negro and white Americans formed the Congress of Racial Equality to battle for democracy at home. Writer Helen Buckler describes the group's use of "disciplined, nonviolent action" in its first "sit-in."*]

In Chicago, late one night in the spring of 1942, two men, one white, one Negro, entered a small, but well set-up coffee shop in a good residential neighborhood. They asked for a cup of coffee and were refused service. Several ensuing interviews with the management failed to dislodge the policy of discrimination, which was said to be due to the unwillingness of patrons to eat beside Negroes. . . . It was suggested that the management try serving Negroes for a short period, and if the trial resulted in loss of business, the loss would be made good. The management refused to experiment.

After several weeks of such efforts, during which the management had put up a sign reading, "We reserve the right to seat our patrons where we choose," a group of twenty-one persons entered the coffee shop in the late afternoon. Among them were university students, business and professional people, men and women, a young minister or two. The majority were white, but included in the group were Negro men and women. . . .

The management immediately asked the Negro men, who had seated themselves at the counter, to descend to the basement where, it was said, Negroes were served. They refused, saying they wished to sit with their friends. . . . Whereupon the management telephoned for the police.

Meanwhile, though food had been placed before the whites in the group, they would not eat unless their Negro companions were served. All maintained an unruffled demeanor. . . . Two police officers arrived. . . . Asked by the management if they would not eject the group on the grounds that the coffee shop reserved the right to seat its patrons where it wished, the officers replied, "There is nothing in the law that permits us to do that," and they left. After an hour the management, seeing that this new style sit-down strike was costing business, capitulated and served the entire twenty-one.

. . . subsequent visits to the coffee shop found the management amiably serving all alike—nor did there appear to be any fall-off in business.

Helen Buckler, "The CORE Way," *Survey Graphic* (February, 1946), p. 50. Reprinted by permission.

## The Men Who Landed in France on D-Day

[*General Dwight D. Eisenhower, in charge of the Allied invasion of France in June, 1944, later addressed the Negro battalion that took part in the landings.*]

Your battalion landed in France on June 6 under artillery, machine-gun, and rifle fire. Despite the losses sustained, the battalion carried out its mission with courage and determination and proved an important element to the air-defense team. The cheerfulness and devotion to duty of officers and men have been commented on by the personnel of other units.

. . . I commend you and the officers and men of your battalion for your fine effort, which has merited the praise of all who have observed it.

Helen Gahagan Douglas, "The Negro Soldier," *Remarks of Hon. Helen Gahagan Douglas* (Washington, 1946), p. 5. Reprinted from *The Congressional Record.*

## General Eisenhower Discusses His Troops

[*At a June 15, 1945 press conference, General Eisenhower was asked what contribution Negro soldiers made in the European theater of operations. This was his answer.*]

To start with, I would like to say this: That I do not differentiate among soldiers. I do not say white soldiers or Negro soldiers and I do not say American or British soldiers. To my mind, I have had a task in this war that makes me look upon soldiers as soldiers. Now, I have seen Negro soldiers in this war and I have many reports on their work where they have rendered very valuable contributions and some of them with the greatest enthusiasm. In late November, when we were getting short of reinforcements, replacements, some 2,600 Negro soldiers volunteered for front-line service [in the Battle of the

Bulge] and they did good work. All my commanders reported that these volunteers did excellent work. But their major job has been in Service of Supply, engineer units, quartermaster units, ordinance units. There, so far as I know and certainly as far as any official reports, they have performed equally with every kind of ordinance battalion, quartermaster battalion, and engineer battalion. They have done their job and they have done the job given them.

Helen Gahagan Douglas, "The Negro Soldier," *Remarks of Hon. Helen Gahagan Douglas* (Washington, 1946), p. 6. Reprinted from *The Congressional Record*.

## *The 332nd Wins the Distinguished Unit Citation*

[*President Franklin D. Roosevelt awarded the all-Negro 332nd Fighter Group a Distinguished Unit Citation in 1945. It read:*]

On March 24, 1945, fifty-nine P-51 type aircraft were airborne and set course for the rendezvous with the bomber formation. Through superior navigation and maintenance of strict flight discipline, the group formation reached the bomber formation at the designated time and place. Nearing the target approximately 25 enemy aircraft were encountered which included ME-252s which launched relentless attacks in a desperate effort to break up and destroy the bomber formation.

Displaying outstanding courage, aggressiveness, and combat technique, the group immediately engaged the enemy formation in aerial combat. In the ensuing engagement that continued over the target area, the gallant pilots of the 332nd Fighter Group battled against the enemy fighters to prevent the breaking up of the bomber formation. . . . Through their superior skill and determination, the group destroyed three enemy aircraft, probably destroyed three [more], and damaged three. Among their claims were eight of the highly rated enemy jet-propelled aircraft, with no loss sustained by the 332nd Fighter Group.

Leaving the target area and en route to base after completion of their primary task, aircraft of the group conducted strafing attacks against enemy ground installations and transportation with outstanding success. By the conspicuous gallantry, professional skill, and determination of the pilots, together with the outstanding technical skill and devotion to duty of the ground personnel, the 332nd

Fighter Group has reflected great credit on itself and the armed forces of the United States.

United States Department of War, *Press Release*, October 16, 1945.

## Bravery in the European Theater of Operations

*[Charles L. Thomas, a 24-year-old commander of a tank destroyer company in France, and Captain Charles Gandy of the 92nd Division, were two of the many Negroes serving in the United States Army to win decorations for bravery in action. Captain Thomas won the Distinguished Service Cross for "extraordinary heroism in action" for the following action:]*

Sustaining wounds in the chest, legs, and arms, the Negro officer won the Army's second highest decoration by literally shooting his way through the Siegfried line last December in a blaze of fire from enemy rockets, artillery and machine guns.

He [Captain Charles Gandy] led his company out in broad daylight and . . . by personal example and leadership, succeeded in getting his entire company across a canal, with an abrupt 12-foot wall. This was accomplished in rain and under extremely heavy fire. . . . Captain Gandy went forward alone to reconnoiter [and while] engaged in this activity, he was mortally wounded by enemy machine-gun fire. His outstanding gallantry and leadership in combat exemplified the heroic traditions of the United States Army.

Citations in *The Congressional Record*, 79th Congress, First Session, pp. 7421-7422.

## Integration During the Battle of the Bulge

*[This was the way the Paris edition of the United States Army's* Stars and Stripes *reported the mixing of Negro and white units during the decisive Battle of the Bulge.]*

Negro doughboys are participating in the eastward sweep by General Hodges' forces. . . .

If comments of white personnel of these divisions are any indication, the plan of mixing white and colored troops in fighting units, a departure from previous United States Army practice, is operating successfully.

Negro reinforcements reported a sincere, friendly welcome everywhere. They also spoke of excellent relations with their white fellow-doughs, of the making of inter-racial friendships.

The integration of the Negro platoons into their units was accomplished quickly and quietly. There was no problem. . . .

"I was damned glad to get those boys," said the CO of K company, Capt. Wesley J. Simons, of Snow Hill, Md. "They fit into our company like any other platoon, and they fight like hell. Maybe that's because they were all volunteers and wanted to get into this."

Alan Morrison, *Stars and Stripes*, Paris Edition, April 6, 1945.

# Senator Maybank Defends the Southern Way of Life

[*Throughout World War II, all efforts to secure equal rights for Negroes were met by the opposition of Southern Senators and Congressmen. One of these, Maybank of South Carolina, attacks "these agitators" who wish to extend democracy.*]

. . . our custom of segregation . . . has proved mutually satisfactory to the vast majority of both races in South Carolina. . . .

In my opinion these agitators are making a serious mistake, when during stress of war they seek by law to abrogate customs which are as old and deep-rooted in the South as our civilization itself. . . .

Mr. President, the white people of the South will not accept these interferences. We are proud of our section. We know what is best for the white people and the colored people. We are going to treat the Negro fairly, but in so doing we do not intend for him to take over our election system or attend our white schools.

Regardless of any Supreme Court decisions and any laws that may be passed by Congress, we of the South will maintain our political and social institutions. . . .

---

*The Congressional Record*, Vol. 90, Part III, 78th Congress, Second Session, p. 3432.

## *Robert C. Weaver, Government Official*

[*In January, 1966 Robert C. Weaver became the first Negro Cabinet member in American history. His nomination by President Johnson was unanimously confirmed by the United States Senate. A few years before this, after three decades of faithful government service, Weaver described his role as an official and a Negro.*]

I happen to have been born a Negro and to have devoted a large part of my adult energies to the problem of the role of the Negro in America. But I am also a government administrator, and have devoted just as much energy—if not more—to the problems of government administration at the local, state, and national levels.

My responsibilities as a Negro and an American are part of the heritage I received from my parents—a heritage that included a wealth of moral and social values that do not have anything to do with my race. My responsibilities as a government administrator do not have too much to do with my race, either. My greatest difficulty in public life is combating the idea that somehow my responsibilities as a Negro conflict with my responsibilities as a government administrator: and this is a problem which is presented by those Negroes who feel that I represent them exclusively, as well as by those whites who doubt my capacity to represent all elements in the population. The fact is that my responsibilities as a Negro and a government administrator do not conflict: they complement each other. . . .

What are the responsibilities of Negro leadership? Certainly the first is to keep pressing for the status of first-class citizenship for all—an inevitable goal of those who accept the values of this nation. Another is to encourage and help Negroes to prepare for the opportunities that are now and will be open to them.

The ultimate responsibilities of Negro leaders, however, are to show results and to maintain a following. This means that they cannot be so "responsible" that they forget the trials and tribulations of those less fortunate or less recognized. They cannot stress progress —the emphasis that is so palatable to the majority group—without, at the same time, delineating the unsolved business of democracy. They cannot provide models that will have any meaning for their followers unless they can bring about social changes that will facilitate the emergence of these models from the *typical* environment of the Negro community. . . .

Most Negroes in leadership roles have made clear that they and those who follow them are part of America. They have striven for realization of the American dream. But they cannot succeed alone. Sophisticated whites realize that the status of Negroes in our society depends not only on what the Negro himself does to achieve his goals and to prepare himself for opportunities, but even more, on what all America does to expand these opportunities. The quality and character of future Negro leadership will be determined by how effective those leaders who relate to the *total* society can be in satisfying the yearnings for human dignity that lie in the hearts of all Americans.

*The Negro as an American*, Occasional Papers of the Fund for the Republic, 1963, pp. 3-8.

## Defending the Flag in Ghana

[*On February 4, 1964, Adger Emerson Player, a Negro member of the American Embassy staff in Accra, Ghana, kept an anti-American mob from desecrating the American flag. His bravery received wide publicity and the special thanks of President Lyndon B. Johnson. Player explained his action in a letter to a California Congressman.*]

Dear Sir: I have been the subject of much publicity since February 4, 1964. . . .

President Johnson wrote that I "have the gratitude of freemen everywhere who respect the principles and ideals for which our flag stands." The American dilemma is still the contradiction of racial bondage, injustice, and inequality as practiced by some Americans with the American principles of liberty, justice, and equality. I would like to set the record straight regarding what I consider the true meaning of my action.

My action was something that any American—black or white —would have done. However, my raising of the flag decreases in real significance when compared with the real acts of heroism and sacrifice by countless American Negroes who since August 1619 and continuing through today have lost their lives because they asserted their God-given rights as human beings and as Americans. I did only what American Negroes have been doing from the very beginning of the history of the United States—loyally defending the country that our ancestors made along with other Americans of all origins and races. This is our country in every respect. We have a perfect right to defend it. In addition, we must honor those Negro Americans of yesterday who sowed American and foreign soil with their lives so that generations of today and tomorrow may reap the rewards, benefits, duties, and responsibilities of free men and women. These—our ancestors—were real heroes and courageous American Negroes whose names have been hidden in American history far too long. . . .

I hope that all the words of praise for my deed in raising the American flag in Ghana will be translated now in the United States into respect and full acceptance of American Negroes. If this full respect and acceptance does not take place, then one must draw the sad conclusion—as many American Negroes and other people throughout the world will—that the American flag was raised once again in vain.

Sincerely yours,

*Adger Emerson Player*

American Embassy, Accra, Ghana.

*The Congressional Record*, 88th Congress, Second Session, Appendix, A1041.

# Dr. Bunche Receives the Nobel Peace Prize

[*Ralph J. Bunche grew up in poverty—he sold newspapers and shined shoes to help his family. He worked his way through college as a janitor and received a Ph.D. degree from Harvard. For his outstanding contribution to peace in solving the 1948 dispute between the Arabs and Jews in the new state of Israel, he was awarded the Nobel Peace Prize. This is how the* Voice of America *carried the news to the world.*]

"I am flabbergasted!" said Ralph J. Bunche, when told he had been awarded the Nobel Peace Prize.

But his friends and co-workers in the United Nations, where Dr. Bunche directs the Department of Trusteeships, were not surprised. They and other international observers fully expected that Dr. Bunche's valiant efforts to end hostilities in the Holy Land would earn a just recognition.

Dr. Bunche acknowledged the praise:

"I wish to say that my peace efforts flowed from the strength of the United Nations."

But the legions of men and women who had followed his trials and triumphs were not satisfied with this explanation. In appreciation of Dr. Bunche's personal achievements as a U.N. mediator, they bestowed more than sixty awards and degrees on him.

*Voice of America*, English edition (July-August, 1951), p. 15.

# The War in Korea and Sergeant Cornelius H. Charlton

[*The outbreak of war in Korea in June, 1950 brought the armed forces of the United States—and, later, the United Nations—to that small nation near China. Two Negro G.I.'s won the Congressional Medal of Honor in Korea, but lost their lives in action. One was Cornelius H. Charlton. His award read:*]

Sergeant *Cornelius H. Charlton* . . . distinguished himself by conspicuous gallantry and intrepidity above and beyond the call of duty in action against the enemy near Chipo-ri, Korea, on 2 June 1951. His platoon was attacking heavily defended hostile positions on commanding ground when the leader was wounded and evacuated. Sergeant *Charlton* assumed command, rallied the men, and spearheaded the assault against the hill. Personally eliminating two hostile positions and killing six of the enemy with his rifle fire and grenades, he continued up the slope until the unit suffered heavy casualties and became pinned down. Regrouping the men, he led them forward only to be again hurled back by a shower of grenades. Despite a severe chest wound, Sergeant *Charlton* refused medical attention and led a third daring charge which carried the crest of the ridge. Observing that the remaining emplacement which had retarded the advance was situated on the reverse slope, he charged it alone, was again hit by a grenade, but raked the position with a devastating fire which eliminated it and routed the defenders. The wounds received during Sergeant *Charlton's* daring exploits resulted in his death, but his indomitable courage, superb leadership, and gallant self-sacrifice reflect the highest credit on himself, the Infantry, and the military service.

*General Orders No. 30*, Department of the Army (Washington, March 19, 1952).

# 19

# America's Civil Rights Revolution

GREAT social revolutions are not born in a day, a year, or even a decade. When they do happen, people begin to realize they came from long-ignored smoldering fires. The civil rights crisis of the 1960's had its roots deep in America's struggle for freedom and justice. It was first born in the fierce resistance of Africans aboard the ships of the slave trade and on the plantations of the New World. The descendants of these Africans gained renewed hope and courage from the ringing words of the Declaration of Independence and from the efforts of fearless Negro and white abolitionists.

The Negro revolution of today can trace its demands for equality to the fiery words hammered out by William E. B. Du Bois. "The problem of the twentieth century," wrote this gentle scholar in 1903, "is the problem of the color-line." Only equality, he pointed out during most of his 95 years on earth, would make the dream of America a reality for all. On the day he died in 1963, hundreds of thousands of Americans were moving toward Washington, D.C., to voice their protest against all color-lines in the United States. They were taking part in a long historic process, deeply embedded in their nation's history. And they were contributing to the fulfillment of America's commitment to equal justice for all.

*Congressman Adam Clayton Powell addresses a 1942 protest meeting in a Washington church. Powell was an early civil rights leader.*

## The Supreme Court Decision of 1954

Shortly after high noon on Monday, May 17, 1954, members of the Supreme Court, spectators, and reporters sat solemnly listening to Chief Justice Earl Warren read the Court's decision in the *Brown* case. High above the entrance to the building is the motto, "Equal Justice Under Law." Inside the marble meeting room more than a half century of legal segregation was being overturned by the unanimous decision of the nine justices. The heart of the decision was in the sentence: "Separate educational facilities are inherently unequal." One year later the Court ruled that all school districts must desegregate "with all deliberate speed."

Within a year after the 1954 decision more than 500 school districts in the North and upper South had quietly desegregated. In the cities of Baltimore and Washington, D.C., Negro and white children sat side by side for the first time in history. Virginia, leader of the South, appeared calm and thoughtful after the *Brown* decision. Governor Thomas Stanley commented: "We will consider the matter and work toward a plan which will be acceptable to our citizens and in keeping with the edict."

Everywhere in the upper South the pattern was the same. Children and parents of both races accepted the change more easily than anyone would have predicted. Only where there was organized opposition by white "segregationists" was there trouble. In Hoxie, Tennessee 26 Negroes were enrolled in a white school system of 800. There was no opposition until a few white parents began to stir others with fears of interracial marriages. When a group of white parents demanded that the Board of Education halt integration, the Board held firm and peaceful integration continued. The issue died.

In September, 1956 John Kasper, an anti-Negro agitator from New Jersey, went to Clinton, Tennessee to fight the integration of the new high school. He began by calling white parents on the telephone and warning them of what would happen to their children in the integrated high school. Some hung up on him. But others listened and began to worry. In the school a few white students formed a "White Youth Council" to annoy the Negro students and keep other whites from befriending them. The principal reported, "When the Negro kids came in, the others were real nice and friendly until the White Youth Council was formed." But Kasper was finally jailed and some of the students banded together to oppose the White Youth Council. "We finally got tired of them taking advantage of the Negro students," explained a white student.

In the Deep South, open and complete defiance of the Supreme Court decision began to develop as soon as it was announced. Georgia's Governor Herman Talmadge declared that his state would "not tolerate the mixing of the races in the public schools or any other tax-supported institutions." Except for a few districts in Texas, no Negro was admitted to schools in the Deep South until the districts had been compelled to admit them by federal court orders.

In many places, White Citizens Councils battled school integration by threatening loss of business to persons employing those who supported compliance with the court decision. The Ku Klux

Klan became more active, using terror and violence to silence the voices that called for peaceful acceptance of the *Brown* decision.

Defiance of the Supreme Court was spurred by a "Southern Manifesto" issued by 96 Southern Congressmen in March, 1956. It denounced the *Brown* ruling and called for "all lawful means to bring about a reversal of this decision which is contrary to the Constitution. . . ." The pace of integration began to slow down considerably. While 200 new school districts had integrated in 1956, only 38 new ones had done so a year later.

The first important test of the power of the federal backing for integration came in September, 1957. Governor Orval Faubus of Arkansas interfered with a court order directing the Central High School in Little Rock to admit nine qualified Negro pupils. Faubus warned of bloodshed if the nine entered the high school and called out National Guard troops to protect the school.

The Governor's fearful announcements brought out large crowds of segregationists in front of the high school. When one of

*The 101st Airborne Division escorts Negro students into Central High School in Little Rock, Arkansas.*

the nine students, fifteen-year-old Elizabeth Eckford, tried to enter the school, she was halted by a National Guardsman. "When I tried to squeeze past him he raised his bayonet and then the other guards closed in and they raised their bayonets." A jeering crowd ("Lynch her!") followed her as she walked bravely to the bus stop. A white Northern reporter put his arm around her and whispered "Don't let them see you cry." A white woman placed her aboard a bus. Elizabeth Eckford's heroism in the face of both the National Guard and the mob was carried to the far corners of the earth by radio and television. News of Governor Faubus' defiance of court orders was also heard around the world.

President Dwight D. Eisenhower, reluctant to use federal force to compel a state to cooperate with court orders, had to support the decisions of the courts. The President had often said: "I do not believe you can change the hearts of men with laws and decisions." But in September, 1957 he finally ordered 1,000 of the crack 101st Airborne Division into Little Rock to protect the nine students and to enforce the court order.

Paratroopers guarded the entrances to Central High School and twenty-four were stationed in the hallways. The nine Negro students were brought to school by the United States Army. When some white students called for a "walkout" less than sixty out of the 1,800 students left school. Others invited the new students to join the Glee Club or sat with them at lunch.

But the troublemakers did not quit. They singled out Minnejean Brown, 16, and cursed, tripped, or pushed her at every opportunity. After five months of this abuse, her patience came to an end. When another girl spilled hot soup on her in the school cafeteria, she struck back. The principal suspended both pupils. Minnejean Brown entered the private Lincoln School in New York City and graduated a year later, high in her class.

Governor Faubus' interference continued. He closed the Little Rock schools, and for more than a year they remained closed. But when the Board of Education forced the opening of the schools again, small "token" groups of Negro pupils were present in several of the city's schools.

The crisis at Central High School focused the nation's attention on the question of civil rights and the enforcement of the 1954 *Brown* decision. In 1957 Congress passed the first law since Reconstruction to protect the rights of America's Negroes. It provided the

Attorney General with greater power than he had ever had to halt interferences with school desegregation, and established a Civil Rights Commission to report to the President on what progress was being made toward equality. The law was guided through Congress by Senator Lyndon B. Johnson of Texas. In 1960, another civil rights law was introduced by Senator Johnson and was guided through Congress by Senators John F. Kennedy and Lyndon B. Johnson.

The 1957 law also provided that cases involving a denial of voter rights be tried in federal, rather than state courts. It made the 1939 civil rights section of the Department of Justice a full division and provided it with additional staff and funds. The 1960 Civil Rights Act further strengthened the 1957 act by providing for federal referees in cases where voting rights were denied. It also made sure that Southern voter registrars could not evade the law by hiding the records or resigning suddenly when faced with an investigation by the Attorney-General's office.

## *The Montgomery, Alabama Bus Boycott*

On December 1, 1955, Mrs. Rosa Parks boarded a bus in Montgomery, Alabama, the first capital of the Confederacy, and took a seat near the front. When a white man entered the bus and found no empty seats, the bus driver asked Mrs. Parks to move to the rear so that the gentleman could have her seat. There was nothing unusual in this request, for Negroes were expected to give up their seats and follow the bus driver's orders. But Mrs. Parks refused. "I don't really know why I wouldn't move. There was no plan at all. I was just tired from shopping." Mrs. Parks was arrested on the spot for breaking the segregation law and taken to police headquarters to be fingerprinted.

The night after Mrs. Parks' arrest, the Reverend Martin Luther King, Jr., 27, called a meeting of church leaders in his Baptist church. The entire group agreed to ask all Negroes to stay off the buses the day Mrs. Parks came to trial. On that fateful December 5, Dr. King got up early and went to check on the progress of the boycott. He wrote of this incident in *Stride Toward Freedom*.

> I jumped in my car and for almost an hour I cruised
> down every major street and examined every passing

bus. During this hour, at the peak of the morning traffic, I saw no more than eight Negro passengers riding
the buses. By this time I was jubilant. . . . A mir-
acle had taken place.

And a new and powerful American leader had been born!

Ninety per cent of the Negroes stayed off the Montgomery
buses that day and continued to stay off them month after month,
for more than a year. People organized car pools; others walked
great distances to work. The bus company lost 65 per cent of its
business and had to cut schedules, lay off drivers, and raise fares.
The businesses of the white merchants suffered.

The city in which Jefferson Davis took the oath of office as
President of the Southern Confederacy had become a scene of a nonviolent battleground for human rights. The Southern whites learned
again that their picture of the Negro as content under segregation
and happy without equal rights was a lie. The Negroes had discovered the devastating weapon of the economic boycott used so effectively by American colonists against the British before the Revolution.

*Dr. Martin Luther King, Jr., speaks to a group of young admirers.*

After the boycott had been under way for 80 days, a desperate city administration ordered the arrest of Dr. King and 100 other Negro leaders. Dr. King told a packed meeting the next night that the boycott would continue no matter how many of its leaders went to jail. The conflict, he pointed out, was not "between the white and the Negro" but "between justice and injustice." He called upon his followers to love rather than to hate those who opposed them.

> If we are arrested every day, if we are exploited every day, if we are trampled over every day, don't ever let anyone pull you so low as to hate them. . . . We must realize so many people are taught to hate us that they are not totally responsible for their hate.

The bus boycott went on until final victory. In November, 1956, the Supreme Court ruled that bus segregation violated the United States Constitution. The Montgomery bus company agreed not only to end segregation but to hire Negro drivers and treat all passengers with equal respect.

As the day approached for the integration of the buses, Negro churches instructed their members to sit where they pleased but not to strike back if beaten. At 5:55 in the morning of December 21, 1956, Dr. King and Reverend Glen Smiley, a white friend, boarded the bus near Dr. King's house. As Dr. King paid his fare the bus driver said, "We are glad to have you this morning." Dr. King and Reverend Smiley rode into history, sitting side by side. During that 1956 season of "peace on earth and good will toward men," a new day had begun to dawn in Alabama. The city of Montgomery had produced the most important civil rights leader of the day and the most effective weapon of protest yet devised.

The technique of nonviolence was used most effectively by college students staging "sit-ins." On February 1, 1960 the manager of a five and ten cent store in Greensboro, North Carolina watched four Negro college students who sat on the stools at his lunch counter and who insisted on each being served a cup of coffee. He turned to a reporter and said: "They can just sit there. It's nothing to me." The students continued to sit, returned the next day, and sat some more. By the fourth day some whites joined the "sit-in." After several months of this, the lunch counter was opened to Negroes as well as whites.

The sit-ins immediately spread to hundreds of other Southern cities and almost always they were led by students from high schools or colleges. In the first six months of the new campaign, over 1,600 young men and women, Negro and white, were arrested for taking part in lunch counter sit-ins. But it was now possible for Negroes to sit on the stools of more and more Southern lunch counters and order whatever they pleased.

Many of the sit-ins were led by members of the Congress of Racial Equality (CORE), an interracial organization that had used nonviolent techniques to smash racial bars since the early days of World War II. As a reminder of their nonviolent purpose each CORE member carried a card which read:

> Don't strike back or curse if abused;
> Don't laugh out;
> Don't hold conversations with floor workers;
> Don't block entrances to the stores or aisles;
> Show yourself courteous and friendly at all times;
> Sit straight and always face the counter;
> Remember love and non-violence;
> May God bless you.

While these demonstrators were often abused by segregationists, by not fighting back they increasingly won sympathy and support for the justice of their cause.

## The Federal Government Takes Action

Since the end of Reconstruction American politicians had tried to ignore the Negro drive for rights. Some tiptoed around it while others denounced it as "dividing the country." The 1954 Supreme Court decision and the attempts of Southern states to avoid compliance made it increasingly difficult for federal officials to avoid the issue. American Negroes now had the full support of the Constitution.

Although President Dwight D. Eisenhower did not speak in favor of the *Brown* decision, he ordered the integration of 47 veterans' hospitals and the Navy Yards of Norfolk and Charleston. He also had the Washington, D.C. schools speedily desegregated. In both the 1952 and 1956 Presidential campaigns, however, neither President Eisenhower nor Democratic candidate Adlai Stevenson had taken a strong position on civil rights nor told how he intended to enforce equality.

By the election of 1960, however, the civil rights issue had become very important and the "Negro vote" had become crucial. Vice-President Nixon courted the white Southerners and made few appeals to Negro voters. But Senator John F. Kennedy stated his belief that the President must "wage the struggle for equal rights." Fast-moving events on the civil rights front soon tipped the balance to candidate Kennedy.

Reverend Martin Luther King was jailed for leading a demonstration in Georgia. Senator Kennedy called Mrs. King and asked if he could aid her husband and said that he would be happy to do whatever he could to help. Robert Kennedy, his campaign manager, phoned a Georgia judge, and Dr. King was released on bail. Newspapers, radio, and television carried the news to all parts of the nation.

For many Negroes, Kennedy was clearly the candidate "who cared" about Negro rights. By the narrowest of margins, the Negro vote being crucial in several states, John F. Kennedy was elected President of the United States.

In the 1964 election, 95 per cent of the Negro voters helped give President Lyndon B. Johnson his overwhelming victory over Senator Barry Goldwater. While Goldwater had defended "states' rights" and opposed civil rights laws, President Johnson had pledged his administration to carry out a program of complete equality of rights for all.

By 1965 Negro voting power, which had been growing steadily since World War I, was obvious from coast to coast, especially in the great industrial centers of the nation. Six Negroes sat in the United States Congress. Representative Adam Clayton Powell of New York was chairman of the important Committee on Education and Labor, and Congressman William Dawson of Illinois, grandson of slaves, was chairman of the Committee on Government Operations. Ninety-four Negroes served in the legislatures of 24 states. In Georgia Senator Horace T. Ward beat his white opponent by a two-to-one margin in a district where a majority of the voters were white. Ward was one of two Negro Senators serving in Georgia's legislature. Others served in the legislatures of Delaware (3), Kentucky (2), Maryland (4), Missouri (8), Oklahoma (4), and Tennessee (1). Illinois had eleven Negro legislators. Even some of the states with few Negroes had Negro representatives in the state houses (Nebraska, Colorado, Washington, Kansas, and Wisconsin). Eleven of these 94 state representatives were women.

*Senator Edward E. Brooke of Massachusetts, first Negro elected to the Senate since B. K. Bruce left in 1881.*

In 1966 Edward W. Brooke of Massachusetts became the first Negro elected to the United States Senate since Reconstruction. Brooke had attended the segregated schools of Washington, D.C., and then won the Bronze Star for his intelligence work with Italian partisans during World War II. He won election as Attorney General of his state (2 per cent Negro population) before he was elected to the Senate by a huge majority.

## The Kennedy Administration in Action

In the spring of 1961 the Kennedy administration had been in office only a few months when it was presented with its first civil rights crisis. James Farmer, Director of CORE, led a group of Negro and white "Freedom Riders" into the South. They began a series of bus rides to make sure that bus terminals in the deep South were not segregated. One bus was set afire. On Mother's Day, 1961, James Peck, a white Freedom Rider, was almost beaten to death in Birmingham. He said that as he stepped from a bus "six of them started swinging at me with fists and pipes. . . . Within seconds I was unconscious on the ground." His head wounds required 53 stitches. Attorney General Robert Kennedy sent United States marshals to protect other riders and personally planned some of the trips through the South to prevent further violence.

*James Meredith graduates from "Ole Miss." After his graduation he continued to play an important part in civil rights activities in both the South and the North.*

The next great test for the federal government came on the long night of September 30, 1962, when James Meredith, son of a Mississippi farmer, entered the University of Mississippi to complete his studies. Meredith had to be brought onto the campus protected by 500 marshals.

That night, as President Kennedy addressed the country on television and radio, calling for peace and order, the marshals were holding off a mob of 2,500 Mississippians determined to either drive Meredith from the campus or kill him. Meredith, however, reported: "I think I read a newspaper and went to bed around 10 o'clock. . . ." He added, "And I slept pretty well all night."

By morning two men lay dead, shot by the rioters, scores of marshals and citizens had been injured, and many cars and buildings had been damaged. But James Meredith was enrolled at "Ole Miss" despite the violence and the estimated cost of almost half a million dollars. Student Meredith ignored some nasty pranks and said of the students: "Most I'd say—have been courteous, and the faculty members certainly have."

On August 18, 1963, James Meredith lined up with his fellow classmates to receive his diploma. It was a bright, sunny Southern day.

## 1963: The Year of Decision

On the 100th anniversary of the Emancipation Proclamation, the civil rights drive was picking up momentum from Negro and white citizens. For many progress was slow, too slow. Ten years after the *Brown* decision of the Supreme Court had ordered the integration of the schools, only 1.06 per cent of the South's Negro school children sat in classes with whites. The strategy of the civil rights movement, now led by Martin Luther King, was to strike at the most segregated city in America, Birmingham, Alabama.

This Southern steel city has had a long history of racial injustice, unequaled in the nation. It has been the scene of 60 unsolved anti-Negro bombings since the end of World War II. Birmingham officials had banned a children's book that showed black and white rabbits playing together. Its leading law enforcement official, Eugene "Bull" Connor, readied his weapons for the demonstrators and said, "I got plenty of room in the jail." As it turned out, he would need every bit of jail space.

On April 3, 1963 Dr. Martin Luther King and his aides arrived in Birmingham to plan their most ambitious program of resistance to segregation and discrimination. Fearing their phones were tapped, they used code names—King was called "JFK" and demonstrators were "baptismal candidates." Arrests of demonstrators began with the first demonstrations. Orderly, well-dressed Negroes were loaded into patrol wagons when they tried to march into downtown Birmingham. The charge was "parading without a permit."

As more and more Negroes joined the marching, singing groups into Birmingham, the shopping area suffered a severe drop in sales. To stem this mounting tide of humanity, Connor ordered the police to use their trained dogs against the paraders. The dogs were first used on Palm Sunday.

Next the city government secured a court order banning further marches. For the first time Reverend King and his group decided to disobey a court order. "We did not hide our intentions," King wrote

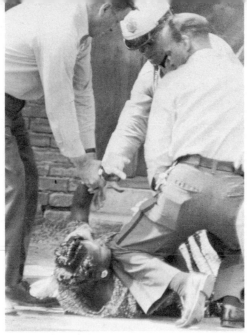

*Three Birmingham, Alabama policemen subdue a woman demonstrator.*

in *Why We Can't Wait.* "In fact, I announced our plan to the press, pointing out that we were not anarchists advocating lawlessness, but that it was obvious to us that the courts of Alabama had misused the judicial process in order to perpetuate injustice and segregation." On Good Friday, Dr. King and Reverend Abernathy were arrested for leading a march into the center of Birmingham.

A concerned President Kennedy called Mrs. King to promise whatever help was possible, and Attorney General Robert Kennedy called Birmingham and had Dr. King released from solitary confinement. In eight days Dr. King was free and the marches continued. So did the arrests. Before the crisis ended with the surrender of the Birmingham officials, 3,300 others, many of them schoolchildren, had been jailed.

On May 7, a stunned nationwide television audience watched high-pressure hoses shoot powerful jets of water on carefully attired Negro demonstrators. Men and women were swept into the gutter or struck down. One jet tore the bark off a tree, and another sent Reverend Fred Shuttleworth crashing into the side of a building. Birmingham police then beat their way into the demonstrators, swinging their clubs.

A few days later the home of Dr. King's brother was bombed, and the parents and their five children narrowly escaped death. A series of bomb blasts rocked the Negro areas of the city a few days after that. As the infuriated inhabitants moved into the streets, police sealed off the Negro sections and drove the people off the streets. On a few occasions, such as this one, Negroes responded to violence with violence. But it was the restraint of the Negroes, when contrasted with the violence launched by "Bull" Connor, that made Dr. King's Birmingham campaign a success. President Kennedy later told King that Connor's police dogs and fire hoses had done as much to advance the cause of Negroes as had Lincoln's Emancipation Proclamation.

Segregation in Birmingham was dying despite the confusion and violence. A white city businessman asked: "Are the Negroes I see around town walking a little straighter these days?" And Birmingham, wrote Dr. King, "was a fuse—it detonated a revolution that went on to win scores of other victories."

In the months following the dramatic events in Birmingham, 800 civil rights demonstrations took place in cities and towns of the South and North. Increasing numbers of white clergymen and citizens of all faiths joined in the civil rights campaign. Dr. Eugene Carson Blake, head of the United Presbyterian Church, was quoted in *Time* magazine as saying: "Some time or other, we are all going to have to stand and be on the receiving end of a fire hose." Then he joined two dozen other clergymen in a protest march and was arrested.

The events in Birmingham brought a demand from President Kennedy for Congress to pass a civil rights law which would open public facilities to all Americans. Our people, the President told the nation, "for all its hopes and all its boasts, will not be fully free until

*Reverend Martin Luther King, Jr. (right), and Reverend Ralph Abernathy (at his side) lead a Birmingham march in violation of a court order. They and fifty-one other demonstrators were arrested.*

all its citizens are free. . . . Now the time has come for this nation to fulfill its promises." The urgency of his demand for action was underscored by the assassination of Medgar Evers, a veteran of World War II and a Mississippi civil rights leader. He was shot in the back just 24 hours after the President's talk.

In 1964 Congress passed the civil rights law President Kennedy had been asking for. President Johnson, who had taken over the battle for the civil rights bill when Kennedy was assassinated, signed it into law on July 4, 1964. It provided for the complete integration of public facilities and schools. Federal funds, under this statute, could be withheld from any project which did not take steps to end discrimination. Neither unions nor businesses of over 25 employees could practice discrimination. Greater powers were provided for the Justice Department in dealing with those who broke the law and new government agencies were created to carry out parts of the new law.

In 1965 President Johnson signed a voting rights bill that provided federal registrars in any section of the South where Negroes were denied the right to register and vote. Immediately after the passage of the law, government registrars went South and began to register thousands of new voters.

## Action in the North

By 1963 Negro leaders turned their attention to the vast problems of the Negroes in Northern ghettos. One-third of the country's Negroes are packed into Northern cities. Grinding poverty, more than civil rights, was their special problem. In a nation of abundance, they were among "the other America" who lived without jobs, decent homes—and hope.

The discrimination that faced the Northern Negro was not written into law as it was in the South. In the North most people claimed to believe in equality. But the best jobs, neighborhoods, and schools were closed to the Negro just the same.

During the 1960's, the frustration in the Negro ghettos of the North brought new members to extremist groups such as the Black Muslims. This group boldly asserted the superiority of the black man and told Negroes to live apart from whites. White newspapers featured the Muslims' racism and their training for defense against

*Malcolm X addresses a Harlem rally in 1963, supporting efforts to integrate Birmingham, Alabama.*

whites. Little was written about their amazing success in reforming criminals and dope addicts, teaching Negroes about the role of the Negro in Africa and America, and stressing better health habits and stronger family ties.

The most articulate spokesman for the Muslims was Malcolm X, a self-educated man with a criminal past. Recruited in prison, Malcolm X became a Muslim leader upon his release in 1952. But a trip to Africa in 1964 convinced him that hatred of the white man "didn't bring us anything." He began to "see things on a broader scale." He emphasized "human rights" rather than civil rights and refused to attack whites. "If you attack him because he is white, you give him no out. He can't stop being white. We've got to give the man a chance."

But before Malcolm X could carry his new crusade much further, he was assassinated as he began making a speech to his New York followers. At his grave, Negroes refused to let white gravediggers bury their leader. His black followers, some with shovels and others with handfuls of earth, buried Malcolm X.

The Northern ghetto dwellers began to move into action, sometimes under careful direction, sometimes spontaneously. In New York two school boycotts, which kept thousands of children out of school, were used to dramatize the city's slowness in improving schools in Negro neighborhoods and in integrating all schools. To

*Poverty is still the lot of two-thirds of today's Negroes, such as this Atlanta, Georgia family.*

dramatize job discrimination, civil rights groups picketed unions and businesses and white and Negro men chained themselves to machines or stood in the paths of bulldozers.

Summer riots in 1964, 1965, and 1966 further dramatized the futility of life in the Northern ghettos. In a dozen cities young men, often unemployed, smashed cars and store windows and pelted police with stones and bottles. In Watts, California 34 (mostly Negro) were left dead and thousands were left homeless, after 6 days of shooting, burning, and looting. When a group of Harlem rioters were asked to return to their homes, they answered, "Baby, we are home!" President Johnson knew that federal money could provide hope for these desperate people, as well as build pleasant neighborhoods to replace crumbling slums. His "War on Poverty" was supposed to accomplish what civil rights laws could not do.

Each time the Northern Negro took a step toward equality he found his way blocked by groups of whites. When New York Negroes organized a school boycott, whites organized a counterboycott. They saw Negro advancement as a threat to their position. One white group that picketed Negroes called itself SPONGE or "The Society for the Prevention of Negroes Getting Everything." While most Northern whites were willing to concede "token" integration, complete equality frightened them. Some openly admitted they did not want their children associating with Negroes anywhere, anytime.

While some people called this opposition to Negro equality "the white backlash," others pointed out that it had always been present in American life—and had been a major factor in halting Negro progress.

As in the South, the schools became the focus of Negro leaders —and the white opposition. In New York the dispute arose over transferring Negro students to schools in white neighborhoods and moving white students to schools in Negro neighborhoods. "Why do we have to sacrifice our kids," said one mother, "because the Negro was mistreated for many years?"

In many districts with almost equal numbers of Negroes and whites, integration was successful and the reports were encouraging. Integration did not lower academic standards. Teachers found that mixed classes added a new dimension to the experience of the students. As in the South, the children accepted each other far better than their worried parents. The dire predictions of the white adults did not come to pass. And while students still chose to sit near their older friends, mixing became easier and more natural.

## America's Largest Protest March

Beginning in the 1960's a new and determined young army of college students of all races and religions entered the South to teach a new freedom to long-oppressed Negroes. These new "carpetbaggers" were trained in nonviolence and came armed with thick books and high ideals. They helped the local Negroes establish libraries, community centers, and "Freedom Schools." Their classes met under trees until rooms could be found. Negro children learned to read and write, to understand the rights of American citizens, and the role that Negroes have played in American history.

The schools and the teachers lived under a reign of terror similar to that of the Reconstruction period. Buildings were bombed and civil rights workers beaten or murdered. But every act of violence only seemed to convince these young men and women of the rightness of their cause. As his deputies tried to intimidate a 1962 meeting of Georgia Negroes, Sheriff Z. T. Mathews told a reporter: "We want our colored people to go on living like they have for the last 100

*A voter-registration worker talks with a cotton picker in the Deep South. From 1964 to 1966 a small army of civil rights workers went south to aid in registering Negro voters or in teaching in "freedom schools." Some lost their lives; others were beaten or jailed.*

years." But American Negroes had no intention of doing that, no matter what the cost.

To dramatize their demand for equality to the nation, civil rights leaders planned a gigantic march on Washington for August 28, 1963. The five major Negro organizations agreed to support the idea of Asa Philip Randolph, 75, who had called off another march in 1941 only when President Franklin D. Roosevelt complied with its objective of eliminating discrimination in defense industries. With the massive support of Martin Luther King's Southern Christian Leadership Conference, Roy Wilkins' NAACP, James Farmer's CORE, Whitney Young's Urban League, and John Lewis' Student Non-Violent Coordinating Committee, men and women went into action. Additional aid came from Catholic, Protestant, and Jewish leaders.

*A smiling President Kennedy congratulates leaders of the 1963 March on Washington. From left to right: Whitney Young, Jr. (National Urban League), Reverend Martin Luther King, Jr. (Southern Christian Leadership Conference), Rabbi Joachim Prinz (American Jewish Congress), A. Philip Randolph (director of the March), President Kennedy, Walter Reuther (President of United Auto Workers), Roy Wilkins (NAACP). America's largest protest march was conducted without incident or violence.*

On the day of the march, buses, trains, cars, and planes brought Washington its greatest crowd in history. Housewives and Congressmen, sharecroppers and celebrities, civil rights workers and clergymen of all religious faiths were among the quarter of a million people who gathered before the Lincoln Memorial that day. Television cameras brought the story to the far corners of the world.

The immense crowd listened to Dr. King's vision of an America free from bigotry: "I have a dream that my four little children will one day live in a nation where they will not be judged by the color of their skin but by the content of their character." They listened to men who long had been on the firing line of racial progress such as Randolph, Wilkins, and Young. (James Farmer was in a Louisiana jail for having led the civil rights drive there.) They heard from John Lewis, 23, whose SNCC had brought hundreds of young people into the South, new "carpetbaggers" who had come to build schools and to encourage people to register for voting.

Although some fearful voices had predicted violence that day, the mood in Washington was far different. Emily Rock, 15, of Woodlands High School, New York recorded her thoughts:

> I have never seen such a crowd of people as there were that day. There was a special feeling of closeness. I have never felt so small and yet part of something so immense, wonderful, and grand.
>
> I had a feeling of pride for my race and for the whites who thought enough to come. And there was a sense of triumph. We had proved by being orderly, nonviolent, and determined that we were not the kind of people our enemies said we were.
>
> All around, in the faces of everyone, there was this sense of hope for the future—the belief that this march was the *big* step in the right direction. It could be heard in the voices of the people singing and seen in the way they walked. It poured out into smiles.

*Emily Rock. At graduation she was chosen school valedictorian.*

The battle for equal rights did not conclude on that August afternoon in 1963. There were other marches—and other murders. But Emily Rock was right. The "hope for the future" that was present on that day will make for a better tomorrow.

*There were other marches. This one from Selma to Montgomery, Alabama was preceded by the murder of a clergyman and followed by the murder of a housewife. Both victims were white people who came south to help Negroes gain their rights as Americans.*

# The NAACP Greets the New "Law of the Land"

*[It was NAACP Chief Counsel Thurgood Marshall and two other Negro lawyers who successfully carried the* Brown *case to the Supreme Court in 1954. An NAACP conference meeting in Atlanta, a few days after the historic decision outlawing school segregation was handed down, expressed the confidence of the organization that rapid compliance would be forthcoming.]*

All Americans are now relieved to have the law of the land declare in the clearest language: ". . . in the field of public education the doctrine of 'separate but equal' has no place. Separate educational facilities are inherently unequal." Segregation in public education is now not only unlawful; it is un-American. True Americans are grateful for this decision. Now that the law is made clear, we look to the future. Having canvassed the situation in each of our states, we approach the future with the utmost confidence. . . .

We stand ready to work with other law abiding citizens who are anxious to translate this decision into a program of action to eradicate racial segregation in public education as speedily as possible. . . .

While we recognize that school officials will have certain administrative problems in transferring from a segregated to a non-segregated system, we will resist the use of any tactics contrived for the sole purpose of delaying desegregation. . . .

We insist that there should be integration at all levels, including the assignment of teacher-personnel on a nondiscriminatory basis. . . .

We look upon this memorable decision not as a victory for Negroes alone, but for the whole American people and as a vindication of America's leadership of the free world.

Lest there be any misunderstanding of our position, we here rededicate ourselves to the removal of all racial segregation in public education and reiterate our determination to achieve this goal without compromise of principle.

---

"*The Atlanta Declaration*," cited in *The Crisis*, Vol. 61 (June-July, 1954), pp. 358-359. Reprinted by permission.

# Voices from Central High School

[*The battle of Central High School was fought in the minds of its pupils as well as in the hallways and out in the streets of Little Rock, Arkansas. Mrs. Jorunn Ricketts, a Norwegian correspondent, invited six of the students at the high school to take part in a broadcast discussion for the National Broadcasting System. There were three white girls (Sammy Dean Parker, Kay Bacon, and Robin Woods), a white boy (Joseph Fox), and two Negroes (Ernest Green and Minnijean Brown).*]

*MRS. RICKETTS:* Do you think it is possible to start working this out on a more sensible basis than violent demonstration?

*SAMMY:* No, I don't because the South has always been against racial mixing and I think they will fight this thing to the end. . . . We fight for our freedom—that's one thing. And we don't have any freedom any more.

*ERNEST:* Sammy, you said that you don't have freedom. I wonder what do you mean by it—that you don't have freedom? You are guaranteed your freedoms in the Bill of Rights and your Constitution. You have the freedom of speech—I noticed that has been exercised a whole lot in Little Rock. The freedom of petition, the freedom of religion, and the other freedoms are guaranteed to you. As far as freedom, I think that if anybody should kick about freedoms, it should be us. Because I think we have been given a pretty bad side on this thing as far as freedoms.

*SAMMY:* Do you call those troops freedom? I don't. And I also do not call free when you are being escorted into the school every morning.

*ERNEST:* You say why did the troops come here? It is because our government—our state government—went against the federal law. . . . Our country is set up so that we have forty-eight states and no one state has the ability to overrule our nation's government. I thought that was what our country was built around. I mean, that is why we fight. We fought in World War II together—the fellows that I know died in World War II, they died in the Korean War. I mean, why should my friends get out there and die for a cause called "democracy" when I can't exercise my rights—tell me that.

*ROBIN:* I agree with Ernest.

*JOE:* Well, Sammy, I don't know what freedom has been taken away from you because the truth there—I know as a senior myself—the troops haven't kept me from going to my classes or participating in any school activity. I mean, they're there just to keep order in case—I might use the term "hotheads"—get riled up. But I think as long as—if parents would just stay out of it and let the children of the school at Central High figure it out for themselves I think it would be a whole lot better. I think the students are mature enough to figure it out for themselves. . . . As far as I'm concerned, I'll lay the whole blame of this trouble in Governor Faubus's lap.

*SAMMY:* I think we knew before this ever started that some day we were going to have to integrate the schools. And I think that our Governor was trying to protect all of us when he called out the National Guard—and he was trying to prepare us, I think.

*ERNEST:* . . . Well, I have to disagree. . . . I know a student that's over there with us, Elizabeth [Eckford], and that young lady, she walked two blocks, I guess—as you all know—and the mob was behind her. Did the troops break up the mob?

*ROBIN:* . . . and when Elizabeth had to walk down in front of the school I was there and I saw that. And may I say, I was very ashamed—I felt like crying—because she was so brave when she did that. And we just weren't behaving ourselves—just jeering her. I think if we had had any sort of decency, we wouldn't have acted that way. But I think if everybody would just obey the Golden Rule—do unto others as you would have others do unto you—might be the solution. How would you like to have to . . . walk down the street with everybody yelling behind you like they yelled behind Elizabeth?

*MRS. RICKETTS:* Sammy, why do these children not want to go to school with Negroes?

*SAMMY:* Well, I think it is mostly race mixing.

*MRS. RICKETTS:* Race mixing? What do you mean?

*SAMMY:* Well, marrying each other.

*MINNIJEAN:* Hold your hand up. I'm brown, you are white. What's the difference? We are all of the same thoughts. You're thinking about your boy—he's going to the Navy. I'm thinking about mine—he's in the Air Force. We think about the same thing.

*SAMMY:* I'll have to agree with you.

498 / EYEWITNESS: *The Negro in American History*

*ERNEST:* Well, getting back to this intermarriage and all that. I don't know [where] people get all that. Why do I want to go to school? To marry with someone? I mean, school's not a marriage bureau. . . . I'm going there for an education. Really, if I'm going there to socialize, I don't need to be going to school. I can stand out on the corner and socialize, as far as that.

*MINNIJEAN:* Kay, Joe, and Robin—do you know anything about me, or is it just that your mother has told you about Negroes? . . .

*MRS. RICKETTS:* . . . have you ever really made an effort to try to find out what they're like?

*KAY:* Not until today.

*SAMMY:* Not until today.

*MRS. RICKETTS:* And what do you think about it after today?

*KAY:* Well, you know that my parents and a lot of the other students and their parents think the Negroes aren't equal to us. But —I don't now. It seems like they are, to me.

*SAMMY:* These people are—we'll have to admit that.

*ERNEST:* I think, like we're doing today, discussing our different views . . . if the people of Little Rock . . . would get together I believe they would find out a different story—and try to discuss the thing instead of getting out in the street and kicking people around and calling names—and that sort of thing. If . . . people got together it would be smoothed over.

*KAY:* I think that if . . . our friends had been getting in this discussion today, I think that maybe some of them—not all of them —in time, they would change their mind. But probably some of them would change their mind today.

*SAMMY:* I know now that it isn't as bad as I thought it was— after we got together and discussed it.

*KAY:* [Sammy and I] We both came down here today with our mind set on it [that] we weren't going to change our mind that we were fully against integration. But I know now that we're going to change our mind.

*MRS. RICKETTS:* What do your parents say to that?

*KAY:* I think I'm going to have a long talk with my parents.

---

# A Presidential Aide Recalls the 1960 Election

[*In 1956, E. Frederick Morrow became the first Negro Presidential aide in history. He was appointed by President Dwight D. Eisenhower and he later served in the 1960 presidential campaign of Richard Nixon.*]

Late in the campaign I joined the Nixon entourage on the road. Unlike the Eisenhower campaigns of '52 and '56, I was never seen with the Vice-President. I rode in caravans in a rear car and was never called into parlays or strategy meetings.

In the closing days of the campaign, Reverend Martin Luther King, Negro idol and civil rights leader, was thrown in jail in Atlanta on a trivial charge. It was an international sensation. It was the moment for American leadership to speak.

I begged the Nixon managers, by memo and in person, to have the Vice-President make a statement deploring the situation under which King was jailed. They demurred. They thought it bad strategy.

The next day I joined the Nixon campaign train in Illinois. I urged his press secretary to have him take some action. I even drafted a telegram for the Vice-President to send to the mayor of Atlanta. The press secretary put the draft in his pocket to "think about it."

Twenty-four hours later, King was freed from jail. His freedom came after the intercession of the Democratic presidential candidate, John F. Kennedy. He had scored tremendously, not only by wiring the mayor of Atlanta, but by phoning King's wife to express his concern and ask if he could be of assistance. And his brother Robert had apparently talked to other Atlanta officials.

*This action won the election.* Kennedy's action electrified the entire Negro community and resulted in tens of thousands of Negro voters going over to the Democrats' banner. . . .

The results of this campaign should hold many valuable lessons for Republican leaders and politicians. The strategy of wooing the solid South and ignoring the available Negro vote was a costly blunder. . . .

E. Frederick Morrow, *Black Man in the White House* (New York: McFadden Books, 1963), pp. 213-214.

## A "Freedom Ride" Reaches Birmingham

[*On May 4, 1961, a group of Freedom Riders took buses southward to test the South's compliance with federal court orders which forbid segregation on buses or in terminals. James Peck, white, and Charles Person, Negro, were among the group that arrived in Birmingham, Alabama on Mother's Day, 1961. Peck tells the story.*]

Upon my arrival in Birmingham, I could see a mob lined up on the sidewalk only a few feet from the loading platform. Most of them were young—in their twenties. Some were carrying ill-concealed iron-bars. A few were older men. All had hate showing on their faces.

I looked at them and then I looked at Charles Person, who had been designated as my team mate to test the lunch counter. Person, a slim youth, quiet and determined, had been jailed-in for sixteen days during the campaign to desegregate Atlanta lunch counters. . . .

Now we stood on the Birmingham unloading platform with the segregationist mob only a few feet away. I did not want to put Person in a position of being forced to proceed if he thought the situation too dangerous. When I looked at him, he responded by saying simply, "Let's go."

As we entered the white waiting room and approached the lunch counter, we were grabbed bodily and pushed toward the alleyway leading to the loading platform. As soon as we got into the alleyway and out of sight of onlookers in the waiting room, six of them started swinging at me with fists and pipes. Five others attacked Person a few feet ahead. Within seconds, I was unconscious on the ground.

I learned only later that the mob went on to assault Tom Langston of the *Birmingham Post-Herald* and smashed his camera. Langston had been sufficiently quick-witted to remove his film, and the photo of my beating, clearly showing the hate-filled expression of my assailants, appeared in the next morning's *Post-Herald* and in many newspapers throughout the country. Then, Clancy Lake, a radio newsman, was attacked as he sat in his car, broadcasting an account of the onslaught.

When I regained consciousness, the alleyway was empty. Blood was flowing down my face. . . .

. . . I did not realize how seriously I had been hurt. My head required fifty-three stitches. [Person did not require hospitalization.]. . . .

James Peck, *Freedom Ride* (New York: Grove Press, 1962), pp. 98-99.

## *James Meredith Attends "Ole Miss"*

[*James Meredith, 29 and an Air Force veteran, entered the University of Mississippi in the fall of 1962. The Governor of the state opposed his admission and a riot that led to two deaths greeted his arrival. But on the day after the riot, he began attending classes with the all-white student body and faculty.*]

Monday morning at eight o'clock I registered, and at nine I went to class in Colonial American History. I was a few minutes late, and I took a seat at the back of the room. The professor was lecturing on the background in England, conditions there at the time of the colonization of America, and he paid no special attention when I entered. I think there were about a dozen students in the class. One said hello to me, and the others were silent. I remember a girl—the only girl there, I think—and she was crying, but it might have been from the tear gas [used by the United States marshals the night before] in the room. I was crying from it myself.

I had three classes scheduled that day. I went to two, and the third didn't meet because there was too much gas in the room. No marshals were in the classrooms with me, nor were they all week. . . .

As far as my relations with the students go, I make it a practice to be courteous. I don't force myself on them, but that's not my nature anyway. Many of them—most, I'd say—have been courteous, and the faculty members certainly have been. When I hear the jeers and the catcalls . . . I don't consider it personal. I get the idea people are just having a little fun. I think it's tragic that they have to have this kind of fun about me, but many of them are children of the men who lead Mississippi today, and I wouldn't expect them to act any other way. . . .

It hasn't been all bad. Many students have spoken to me very pleasantly. They have stopped banging doors and throwing bottles into my dormitory now.

One fellow from my home town sat down at my table in the cafeteria. "If you're here to get an education, I'm for you," he said. "If you're here to cause trouble, I'm against you." That seemed fair enough to me.

---

James Meredith, "I'll Know Victory or Defeat," *The Saturday Evening Post*, Vol. 235 (November 10, 1962), p. 17. Reprinted by permission of James Meredith.

## The Battle of Birmingham in 1963

[*Mary Hamilton, 18, was one of many young Negro civil rights workers who led the Negro groups marching into downtown Birmingham during the spring of 1963. She describes her arrest to a reporter for Pacifica Radio.*]

I had been helping out with the demonstrations in one way or another. And on Monday I was asked to help clear the sidewalks of the pedestrians so the Freedom March—so the demonstrators—could walk on the sidewalk without interference. . . . Generally the case is when they [the police] see an organizer around, they, if they can, they will arrest you. So I had been ordered by the police to stay off the sidewalk.

I had really stepped up on a ledge as the demonstrators were walking towards us. And I lost my balance. It was really this simple. I had lost my balance and stepped down to gain my balance. And the minute I stepped down on the sidewalk I was nabbed—and placed in a police car. I was arrested.

At that time about eighty people were arrested. Two groups were placed in two different buses. We were taken to the city jail. These demonstrators were—the average age range I would say was about, um, seventeen. . . .

All, all of the girls were placed in the downstairs cell block. It then began to rain and so we all climbed up and looked out the window. And here were these children—a good two hundred children out in the rain—just being drenched. The rain was coming down in torrents. And people were milling about and the police were out trying to drive people away. There was plenty of room in the cell block which I was in, to put these children. But instead the police preferred to leave them out. And it rained on those children two hours.

So we began banging on the—there were steel doors. So a mob of policemen came in. One of them said, "Well, we know what to do with the whole group." So they herded us all into solitary confinement cells, which were about two by two. You could take two steps, two short steps, in both directions. . . . There were from twelve to fifteen of us in these cells. We were left in there a good two hours. . . . We were uncomfortable . . . and so after about three hours we began banging on the walls of the cell. And of course there was a big noise and everything.

Policemen crowded in again—suddenly. There seemed to be a characteristic about these cops—they can never be alone by themselves and they must always come with their guns, their clubs, and their helmets. Anyway, they all herded into the cell and wanted to know what was up. And I told them, I said: "The girls have been in here for five hours without bathroom facilities and without water—and you can't treat people this way." And I just went on like this. So they took all the girls out except me. . . .

---

"Freedom Now" presented on *Pacifica Radio* (WBAI in New York). Reprinted by permission.

## President John F. Kennedy Calls for Equal Rights

[*In June of 1963 it was clear to all that the civil rights crusade had become a revolution. President Kennedy spoke to a nationwide television and radio audience on June 12 and put the civil rights issue in terms never before used by an American President.*]

. . . This Nation was founded by men of many nations and backgrounds. It was founded on the principle that all men are created equal, and that the rights of every man are diminished when the rights of one man are threatened.

Today we are committed to a worldwide struggle to promote and protect the rights of all who wish to be free. And when Americans are sent to Vietnam or West Berlin, we do not ask for whites only. It ought to be possible, therefore, for American students of any color to attend any public institution they select without having to be backed up by troops.

It ought to be possible for American consumers of any color to receive equal service in places of public accommodation, such as hotels and restaurants and theaters and retail stores, without being forced to resort to demonstrations in the street, and it ought to be possible for American citizens of any color to register and to vote in a free election without interference or fear of reprisal.

It ought to be possible, in short, for every American to enjoy the privileges of being American without regard to his race or his color. In short, every American ought to have the right to be treated as he would wish to be treated, as one would wish his children to be treated. But this is not the case.

The Negro baby born in America today, regardless of the section of the Nation in which he is born, has about one-half as much chance of completing a high school education as a white baby born in the same place on the same day, one-third as much chance of completing college, one-third as much chance of becoming a professional man, twice as much chance of becoming unemployed, about one-seventh as much chance of earning $10,000 a year, a life expectancy which is 7 years shorter, and the prospects of earning only half as much.

This is not a sectional issue. Difficulties over segregation and discrimination exist in every city, in every State of the Union, producing in many cities a rising tide of discontent that threatens the public safety. Nor is this a partisan issue. In a time of domestic crisis men of good will and generosity should be able to unite regardless of party or politics. This is not even a legal or legislative issue alone. It is better to settle these matters in the courts than on the streets, and new laws are needed at every level, but law alone cannot make men see right.

We are confronted primarily with a moral issue. It is as old as the scriptures and is as clear as the American Constitution.

The heart of the question is whether all Americans are to be afforded equal rights and equal opportunities, whether we are going to treat our fellow Americans as we want to be treated. If an American, because his skin is dark, cannot eat lunch in a restaurant open to the public, if he cannot send his children to the best public school available, if he cannot vote for the public officials who represent him, if, in short, he cannot enjoy the full and free life which all of us want, then who among us would be content to have the color of his skin changed and stand in his place? Who among us would then be content with the counsels of patience and delay?

One hundred years of delay have passed since President Lincoln freed the slaves, yet their heirs, their grandsons, are not fully free. They are not yet freed from the bonds of injustice. They are not yet freed from social and economic oppression. And this Nation, for all its hopes and all its boasts, will not be fully free until all its citizens are free.

We preach freedom around the world, and we mean it, and we cherish our freedom here at home, but are we to say to the world, and much more importantly, to each other that this is a land of the free except for the Negroes; that we have no second-class citizens except Negroes; that we have no class or cast[e] system, no ghettoes, no master race except with respect to Negroes?

Now the time has come for this Nation to fulfill its promise. The events in Birmingham and elsewhere have so increased the cries for equality that no city or State or legislative body can prudently choose to ignore them.

The fires of frustration and discord are burning in every city, North and South, where legal remedies are not at hand. Redress is sought in the streets, in demonstrations, parades, and protests which create tensions and threaten violence and threaten lives.

We face, therefore, a moral crisis as a country and as a people. It cannot be met by repressive police action. It cannot be left to increased demonstrations in the streets. It cannot be quieted by token moves or talk. It is a time to act in the Congress, in your State and local legislative body and, above all, in all of our daily lives.

It is not enough to pin the blame on others, to say this is a problem of one section of the country or another, or deplore it. A great change is at hand, and our task, our obligation, is to make that revolution, that change, peaceful and constructive for all.

Those who do nothing are inviting shame as well as violence. Those who act boldly are recognizing right as well as reality.

Next week I shall ask the Congress of the United States to act, to make a commitment it has not fully made in this century to the proposition that race has no place in American life or law. . . .

---

John F. Kennedy in *Public Papers of the Presidents of the United States*, Vol. III (Washington, 1964), pp. 236-237.

# The Mind of the Ku Klux Klan

*[The Negro's demand for equal justice has always infuriated the Ku Klux Klan. Since the 1954 Supreme Court decision and the civil rights crusade, Klan activity has increased. In the summer of 1964, shortly after the bodies of three young civil rights workers, Michael Schwerner, James Chaney, and Andrew Goodman were found, the Klan issued a newsletter giving their side of the murder. It was written in question (Q) and answer (A) form.]*

Q. What is your explanation of why there have been so many National Police Agents [F.B.I.?] involved in the case of the "missing civil rights workers?"

A. First, I must correct you on your terms. Schwerner, Chaney and Goodman were not civil rights workers. They were Communist Revolutionaries, actively working to undermine and destroy Christian Civilization. The blatant and outlandish National Police activity surrounding their case merely points up the political overtones of the entire affair. . . .

Q. By "political overtones" do you mean that the case has a bearing on the forthcoming elections?

A. It is doubtful that the case itself will be made an issue in the election. However, the incumbent in the White House [Lyndon B. Johnson] is a communist sympathizer, as proven by his numerous acts of treason, and his sole chance of victory in the November election will depend upon his being able to hold his communist-liberal block together by continuing to support and protect all Domestic Communists. . . .

Q. Isn't it unlikely that the Communists would do that [kill the three civil rights workers themselves] in this case? Schwerner was a valuable man?

A. Not at all. The Communists never hesitate to murder one of their own if it will benefit the party. Communism is pure, refined, scientific Cannibalism in action. A case in point is the murdered Kennedy. Certainly, no President could have been a more willing tool to the Communists than was the late and unlamented "Red Jack." He cooperated with them at every turn. Yet . . . he was callously given up for execution by those whom he had served so well. . . .

*Q.* Do the White Knights of the KU KLUX KLAN advocate or engage in unlawful violence?

*A.* We are absolutely opposed to street riots and public demonstrations of all kinds. Our work is largely educational in nature. . . . All of our work is carried on in a dignified and reverent manner. . . . We are all *Americans* in the White Knights of the KU KLUX KLAN of Mississippi.

*The Klan-Ledger*, Special Neshoba County Fair Edition.

## Malcolm X Explains Black Nationalism

[*Malcolm Little left high school at 15 and was jailed at 21 for burglary. In jail he was converted to the Black Muslim movement and changed his last name to "X." After his release from prison in 1952, he became the most articulate American spokesman for black nationalists. A year before his assassination, he outlined his views in these words.*]

The political philosophy of black nationalism means: we must control the politics and the politicians of our community. They must no longer take orders from outside forces. We will organize, and sweep out of office all Negro politicians who are puppets for the outside forces. . . .

. . . Whites can help us, but they can't join us. There can be no black-white unity until there is first black unity. There can be no workers' solidarity until there is first some racial solidarity. We cannot think of uniting with others, until after we have first united among ourselves . . . .

Concerning nonviolence: it is criminal to teach a man not to defend himself when he is the constant victim of brutal attacks. It is legal and lawful to own a shotgun or a rifle. We believe in obeying the law.

In areas where our people are the constant victims of brutality, and the government seems unable or unwilling to protect them, we should form rifle clubs that can be used to defend our lives and our property in times of emergency. . . . When our people are being bitten by dogs, they are within their rights to kill those dogs.

We should be peaceful, law-abiding—but the time has come for the American Negro to fight back in self-defense whenever and wherever he is being unjustly and unlawfully attacked.

If the government thinks I am wrong for saying this, then let the government start doing its job.

---

Statement by Malcolm X delivered to a New York press conference, March 12, 1964.

## "I Shall Cast My Lot with the Leadership of My Community"

[*As the Civil Rights Law of 1964 speeded toward passage on July 2, 1964, Congressman Charles Longstreet Weltner of Atlanta, Georgia rose to speak. "His fellow Southerners sat stunned," wrote a reporter, as the Representative told why he had changed his mind.*]

Mr. Speaker, over 4 months ago, the civil rights bill came to this floor. Its stated purpose, equality of opportunity for all Americans, is a proper goal. But I questioned its means, and voted against passage. Now, after the most thorough and sifting examination in legislative history this measure returns for final consideration. It returns with the overwhelming approval of both Houses of Congress.

Manifestly, the issue is already decided, and approval is assured. By the time my name is called, votes sufficient for passage will have been recorded.

What, then, is the proper course? Is it to vote "no," with tradition, safety—and futility?

I believe a greater cause can be served. Change, swift and certain, is upon us, and we in the South face some difficult decisions.

We can offer resistance and defiance, with their harvest of strife and tumult. We can suffer continued demonstrations, with their wake of violence and disorder.

Or, we can acknowledge this measure as the law of the land. We can accept the verdict of the Nation.

Already, the responsible elements of my community are counseling this latter course. And, most assuredly, moderation, tranquillity, and orderly processes combine as a cause greater than conformity.

Mr. Speaker, I shall cast my lot with the leadership of my community. I shall cast my vote with that greater cause they serve. I will add my voice to those who seek reasoned and conciliatory adjustment to a new reality.

And finally, I would urge that we at home now move on to the unfinished task of building a new South. We must not remain forever bound to another lost cause.

---

Representative Charles Longstreet Weltner, *Report from Washington* (Washington, July 24, 1964). Reprinted from *The Congressional Record.*

# Langston Hughes Views Harlem Riots

[*During the summers of 1964 and 1965, riots erupted in many Northern Negro ghettos. Langston Hughes, poet, playwright, reporter, and author takes a satirical look at the background of the Harlem riot of 1964.*]

Opinion in Harlem is divided as to whether or not riots do any good. Some say *yes*, they achieve concrete results in community improvements. Others say *no*, they set the Negro race back 50 years. Those who disagree say, in effect, "But Negroes are always being set back 50 years by something or another, so what difference does a riot make?"

Old-timers who remember former riots in Harlem say, "White folks respect us more when they find out we mean business. When they only listen to our speeches or read our writing—if they ever do—they think we are just blowing off steam. But when rioters smash the plate glass windows of their stores, they know the steam has some force behind it. Then they say, 'Those Negroes are mad! What do they want?' And for a little while they will try to give you a little of what you want.

"After every riot in Harlem, the whites respect you more. After that big riot in 1935, the white-owned shops all along 125th Street that would not hire Negro clerks, began to hire at least one. We got a great many jobs out of that riot that we couldn't get before in our own community because the clerks, cashiers and everything were all white."

The big riot in 1943, which grew out of a white policeman shooting a black soldier at 126th Street and 8th Avenue during a period of much police brutality in the area, produced remarkable changes in police attitudes in Harlem, and resulted in a number of additional Negro officers being added to the force.

Chocolate and vanilla teams of policemen appeared on uptown streets walking together. Squad cars became integrated. And a white policeman would often grant his Negro colleague the courtesy of making the arrest, if an arrest had to be made. And for a long time, after the '43 riots, seldom did Negro or white cops beat a culprit's head in public—as they frequently did before the riots. . . .

After the 1943 riots, one night on Lenox Avenue, I saw two white policemen attempting to push a young Negro into a squad car. The man refused to get in. Each time the police tried to force him, he would spread out his arms and legs or twist his body so that they could not get him through the door. With a crowd of Negroes all around, the white cops seemingly did not dare hit the Negro. But, to their fortune a colored policeman on foot arrived. He simply said, "Get in that car fellow!" The Negro got in, and the car sped away with its prisoner.

Folks in the crowd said, "You see—since the riots, they sure do arrest you politely. Now his head won't be cracked, till they get him down to the precinct house." The riots of 1943 almost ended *public* police brutality on the streets of Harlem.

Out of our 1964 riot this week I do not know what concrete results will come but certainly its repercussions have already reached into high places. No less an authority than President Johnson has spoken from the capital saying grandiloquently, "Violence and law-lessness cannot, must not, and will not be tolerated." Some Harlemites interpret this to mean that there will be no more head-bustings on the part of the police, or shooting of adolescents, black, white, or Puerto Rican by men representing New York's Finest. "American citizens have a right to protection of life and limb," continued the President, "whether driving along a highway in Georgia, a road in Mississippi, or a street in New York City."

. . . Negroes have been asking for years that Georgia and Mississippi be made safe—and getting no results from federal or state governments. But now, after a weekend of rioting in Harlem, you see what the President says! The riots have already produced one good result. . . .

---

Langston Hughes, "Harlem III," *New York Post*, July 23, 1964, p. 29. Reprinted by permission of Harold Ober Associates.

# *Martin Luther King Explains Nonviolent Resistance*

[*In this selection, especially prepared for this volume, Dr. King tells of the theory of nonviolence on which his leadership in the civil rights struggle is based.*]

During my freshman days in 1944 at Atlanta's Morehouse College I read Henry David Thoreau's essay *On Civil Disobedience* for the first time. Here, in this courageous New Englander's refusal to pay his taxes and his choice of jail rather than support a war that would spread slavery's territory into Mexico, I made my first contact with the theory of nonviolent resistance. Fascinated by Thoreau's idea of refusing to cooperate with an evil system, I was so deeply moved that I reread the work several times.

A few years later I heard a lecture by Dr. Mordecai Johnson, President of Howard University. Dr. Johnson had just returned from a trip to India and he spoke of the life and teachings of Mahatma Gandhi. His message was so profound and electrifying that I left the meeting and bought a half-dozen books on Gandhi's life and works.

Before reading Gandhi, I had believed that Jesus' "turn the other cheek" philosophy and the "love your enemies" philosophy could only be useful when individuals were in conflict with other individuals—when racial groups and nations were in conflict, a more realistic approach seemed necessary. But after reading Gandhi, I saw how utterly mistaken I was.

During the days of the Montgomery bus boycott, I came to see the power of nonviolence more and more. As I lived through the actual experience of this protest, nonviolence became more than a useful method; it became a way of life.

Nonresistance attacks the forces of evil rather than the persons who happen to be doing the evil. As I said to the people of Montgomery: "The tension in this city is not between white people and Negro people. The tension is at bottom, between justice and injustice, between the forces of light and the forces of darkness. And if there is a victory, it will be a victory not merely for fifty thousand Negroes but a victory for justice and the forces of light. We are out to defeat injustice and not white persons who may be unjust."

It must be emphasized that nonviolent resistance is not for cowards. *Nonviolent resistance does resist.* If one uses this method because he is afraid or merely because he lacks the weapons of violence, he is not truly nonviolent. That is why Gandhi often said that if cowardice is the only alternative to violence, it is better to fight. He made this statement knowing that there is always another choice we can make: There is the way of nonviolent resistance. No individual or group need submit to any wrong, nor need they use violence to right a wrong. This is ultimately the way of the strong man.

The nonviolent resistance of the early Christians shook the Roman Empire. The nonviolence of Mahatma Gandhi and his followers had muzzled the guns of the British Empire in India and freed more than three hundred and fifty million people from colonialism. It brought victory in the Montgomery bus boycott.

The phrase "passive resistance" often gives the false impression that this is a sort of "do-nothing method" in which the resister quietly and passively accepts evil. But nothing is further from the truth. For while the nonviolent resister is not physically aggressive toward his opponent, his mind and emotions are always active, constantly seeking to persuade his opponent that he is wrong—constantly seeking to open the eyes of blind prejudice. This is not passive nonresistance to evil, it is active nonviolent resistance to evil.

Nonviolence does not seek to defeat or humiliate the opponent, but to win his friendship and understanding. The nonviolent resister not only refuses to shoot his opponent but he also refuses to hate him. To strike back in the same way as his opponent would do nothing but increase the existence of hate in the universe. Along the way of life, someone must have sense enough and morality enough to cut off the chain of hate.

In the final analysis all life is interrelated. All humanity is involved in a single process, and all men are brothers. To the degree that I harm my brother, no matter what he is doing to me, to that extent I am harming myself. Why is this? Because men are brothers. If you harm me, you harm yourself.

## A President Announces "We Shall Overcome"

[*The 1965 march of Selma Negroes demanding the right to vote was attacked by Alabama state troopers, and two white supporters of Negro rights were killed, one a minister from Boston and the other a Detroit housewife. President Lyndon B. Johnson called on Congress to enact a law that would allow all people to vote regardless of their race. His speech to a joint session of Congress was carried by radio and TV to the far corners of America and the world.*]

I speak tonight for the dignity of man and the destiny of democracy. . . .

There is no Negro problem. There is no Southern problem. There is no Northern problem. There is only an American problem. And we are met here tonight as Americans, not as Democrats or Republicans, we are met here as Americans to solve that problem. . . .

Every device of which human ingenuity is capable has been used to deny this right [to vote]. The Negro citizen may go to register only to be told that the day is wrong, or the hour is late, or the official in charge is absent. And if he persists and if he manages to present himself to the registrar, he may be disqualified because he did not spell out his middle name or because he abbreviated a word on the application. And if he manages to fill out the application he is given a test. The registrar is the sole judge of whether he passes this test. He may be asked to recite the entire constitution, or explain the most complex provisions of state laws. And even a college degree cannot be used to prove that he can read and write.

For the fact is that the only way to pass these barriers is to show a white skin. . . .

Wednesday I will send to Congress a law designed to eliminate illegal barriers to the right to vote. . . .

But even if we pass this bill, the battle will not be over. What happened in Selma is part of a far larger movement which reaches into every section and state of America. It is the effort of American Negroes to secure for themselves the full blessings of American life.

Their cause must be our cause too. Because it is not just Negroes, but really it is all of us, who must overcome the crippling legacy of bigotry and injustice. And we shall overcome. . . .

The real hero of this struggle is the American Negro. His actions and protests, his courage to risk safety and even to risk his life, have awakened the conscience of this nation. His demonstrations have been designed to call attention to injustice, designed to provoke change, designed to stir reform. He has called upon us to make good the promise of America. And who among us can say that we would have made the same progress were it not for his persistent bravery, and his faith in American democracy. . . .

Lyndon B. Johnson, Remarks of the President to a Joint Session of Congress (Washington: Office of the White House Press Secretary, March 15, 1965), pp. 1-5.

# Index